Rational Lives

American Politics and Political Economy
A series edited by Benjamin I. Page

Dennis Chong

Rational Lives

Norms and Values in Politics and Society

THE UNIVERSITY OF CHICAGO PRESS

CHICAGO AND LONDON

Dennis Chong is professor of political science at Northwestern University.

The University of Chicago Press, Chicago 60637
The University of Chicago Press, Ltd., London
© 2000 by The University of Chicago
All rights reserved. Published 2000
Printed in the United States of America
10 09 08 07 06 05 04 03 02 01 00   5 4 3 2 1

ISBN (cloth): 0-226-10438-9
ISBN (paper): 0-226-10439-7

Library of Congress Cataloging-in-Publication Data

Chong, Dennis.
    Rational lives : norms and values in politics and society / Dennis Chong.
        p.   cm.
    Includes bibliographical references and index.
    ISBN 0-226-10438-9 (alk. paper) — ISBN 0-226-10439-7 (pbk. : alk. paper)
    1. Rational choice theory.   2. Political psychology.   3. Political sociology.   I. Title.
    HM495.C47   2000
    306.2—dc21   99-044629

To my mother, May Chong, and in memory of my father, Ging Chong

CONTENTS

FIGURES

ACKNOWLEDGMENTS

In the course of writing this book, I was fortunate to receive the support of many friends and colleagues. For their comments, questions, and suggestions, which I found to be helpful in ways, large and small, my thanks to Chris Achen, David Austen-Smith, Jay Casper, Phil Charko, Jack Citrin, Patti Conley, Chris Day, Marissa Martino Golden, Russell Hardin, Jim Johnson, Jack Knight, Jim Kuklinski, Antonia Maioni, George Marcus, Anna-Maria Marshall, Pierre Martin, Doug McAdam, Herbert McClosky, Melissa Miller, Ben Page, Theresa Parker, Barry Preisler, Lynn Sanders, David Sears, Bob Shapiro, John Sprague, Michael Taylor, Michael Wallerstein, and Yael Wolinsky.

A special note of appreciation to Jim Kuklinski, Michael Taylor, and Yael Wolinsky for providing me with detailed comments on the entire manuscript.

One of the themes of this book is that decisions made long ago often figure in the choices that we elect to make today. It is only fitting therefore to mention three professors of mine who have been inspirations and examples to me and who played important roles in shaping how I think about the social sciences. The instruction that I received from Jean Laponce at the University of British Columbia, John Meisel at Queen's University, and Herbert McClosky at the University of California, Berkeley shows that some lessons really do last a lifetime.

I also received excellent research assistance while writing this book. Beth Durkac helped me in countless ways as my research assistant when she was a political science major at Northwestern. For my research on the Apple Computer controversy in Texas, I benefited from the assistance of Anna-Maria Marshall, who at the time was a doctoral student in political science. The analysis of this case in Chapter 5 draws on our paper, "When Morality and Economics Collide (or Not) in a Texas Community" (*Political Behavior* 21 [1999]: 91–121). For their hospitality and cooperation, I'd like to thank the many individuals in Williamson County who agreed to be interviewed for this case study.

The College of Arts and Sciences at Northwestern University provided me with generous research support and a year's leave from teaching in 1997–98.

The Institute for Policy Research at Northwestern also contributed financial support for elements of this research.

At the University of Chicago Press, Executive Editor John Tryneski guided me toward completion of this book, meeting regularly with me at conferences and asking me about the book's progress over our many lunches together. I was going to say that he offered a combination of inducements and admonitions along the way, but in thinking back, I recall that it was always words of support and encouragement. Claudia Rex, the production editor on the book, is reason alone to publish at the University of Chicago Press. She read the manuscript as carefully as anyone and her observations about its structure and style improved the final product. All I can say is that it is nice to work with someone who knows what she is doing.

The Museum of Modern Art in New York and Artists Rights Society, the representatives of Balthus, kindly provided permission to use, for the cover art, Balthus's painting, *La Rue,* which depicts nine oddly choreographed people seemingly going about their ordinary lives on a Parisian street. (I understand the thin cardboard figure in front of the store is not supposed to be a cardboard cutout at all, but a real person.)

I dedicate this book to my parents, who confronted prejudice but taught tolerance, and who endured much harder lives so that their children might enjoy easier ones.

Dennis Chong

October 1999
Evanston, Illinois

INTRODUCTION

Entities should not be multiplied unnecessarily.

William of Ockham

Conflict between groups over the norms and values that govern society is often said to be one area of life that is not readily explained by economic or rational choice models. Political activism on these issues, the argument goes, is more likely to be motivated by expressive desires, symbolic goals, and long-term values than by pocketbook or instrumental calculations. According to this view, economic models are best suited to studying conflicts over material interests rather than differences over ways of life.

The idea of "status politics," for example, has been used to explain attempts by groups to pass laws that certify their cultural values and beliefs as the dominant norms of society. Such groups presumably are pursuing, not material benefits from the government in the form of tax breaks and other economic concessions, but status or recognition through government regulation of lifestyles. In a classic formulation, the historian Richard Hofstadter wrote: "Besides their economic expectations, people have deep emotional commitments in other spheres—religion, morals, culture, race relations—which they also hope to see realized in political action. Status politics seeks not to advance perceived material interests but to express grievances and resentments about such matters, to press claims upon society to give deference to non-economic values. As a rule, status politics does more to express emotions than to formulate policies."[1]

In general, theories of action that give priority to group ties and values have been dubbed "sociological" or "social-psychological" explanations.[2] In their ideal form, sociological explanations ground the motivation for people's behavior in their attachment to social norms, values, and group identifications rather than in their assessments of costs and benefits. Political preferences are akin to cultural tastes: "Both have their origin in ethnic, sectional, class, and family traditions. Both exhibit stability and resistance to change for individuals but flexibility and adjustment over generations for the society as a whole. Both seem to be matters of sentiment and disposition rather than 'reasoned preferences.' . . . Both are characterized more by faith than by conviction and by wishful expectation rather than careful prediction of consequences. The preference for one party rather than another must be highly similar to the preference for one kind of literature or music rather than another."[3]

Preferences and actions in the sociological model are determined by the norms and values that have been inculcated through the family, school, church, and other groups and institutions that shape people's socialization. Those who have internalized democratic norms, for example, are more likely to be tolerant of nonconformity; racial policy preferences depend on general beliefs in equality and individualism; and attitudes toward abortion and women's rights are shaped by religious upbringing. In her autobiography, Sarah Boyle, a member of a privileged white Virginian family, traced her willingness to support the civil rights movement in the 1950s, despite hostile opposition from most of the community, to the enduring lessons conveyed by her father: "he instilled in me a conviction that the only thing which really matters in anyone's life is a consistent choice of right over wrong."[4] Her father was the source of many traditional adages—about being honest, doing one's share, and persevering in the face of great odds—that she took to heart and used to guide her choices throughout her life.[5]

Apparently no one is exempt from the elementary principle of political socialization that attitudes and values are likely to be related to social origins. In the Tibetan Buddhist religion, for example, when the Panchen Lama dies, he is reincarnated as an infant.[6] The location and identity of the reincarnated Lama can be discovered through a series of divine signs. Using these leads, senior lamas locate a number of children who meet the criteria supplied by the oracles, and one of these children is eventually selected as the reincarnated Lama on the basis of his ability to recognize a variety of objects that belonged to the deceased lama. In theory, the new lama could be located anywhere, but political and religious leaders remain acutely aware that the geographical location of the new lama could hint at his future political inclinations. Therefore, when the Panchen Lama died in 1989, the whereabouts of the reincarnated Lama generated much political controversy because the Panchen Lama would be an influential voice on the question of Tibet's future relationship with China. If the Panchen Lama turned out to be a boy in China with parents who supported the Beijing government, he would probably favor maintaining existing ties to China. But if he were plucked from a family of anticommunist Tibetan exiles in India, he would be inclined to support the movement for political independence when he grew up. Knowing what was at stake, religious and political authorities fought over where they should concentrate their search. All of which might lead one to ask, Whatever happened to the idea of the One True Panchen Lama?

Economic explanations presume that people are instrumentally rational, meaning that they take actions only insofar as those actions secure desired, typically private ends. Behavior is motivated by the relative attractiveness of different alternatives instead of being driven by internal values, identities, and dispositions. In the economic view, individuals show no sentiment in discarding existing norms and practices when they cease to serve their interests, whereas in the sociological view, changing behavior requires changing underlying values and dispositions.[7]

Values and dispositions, however, are said to be difficult to change, which is why cultural inertia will often prevail over self-interest.[8] The origins of "cracker culture" illustrate the transatlantic inertia of Old World customs, practices, traits, and dispositions brought to the United States by British settlers in the eighteenth century. Because the English settled disproportionately in the northeast, while those of Celtic origin tended to settle in regions to the South and West, British cultural cleavages were in significant ways reproduced in this country: "British immigrants—English and Celtic—brought with them to America their habits and values as well as their old feuds, biases, and resentments."[9]

In the sociological view, people follow established traditions and conform to social norms in a relatively reflexive fashion. They pass on to subsequent generations those beliefs and values that they were raised to support. They continue to subscribe to those values even after the values have been made dysfunctional by changing circumstances. Oscar Lewis's idea of a "culture of poverty," derived from his studies of Latin America, is among the more controversial claims that values persist to the detriment of their bearers. "The culture of poverty," Lewis wrote, "is not only an adaptation to a set of objective conditions of the larger society. Once it comes into existence it tends to perpetuate itself from generation to generation because of its effect on the children. By the time slum children are age six or seven they have usually absorbed the basic values and attitudes of their subculture and are not psychologically geared to take full advantage of changing conditions or increased opportunities which may occur in their lifetime."[10]

Despite the infiltration of economic reasoning in many social science fields outside economics, research on political attitudes, values, and preferences has largely resisted explanations based primarily on self-interested motivations. The received view of the field continues to be that, with few exceptions, self-interested motivations do not significantly affect political orientations and preferences on social policies.[11] By instead emphasizing political socialization, symbolic values, group loyalties, personal traits and dispositions, and social conformity, research on political attitudes and values continues to reflect its sociological and social psychological heritage.[12]

My priority in this book is to steer the discussion back in the direction of rational choice, not necessarily all the way, but in a manner that shows why instrumental reasoning must be an essential component of any interesting theory of norms and values. The best evidence for the sociological model, and against the economic model, is that values and group identifications often seem to develop without respect to self-interest and to motivate actions that ignore costs and benefits. One aim of this book is to discuss how *some* of this behavior can be accounted for in rational choice terms, although ultimately I believe the sociological view has merit. The book's main argument, however, is that *there is a large element of rationality underlying value formation and change, group identification, and conflict over social norms and lifestyles.* But the rationality is not crudely objective in the sense that we choose our beliefs, values, and social practices in the same way that we make purchases in a store. Rather, we are rational in the sense of trying to identify and follow our interests within our limitations of experience and our relatively shortsighted ability to make prognoses over the life course. Interests are an essential part of the explanation whether they enter through the front door, as a conscious element in developing norms, or through the back door, as a past investment in personal development that motivates individuals to sustain the institutions that they have built their lives around, whether or not those institutions are the product of rational action.

Inevitably, personal rigidities due to traits and dispositions, habits, and addictions creep into the process and inhibit our ability to make rational choices. Moreover, attachment to an accustomed way of life tends to be strengthened by rationalization and selective perception, which lead people to believe that their social norms and practices are superior to alternative ways of life and are essential to political and economic progress. Popular subscription to such ethnocentric beliefs provides some of the animus behind defense of the status quo. Many instances of behavior are subjectively rational in the sense that the actors believe they are choosing the best alternative, but their reasoning is flawed or their method of gathering information is biased. Therefore they can be said to be doing the best they can given their understanding of their situation, but their basic understanding is not rigorous. It becomes difficult to disentangle whether the reasons and justifications that people provide to explain their actions are rationalizations after the fact or if the reasons provided are indeed the main causal force. Such reasons, however, are not merely redundant, but at a minimum intensify and justify the position or action taken.

Nevertheless, by giving short shrift to the role of interests, the sociological approach fails to provide a coherent explanation of how social norms and values are formed and perpetuated and why they represent a continual source of conflict. Any theory of conflict between groups seeking either to change or to preserve the values that regulate society needs to take stock of the instrumental power of social norms and values in addition to people's emotional and intellectual attachment to their way of life. I will not simply recast a story of how norms are developed along lines that are consistent with a rational choice explanation but will argue that an explanation of social conflict that does not treat norms and values strategically leaves gaps in our understanding of the reasons why people defend their culture and the circumstances in which they will seek to impose their norms and values on others.

Social norms and values establish ideal forms of behavior, assign priority to different points of view and ways of life, and affect individual choice by coordinating expectations and increasing the attractiveness of certain alternatives over others. They are manifest in all walks of life: in our personal relationships, families, churches, schools, places of employment, at social functions, on the street, and in the marketplace. For norms to be effective, there must be widespread agreement that a general consensus exists around them and social sanctions for failure to comply with them. Some social norms are backed by the force of legal authority, but not all laws have the characteristic of social norms. Many laws are foreign to people insofar as they do not resonate like a social norm and do not strike people as obviously right or wrong.[13]

We have to recognize that social norms and values not only coordinate behavior in groups, but also create incentives that affect the kinds of life choices—many of which are irreversible--that people make in their personal development. They influence individual decisions (and rational calculations) by providing sanctions for nonconformity and information about how people are expected to behave. Because norms and values affect individual choices and social outcomes, they will themselves be subject to conflict. We would expect that rational individuals would prefer social institutions that promote benefits for themselves rather than for the society at large. They will prefer norms that influence other people to make choices that produce social outcomes favorable to themselves. Therefore, resistance to new norms will originate most strongly from individuals who are ill-equipped to deal with changes in the status quo and who benefit from the political coordination that is supplied by existing values and norms.

Giving a more central role to self-interest not only improves explanation but also yields a far more interesting and fruitful theory. While status concerns and longstanding prejudices certainly play an important role in conflicts over values and lifestyles, it is hard to formulate a dynamic theory of social conflict without incorporating interests and strategic calculations.[14] The deductive power of a purely sociological or psychological theory is limited insofar as its major claims consist of an inventory of causal relationships correlating values either with other values or with actions. There are surprisingly few mechanisms involving group dynamics and political mobilization in theories that are centered on social values. Relying exclusively on values to explain social behavior therefore essentially reduces analysis of social conflict to studying internal dispositions and habits and value differences across groups as opposed to social processes in which people's choices are interdependent and their decisions to identify with groups and remain loyal to them are affected by strategic considerations of the consequences of following one norm or another.

An Overview

In chapter 1, I begin by outlining a rational choice model that will provide the framework for the analysis in this book. In the model, it is assumed that rationality is based on subjective calculations of self-interest, that individuals are motivated by both material and social goals, and that calculations of interest are contingent on the history of one's choices, including the values, identifications, and knowledge that one has acquired through socialization.

I then examine alternative noninstrumental theories that are centered on status and symbolic values. The theory of status politics focuses on expressive motives behind collective defense of cultural beliefs and symbols. Symbolic politics theory argues that long-term values are more influential than self-interest in determining mass policy preferences. Both of these theories make important contributions by identifying social psychological motives and mechanisms that tend to be overlooked by rational choice theory, but they also fall short, paradoxically, of providing coherent explanations for why people pursue status and how social values change.

Although the theory of status politics raises some intriguing questions about why people defend cultural values and practices that are not obviously connected to material consequences, I argue that cases of status politics can be explained by an instrumental theory of action and do not merit a special model. Defense of a way of life is related instrumentally to political and economic interests because social and political relationships are built upon a foundation of common norms and values.

The theory of symbolic politics also challenges the role of self-interest in determining political preferences. This research demonstrates persuasively that objective measures of self-interest will often be weak predictors of policy preferences when values such as political ideology and racial prejudice are taken into account. However, in my opinion, this theory takes an excessively narrow view of rational behavior and, because of its emphasis on psychological mechanisms, does not provide an adequate explanation of value formation and change. Although value change is difficult because individuals have a strong interest in coordinating their beliefs and preferences with other members of their reference groups, longitudinal studies conducted over the life span indicate that when people change reference groups and acquire new interests, their values change accordingly.

Chapter 2 outlines an instrumental theory of opinion and value formation based on social group influences. According to this theory, people join groups and conform to group norms because groups provide individuals with social and material benefits that they cannot obtain on their own. Through social conformity, people gain acceptance into their reference groups (i.e., status), identify their interests, and acquire the knowledge and values that they require to make decisions. Some group norms and values are followed because they benefit group members, but even when the substance of the group norm does not directly serve one's interest, it can be in one's interest to conform to group norms when the norm is enforced by social pressure or when the norm represents a social convention that everyone has an interest in supporting so long as others do so.

On the basis of these premises, I develop a general model of individual choice that can be applied to preferences among policies, attitudes, norms, and identifications. The model presented here combines a social psychological model in which identities and values are internalized through socialization with an economic model in which belief and value formation are motivated by external or instrumental benefits. The model assumes that individual choice depends on two factors: (1) the material and social incentives associated with the alternatives that one faces; and (2) past investments in values, group identifications, and knowledge that may create an underlying disposition in favor of a particular alternative. In contrast to symbolic theories, this is an explicitly dynamic model that explains both stability and changes in preference. Preferences are stable when incentives and dispositions remain constant. On the other hand, new incentives produced by institutional change or by social mobility from one group to another will lead gradually to the formation of new values. People are therefore partly pushed by internal predispositions and partly pulled by the costs and benefits of the options they face. Using these two mechanisms, the model yields a number of deductions about socialization and conformity, the development of norms and conventions, the diffusion of ideas, patterns of public opinion formation, habitual versus rational choice, partisan and ideological choice, and the circumstances in which principles may prevail over self-interest.

Chapters 3 and 4 use the model of individual choice to analyze conflict over social norms. Chapter 3 identifies several mechanisms that explain people's attachments to a way of life and their resistance to cultural change. First, norms and values coordinate people's beliefs, expectations, and choices and reduce uncertainty about how others will behave in different social situations. Competing norms produce coordination problems that raise transaction costs and hinder communication and social interaction.

A second mechanism that strengthens attachment to a way of life is ethnocentrism, a tendency to attribute greater value to those groups and norms with which one is familiar. Ethnocentric beliefs stem from psychological biases in gathering and interpreting information about one's own culture and the norms and practices of those who are different. Although ethnocentrism rests on an irrational foundation, it can be placed in the service of quite rational political strategies aimed at tangible goals.

Third, attachment to cultural norms and practices is reinforced by earlier investments and decisions based on those norms. By building their lives around the prevailing norms, people develop stakes in the status quo and self-interested reasons to oppose new norms that may reduce their opportunities and status. A different socialization might have better equipped a person to adapt to the new norms, but he is nevertheless constrained by his past development and what is rational for him now is contingent on his earlier decisions.

In Chapter 4, I discuss how social and cultural divisions are further reinforced by political mobilization. Political entrepreneurs mobilize the public for collective goals by taking advantage of existing group identifications and values. When individuals are already united by beliefs, values, social norms, and group identities that they share as a result of common socialization processes, political coalitions can be readily built upon the foundation of this consensus. Political entrepreneurs therefore sometimes merely have to find a way to capitalize on existing community resources by creating focal points or frames of reference for mass coordination around common beliefs and group identities.

Competing frames of reference encourage people to draw different interpretations of a given conflict—its scope, the parties that will be affected, the interests at stake, the applicable principles. As E. E. Schattschneider emphasized, "Political conflict is not like an intercollegiate debate in which the opponents agree in advance on a definition of the issues. As a matter of fact, the definition of the alternatives is the supreme instrument of power."[15] Whichever side in a conflict is able to establish the terms on which the conflict will be fought gains a decided advantage in garnering popular support for its position. While political leaders aim to coordinate public opinion around frames of reference that serve their own positions, the best they can do sometimes is steer the public in directions that it is already predisposed toward.

In a society organized along racial lines, for example, racially based political appeals will be commonplace. Such political strategies, however, will tend to shore up group boundaries by offering political benefits in exchange for allegiance to group values. Racial prejudice will acquire more currency if winning political coalitions derive much of their appeal from a racist platform. Fortunately, not all political coordination will center on group interests or demagoguery. In a society that consists of numerous, overlapping groups defined by conflicting norms, values, and interests, political leaders must often base their appeals on more neutral principles and ideological values in order to broaden their coalitions.

Chapter 5 chronicles a controversy over economic interests and cultural values that took place in 1993 in Williamson County, Texas. A routine tax rebate plan designed to attract Apple Computer to this growth-oriented community ran aground when attention was focused on the company's policy of extending health insurance to the unmarried domestic partners of its employees. Although most county residents favored economic development, many feared that Apple's policy would attract homosexuals and unmarried heterosexual couples who would not conform to the community's conservative norms. I went to Texas to analyze how this controversy played out and to learn how individuals reconciled their material interests and moral values in deciding where they stood on this issue. Using interviews with central participants, county survey data, and letters written to public officials by concerned citizens, I investigate the reasons that people offer in explaining why it is important to them that their community maintains a consensus around common social norms and values. In the process, I uncover the social theories that they hold about the causal connections between cultural values, social order, political outcomes, and economic progress.

Given the variety of forces that secure and reinforce the status quo, how do social values change? In chapter 6, I build on the model of individual choice developed in chapter 2 and develop a model of social change to explain the development of new social norms and values. I use this model to analyze the diffusion of new norms of racial equality in the post–World War II period. Given the virtually unanimous support in the South for racial segregation, the changes that occurred in racial norms and values within a relatively short time frame is a remarkable illustration of the possibility of changing social values. Southern communities tried to close ranks in defense of their traditional norms, but the cost of resistance eventually proved to be excessive.

In general, new values typically call for a new repertoire of social and economic skills that will place certain members of society at a competitive disadvantage. Therefore, we would expect that some individuals will cling to their existing beliefs and values until the pressure (or incentive) for change grows too strong to resist. For a new norm to take hold, there must be a corresponding realignment of interests and incentives favoring it over the old norm. The basic idea of the model is that normative change requires institutional incentives and sanctions that not only alter patterns of social interaction but also instigate changes in popular attitudes. People change both their attitudes and their behavior when changes in social and legal institutions make it detrimental for them to continue to conform to old norms. Psychological adjustment is critical to smoothing the transition from the old to the new norm. Without the adaptation of underlying attitudes, conformity to the new norm is maintained by strictly external incentives, and any relaxation of those sanctions will lead to a reversion to past behavior.

I conclude in chapter 7 by reviewing the arguments in the book and providing some final reflections on the contrasts between instrumental and expressive explanations of social action, the falsifiability of rational choice models, and the normatively beneficial consequences of assuming that people's choices and actions are motivated by an underlying rationality.

CHAPTER ONE

Interests versus Values

For in most social situations, if not in all, there is an element of rationality.

Karl Popper

Rational choice theory, it seems to me, has considerable intuitive plausibility and, at the very least, is a compelling point of departure for social analysis, even when applied to noneconomic phenomena such as decisions regarding lifestyles. Individual actions are seldom perfectly rational, but there is an essential degree of rationality in most behavior. We are rational in the sense of doing the best we can for ourselves within the confines of our knowledge and beliefs about the way the world works. Unless we assume that people are essentially rational actors whose beliefs, desires, and behavior are coherent, we have limited ability to make sense of their actions.[1] Analysts therefore do well to see how far this idealized explanatory model comports with actual behavior.[2]

I will begin this chapter by discussing the premises underlying rational choice theory. Then I will evaluate competing sociological and social-psychological theories based on symbolic and expressive motives rather than instrumental calculations—focusing especially on theories of status and symbolic politics, which have raised doubts about the role of self-interest in political decision making. In my view, symbolic and expressive theories both advance and hinder our understanding of decision making. They demonstrate persuasively that people weigh social considerations in addition to economic concerns, and that objective indicators of material self-interest are often weak predictors of individual choice when matched against subjective values. But these insights are obtained at a high price. The theories we employ to explain social behavior guide the focus of our analyses. By using group identifications and values to explain preferences, symbolic and expressive theories turn our attention inward toward psychological factors at the expense of political and economic forces and, by assuming that identifications and values are resilient in the face of changing incentives, they direct us away from processes of value formation and change. A sufficient defense of these theories would be that they are true, or at least are supported by the available evidence, thus closing off some of the interesting avenues suggested when we assume rational action. However, there are anomalies in the evidence that I believe point to a need for an alternative model. In my critique, I will recommend that a good place to start in filling the void left by symbolic and expressive theories is to examine value change and the pursuit of status as forms of instrumental action.

The brass ring will go to a theory that is sufficiently dynamic to accommodate both stability and changes of preferences and which also is able to incorporate such social-psychological factors as group identifications and ideological values into a model of individual choice. In this chapter, I begin by proposing a rational choice model that takes into account social incentives and psychological dispositions in addition to material incentives. As we shall see, a model that combines both incentives and dispositions can address some of the challenges to rational choice that have been raised by studies of symbolic politics. I will also show that such a model can provide a better explanation of social conformity, the formation of norms and conventions, and social change.

RATIONAL CHOICE

Individuals act rationally when they choose the best available means to achieve what they understand to be in their interest. While we may speak about objective interests as though they were unproblematic, most examples of rational choice reasoning rely on importing assumptions about a person's goals and his knowledge and beliefs about the world, without which no specific predictions or deductions can be drawn. In Herbert Simon's terminology, the analysis assumes *procedural* rather than *substantive* rationality. In evaluating whether a choice is substantively rational, we need only assess whether an individual chooses optimally given his goals and the objective characteristics of the situation. In contrast, procedural rationality takes into account the individual's frame of mind, his conceptualization of his predicament, and his aptitude for evaluating the information and options available to him.[3]

When we say that an option or policy is in someone's interest, we mean that pursuit of that policy will increase the likelihood that he will get something he wants for himself—whether that something is money, or power, or status. The key phrase is "for himself." If someone does something in order to obtain goods for others, then he is acting in their interest and not his own.[4] Russell Hardin classifies actions taken in order to promote group interests despite individual costs as "extrarational," and actions taken by individuals that do not further either individual or group interests as "irrational."[5] That we expect people to pursue self-interest more commonly than the interests of others is evident in the admiration given to those who act altruistically.

Because people can be mistaken about the consequences of their choices, it still is useful to make an analytical distinction between their *perceived* and *objective* interests. Indeed, society routinely assumes that some people cannot be trusted to recognize and guard their interests, especially minors, the elderly and infirm, and those with mental deficiencies. In such cases, parents, guardians, or the state assume the role of identifying and defending the interests of these persons. By maintaining a distinction between people's preferences and their objective interests, we leave open the question of whether preferences are shortsighted or distorted by limited experiences.

A more stringent criterion of rationality to keep in mind in the course of the analysis is that rational action is goal-directed behavior based on rational beliefs about the relationship between means and ends. Whether beliefs are rational depends on the reasons for holding them; beliefs must stem from processes of information gathering and analysis that are reliably related to generating accurate or true beliefs.[6] For instance, rational assessment of evidence can readily be built upon irrationally formed premises. Increase Mather was vigilant during the Salem witch trials about applying appropriate, quasi-scientific standards of evidence to prosecute suspected witches and wizards. Mather knew that accusations of witchcraft could be easily fabricated because there were instances of fakery on record. Therefore he scrupulously challenged unsubstantiated accusations of witchcraft, though he never questioned that witches existed or doubted that proven cases of witchcraft deserved harsh punishment.[7]

For rational choice models to have greater explanatory value, they need to incorporate two additional assumptions about how interests are calculated.[8] First, *individual calculations of self-interest weigh social pressures and incentives alongside more tangible material factors.* Our dependence on groups means that we must think about how our actions influence our social relationships. Many actions are taken with an eye toward how they might affect our reputations with other group members. We care not only about the most efficient means of pursuing our goals but also about the effect of our behavior on our standing within our groups, since what we do today conveys information about ourselves that will affect how others will act toward us in the future.

If we restrict the goals that rational individuals pursue to material benefits, we are likely to have a parsimonious and testable model, but one that will in all likelihood be readily falsified in the study of politics and sociology. John Harsanyi recognized this shortcoming years ago when he suggested that rational choice models would have limited application beyond economic choices unless they assumed that individuals were motivated by both material goals and a desire for social status.[9] People use the power wielded by groups to obtain benefits for themselves; they also take pleasure in maintaining affiliation and good relations with their friends, neighbors, and associates. Therefore, some of the utility of group memberships stems straightforwardly from the assistance that groups provide in achieving individual goals, such as obtaining a job or acquiring information, but there is also utility associated simply with being able to share ideas and engage in recreation and common activities with other people.

Second, *current interests are contingent on past decisions.* The value of different present-day alternatives depends on choices—to obtain education, skills, knowledge—made in the past that affect an individual's capacity to take advantage of current opportunities. Similarly, the development of social psychological dispositions—group memberships, values, identifications—represent past choices that will have a bearing on the attractiveness of contemporary ones. Early life decisions create or foreclose opportunities later in life and increase or limit one's ability to adapt to social change.[10] We cannot readily change the person we have spent a lifetime becoming. If we have developed personal aptitudes and characteristics well suited to some environments but not others, this will affect our receptivity to new norms, institutions, and technologies. Unfortunately, the investments we make in acquiring skills, knowledge, and other personal dispositions are made with varying degrees of foresight, depending on our level of sophistication and our ability to anticipate future circumstances and needs. The constraints imposed by past decisions can sometimes be undone by current choices, but one may reach a stage of life when it is no longer economical to change, so the rational choice may instead be to try to make the best of one's earlier investments.

Individual Choices and Collective Outcomes

Like any good theory, rational choice theory raises interesting issues for study and charts a program and methodology of research. By tracing social institutions, collective action, and social change to the actions of individuals, the theory follows the principle known as *methodological individualism.* People's actions are in turn explained by their preferences, beliefs, opportunities, and choices. Rational choice theory thus reframes many conventional research questions by asking how rational individuals would behave in different environments of choice and what the collective outcome of those choices will be. This approach was essential in pointing out the difficulty of motivating self-interested actors to take collective action on behalf of public goods. Instead of assuming, as earlier group theories did, that individuals will naturally take action that is in their collective interest, rational choice theory implied that individuals paradoxically will refrain from contributing even if they stand to benefit from the collective good. Because people can potentially receive the benefits of these goods without paying for them, they will not readily contribute to their provision.

The logic of collective action, which has proved applicable to a remarkably broad range of social and economic situations, proceeds from the assumption that cooperation must be explained in terms of the individual's cost-benefit calculus rather than the group's, since the group as such is not rational, but can only consist of rational individuals.[11] In such classic examples of collective action problems as preserving the environment, maintaining a common natural resource, participating in national defense, and engaging in social protests, group members gain when all individuals do their share, but the marginal benefit of a single contribution is outweighed by its cost. What is best for the group therefore is not necessarily best for the individual. Studies of collective action using laboratory experiments, game theory, and historical cases have tried to identify the conditions under which rational actors are likely to cooperate when they have a strong incentive to be free riders. Collective action problems are typically solved by changing the incentive structure facing individuals or by inducing cooperative behavior through repeated social interaction. In the political realm, it also appears that social norms, principled commitments, and expressive or symbolic benefits are often needed to motivate participation in collective action. Whether inclusion of these elements stretches the rational choice model or breaks it is the source of much controversy in the field.[12]

Likewise, the related puzzle of why people bother to vote had not greatly troubled students of elections before the problem was reexamined from the perspective of rational choice. Sociologists and political scientists traced group variation in voter turnout to differences in the extent to which group economic and noneconomic interests were made salient in electoral campaigns. Farmers, for example, were thought to turn out more than average because they were especially vulnerable to government economic policies. In general, those who paid close attention to politics, such as lawyers, professors, and business people, voted more frequently, because they saw more clearly than others the costs and benefits of alternative policies. From this perspective, the motivation to vote may also stem from an interest in furthering moral and religious convictions through government action, or from social pressure to abide by group norms. Although the discussion in this literature was conducted at the group level, the implication was that voting was instrumental in that individuals acted according to their broadly defined group interests.[13]

The rational choice account of voting, however, reveals that the policy benefits that one can expect from voting will almost always be insufficient to repay the cost of gathering information and going to the polls. This implies that people require other inducements to vote, such as civic duty, social pressure, the value of exercising voice, and the like. Thus far, we have no powerful theory—rational choice or any other kind—about how these factors motivate individual action. Since the problem of voter turnout has not been solved by any rival theory, it is not, strictly speaking, an "anomaly" for rational choice theory, but simply an unsolved problem for all relevant theories. A theory is presented with an anomaly only when it fails to account for a problem that another theory has already solved. An unsolved problem is less damaging to a theory than an anomaly, because theories are judged by their comparative explanatory power.[14] The fact that rational choice theory has fallen short in explaining voter turnout, therefore, is no reason to abandon the theory. Until there is a rival theory that provides a consistent explanation for voting and other forms of political action, it will not be the problem that ate rational choice.[15]

Causal Mechanisms

Some of the discoveries of rational choice theory may appear merely to restate earlier observations or to be obvious. But even when deductions from a particular model reproduce what is already known, rational choice theory is valuable for specifying a causal mechanism behind the phenomenon in question.[16] Exploration of this underlying mechanism sheds light on the range of circumstances in which the regularity will hold and when it is likely to be contradicted. In the study of social movements, it frequently has been observed that collective action piggybacks on existing community organizations. People who were affiliated with churches and fraternal organizations, for instance, were more likely to be active in the civil rights movement.[17] This is the kind of empirical regularity that is commonplace in social science research. Stated in this form, we do not know specifically what it is about organizational membership that facilitates contributions to public goods. One possible mechanism is that cooperative conventions created out of self-interest within enduring community networks and organizations provide the foundation for large-scale cooperation. Contingent cooperation in large-scale ventures is facilitated when collective action comprises a federated network of community groups and organizations.[18] Monitoring is feasible in these smaller groups, and cooperation or defection can be rewarded or punished in the course of everyday interaction with friends and associates. A person who refuses to contribute to a community-wide effort may suffer damage to his reputation and lose companionship and future opportunities for beneficial exchanges with those in his immediate reference groups.[19] Rational choice theory therefore leads the researcher to examine whether social institutions and patterns of social exchange within communities create favorable conditions for cooperative behavior.

By exploring the mechanism of rational calculation in repeated social interaction, we can derive further hypotheses about circumstances that would theoretically foster cooperation by lengthening people's time frames. The addition of a lower-level mechanism to explain a social regularity is therefore not simply philosophically satisfying in the sense of offering microfoundations; rather, further exploration of the implications of this individual-level mechanism yields other deductions about the relationship between structural conditions and aggregate outcomes.[20] For example, black migration to cities and burgeoning black college attendance between the 1930s and 1950s would be expected to promote collective action by creating structural conditions that permitted regular social exchange and community building among blacks.[21] In contrast, organizations whose members pay dues but enjoy few opportunities for direct social exchange are predicted to be not as conducive to promoting collective action.

Alternative social science theories, such as structural explanations, are frequently imprecise about causal mechanisms. Such explanations would often be strengthened if they more explicitly considered the role of individual choice. The causal impact of structural change on revolutionary collective action, for instance, depends crucially on how people experience their social arrangements and how their beliefs about their condition and opportunities change as a result of changes in state capacity or social and economic relations. People's beliefs affect their ability to develop effective organizations and to overcome collective action problems in their struggle against the state.[22]

Similarly, functionalist explanations of social institutions that point to how such institutions contribute to the maintenance of society gloss over the mechanisms by which individuals create and defend such arrangements. According to Kingsley Davis and Wilbert Moore's functionalist account of social stratification, for example, a status system guarantees that adequate incentives are available to attract the most able individuals to the most important social positions.[23] In the interest of society, individuals with the necessary aptitudes must be given an incentive (such as higher income and status) to undergo the education and training that are required for such occupations. However, the standard critique of functionalist explanations holds that we cannot account for a system of social stratification by pointing to how it serves the general interests of society. One must still ask how and why individuals support such a social arrangement. Individuals must have a personal reason, rooted in self or group interest, for acquiring status and for granting it to others, because "social needs can affect individual behavior only as far as they are translated into individual motivations."[24] This is why, within every social group (street gangs and criminal organizations included), individuals pursue status for its attendant benefits and status is granted only to individuals whose actions further the interests of those bestowing the status.

Finally, as we shall see in chapter 2, social-psychological theories that attempt to explain conformity in small groups on the basis of patterns of identification and social contact (e.g., reference group theory), underspecify the causal relationships between membership and beliefs. Again, one must incorporate strategies, choices, and interests to explain how individuals identify themselves and to account for the ideas and values to which they are likely to conform.

Cultural Inertia and Habit

One would think that former Oregon Senator Bob Packwood, while dogged by charges that he had a history of making unwanted sexual advances to women and under investigation by the Senate Ethics Committee, would have stopped telling jokes about sex in public and resisted the temptation to compliment pretty women. Indeed, a person accused of sexual misconduct might be expected to smarten up and become especially vigilant about his own behavior, especially around women. But apparently Packwood remained prone to such lapses, forcing his chief of staff to watch sternly over him and step in whenever she saw that he was about to cross the line.[25]

Habits learned, ingrained, and positively reinforced over a lifetime die hard. When Packwood was growing up, he was painfully shy. Aware that he was socially inept, he read Dale Carnegie's *How to Win Friends and Influence People* to learn ways to become more popular. Apparently, he collected bawdy jokes in a notebook and systematically committed them to memory, perhaps because he found it easier to fit in by being funny. For much of his adult life, the training he undertook to improve his social skills served him adequately. He never came close to being comfortable with the glad-handing that politicians are famous for, but he took steps to develop appealing personal characteristics that he knew he would need in greater measure to be successful. The irony in Packwood's case is that when times changed, and relationships between the sexes in and out of the workplace were redefined, the traits that Packwood so deliberately learned to smooth his path continued to rule him, prompting behavior that was no longer tolerated. Values and dispositions that he cultivated over a lifetime were stubbornly unresponsive to his new interests.

Just as Packwood had difficulty shaking his old style, inner-city youths, who must project fearlessness—by the clothes they wear, the language they use, and the way they move—in order to survive on the street, have trouble adjusting to the norms of "decent" behavior required at school and on the job. As Elijah Anderson explains, "The street-oriented youth . . . has made the concept of manhood a part of his very identity; he has difficulty manipulating it—it often controls him." The street code that inner-city youths are socialized to follow is adaptive in the environment in which they operate, but detrimental outside it. [26]

If there is a single lesson to draw from the sociological model, it is that individuals often make choices largely out of habit or inertia without engaging in much, if any, strategic calculation. In practice it may be indeterminate whether habit reflects a prior commitment to a course of action involving some earlier measure of rational reflection or if it merely reflects mindless repetition; nevertheless, it seems that with changes in the available choices, behavior often displays more rigidity than economists acknowledge.

The inertia contained in beliefs and values can prevent people from recognizing that conditions have changed. Scottish and Irish immigrants, for example, accustomed to wood shortages in the Old World, continued to build small houses in this country even though wood was abundant in their new surroundings.[27] Before the advent of modern protective masks and helmets, National Hockey League goaltenders perfected a "stand-up" style of defending the net in order to guard their exposed faces from errant sticks and skate blades. But the upright style eventually came to be regarded as a superior goaltending technique irrespective of its self-preservationist origins, so that new goaltenders were schooled in this method long after improved head and face protection rendered it unnecessary. The stand-up style did not diminish in popularity until some innovative goaltenders capitalized on the new equipment and enjoyed success using less inhibited techniques.[28] As Jon Elster observed, "People sometimes act stupidly out of stupidity and rigidly out of rigidity. Inertia may be a rational way of coping with a too rapidly changing environment, but it may also be just what it is: inertia."[29] Beliefs and values are rooted in emotions and sensibilities that are not easily controlled or altered voluntarily. They have a hold on the mind that may not be loosened by new circumstances and changes in incentives. Cultural practices, therefore, tend to persist even after the environmental constraints that gave rise to them no longer exist.

A major criticism of rational choice theory is that people often seem to be guided more strongly by enduring values and group attachments than by self-interested instrumental calculation. A great variety of noneconomic theories of politics have been popular in political science and sociology at different junctures. In the aftermath of World War II, psychological explanations centering on personality traits and political attitudes were used to explain behavior as diverse as fascism, modernity, and democratic stability. In the 1950s and 1960s, symbolic and expressive theories of social movements and political extremism dominated the study of mass behavior and served as antecedents to more recent noninstrumental theories.[30]

In the following sections, I will take a closer look at theories of status politics[31] and symbolic politics[32] to show how noninstrumental theories contrast with rational choice theory. *Status politics* describes collective action aimed at preserving the social status of a group's way of life. Group norms and values are defended because they offer more prestige than alternative ones. *Symbolic politics* revolves around psychologically ingrained attachments to general social values produced by early childhood socialization. Such symbolic attitudes act like defense mechanisms to shield the bearer from disturbing information about himself and the world. There is no correspondence between the attitude and the actual state of the world; rather, such attitudes reflect inner tensions and needs, as when personal frustrations and fears are displaced into prejudices against racial and ethnic minorities. The targets of aggression are merely scapegoats.[33]

In neither theory are the group attachments grounded in self-interest, nor are the values held and defended instrumental to attaining material goals. The status theory therefore emphasizes the social significance of certain values and ways of life; the symbolic theory emphasizes their psychological significance. Both theories focus on the resentments that surface when traditional ways of life are threatened; neither theory leaves much room for the operation of self-interest in developing and maintaining attachments to a way of life or in shifting allegiance to new values.

STATUS POLITICS

Status politics are essentially group politics organized along social rather than economic dimensions. The historian Richard Hofstadter and the sociologist Seymour Martin Lipset advanced the theory to explain conservative and reactionary American politics in the 1950s. The sociologist Joseph Gusfield developed a variation of the theory in his account of the turn-of-the-century temperance movement.

Gusfield contended that Prohibition and temperance were struggles between new and traditional groups over the legitimacy and status of their respective habits and lifestyles: "The agitation and struggle of the Temperance adherents has been directed toward the establishment of their norms as marks of social and political superiority." Each side in the conflict tried to use public policy to assert its preeminence in the social order: "Status issues indicate, by their resolution, the group, culture, or style of life to which government and society are publicly committed. They answer the question: On behalf of which ethnic, religious, or other cultural group is this government and this society being carried out? We label these as *status issues* precisely because what is at issue is the relevant groups in the status order of the society."[34]

Gusfield argued that status issues are not pursued in order to enhance one's economic position. Rather, "a political issue becomes one of status when its tangible, instrumental consequences are subordinated to its significance for the conferral of prestige. . . . The argument is less over the effect of the proposed measures on concrete actions than it is over the question of whose culture is to be granted legitimacy by the public action of government."[35] The status obtained through the government's affirmation of the group's values is valuable in itself: "The fact of affirmation is a positive statement of the worth or value of the particular subculture vis-à-vis other subcultures in the society. . . . It demonstrates their dominance in the power structure and the prestige accorded them in the total society."[36]

In his analysis of the sources of conservative activism in the postwar period, Hofstadter acknowledged that political and economic grievances about taxes, inflation, and the quality of life in cities constituted part of the motivation, but he was not persuaded that the essential features of the movement could be accounted for in material terms. In addition to these tangible concerns, there were cultural and symbolic elements driving political action that did not easily lend themselves to economic interpretation—"among them the sheer weight of habit and party loyalty, ethnic origins and traditions, religious affiliations and religious styles, racial and ethnic prejudices, attitudes toward liberty and censorship, feelings about foreign policy quite unrelated to commercial goals and of dubious relationship to the national interest."[37]

There were in particular several anomalies concerning the 1950s conservative political movement, such as why its proponents reacted to international insecurity and instability by demanding rigid domestic conformity, or why so much suspicion was directed at the government, almost irrespective of the partisanship of the incumbent administration: "None of [the tangible factors] seem to explain the broad appeal of pseudo-conservatism, its emotional intensity, its dense and massive irrationality, or some of the peculiar ideas it generates. Nor will they explain . . . why the rank-and-file janizaries of pseudo-conservatism are so eager to hurl accusations, write letters to congressmen and editors, and expend so much emotional energy and crusading idealism upon causes that plainly bring them no material reward."[38]

Hofstadter postulated that episodes of status politics alternated with conventional interest politics, depending on the condition of the economy. In a troubled economy, groups direct their energies toward programmatic and legislative solutions for their material grievances; the government is looked to for a remedy. In times of economic prosperity and social mobility, some social groups become vulnerable to changes in the social order and resort to desperate measures to retain their social position. Hofstadter suggests that certain poorly understood psychological dynamics are at work: "For the basic aspirations that underlie status discontent are only partially conscious; and, even so far as they are conscious, it is difficult to give them a programmatic expression. . . . Therefore, it is the tendency of status politics to be expressed more in vindictiveness, in sour memories, in the search for scapegoats, than in realistic proposals for positive action."[39]

Although several researchers have made use of the concept of status politics, they do not all share the same position on the degree to which such behavior is expressive or instrumental. Gusfield distances himself from the view of Hofstadter and Lipset that status politics are spurred exclusively by expressive and psychological motives. His version concentrates on non-class-based group conflict that is aimed, not directly at generating material benefits, but rather at using state action to alter the meanings and significance of certain social behaviors. Gusfield emphasizes that between expressive and class politics there is a symbolic realm pertaining to people's social status, and whereas Hofstadter and Lipset view status politics as reflecting irrational motives, Gusfield maintains that people understandably have an interest in protecting and enhancing their status.

But a reluctance to link the symbolic realm to tangible interests results in a curiously abbreviated theory which suggests that there are sufficient symbolic reasons for people to wish to defend their culture. It would appear that a more promising line of inquiry would be to assume that status and prestige are rationally sought and that they are instrumental to other political and economic goals in society. The pursuit of esteem and status depends on the ability to use one's status to obtain a variety of other valued goods.

The crux of the issue concerning status politics, therefore, is in what sense it merits a special category: Why do people care about acquiring status if status is not translatable into other benefits? If the social issues defining status politics are essentially expressive rather than instrumental, then why do the symbols and values underlying these issues reliably transmit across generations, and why does it matter whether individuals conform to them? Are there material consequences to having one set of cultural norms and symbols predominate over another? Why do groups develop strong attachments to their norms and practices?

The temperance movement is the classic case study of a status issue, and the politics of that era offer a vivid example of how ideas about culture become entangled with political and economic goals. As new ethnic groups in the United States began to acquire more political power in the cities, nativist groups felt their control over culture *and* politics wane.[40] Traditional practices and ways of life were being transformed by new technologies, ascendant groups, and broad-scale social changes.

In the 1920s, the old guard of white, Anglo-Saxon, Protestant families fought against encroaching social change on a number of fronts and were sometimes successful in delaying reform: "Small-town and rural Protestants were waging a vigorous defense of their cultural values against their rapidly gaining foes—the advancing Catholics and minority ethnic groups on one side and the modernists in religion and secularists in intellectual culture on the other. The Ku Klux Klan, Prohibitionism, the campaign against evolution in the schools, anti-Catholicism and the whispering campaign against Al Smith were all aspects of this struggle."[41]

The temperance movement should be viewed in the context of this broader reaction against new political and economic forces in American society. Nativist groups supported Prohibition in an attempt to enforce the moral values of the traditional culture. They believed that drinking was symptomatic of a general moral decline that was eroding American society, but they also believed that alcohol was itself the cause of real social problems. Alcohol was a symbolic issue in that it exemplified the contrasting lifestyles of competing factions, but it was a real issue in the sense that people thought there were harmful social consequences associated with drinking. Drinking and drunkenness were elements of the increasing sense of disorder in American cities. The effort to control the use of alcohol was therefore not expressive action that was unrelated to perceived social ills.

In a new epilogue written more than twenty years after the original publication of his book, *Symbolic Crusade,* Gusfield amends the details of his account of the temperance movement by giving greater weight to people's concerns that drinking caused crime, poverty, sloth, immoral behavior, and the decline of religious belief.[42] When community institutions such as the church proved incapable of solving the problems associated with alcohol consumption, people demanded government intervention. When national prohibition took effect in 1920, liquor bans already existed in two-thirds of the states, but teetotalers believed that national enforcement was needed to bring the problem under control. Ultimately, the Eighteenth Amendment was repealed in response to conventional economic arguments that the liquor industry would generate needed jobs during the Depression.[43]

But the disposition toward alcohol was only one element in the sociopolitical divide along fundamentalist-secular, liberal-conservative, traditional-modernist, local-cosmopolitan, and urban-rural lines. The fate of Prohibition depended on whether "the power of the Protestant, rural, native American was greater than that of the Eastern upper classes, the Catholic and Jewish immigrants, and the urbanized middle classes. This was the lineup of the electoral struggle."[44] The issue was not only whether alcohol consumption would be permitted, but whose way of life would prevail: which curriculum would be taught to schoolchildren, what standards of sexuality and morality would be reinforced, how much immigration would be permitted, what regions of the country would be most influential, which groups would dominate the Democratic party. Thus, it would appear that the tangible implications of changes in status and prestige are more significant than the symbolism of being able or unable to enforce group norms. Status is a barometer of a group's resources and power.

Symbolic Politics

Prejudice is the reasoning of the stupid.

Voltaire

Many of the kinds of political issues that animated ideological conflict in the 1950s and inspired social psychological theorizing have hardly waned with time, but instead have been renewed and updated in today's political climate. Current cultural debates center on the legality of abortion, government funding of controversial forms of artistic expression, the place of gays and lesbians in society, policies aimed at promoting equality for women and minorities, the defense of traditional values in education and the family, concern over violence and sex in films and television, and so forth. But analyses of these contemporary conflicts still hark back to the notion that to understand cultural political conflict, one will have to focus on the expressive and symbolic attachment that people have to their way of life, which is assumed to be distinct from instrumental action.[45] Jack Citrin and Donald Green, for example, say that we can explain these controversies only by acknowledging that people give priority to their cultural norms. Robert Abelson contends that the actions that people take on such issues are motivated by noninstrumental, expressive concerns.[46] Therefore, the theoretical tradition that defines status politics lives on in contemporary research.

The most popular current version of expressive and symbolic theorizing in political science has an even more pronounced psychological bent than did the earlier sociological theories focusing on status discontent. Some of the strongest empirical claims for the resilience of group identifications and social values are found in a collection of studies accumulated over the past twenty years which argue that there is at best a tenuous connection between people's life circumstances (or self-interests) and their public policy stands.[47] Instead, the studies suggest that so-called symbolic orientations like political ideology, party identification, racial tolerance, and other general values bear most of the responsibility for shaping policy preferences.

Adherents of the symbolic theory have tried to assess the relative influence of values and self-interest on policy preferences by looking at how choices are affected by variation in the costs and benefits of alternative policies. Self-interest is usually measured narrowly in terms of an individual's objective interest, with interest being defined as short-term, material benefits for oneself or one's family. This is a reasonable starting point for investigating the extent to which people's policy stances are instrumentally motivated. However, we should keep in mind that there are alternative assumptions (namely, those mentioned earlier) that can be made about the nature of rational calculation, which I will return to after discussing the results of these studies.

Because the studies just mentioned are cross-sectional, we only see how cross-sectional variation in the costs and benefits of policy alternatives affects marginal distributions of opinion. For example, does having a school-age child affect whether one supports school busing beyond the influence of one's ideological and racial beliefs? The verdict of theorists of symbolic politics is that deep-seated values influence preferences more than the objective costs of the policy. The same is true on issues of law and order, government employment policy, health insurance, and many other policy matters that have been tested in this fashion as part of the research program. A crime victim who behaves according to a narrowly defined self-interest model presumably updates his information about the relative safety of his community and neighborhood after having been victimized; however, survey data show that whether or not one has been victimized actually makes little difference to attitudes on gun control and criminal sentencing. Similarly, whether one has health insurance or is employed seems to make only a marginal difference (albeit sometimes statistically significant) to whether one supports government programs to provide health coverage and jobs. In general, variation in the costs and benefits of policies seems to influence choices weakly if at all. Personal circumstances bearing on an issue typically have a smaller effect than symbolic attitudes and demographic factors.

Surprisingly, perhaps, studies show that a white respondent's belief that he or a member of his family will lose a job, a promotion, or a place in college to an equally or less-qualified black person does not significantly affect a variety of racial policy positions—including attitudes toward preferential hiring and college quotas—once *racial resentment* is added to the equation. Racial resentment is a symbolic value that is postulated to be the cause of both perceived threats and racial policy stances.[48] Racial threat is "a product not so much of the social circumstances white Americans find themselves in, but how they look at the social world, and especially whether or not they regard

blacks with suspicion and resentment." Consequently, "when faced with policy proposals on school desegregation or affirmative action, whites and blacks
come to their views without calculating what's in it for them."[49]

The considerable body of research on symbolic politics indicates that measures of objective self-interest will generally be weak influences on individual
policy preferences when contrasted with social values. Those unfamiliar with
this empirical research may be prone to thinking that individual behavior is
more adaptive than it tends to be. In this view, the person who loses his job
will suddenly want the government to provide everyone with a guaranteed
job; the parents who produce a new child will reverse their stand on busing
and now oppose it because they are at risk; the liberal who gets mugged one
evening wakes up as a conservative who is opposed to gun control, advocates
mandatory prison terms, and calls for the death penalty. Instead, personal dispositions, including social values and group identifications, can dominate individual choice at the expense of apparent objective incentives.

Why does self-interest appear to have so little effect on opinion? Using
phrasing reminiscent of Talcott Parsons,[50] two principal exponents of the theory of symbolic politics, Donald Kinder and David Sears, suggest that "one
possibility is that self-interest is typically overwhelmed by long-held, emotionally powerful predispositions. According to this account, people acquire predispositions (like racial prejudice or nationalism) early in life that shape their
political views in adulthood. Interpretation and evaluation of political events
are essentially affective responses to salient symbols that resemble the attitude
objects to which similar emotional responses were conditioned in earlier life.
Whether or not the event has some tangible consequence for the citizen's
personal life is irrelevant; the pertinent personal stake is a symbolic one, which
triggers long-held, affect-laden, habitual responses."[51]

In other words, early socialization shapes the values and partisan affiliations
that a person adopts. These inclinations and attachments, according to the
theory, tend to persist throughout one's life and to color one's interpretation
and evaluation of political issues. The symbols associated with a political issue
evoke the relevant underlying predispositions that give rise to one's response.
"Busing" and "integration," for example, are racial symbols that activate a
person's racial tolerance or prejudice.[52] There is limited scope for the operation
of self-interest when choices are conditioned in this manner.

DOES RATIONAL CHOICE THEORY SURVIVE THE CHALLENGES POSED BY THE SYMBOLIC POLITICS RESEARCH?

I think not only that rational choice can be sustained but also that proper
recognition of the significance of the work of symbolic theorists ought to result

in a more realistic and robust rational choice model. First, studies of symbolic politics identify the kinds of rational choice assumptions that will not hold up to real decision making. Second, they point to the kinds of social psychological factors that need to be accommodated within a rational choice model if it hopes to achieve a modicum of explanatory power in the political and sociological realms. But if these adjustments are made, we should end up with a model that has stronger properties than either spare economic models or less flexible noninstrumental models.

First, let us be clear about what studies of symbolic politics do and do not demonstrate about the weakness of self-interest. There are assorted methodological issues about the setup of the tests in this research that should make us cautious about interpreting their results as a refutation of rationality or, at least, of self-interest. In addition to issues of internal validity, I raise questions about the formal limitations of expressive and symbolic theories to explain behavior. I will break these issues into five categories: (1) whether objective or subjective indicators are better measures of self-interest, (2) whether material goals exclusive of social incentives adequately measure self-interest, (3) whether rationality means the same thing in survey responses as in actual behavior, (4) whether motivation from values is exclusive of rational calculation, and (5) whether the theory underlying symbolic values is a good theory of value formation and change. I will comment on these issues here before developing an alternative theory of value formation based on these observations in the next chapter.

Objective versus Subjective Self-Interest

Tests of self-interest in mass surveys commonly measure self-interest without considering what people believe about their situations; instead, researchers try to infer self-interest from a person's objective characteristics or reported experiences.[53] But the validity of some of the assumptions used to establish a person's objective interest is debatable. A proper test of self-interest requires that different individuals are differentially rewarded by the alternatives, so that those individuals who stand to gain the most from a particular option will be its strongest supporters. However, when an individual has no direct stake in an issue, researchers assume that he or she will take a position opposed to those with a putative interest. So, for example, we are told to assume that people without children will have a greater interest in supporting busing than those with children. But it is not clear why this should be the case. Those without children may include both disinterested spectators and coopted neighbors of people with an interest in one side of the controversy or the other. The former group might judge busing to be a failure just as strongly as the parents who oppose it; the latter group may simply be pressured to support their friends. (I will elaborate on these dynamics below.) Still another possibility, of course, is that childless residents may oppose busing because they fear a drop in property values or for some other self-interested reason, in which case they are not disinterested but interested for reasons not measured by the survey.

Similarly, we might question the premise behind why we would expect those who reside in neighborhoods with higher crime rates to be more prone to seek harsher penalties for criminal offenders. Residents of low-crime areas may be just as concerned about crime, even if they are less likely to be victimized, and they may be just as likely to favor tough sanctions; there is nothing irrational about their opinion. The implicit assumption underlying this test is that objective danger is correlated with fear, which in turn is correlated with opinion. But rational individuals in low-crime areas do not pay any direct cost for demanding longer prison sentences (there may be tax consequences, but these are hard to estimate); opinions are virtually free of charge.

When any one of two or more competing policy alternatives can plausibly be pursued out of self-interest, we cannot specify a priori which is the self-interested choice. One study hypothesized that self-interested victims of crime would be more *opposed* to gun control, but found no relationship.[54] Another study, however, expected just the opposite—that people who had been threatened by a gun would be more *supportive* of gun control.[55] In fact, self-interested individuals who wish to be protected from crime might reasonably take either side of the gun control debate; some will think that taking guns out of the hands of criminals will reduce crime, while others will think that putting guns in the hands of law-abiding citizens will ward off criminals.

In general, there is confusion among proponents of symbolic politics about what constitutes self-interested behavior and little appreciation for collective action problems. For example, Sears and Funk are puzzled by the lack of political activism against nuclear weapons, concluding *incorrectly* that participation is the rational choice for self-interested individuals: "People do not perceive as serious problems issues that objectively should stimulate widespread self-interested revolt. . . . One might think humans would be united in vehement opposition to weapons that could eradicate all human civilization and indeed life on this planet. Yet researchers have consistently found very little public concern about them."[56]

The influence of costs and benefits on policy positions would probably be much greater if people had better information. There is a strong relationship, for example, between home ownership and support for property tax cutbacks because people can readily see the economic ramifications of this issue.[57] On many issues, however, uncertainty surrounding the various alternatives makes it difficult for people to know what policy is best for them. In such instances, the "best choice" may owe more to persuasion than it does to objective evidence.

Studies based on mass surveys of the relationship between self-interest and policy choices generally ignore the influence of subjective beliefs about the alternatives on individual choice. But this has not prevented proponents of symbolic explanations from citing the importance of information and subjective beliefs to explain why the self-interested choice has not prevailed in numerous studies. On many issues investigated, it is conceded that people do not have a clear idea of the stakes involved or of the relationship between alternatives and outcomes.[58] Yet there has been no suggestion that the design of the surveys should be modified to ascertain what information people have about alternative possibilities in order to test whether they follow their subjective interests. Instead, researchers have intentionally favored objective measures of self-interest over subjective measures which supposedly pose a "threat to unequivocal causal interpretations."[59] For example, since doctors who oppose national health insurance are expected to rationalize their position by saying that such a scheme will cost them money, researchers are reluctant to examine the relationship between medical students' beliefs about the effect of national health insurance on doctors' earnings and their attitudes toward the policy. Rather, the measure of self-interest preferred by researchers is the medical students' degree of financial indebtedness resulting from their education. Not surprisingly, beliefs turn out to influence policy attitudes, because they represent what students think is in their interest, whereas the objective indicator (student loans) does not.[60]

Likewise, it is assumed that those without health insurance or employment, if they are self-interested, should support government intervention in those areas. But what is missing in tests comparing the relative influence of self-interest and symbolic values is an assessment of how people in a given objective state evaluate the alternatives they face—for example, how the uninsured regard the prospect of government health insurance as opposed to private insurance, or how the unemployed view government policies to combat unemployment. Conservatives who lose their health insurance coverage might still oppose a national plan because they believe the state cannot efficiently manage such programs. Is it thus accurate to say that such people go against their self-interest in favor of their conservatism? Perhaps a better question is whether there are individuals who believe in state intervention and who believe they would benefit from such programs but still prefer that the government do nothing. Such individuals would not possess coherent beliefs, desires, and preferences.

Social science generalizations, as Simon noted, typically rely on implicit assumptions about the state of mind of individual decision makers. Assumptions have to be imported about people's decision-making rules; otherwise, there is no way to go from the objective situation to the individual's choice. For example, election studies indicate that one explanation for the general weakness of economic self-interest as a determinant of individual voting behavior is that people often take responsibility for their own economic status. In the United States, there is a strong bias in the political culture in favor of economic individualism. People are taught to believe that they are in control of their own destinies and that they succeed or fail largely on their own effort. They are therefore reluctant to connect their perception of their own economic situation to their rating of the health of the economy in general. To the extent that individuals absolve the government of responsibility for their economic status, they will not cast a vote based on changes in their financial state. Individuals who believe in the work ethic and who have faith that the marketplace offers equality of opportunity will not translate their economic grievances into political behavior.[61]

Such studies reinforce why it is difficult to assess straightforwardly whether people pursue their interests. Perceived interests depend on the explanation that one provides for one's current status. Differences in beliefs about how the world functions have significant implications for the prescriptions that people draw for their own predicaments.

Material versus Social Benefits

A narrow focus on short-term, material benefits also rules out social incentives from the purview of the rational actor. Social incentives may be immediate pressures and threats imposed by others. Consideration of social relationships may also factor into long-term strategies for obtaining self-interest. People will sometimes defend values that appear to run against their immediate self-interest in order to preserve social relationships and reputations that return long-term benefits.[62]

Because internal group dynamics may create relatively homogeneous preferences, the relationship between policy preferences and tangible economic or social interests may be apparent only when comparisons are drawn across social groups. On any given issue, most members of a social class may share the same interest, but some members of the class may, for idiosyncratic reasons, find that they do not have the same stake as other group members. But even group members with less to defend may still feel that they are better off conforming with the group norm.

For example, the working class as a whole is more likely to oppose busing than the middle class, because its members have fewer options and resources than middle-class families and are more likely to be affected by any scheme designed to reduce racial imbalance within school districts.[63] Higher-income families can move to the suburbs or enroll their children in private schools to avoid such schemes. Consequently, the middle class can afford to endorse racial norms that are more liberal and tolerant because its members generally are less susceptible to busing. In contrast, within the working-class milieu racial norms are less tolerant and there are strong pressures on individuals to oppose school busing. In this fashion, narrow self-interest (that is, interests defined without considering one's ongoing relationships with others) may be compromised by social influences that encourage conformity to group interests.

The manner in which social pressure compromises narrow self-interest is depicted in Jonathan Rieder's description of white opposition to blacks' moving into the Canarsie neighborhood in the late 1970s.[64] Canarsie residents could not easily move to other neighborhoods because of rising interest rates that made selling and purchasing prohibitively expensive. They therefore tried to prevent home sales to blacks and opposed a school busing plan intended to bring about greater racial integration.

Individuals with the largest investments applied social pressure on others to resist change. Tactics used to prevent home sales to blacks included threatening sellers and their families and real estate agents. Neighborhood organizations monitored sales and kept tabs on residents: "Voluntary groups . . . served as early warning systems, which permitted compensatory action by factions wishing to reverse a sale, and they refined guesswork about the likely conduct of neighbors." It was a tipoff in Canarsie if a resident refused to join the neighborhood association: "Residents who did not join a block association were marked off as risky mavericks to be watched more carefully."[65]

Sellers who did not have strong social ties in the neighborhood were the hardest to influence: "Residents who were not involved with neighbors could go about the business of selling without the pressures generated by social entanglements."[66] People who did not have school-aged children sometimes caved in to pressure from neighbors. One neighborhood vigilante described his tactics: "Sometimes you have to use forceful methods with them, you have to be firm with the sellers. You explain to them, 'Hey look, you raised your kids, you're on your way to Florida, but many of us still have children here. You got your price, but I need mine.' You make threats over the telephone, you threaten their children. That's okay, 'cause they are threatening other people's children. It's self-protection for the staying."[67]

Pressure on sellers to sell only to whites was strongest when few sales to blacks had been completed, for once a number of homes had been sold to blacks on a particular block, there was little effective leverage that "stayers" could maintain against "movers." Each wave of sales and departures increased the motivation for those who remained to follow suit. There was no reason for a person to hold out against residential integration when many of his neighbors had flown the coop. Economic self-preservation became the controlling motive, and there was no longer any normative pressure against selling to a black family. The value of group affiliations diminishes as neighbors depart, and with it the incentive for individuals to conform.

Opinions and Behavior

The symbolic politics research has generally examined the influence of symbolic values and self-interest on other values rather than on actual behavior. Broad value orientations are especially likely to prevail in surveys of policy attitudes that allow people the luxury of expressing opinions for reasons unrelated to material self-interest. In one study of the link between attitudes and behavior, Donald Green and Jonathan Cowden found a significant relationship between self-interest and actual participation in antibusing protests, but no relationship between self-interest and expressed opinions on the busing issue.[68] They conclude that people are less rational, or less self-interested, when they form and express opinions than when they take political action.[69]

I believe, on the other hand, that there is a more parsimonious way to describe what happens than to treat individuals in dichotomous terms, operating according to one model in surveys and another when they act. In surveys, people who oppose busing—an opposition that is a product of group conformity—say so; it is the side that they want to be seen to be on. Their friends oppose busing; the politicians they admire oppose busing. They get net benefits by indicating that they too are opposed. Within affected communities, expressions of opposition to busing in public opinion surveys can reflect sincere dislike for busing schemes as a result of regular group dynamics and social influence processes. In other words, when adopting opinions that have no direct or immediate consequences, there will often be mitigating social forces that interfere with the operation of objective individual interests.

But political activity is more costly than simply expressing one's opinion. Those who become involved in protests need additional incentives or benefits to offset the higher costs. Naturally, parents in predominantly white neighborhoods who lack the resources to enroll their children in private schools are more likely to act because they stand to gain more by preventing busing from occurring in their district. Efforts to deny any role for self-interest in this issue are curious, because casual observation indicates that busing controversies exploded in communities hit by court-ordered busing plans, but they rarely occurred when the threat of busing was remote. Therefore, at the community level of analysis, one finds good intuitive evidence that active opposition to busing was related to the threat of busing.

Social factors, however, can also undercut the relationship between narrow self-interest and protest activity. People who do not have children or who can transfer their children to private schools will sometimes be drafted nevertheless by their neighbors to engage in protest. Such individuals will go along for the same reason that they will be inclined to agree with the predominant community view on the issue. Their rational choice must give due weight to their ongoing social relationships within the community.[70]

Are Value-Based Motives Necessarily Noninstrumental?

Relegating self-interest—as the symbolic politics literature does—to residual short-term material and personal concerns virtually ensures that self-interest will take a back seat to general values and dispositions in their relative explanatory power. A similar bias undercut early research on the prevalence of policy voting, when partisan voting was kept separate conceptually from issue voting. Critics rightly argued that party-line voting was not inconsistent with an economic approach: "Most voters will only learn enough to form a very generalized notion of the position of a particular candidate or party on some issues, and many voters will be ignorant about most issues. The investor-voter will use partisan and ideological labels as practical solutions to the problem of costly information."[71] Ideologies, like party cues, are shorthand versions of political platforms. Parties differentiate themselves by their ideological stances and form ideologies with an eye toward attracting voters. For voters, knowledge of a party's ideology and of the correspondence between that ideology and the ideal social state will be a sufficient basis for voting so long as there is consistency between the stated policies of a party and its actions in office.

In the research on symbolic politics, the same criticism can be levied. A person's racial tolerance or political ideology may be a better predictor of his views on school busing than whether he has school-age children, but, as I will show, there is no reason to assume that developing and following such values occurs independently of interests. The pursuit of values may accord with rational action if we consider what values embody and what it means to follow one's values. Values explain by offering reasons for individual action that go beyond merely summarizing the behavior itself. While the best evidence for motivation by a particular value may be a pattern of consistent behavior, a reference to values focuses on a particular reason for the person's actions rather than on alternative reasons.[72]

Ideologies represent the broadest kinds of values that people employ in their decision making. In their most advanced form, they are coherent systems of belief pertaining to the nature of man, the rights of citizens, the ideal way to organize society, the proper role of the state, the wisdom of programmatic change, and the prerequisites of a good society. But even people who are not ideologues may still have attitudes and feelings that incline them toward different ideological camps.[73] The prevailing social psychological view is that general ideological leanings are acquired very early in life, mainly from parents, while particular views on political subjects remain hazy in the years prior to adulthood.[74]

Ideological values therefore entail preferences for bundles of goods. People have first-order desires as well as reflective second-order desires about desires (or metapreferences).[75] Switching from being a meat eater to being a health-conscious vegetarian represents a change in lifestyle, not simply a change of a single preference ordering. Each lifestyle is accompanied by an overall set of preferences that one conforms to if the lifestyle is followed. But if one abandons a lifestyle for another, then a substitute set of preferences is followed. An ideology similarly consists of principles that order preferences on numerous dimensions. As a constellation of values, a political ideology is designed to guide one's actions over the long haul. Ideological orientations allow a person to make choices readily without engaging in elaborate calculations; thus it is self-defeating to develop such orientations but then to ignore them in specific instances (in this sense, they can override an objective self-interest). If it is rational to develop a general orientation rather than to treat issues in a piecemeal manner, then it can be rational to allow that orientation to guide choices across a variety of issues. Isolated short-term factors that could potentially change one's values (losing one's job, being robbed, etc.) are likely to be resisted, because the utility of a general orientation is compromised if it is too easily altered by singular experiences.

The connection between ideological values and the material interests of individuals is seldom straightforward. For pragmatic reasons, liberal and conservative ideologies in American politics are not aimed simply at one class, but instead offer prescriptions on a variety of issues in both economic and noneconomic realms about how to improve conditions for a diverse cross-section of society. An ideology is intended to hold together a broad electoral coalition. It is not obvious, therefore, that there need be sharp class differences in support for liberalism and conservatism, since both philosophies claim to be best for society as a whole, as well as for the constituent groups in the society. People will be subject to persuasion and manipulation by political leaders about where their interests lie. Therefore, while the socioeconomic biases of ideological and partisan identification are often consistent with a self-interest model (e.g., higher-income persons more strongly endorse laissez-faire market principles), the correlations are far from perfect because, on many topics, there is considerable room for debate about which ideology best serves different socioeconomic groups.[76]

In addition to any direct material interest that is served by an ideology, we also have an interest in establishing a coherent understanding of society so that we can make decisions. Instead of viewing ideological values as fixed psychological states or symbolic values, we might consider them to be general beliefs about social causality. People have a rough understanding about what kind of government serves their individual and group interests—they might, for instance, feel strongly one way or another about government intervention in the economy.

The self-interested position associated with an issue may be hard to discern independently of one's ideological orientation. We have to trace the intermediate links between a person's predicament, his reasons and assessments regarding that predicament, and his evaluation of what needs to be done. Much of this information may be bound up in a person's ideological orientation, which cannot be inferred directly from his specific life circumstances. Ideological values therefore shape both preferences and beliefs about the feasible set of alternatives. That such values guide choice accords with an economic model of decision making in which people are optimizing among the available alternatives given their knowledge and beliefs. There are numerous issues on which the empirical evidence does not point to any definitive conclusion about the consequences of one policy versus another. It is arguable that there is as much doubt about the effects of alternative economic policies as there is about different social and cultural policies. On all such issues, one's position may be guided strongly by one's ideological beliefs.

A Washington insider goes further by arguing that, in contemporary American politics, there is a greater consensus on what needs to be done in the social realm than in the economic realm: "It's not the social issues that are phoney baloney. The economy is the snake-oil issue, the smoke-and-mirrors issue. On the other hand, in the realm of social issues, the issues are real, and some consensus lives."[77] People are convinced that discipline, hard work, honesty, and morality contribute to social stability and economic progress. In contrast, on issues of taxes, free trade, the dollar's exchange rate, the deficit, foreign investment, and other material issues, economists disagree over what is best for the country and present contrasting scenarios about the effects of different prescriptions. In recent debates over the merits of raising the minimum wage, for example, opponents claim that the proposed increase would lead to business failures, inflation pressures, and fewer jobs, whereas advocates argue that a higher minimum wage would encourage some people to seek employment who are currently receiving government welfare payments.[78]

Value Theories as Explanatory Theories

There is also a more philosophical question about the versatility of an explanatory social theory centered on symbolic values. We should consider what it means to explain preferences and behavior using symbolic values and whether the theory of symbolic values offers a sufficient explanation of value formation and change.

Value-based theories explain opinions by tracing them to more general values that encompass the specific preferences to be explained. A lack of discriminant validity separating independent and dependent variables invariably detracts from this approach, as there may be some dispute over whether the measures of symbolic attitudes are simply alternative measures for the policy attitudes. For example, prejudice and conservative ideology explain more of the variance in school busing attitudes than whether one is likely to be affected by the policy. But the racial prejudice measures are close proxies of the dependent variable itself. In their 1980 study, Sears et al. measure racial prejudice using items asking respondents "whether or not whites have the right to keep blacks out of their neighborhood," and "whether desegregation or segregation was favored in general." Is it any surprise that this symbolic variable strongly predicts attitudes toward "government intervention in school desegregation"?[79]

Similarly, it is unclear what "racial resentment" represents. Racial resentment is a symbolic attitude indicated by these views: blacks need only make a greater effort to succeed and can work their way up without any special assistance, as did Italians, Jews, and the Irish; slavery and discrimination do not constitute major barriers to black advancement; blacks could learn to survive without welfare support; blacks have not received less than they deserved; blacks do not enjoy less access to government officials than other groups. According to Kinder and Sanders, "racial resentment is not the *only* thing that matters for race policy, *but by a fair margin racial resentment is the most important.*"[80] But if resentment measures something very close to people's policy attitudes, then it is not remarkable to find that resentment levels rather than self-interest explain racial policy preferences. When the explanatory factor is so proximate to the phenomenon to be explained, there is little room left for additional influences.

The Source of Values

Perhaps the most serious shortcoming of the symbolic theory is its rigid conception of social values. If interests truly are irrelevant to value formation, where do such beliefs come from? Sears and Funk reject the possibility that self-interest shapes partisan and ideological preferences, because symbolic predispositions (1) tend to be formed early in life (often before adulthood) and (2) are not easily altered by short-term material concerns.[81]

There are two theoretical problems with this reasoning. It provides at best an abbreviated explanation for the source of values, and it insists that certain immutable elemental beliefs and values learned early in life are retained indefinitely for non-self-interested motives. By turning cultural values and norms into the bedrock of the theory, the symbolic model provides no convincing account of why some attitudes and values are endorsed and promoted rather than others, nor of how these norms and values occasionally change. But anytime we claim to be explaining social values, we really are trying to explain the reasons underlying changes in social values over time. And it is difficult to account for such change without examining the incentives that people have to adopt or reject new values and to promote or prevent value change in others.

Admittedly, it is an exaggeration to say that interests account entirely for the values that people acquire and convey to others during socialization. There is research, for example, showing that people with certain personality characteristics are predisposed to adopt viewpoints that correspond to those traits. Such individuals may therefore be responding more strongly to inner needs than to external incentives. Paul Mussen and Norma Haan, for instance, explore whether there are personality traits that consistently separate liberals and conservatives over the life span.[82] Their data show that liberal and conservative adult political orientations appear to be outgrowths of personality traits first exhibited during childhood and adolescence: "The enduring qualities associated with a liberal sociopolitical orientation are independence, unconventionality in thinking and behavior, rebelliousness, orientation toward philosophical matters, objectivity, willingness to accept one's own motivations and desires as well as responsibility for one's own actions. In contrast, conservatives are, over prolonged periods of time, lacking in independence, submissive, in need of reassurance, moralistic, little given to introspection, and uncomfortable with uncertainty (that is, intolerant of ambiguity)."[83]

In evaluating the rationality of socialization, we should also consider that the values that people transmit are often not communicated in a strategic manner, as in the case of propaganda, but are expressed simply as opinion. Brian Barry notes that "sometimes . . . the explanation [for cultural stability] may be something humdrum like the tendency of parents to bring up children with the same outlook as themselves, or, in some fundamental ways, to reproduce their own childhood."[84] As he points out, parents do not always teach their children to look after their elders in their old age, even though it would be in their interest to do so. I would add that parents unavoidably convey values in their words and actions, whether they mean to or not, and children naturally pick up on their biases. Some values are promoted because parents think it is important that their children hold such beliefs in order for them to become better people; but ideas can also be transmitted unintentionally, as parents who neglect to watch what they say around their children realize.

Moreover, the readiness with which people conform to the patterns of behavior they are exposed to through socialization suggests a biological mechanism. It may be, as Donald Campbell speculated, that blind conformity is biologically adaptive early in life because it improves the rate of transmission from parents to their offspring. In the formative stages of life, it may simply be better to follow one's elders unquestioningly than to stop and assess the conventional wisdom.[85]

But with qualifications such as these in mind, there are still a number of avenues by which choice and self-interest enter into and shape socialization. A difficulty with the argument that general values are acquired early in life and therefore cannot be based on instrumental calculation is that even if we accept its premise, the conclusion does not follow. A child who is socialized to believe in values whose ramifications he does not fully comprehend is conforming at least partly in response to inducements and punishments controlled by his "teachers"—his parents, schoolteachers, and other role models. By the same token, those given the responsibility for socializing children, especially parents, choose to transmit certain values rather than others at least partly because they think these values will be useful for their children.

Mussen and Haan are quick to add that personality factors do not completely determine political orientations but must be examined in combination with the influence of social and economic variables and historical events.[86] Moreover, to the extent that personality traits are "givens," it can be instrumental for people to develop the appropriate social and political beliefs that complement those dispositions, thus allowing them to live comfortably.[87] People can make what we might call rational adaptations to their predispositions. The personally insecure, for example, may want a strictly conformist environment, because they are more relaxed when events are predictable and deviation from the norm is minimized. Here again dispositions and incentives must be analyzed in concert as the individual tries to shape the social and political environment to his personal needs; his interests take account of his personal traits.

Do Values Change?

The theory of symbolic politics assumes that people are especially impressionable in the early years and that they resist influences that might change their views later in life. But in the sociological and psychological literature, there is no decisive evidence on the evolution of basic social and political values over the life course. There is recognition that there may be substantial variation in stability depending on whether we are examining personality characteristics, personal styles, behavioral traits, general values, or specific beliefs and attitudes. There is little agreement among developmental psychologists about the stability over the life span of various kinds of individual traits.[88] Furthermore, "only rarely have sociologists and political scientists been able to demonstrate strong cohort effects on social and political attitude variables," in which a distinctive era leaves a lasting mark on an especially impressionable sector of the population.[89]

Although early learning experiences are critical in shaping initial political orientations, and although such early socialization guides subsequent attitude formation,[90] the few longitudinal studies that have been conducted indicate that values are subject to change in response to changing roles and changes in social institutions throughout life. Life-cycle changes in one's social position and role create new obligations and interests, place one in new social networks, and lead ultimately to the acquisition of new attitudes.[91]

Thus, the Jennings-Niemi panel study of high school seniors and their parents shows that the influence of parents' partisanship on their childrens' diminishes as the children mature and develop their own priorities in adulthood.[92] The socialization literature on the effects of parenthood and aging finds that political interests evolve with changing life roles. Parents develop stronger interests in local politics and community issues dealing with parks, playgrounds, and recreational centers because of their children's needs to play outdoors.[93] Studies of the elderly reveal a correlation between the subjects' health and their political priorities. Those in good health are more concerned with maintaining their standard of living, while those with medical problems give higher priority to health-care issues.[94]

Hence, a plausible explanation for why value changes occur more commonly during one's early years is that roles and status are then in greater flux.[95] There is a succession of significant events as one goes from childhood to adulthood involving education, employment, marriage, and family, and there are corresponding changes in reference groups, priorities, and perhaps social classes. As one grows older, there are fewer major changes in status, which may account for increased attitude stability. Within broad age categories, we might also expect variation in the extent of exposure to attitude-changing events due to socioeconomic or other factors, which would further complicate the relationship between age and value stability.

An ever-present methodological problem is that it is hard to determine whether the observation of greater change in the early developmental years is due to greater individual openness to change in that stage of life or to greater exposure to life-changing events. For example, when the students in the famous longitudinal Bennington College study were first interviewed in the 1930s, they were at a stage in life when they were psychologically open to change and in a community that exposed them to events and experiences that promoted attitude change. Thus we would anticipate on both counts that they would undergo more attitude change than people in less dynamic situations and stages of life. The study indeed powerfully demonstrated how students conformed gradually to the liberal Bennington political culture even though most of the students came from conservative family backgrounds. Scores on measures of political and economic liberalism increased steadily from the freshman to senior classes. In addition, those students who aspired to leadership within the Bennington community, and were thus highly motivated to learn its norms and conventions, were especially likely to recognize and subscribe to the dominant campus values.[96]

Two follow-ups on the Bennington subjects in the 1960s and 1980s found that the sociopolitical values of the subjects showed significant change over time.[97] As the latter study noted, "We can attribute about 40 percent of the variation in 1984 sociopolitical orientations to factors linked to attitude change since the 1930s and 1940s rather than to persistence from early adulthood. . . . There seems to be much more lifelong openness to change than the generational persistence model suggests might be the case."[98] In particular, if role changes are accompanied by changes in one's social networks, then attitude changes are more likely to occur.[99] Of course, there will still be a bias toward attitude stability if people tend to seek out comfortable social environments that confirm and reinforce existing viewpoints. The Bennington women maintained their college political beliefs when they were able to reproduce a similar social network in their lives beyond college. However, when husbands, friends, and grown-up children introduced conflicting political opinions, the women were more likely to change attitudes.[100]

A vivid description of how social and economic pressure from new reference groups induces attitude change is contained in John Dollard's classic ethnography of a small southern town known as "Southerntown" (a pseudonym) in the 1930s. It was conventional wisdom among the townsfolk he interviewed that northerners who moved to the South regularly experienced a change of heart on the race issue. Conversion was not uniform, however, but occurred most readily among those with the greatest dependence on southern contacts, such as the "northerners who had come to do business in the South":

> One man told me that he had changed his views about "niggers" since he had been to Southerntown and had come to feel much as southern people do. It seemed clear, to me at least, why he had drawn new inferences from his experience, and had changed his attitudes to those of the white caste. It seemed very likely that he had to accept southern views

because his social contacts and those of his wife and family were with whites; he could not stand out against the tremendous pressure of white sentiment; and further he could advance his economic interests only by cooperating with the dominant group. A social or economic boycott would quickly end any attempt to remain a Yankee.[101]

Here, then, is an illustration of when interests motivate attitude change. (Another question, which I take up in chapter 2, concerns why the community exerts such strong pressures toward conformity in the first place: what are the possible interests underlying the development and maintenance of homogeneous views, within a small southern town, or in any community?)

For some individuals, social isolation or personal independence alleviates social pressure to conform. Dollard encountered one long-time Southerntown resident who thumbed his nose at the customs and mores of the town. He often welcomed blacks to his home, allowing them to enter through the front entrance rather than the back door as would be customary in other white-owned homes, if the black person was permitted inside at all. He also visited blacks in town and sometimes dined with them. But this man was a financially secure planter who was both willing and able to isolate himself from southern whites because he did not agree with or choose to interact with them.[102]

In a study of the opinions of African Americans, Melissa Miller and I found that basic racial attitudes and identifications are not fixed by early socialization events but instead show signs of transformation throughout the life cycle. While the content and context of early socialization have varying direct and indirect effects on racial identifications and attitudes, contemporary experiences such as church attendance, participation in black interest groups, friendships with whites, and education, employment, and residence in all-black, racially mixed, or predominantly white colleges, workplaces, and neighborhoods have significant additional effects on racial identifications, attitudes toward whites, perceptions of prejudice, and racial beliefs.[103] Thus, whether people retain the group identifications they acquired during childhood depends on the continuing relevance of those groups in their lives. Individuals are more likely to retain their group identifications if membership in those groups continues to be accompanied by such collective goods as community support and political power.

Other studies examining the influence of changes in one's reference groups and station in life have arrived at similar conclusions. Those who experience intergenerational social mobility from the working class to middle class develop more tolerant racial attitudes, thus "striking an average between the views appropriate to their class of origin and those appropriate to their class of destination."[104] When white college students in the 1940s traveled to the South for their education, their racial beliefs grew less tolerant in conformity with their new environment.[105] In 1964, Herbert Hyman and Paul Sheatsley observed that "exposure to integration appears to increase white support for integration. Northern whites who previously lived in the South show nearly as much support for integration and as much belief in comparability of Negro and white intelligence as whites who have always lived in the North.[106] A more recent national study based on the General Social Survey indicates that geographical mobility by northerners to the South and southerners to the North produces partial resocialization of political and social attitudes, including racial orientations. Southerners who move North become more liberal, while northerners traveling the opposite route become more conservative.[107]

In general, the symbolic theory cannot explain the dramatic changes in racial attitudes among white southerners across all age and education categories in response to social and institutional changes in the 1960s and 1970s. If it is indeed the case that racial resentments are the most important factor underlying racial policy views, and that they are not transformed by changes in social conditions, then how do we account for the shifts in opinion toward racial desegregation in schools, housing, and public accommodations in the period following World War II? Furthermore, how do we account for the generational changes in opinion if racial resentment is unaffected by the social and political environment? Are these merely instances of a temporary suppression of resentment rather than of an enduring change?[108] The symbolic theory of racial resentment would seem to lack the dynamic elements to accommodate the kinds of changes in race relations that occurred in the postwar period. (I will return to this issue in chapter 6.)

Thus the strongest claims about value determinism are not supported by the evidence. If values imprint themselves so that, once internalized, they cannot be changed, then people's choices would be constrained. As their stations in life changed, their preferences would display a decreasing correspondence with their interests and social networks. But this extreme thesis cannot be sustained. Many beliefs are held consistently over time because they are never subject to serious challenge. However, studies indicate that values change when the socioeconomic supports for them are undercut. Value change therefore depends on changes in life circumstances and corresponding changes in social relations. Life changes that result in changes in reference groups typically create incentives for movers to modify their views.

TAKING STOCK OF EXPRESSIVE AND INSTRUMENTAL THEORIES

Let me summarize the discussion in this chapter and return the focus to the relative merits of value-based versus interest-based theories. I began with the premises behind rational choice theory and used that perspective to evaluate theories centered on social values and expressive or symbolic action. Theories of status and symbolic politics highlight the importance of group identifications, partisan and ideological values, and cultural norms in decision making. If the kinds of contests over cultural practices that are the focus of status politics are excluded from rational choice analyses, then much of the political realm is effectively beyond the reach of rational choice models. Consequently, if rational choice models are going to have much explanatory power outside economics, they will have to come to terms with these kinds of cases. My purpose in dissecting the findings in the research on symbolic politics was to show, first, that many of the anomalies for rational choice that are posed by this research can be addressed with a slightly broader, more subjective conception of rationality and self-interest and, second, that an expressive theory has severe limitations in explaining dynamic social and political processes.

A group's desire to maintain its cultural practices and social norms is not obviously related to material ends or consistent with self-interested motivation. We require additional specification of why people feel it is important to coordinate around a set of common social norms and cultural practices, as well as why they are motivated to contribute to the maintenance of these collective goods. Symbolic and status theories are unfortunately truncated at their key explanatory variables and do not themselves have much to offer on these issues. Political choice is a function of reflexive symbolic values and group attachments or of a desire to elevate the status of group norms.

The limitations in the theory of symbolic politics stem from its focus on excessively proximate causes. When social incentives and calculations are ignored, strategic elements of values are set aside, and values are used to explain other values, the product is a relatively static theory. The ability to explain policy preferences and opinions with abstract values may inadvertently contribute to a failure to address more general issues of social and political coordination around norms and values. These issues come into focus only when we develop a theory of value formation and change, and such a theory is possible, I would argue, only by incorporating more strategic elements into a model. An expressive, noninstrumental theory relies too heavily on psychological states at the expense of social and political processes.

What we are seeking, therefore, is *a model with interesting mechanisms and moving parts.* The theory will need to take account of status and group identifications and explain the circumstances under which individuals will invest in these goals. More analysis is needed of how people develop a stake in their social norms and practices and how political coalitions build upon common beliefs and values.

The most promising route to developing a more dynamic theory, I believe, is to build a model based on individualistic assumptions that explains why people are motivated to join groups and develop group identifications, and why they defend their social norms and ways of life. In the following chapter, I will provide such a model of the process by which people acquire their cultural beliefs and values. The mechanism that makes the model run is still rational choice, but the twist I will offer is that calculations are made in a cultural context in which individuals are seeking material goals and trying to protect and improve their status in their social groups.

I will argue that coordination around social norms and values and attachment to a way of life serve broader, more utilitarian purposes than the proponents of status and symbolic politics generally acknowledge. Social norms and values shape beliefs and preferences among alternatives; shared preferences support social conventions, create common expectations, and permit coalitions and groups to form.

Coalitions, in turn, provide the foundation of political power. Once coalitions are in place, people who benefit from the status quo will want to maintain them. They will fight to retain the values and practices that made the coalitions possible in the first place. In all communities, there are individuals and groups who have a greater interest than others in protecting traditions, because they will suffer a loss of prestige and opportunities if new values are adopted. Once we give greater weight to the instrumental foundations of social values, a sharp partitioning of political issues between the economic and cultural realms, each with its corresponding explanatory models, is untenable.

CHAPTER TWO

A Model of Individual Choice

When you get to the fork in the road, take it.

Yogi Berra

Symbolic and status theories emphasize that people will develop strong attachments to their cultural values and practices and resist efforts to change them. Research on symbolic values performs an important service by refuting simpler economic theories that assume that objective changes in personal resources and circumstances will automatically affect people's preferences. Instead, people often are influenced by long-standing preferences that are reflected in their political ideologies, partisanship, and social values. These studies confirm that rational choice models will be limited in their ability to explain much political action unless they can accommodate people's social values and their concern for social status. A model based solely on narrow individualistic calculations of self-interest will, as the literature on symbolic politics indicates, often fall short.

A common weakness of value-based theories, however, is that they are insufficiently dynamic. If status motivates people to engage in collective action to preserve their cultural values, then it becomes incumbent upon us to try to make sense of status systems. Specifically, how is status allocated? For what purpose is status acquired? Why do some activities become prestigious? We can go only so far by modeling choice as a function of fixed symbolic attitudes rather than instrumental considerations. A static model built on relatively fixed dispositions encounters difficulty explaining changes in norms and values. If political choices are influenced more strongly by general orientations than by specific circumstances, what factors shape those orientations? Noninstrumental theories are too narrow because they overstate the habitual nature of choice and give insufficient weight to strategic calculations. A more supple theory is required to explain both value stability and change.

In this chapter I will provide a correction by adding dynamic elements to a model of choice that can explain value formation and conformity to social norms. In this alternative model, the role of *incentives* and *dispositions* varies across choices and over time owing to changes in opportunity and individual and social circumstances. I use this model to identify several characteristic routes through which interests and dispositions work in concert to influence conformity to social norms and values. The model folds together sociological dynamics with economic premises by assuming that preferences and beliefs are shaped by social groups and that choices are made on the basis of instrumental cost-benefit considerations.

The strength of my model is that it accommodates both value-based decisions and instrumental choices. People sometimes act habitually and sometimes in response to incentives. More often, both mechanisms are at work. As the sociological model emphasizes, certain enduring personal characteristics—values, identities, traits, capacities—which I will refer to generally as dispositions—will sometimes govern choices at the expense of objective interests. My qualification is only that interests often affect the formation, maintenance, and transformation of these dispositions, so that dispositional explanations do not exclude rational choice. Underlying dispositions cannot be treated merely as givens; instead they are adapted to our circumstances and aid in the pursuit of self-interest. When we take these additional mechanisms into account, our model acquires a significant increase in explanatory power. Decisions can then be represented by the model in terms ranging from the purely dispositional to the purely calculating, with the proviso that dispositionally driven decisions often embody past strategic calculations.

A measure of instrumental calculation plays a role in most of the cases I discuss in conjunction with the model—sometimes involving straightforward calculations of interest, sometimes combining rational calculation with sociological and psychological mechanisms. While I do not claim that all choices regarding social norms and values follow these processes, I suspect that most disputes over social norms and values emanate from conflicts over interests that evolve in the sense described here and according to the dynamics traced by the model.

I proceed in two steps, first by laying out in informal terms some basic assumptions about the reasons why individuals identify with groups and conform to group norms and conventions, and then by translating this process into a mathematical model from which we can draw a variety of inferences about the dynamics of socialization, conformity, value formation and change, and conflicts over norms. I would encourage even nontechnically trained readers to work through the logic of the formal exposition, since the model only requires knowledge of basic algebra. But even those who choose not to should still find the discussion intelligible because, at each step in the development of the model, I will provide an informal translation of the arguments and substantive illustrations of their implications.[1]

DISPOSITIONS AND INCENTIVES

The model presented in this chapter represents individual choices between two alternatives, for example, different opinions, policy positions, social norms, styles, conventions, or reference groups. I will focus on social conformity processes within both small groups and the population at large—how attitudes and values and general political loyalties are developed through social interaction, exposure to information, and strategic calculation. A second application of the model (developed later, in chapter 4) investigates strategies of political mobilization that capitalize on people's common values and group identifications.

The basic dynamic driving the model is that people develop dispositions which shape their choices, but the dispositions are long-term factors (themselves embodying varying degrees of instrumentality) that are combined with the incentives attached to the current choice. These dispositions should be treated as past investments that affect evaluations of current options. *A person's rational choice therefore depends in part on the accumulation of past decisions that have formed his dispositions and in part on the costs and benefits of his present alternatives.*

Unfortunately, almost any policy preference can be transformed into a general value or predisposition, which is a criticism of symbolic theory not unlike the criticism of rational choice theory that almost anything can be transformed into an interest. Thus the choices one faces may simply be a test of one's underlying values, as I noted in chapter 1 in discussing the relationship between affirmative action attitudes and racial attitudes. Once the underlying values are measured in such cases, it is straightforward to predict one's immediate choice, because the latter is an extension of the former. Moreover, sometimes one's beliefs about the effects of alternative choices are part and parcel of one's ideological values. For these reasons, we should not automatically attribute dispositional explanations to nonrational reflexive mechanisms. Nevertheless, it is useful to maintain a distinction between general orientations and capacities that one carries about and specific incentives or considerations that emanate from the alternatives at hand—even if the two categories may in practice overlap.

REFERENCE GROUPS AND CONFORMITY

Admiral Jeremy M. Boorda, Chief of Naval Operations, committed suicide upon discovering that *Newsweek* planned to publish an article questioning his right to wear two Vietnam War combat decorations. Boorda had never received a citation authorizing him to wear the pins so he apparently violated military rules. While suicide may seem a drastic response, Roger Charles, a retired Marine Corps lieutenant colonel, put matters in context, "Your history is on your chest, and there are very precise regulations about this. This is a big deal in the military."[2]

An important contribution of the postwar program of research on opinion formation, conducted by scholars at Columbia University, was to show how a person's attitudes and actions are shaped and reinforced by his so-called reference groups.[3] These groups include not only closely related people (family, friends, classmates, and co-workers) but also more abstract categories of individuals (professions or social classes to which people might aspire) who have a hand in molding attitudes and opinions.

We rely on our reference groups to help us form judgments about others and about the world. People look to others in their immediate social circle for guidance in developing a coherent understanding of events and situations in which they find themselves. Common opinions provide comfort and security to group members by giving "*meanings* for situations which do not explain themselves."[4]

"Conformity," in conventional parlance, refers to the degree to which one identifies with and lives according to the mainstream ways of society. Every society prescribes certain cultural goals and certain approved cultural means to attain them. Anyone who subscribes to a society's cultural goals and makes use of institutionalized means to reach them is conforming to the norms of the society. Nonconformists, on the other hand, have forsaken competing for prestige and status within traditional groups and elected to abide by the norms and values of alternative, less widely esteemed groups.[5] But because both conformists and nonconformists alike abide by the norms and incentives of their respective environments, we can fairly refer to social conformity processes that operate within all social groups.

Most political or social *nonconformity* therefore is really another form of conformity, except that it is aligned with groups that fall outside the mainstream of society.[6] At issue, really, is not whether people are conformists but rather which reference groups they choose to be guided by:

> When nonconformity represents conformity to the values, standards, and practices of an earlier condition of society which are still enduring but not uniformly accepted, it is often described as "conservatism." Pejoratively, and sometimes exactly, it is described as "reactionary," particularly when it constitutes an effort to re-introduce values and practices which have been superseded or have simply fallen into neglect. When nonconformity represents conformity to values, standards, and practices which have not yet been institutionalized but are regarded as making up the normative system of future reference groups, it is often described as "radicalism."[7]

There are thus many groups that might attract the loyalty of individuals. These groups may share certain common norms, but they also promote contrasting norms and values that are particularistic in the sense that they further the interests of their respective group members. Group norms make sense within specific domains, and not outside those contexts, because each group is defined by norms, values, beliefs, and practices that serve its members and confer status upon those who exemplify them. A group's norms serve the interests of group members by coordinating their expectations and by promoting choices that are partial to group members. In the evolution of law school teaching, for example, the case method won out over the older lecture and textbook methods because it gave the legal profession a distinctive academic foundation that restricted and regulated membership. The premise behind the case method was that legal training was rigorously scientific in the sense that one had to work inductively from the history of cases to discern the evolution of legal principles and doctrines governing a sphere of law. "Law . . . was a branch of learning that genuinely demanded rigorous formal training. There was justification, then, for the lawyers' monopoly of practice."[8]

Individuals join groups to obtain benefits they cannot acquire on their own. They conform to group norms because there are social and material advantages to supporting those beliefs and values.[9] They may estimate the relative benefits of alternative norms or they may simply rely on the cues provided by others. Much value formation is not a product of conscious maximization of immediate material benefits. Where decision making does fit this description, we can chalk up these easy cases as supporting rational choice. But value formation is often less deliberate, especially early in life, when alternatives are limited. It is partially informed, bounded by circumstance, and based on following the example of others, especially higher-status group members.

We may therefore support a norm because we recognize the advantages of that norm for ourselves or because we see that other people endorse the norm. Even if individuals do not deliberately calculate that adopting certain norms and values will be instrumental to achieving their goals, they are likely to see that they have an interest in conforming to the norms of a group in which they seek acceptance. Experiments on social conformity support our intuition that nonconformists tend to be less well liked by fellow group members.[10] Conformity signals to others that one is willing to comply with group norms and goals. The specific opinions and tastes that one agrees with may not be as important as the display of conformity itself. Agreement per se conveys one's willingness to fit in and implies support for the goals of the group. An adolescent gang member may succumb to pressure to obtain a tattoo in order to display his willingness to comply with the dictates of the group; the small act of conformity signifies a deeper and more significant character trait that is valued by other gang members.[11] Nonconformity of opinion, on the other hand, is an equally telltale sign that a person is a potential troublemaker whose behavior cannot be reliably predicted.[12]

In the midst of clashes between rivals Inkatha and the African National Congress while apartheid was being dismantled in South Africa, a woman in the Bambayi squatter settlement outside Durban displayed her instinct for survival: "Does she support the ANC? 'If our community requires us to be members of the ANC, we will become members of the ANC.' How about Inkatha? 'If the community sees it right, it can be so.'"[13] When conformity is a litmus test, there can be life and death incentives for expressing the right beliefs. The Cultural Revolution in China wreaked havoc among the masses because the targets of the regime shifted so erratically that people had difficulty identifying the approved ideology. "It was hard to keep track of who was right and who was wrong. 'One day you're black and then you're red and then you're black again.'"[14] The only safe advice was to stay on top of Chairman Mao's pronouncements.

But imitation of others may itself be motivated indirectly by instrumental reasoning. People may follow others whom they believe have a better idea of the alternatives that best serve group members. In this manner, material goals can be reached by following social cues. Tocqueville wrote in *Democracy in America* that "if man were forced to demonstrate for himself all the truths of which he makes daily use, his task would never end. He would exhaust his strength in preparatory demonstrations without ever advancing beyond them. As, from the shortness of his life, he has not the time, nor, from the limits of his intelligence, the capacity, to act in this way, he is reduced to take on trust a host of facts and opinions which he has not had either the time or the power to verify for himself, but which men of greater ability have found out, or which the crowd adopts."[15]

Conformity makes a great deal of sense when there are some members of the group who are better informed about their interests and can offer guidance. By following the lead of those individuals who have greater expertise, people who possess limited information economize on their decision making.[16] While calculation plays a minimal role here, it is difficult to imagine how a more rational calculator might act much differently in such circumstances. Together, group members can make the rational choice without every person in the group making his or her own calculations about the costs and benefits of available alternatives. All that is required is that there are some group members capable of ascertaining what norms and values best advance the interests of group members.

We could devise a model of social conformity in which most people merely copied the behavior of others but nevertheless made choices that were faithful to their own interests because there were rational opinion leaders driving the process. A promising model of social influence therefore assumes that some individuals have sufficient motivation to assess the consequences of political alternatives and to make decisions based on those evaluations, while other individuals are assumed to be reactive.[17] The leaders provide the energy and direction behind the diffusion process. In this manner, the value-formation process obtains a starting point—opinions and evaluations originate from a source—and not everyone is responding to external influences. Some members calculate the relative advantages and disadvantages of different alternatives, while others follow the norms largely out of imitation and conformity to others. If group interests are preeminent, then social mobility between groups will lead to the formation of new interests and political preferences. The concept of interests provides the value-formation process with a mechanism for explaining change. If it were true that values never changed even when they became obsolete or conflicted with new interests, this would constitute strong evidence against an economic model of behavior. Such stability, however, does not seem consistent with evidence showing that people's values change when they change their reference groups and develop new interests.

GROUP DYNAMICS

Every group operates its own internal prestige market, but the groups themselves are part of a larger system of groups. The same groups are not equally appealing to everyone, because different social categories reflect differential power, wealth, and status. We are well aware that some groups clearly are more prestigious than others. Indeed, we are attuned to prestige hierarchies in all walks of life. We develop a fine sense of the types of behavior that receive more prestige than others, and we also acquire an ability to evaluate the values and behavior of others in a manner that brings us esteem.[18]

While groups control their members by providing or withholding esteem, it is the relative status of a group within a social system that determines its attractiveness to others and affects whether present members will be motivated to leave the group. Status can be acquired through individualistic pursuits, but it also depends on group memberships. We deal with one another on the basis of both unique, personal qualities and generalizations inferred from group affiliations. Because our personal status depends in part on individual factors and in part on group standing, it is in our interest that our group status be elevated.

The inclination to identify with new groups or to reform existing groups brings a dynamic element to people's group identifications. Individuals can change their status by moving between groups in the system or by working to improve the status of their current group. When we speak of social mobility, we normally think of socioeconomic or class mobility, but we should also include mobility between ascriptive categories. People can take measures to heighten or conceal their racial and ethnic backgrounds or their sexual identities by modifying their behavior and appearance. By electing to identify more or less strongly with the distinguishing features of a particular social group, people can affect how others perceive them.

Individuals prefer to belong to groups with higher status, but their aspirations must also take into account their abilities and opportunities. We can never be sure that we are competing in the right domain and sometimes we discover that we are where we belong only after we try to move on. After years of writing critically but not popularly acclaimed novels, the author James Wilcox was encouraged by his editor to incorporate more attractive characters and popular themes in his stories. However, his new books failed to sell any better and, as a consequence, his advances grew even smaller. Rather than redouble his efforts, he learned his lesson and gave up the chase. The market's rebuff taught him to ignore commercial considerations and to produce the kind of work he liked best. "It's so little money that I'm going to write this [new book] exactly the way I want. I feel a burden has been lifted. . . . Now I know it's never going to be a big commercial book. In a way, I'm much happier."[19]

Whether people choose to remain in or move out of their current groups depends on their capacities to thrive in different environments. Sometimes we are stuck in the pond that we find ourselves in, either because we do not have the drive to move out, or because we are limited by the skills and resources that we failed to obtain earlier in life and do not now have the luxury of acquiring. Some who claim to be contented with their situation are engaging in rationalization. Thus, while cultural inertia can indicate irrationality, it can also be rational for people who are ill-equipped to live under different conditions to find ways to preserve their institutions and cultural practices. Individuals defend supportive institutions and attack rules and norms that restrict their opportunities.

People must therefore assess, on the basis of their aspirations and abilities, in which domain they wish to compete. They may choose to invest in their current groups or move to alternative groups that offer them more opportunities and resources. If they are restricted from moving, they may work to improve the standing or opportunities of the group they belong to by improving its image. They may choose to segregate themselves within their own communities and build up community resources. They may of course also seek reform of the system to achieve equality of status and opportunity by removing barriers to advancement.

All strategies pursued by individuals and groups will have consequences for the distribution of status and resources among groups in the society. If we are trying to ascertain which individuals and groups will most likely support or oppose change, we should keep our focus on the incentives and opportunities facing different individuals within competing institutions. Individuals whose opportunities improve because they have the requisite skills under the new system will have the easiest time making the transition. Those who are unable to to take advantage of the changes or who will lose privileges or be less competitive will be most inclined to resist.

A MODEL OF INDIVIDUAL CHOICE

To begin, assume that there are two competing alternatives (norms, opinions, beliefs), L and R. I use the the letters L and R intentionally, because they offer a usefully ambiguous mnemonic. They can be construed neutrally, as a choice between any two arbitrary alternatives, such as driving on the L(eft) or on the R(ight) side of the road, or they can take on political content if used to refer to liberal and conservative or L(eft-wing) and R(ight-wing) policies. In developing the model, I will often speak concretely of choosing between competing norms, but we should not forget that the model's empirical referents will be established by the case at hand.

I assume that an individual acquiesces to a group's norms only if there are self-interested reasons to conform. Individuals contribute to the maintenance and fortification of the groups they join in return for status and social acceptance within the group and a share of the benefits that the group produces, including the benefits of knowledge and understanding.[20] Not only is it the case that people depend on the resources provided by groups to achieve their individual interests, but their conception of their interests and their understanding of the social world are shaped by the information that is transmitted through groups as well. People also draw their identities and social standing from the groups with which they associate, and their social interaction is guided by the preconceptions and stereotypes that they hold about others based on their group ties.

Conforming entails following the norms that are directly related to the group's success as well as the more incidental conventions of the group. For example, when slavery came under attack from northern abolitionists, the South closed ranks and clamped down on all manifestations of nonconformity. Even nonconformity on matters unrelated to the crisis appeared treasonous to others, as all actions in this atmosphere were read in terms of one's willingness to defend the interests of the group. To contravene the norms in another realm, however unrelated, cast a measure of doubt on one's reliability. Hence in the South, "The habit [of intolerance] spread in ever widening circles, poisonously. From the taboo on criticism of slavery, it was but an easy step to interpreting every criticism of the South on whatever score as disloyalty—to making such criticism so dangerous that none but a madman would risk it."[21]

It follows that the more an individual relies on a group, the more susceptible he will be to group pressures to conform and the more strongly he will identify with the group. If an individual can survive as well in a group that promotes L as in a group that supports R, then neither group will enjoy monopoly leverage over that individual. An individual who disagrees with the goals of the group or who does not depend on the evaluations of group members will not seek membership. In general, those who can manage easily without the group, for economic or psychological reasons, will be less inclined to bend their beliefs and behavior to the dictates of the group (recall from chapter 1 Dollard's examples of conformity and iconoclasm in the South).[22]

INCENTIVES: THE MEANING OF π

Individual choice between alternatives depends on a combination of incentives and dispositions. Neither factor has priority, so let me discuss each in turn. Individuals take stock of their material and social incentives in deciding whether to conform to L or R. People will coordinate around norms and values because they identify benefits associated with following the prescriptions of those norms or because there are benefits to coordinating with others around some common standard even when the substance of that norm is secondary. Self-interest must factor in not only direct gains to oneself as a consequence of choosing either L or R but also the collateral benefits that might accrue if one shows solidarity with other members of one's social network, even if this occasionally constitutes a material sacrifice for oneself.

Among the signs that a community supports a norm are that people receive social and material benefits for complying with the norm, they (especially group leaders) make arguments defending the norm, and they are seen to conform to the norm. Therefore, let π_L and π_R carry three related interpretations that represent various routes through which an individual ascertains which ideas, values, or norms to support: (a) the proportion of times, respectively, that L and R are rewarded by supportive responses from others or by material benefits, (b) the proportion of times that L and R are promoted by opinion leaders through communications, and (c) the proportion of people who are observed to choose L or R.

The relative frequencies of these events establishes the incentives that one has to conform to either L or R. To the extent that an individual experiences these events, his or her support for the norm or opinion is strengthened. I have in mind three *instrumental mechanisms* to explain social conformity, which can work either separately or in concert with one another, depending on the case at hand. Individuals choose the best alternative by (1) doing what brings the largest stream of benefits (net costs), (2) following opinion leaders who promote group interests, or (3) coordinating their actions with those of others. In the first case, individual choice stems from calculation that L is superior to R, or vice versa; in the second case, there are opinion leaders who inform group members about the alternative that is in their self-interest; and in the third case, self-interest is served by following the example of others, either because the choices made by others offer clues to the best choice, or because one is better off coordinating one's choice with the choice made by most other members of one's group.

The π values will naturally vary with the characteristics of the individual and those of the environment. The probability that a norm, opinion, or social practice is promoted will vary across communities: for example, in homogeneous communities, one is likely to encounter a disproportionate share of either L or R. In addition, individuals may take actions to place themselves within certain kinds of environments that are more compatible with their tastes. Such active choice, however, is less likely to occur early in life. Since children have little control over their socialization, childhood is apt to be a highly insular experience in which individuals are exposed to a steady diet of either L or R, but not both.

Awareness of norms will depend in part on the integration of individuals into the community. Individuals vary in their motivation to follow social affairs and stay abreast of new ideas and changing norms. Those with low motivation to follow politics and social affairs will encounter less L and less R. Social isolates fall beyond social influence and may never get wind of changes in social norms or feel the pressure of public opinion on an issue. These probabilities may also be shifted by political entrepreneurial activity that promotes L or R, thereby increasing the likelihood that people become aware of L or R.

People's prior beliefs may also influence what they pay attention to; to the extent that there is selective exposure, L or R may be favored. The reverse tendency sometimes occurs, though. In the course of his fieldwork, Dollard encountered a southern man who, contrary to the theory of selective exposure, "apparently read *The Nation, The American Mercury,* and other journals that took a radical attitude on the matter of race inequality just to irritate himself."[23]

Reinforcing Only L

Let me postulate how incentives affect preferences. Assume that, in every period n, an individual experiences an "event" that affects his evaluation of L or R. For example, the event may be exposure to an argument from opinion leaders recommending either L or R. If we begin with the simplest case, in a *homogeneous* social group or neighborhood, a single viewpoint—say L— predominates, so that an individual becomes exposed exclusively to the norm or opinion L. Therefore, $\pi_L = 1$ and $\pi_R = 0$, meaning that alternative points of view are simply not represented in this environment. A basic learning process posits that support for L increases each time L is reinforced through argument, benefit, or example. Therefore, in a given period $n + 1$, the probability of choosing L, p_L, equals:

$$p_{L, n+1} = p_{Ln} + a(1 - p_{Ln}) = (1 - a)p_{Ln} + a. \tag{1}$$

Equation (1) states that the probability of choosing L in period $n + 1$ equals the probability of choosing L in the preceding period *plus* some additional increment, $a(1 - p_{Ln})$, resulting from exposure to L or reinforcement of L (e.g., a positive L role model or an argument defending L) in the interval between period n and period $n + 1$. The probability of any particular response is necessarily bounded between 0 and 1, so the incremental increase is a proportion a of the amount of increase that is possible as of period n. I will elaborate momentarily on the substantive interpretation of the coefficient a and the factors affecting its variation.

It is very simple to demonstrate, and intuitively apparent, that in the long run, given this consistent pattern of exposure to pro-L events, the probability of giving an L response will approach unity asymptotically. In general, solving for equation (1), the probability of an L response in any period n will equal:

$$p_{Ln} = (1 - a)^n (p_{L0} - 1) + 1, \tag{2}$$

where p_{L0} is the probability of an L response in period 0 (the start of the process).

Reinforcing Only R

On the other hand, consider the opposite process, in which a person in a contrasting environment becomes acquainted exclusively with the alternative R ($\pi_L = 0$, $\pi_R = 1$). A straightforward formalization is that the probability of supporting L declines by a constant proportion b with each exposure to R. If there are only two possibilities, L and R, so that $p_R = 1 - p_L$, then the decline in support for L simply means that support for R increases:[24]

$$p_{L,\,n+1} = p_{Ln} - bp_{Ln} = (1 - b)p_{Ln}. \tag{3}$$

Equation (3) represents the conditional probability of choosing L in period $n + 1$ given exposure to R between periods n and $n + 1$. Just as the parameter a indexes responsiveness to a pro-L event, the parameter b reflects the receptivity of the individual to an event that promotes R.

By solving for equation (3), it can be shown that the probability of an L response in any period n equals:

$$p_{Ln} = (1 - b)^n p_{L0}. \tag{4}$$

Therefore, as long as b does not equal 0, it is apparent that continual exposure to events promoting R will gradually extinguish the likelihood of an L response on the issue (i.e., $p_{Ln} \to 0$ as $n \to \infty$).

DISPOSITIONS: THE MEANING OF a AND b

The model assumes that the effect of experiencing an L or R event will depend on the state of a person's underlying dispositions, which are represented by the a and b coefficients. Since both a and b must also fall between 0 and 1, they are proportions representing the values and reference-group identifications that make individuals more or less receptive to events and communications promoting L or R. People with dispositions favoring one of the alternatives will be inclined to choose that alternative independent of current incentives. These dispositions may not all point in a uniform direction. Most individuals will have varying degrees of internal cross-pressures—some identities that point them toward L, but others that will compel them toward R.

In certain types of decisions, it is appropriate to think of dispositions as the skills, knowledge, and training a person has received. Whether conceived of as capacities or psychological orientations, dispositions can be treated as the repository of past decisions and investments a person has made. For this reason, they will have a bearing on how an individual responds to current options, because it may be uneconomical to shift the capital that one has spent the better part of a lifetime acquiring.

As we have seen, there is disagreement about whether people respond actively to new life circumstances or simply react on the basis of long-term dispositions and values. An extreme position is that, on some issues, an individual is incapable of changing his views because of the imprint of early learning. If we assume that political orientations become impervious to change past early adulthood, then a and b become fixed after a critical period n'. But as I argued in chapter 1, dispositions such as partisanship and ideology cannot be treated simply as if they were psychological constants. Rather they are built up over the course of socialization and may themselves be a product of instrumental decisions and periodic updating based on new information. It is realistic to assume that both specific preferences (the p values) and more general orientations (the a and b values) are developing simultaneously. At a minimum, when we take into account both enduring socialization and instrumental mechanisms, the a and b parameters can be viewed as representing the strength of one's attachment to group values due to self-interest or to more reflexive mechanisms.

For example, if a and b represent one's political ideology, ranging from liberal to conservative, we can model ideological development in the same manner as any other belief. Ideological choice depends on arguments, patterns of reinforcement of beliefs, and coordination with the beliefs of others. If we assume further (in the particular case of ideology) that a and b are on a continuum, so that increasing the value of a decreases the value of b and vice versa (i.e., $a = 1 - b$), then receptivity to liberal arguments is inversely related to receptivity to conservative arguments. Therefore, even though the manner in which people respond to information promoting L and R will be conditioned by a and b, this information may also produce incremental changes in a and b over time. A person's ideology influences his evaluations of candidates and political issues, but information about the candidates and the issues they support can have a reciprocal influence on his ideology.

In general, values and group identifications are affected by contemporary circumstances that make certain identifications more strategically advantageous than others. Dispositions require periodic reinforcement in order to remain salient: if a disposition is to remain strong and relevant to decision making, there must be sufficient social and political supports underlying it. But even if a and b are conceptualized in purely economic terms, there is good reason to assume that a and b become less malleable because it will be either unnecessary or difficult to shift earlier investments in a way of life. Dispositions will tend to stabilize over time as people acquire the necessary partisan and ideological values and group identifications to make sense of politics and to conform to their reference groups. Some characteristics that influence receptivity to ideas, such as education and formal skills, will be enduring and difficult to alter substantially on short notice. To simplify matters for calculation purposes, I will usually treat the a and b coefficients as constants in the interval that choices are being made even though they are susceptible to varying degrees of influence over the life course.

As I will explain in detail in chapter 4, the a and b values are themselves subject to political persuasion.[25] If people are cross-pressured because they hold multiple values and identifications, their response to new issues can be affected by strategies that make certain identifications more salient than others. Persuasion depends not only on the communicator's being able to bring attention to his message but also on his ability to influence how people are disposed to interpret the message.

EXPOSURE TO BOTH L AND R

Let me now pull together all elements of the model by examining how dispositions and incentives shape individual choice in a *mixed* environment (a more realistic assumption in most cases), in which an individual encounters varying measures of both L and R. Let π_L equal the probability of encountering L, and π_R equal the probability of encountering R. Suppose that, in any given period, one sees either L or R practiced or reinforced, or receives no exposure to either. (This third contingency, in effect a nonevent, allows us to distinguish norms according to their salience to individuals. I exclude the possibility that both L and R will be simultaneously promoted in any interval.) Therefore the probability of conforming to L (and by implication, R) depends on three contingent events, as follows:

$$P_{L,\,n+1} = p(L \text{ response in period } n+1 \,|\, L \text{ event in period } n)$$

$$\times\ p(L \text{ event in period } n)$$

$$+\ p(L \text{ response in period } n+1 \,|\, R \text{ event in period } n)$$

$$\times\ p(R \text{ event in period } n) \tag{5}$$

$$+\ p(L \text{ response in period } n+1 \,|\, \text{no event in period } n)$$

$$\times\ p(\text{no event in period } n)$$

Using equations (1) and (3) and assuming that no exposure to an argument produces no change, we have:

$$p_{L,\,n+1} = [(1-a)p_{Ln} + a]\,\pi_L + [(1-b)p_{Ln}]\,\pi_R \tag{6}$$
$$+\ (1 - \pi_L - \pi_R)p_{Ln}.$$

By rearranging, we can see that equation (6) is a first order difference equation of the form: $p_{n+1} = Ap_n + B$, where $A = (1 - \pi_L a - \pi_R b)$ and $B = \pi_L a$. The solution to equation (6) for any period n equals:

$$p_n = A^n[p_0 - B/(1 - A)] + B/(1 - A). \tag{7}$$

Substituting for A and B, we obtain:

$$p_n = (1 - \pi_L a - \pi_R b)^n\,(p_0 - p^*) + p^*, \tag{8}$$

where

$$p^* = (\pi_L a)/(\pi_L a + \pi_R b). \tag{9}$$

Equations (8) and (9) are key expressions that indicate how dispositions and incentives combine to determine individual preferences between alternatives. The *solution* of the model (eq. 8) allows us to trace the time path of p given different assumptions about the values of the model parameters. If we know the values of π_L and π_R, the state of the underlying dispositions a and b, and the starting value of p at time 0, we can calculate the value of p_n for any period n.

The value p^* represents the *equilibrium* of this social influence process. If the process reaches this state at any time, it remains there in all subsequent periods. Equation (9) is a simple expression that packs a considerable amount of information. *The equilibrium is determined by the relative strength of incentives and dispositions to favor either L or R.* If there is no disposition to favor either L or R—that is, if $a = b > 0$—then preferences are determined entirely by the incentives behind the alternatives as p^* reduces to $\pi_L/(\pi_L + \pi_R)$. There is a nice symmetry between incentives and dispositions insofar as the reverse is also implied: dispositions govern choices when incentives cancel each other out—that is, when $\pi_L = \pi_R$, $p^* = a/(a + b)$.

Whether p^* is ever attained depends on whether the solution sequence $\{p_n\} = p_0, p_1, p_2, \ldots p_n$ converges over time. Since $(p_0 - p^*)$ and p^* are constants, the behavior of this sequence will depend on the behavior of A^n, where $A = (1 - \pi_L a - \pi_R b)$. By assumption, a, b, π_L, and π_R represent probabilities and proportions, so that they will be bounded between 0 and 1, which implies that the value of A will also be constrained between 0 and 1. Therefore, the relevant paths for our purposes are defined by $0 \leq A \leq 1$.

All relevant paths are illustrated in figure 2.1 for different values of A and different starting values p_0. In general, if the absolute value of A is less than 1, the product term in equation (8) approaches 0 in the limit, and $\{p_n\}$ tends toward $p^* = (\pi_L a)/(\pi_L a + \pi_R b)$. Thus, in the subset of cases in which $0 < A < 1$, the time path always converges toward the equilibrium p^*. If $p_0 < p^*$, then $\{p_n\}$ will increase monotonically toward p^* (see fig. 2.1a); if $p_0 > p^*$, then $\{p_n\}$ will instead decrease monotonically toward p^* (see fig. 2.1b).

If $A = 1$, then both $\pi_L a$ and $\pi_L b$ equal 0, since neither dispositions nor incentives take on negative values. When $A = 1$ and $B = \pi_L a = 0$, the time path remains constant at the level of the starting value p_0 (see fig. 2.1c). Finally, if $A = 0$, then $\{p_n\}$ converges immediately on $p^* = B/(1 - A) = B = \pi_L a$ (see fig. 2.1d).

Except in the limiting case where $A = 1$, the predominant forces in the

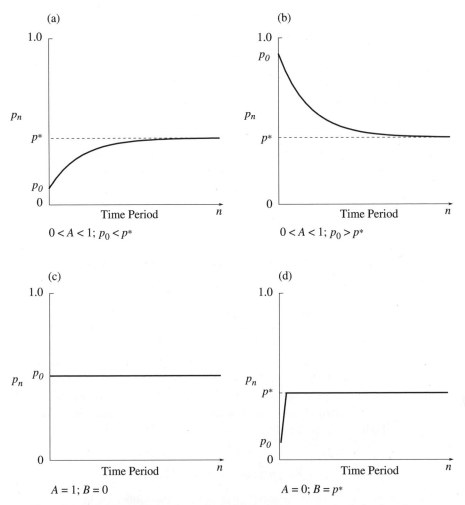

Figure 2.1. Relevant solution sequences $\{p_n\}$ of the equation: $p_{n+1} = Ap_n + B$, where $A = (1 - \pi_L a - \pi_R b)$ and $B = \pi_L a$

model tend to push individual propensities toward the equilibrium value p^*. Consider, however, not the overall equilibrium value, but the two components on which it is based: the disposition to choose L or R and the material and social incentives to make those choices. Both components may recommend the same choice, or they may operate at cross purposes. There can thus be varying "fits" between a person's dispositions and the incentives of his environment.

Since people want to be comfortable in their reference groups and to be rewarded for their choices, they will develop congenial dispositions that allow them to make the appropriate responses in their communities. Strong dispositions make certain choices easier than others. In this regard, formation of dispositions is akin to an investment that is meant to give a person the right identifications, values, and knowledge to permit acculturation into the society.

In a society that rewards L most of the time, it is best for one to be able to choose L most, if not all, of the time by developing the right dispositions that increase the likelihood of selecting L. Someone with strong dispositions toward R will instead be inclined to choose the less rewarded alternative out of habit, contrary values, insufficient capacity, or psychological rigidity. In such cases, a person's dispositions—his values, identifications, and skills— are out of step with the current norms of the community, to some degree. In chapter 3, I will explain how this state of affairs may arise and how it can contribute to group conflict over social norms.

DEDUCTIONS: THE INTERPLAY BETWEEN INCENTIVES AND DISPOSITIONS

Using this model, we can analyze a variety of social processes in terms of the interaction between individual dispositions and social and material incentives. The structure of the model is sufficiently general so that it can be applied to the dynamics of socialization, identity formation, conformity to conventions and norms, social diffusion, cultural inertia, and opinion and value change. All of these processes fit into the model because they can be conceptualized in terms of individual choices between alternative norms, values, identifications, and policies over the life course.

Rational Choice and Habit

First, let me offer a brief discussion employing the model on the contrast between value- and incentive-driven choices. When both dispositions and incentives bear on decision making, a change in the balance between π_L and π_R, while holding a and b constant, is predicted by the model to produce a corresponding change in p^*, which means that increasing the incentive through argument, example, or material or social benefit for choosing an alternative increases the rate of conformity to that alternative. This is clearly a falsifiable implication, because it assumes that shifting incentives should sway one's choice (except in the limiting condition when either a or $b = 0$); for example, if $b > 0$, and $\pi_{R,\,n+1} > \pi_{R,\,n}$, then p^* should decline over time.

When are people more likely to make the rational choice? People are more likely to act instrumentally when the incentives are apparent, there are large consequences to their decisions, and there is a clear relationship between means and ends.[26] When π_L and π_R are indistinguishable or not calculable, then decision making more likely turns on an individual's values and group orientations. Therefore, *the effect of incentives diminishes in relation to standing values and dispositions if there is little or nothing to differentiate between alternative courses of action.* This is a basic rule to memorize, because I will make use of it again below.

In practice, we should also expect that rationality will improve with experience and repetition of choice. Errors of choice will eventually be recognized and corrected. This result is also indicated by the model, as p_L always converges over time toward the more highly rewarded alternative when dispositions are equal and one is amenable to incentives (i.e., $a = b > 0$). Therefore, the individual propensity, p_{L0}, may begin out of equilibrium, but it will approach p^* as a person learns to choose the superior alternative with increasing frequency.

It may, however, be the case that changes in opportunities do not alter choices. In the case of habitual or internalized choice, dispositions developed in favor of either L or R guide choices reflexively, sometimes to the detriment of self-interest. Dispositional explanations assume that responses stabilize and become unresponsive to changes in incentives (the π's) even if incentives may have partly shaped dispositions in the formative life stages. Psychologically internalized feelings of self-esteem or guilt for abiding by the norm or failing to do so may take the place of external incentives. Early learning in this view produces hardened orientations reflected in fixed values of a and b. By definition, a rigid person retains his preferences even if his new environment contains a different incentive structure.

Habitual choice occurs when preferences depend entirely on $a/(a + b)$ and are unaffected by π_L and π_R. Such behavior runs contrary to our assumption that a rational individual remains open to new information and changes in incentives instead of being driven by permanent dispositions that govern choices irrespective of context. As I have noted, however, if these dispositions are formed originally to adapt to the environment (as in the cases of Packwood and the inner-city youth described in chapter 1), then they contain a built-in instrumental rationality, and the habitual response is indistinguishable from the consciously calculated choice, so long as the environment remains constant. To demonstrate: when a and b perfectly reflect the balance of incentives in one's social network, then $a = \pi_L$ and $b = \pi_R$; therefore $a/(a + b) = \pi_L/(\pi_L + \pi_R)$. In other words, the purely disposition-driven choice is indistinguishable from the purely incentive-driven one! In such cases, we can separate habit from rational choice only if we can find a way to observe whether preferences respond to a new balance of incentives.

In principle, the model is falsified when people fail to take advantage of new opportunities. If material incentives are recognized but ignored in favor of group loyalties, if the strength of group identifications do not correspond to the incentives provided for maintaining those ties, if people are not responsive to information that is relevant to their choices, seeing instead what they are predisposed to see, then, in these instances, dispositions are dominating incentives.

But, as I will show in chapter 3, new incentives may not alter the behavior of individuals who calculate that they will fare poorly under the new system. Cultural inertia therefore may stem from rational calculation as well as simple habit. When a person's dispositions reflect adaptation to the incentive structure of the environment, he develops a vested interest in maintaining that environment because he may later be unable to adjust readily to a new environment. The model therefore recognizes that the past decisions a person has made in acquiring knowledge and skills and forming social ties and group identifications affect his assessment of the relative merits of current choices. Someone who has developed the dispositions necessary to succeed in an environment where L is the norm is therefore acting rationally by opposing initiatives to change the norm from L to R.

Principled Choices

Even among rational actors, there are circumstances in which we would expect principled behavior and enforcement of impartial norms. *Public spirited behavior will tend to be displayed and neutral standards applied when private interests are not at risk.* This deduction is simply a corollary of the generalization offered in the last section about the conditions under which rational choice will be muted: when incentives between alternatives cancel each other, then underlying dispositions, including strong moral values, will prevail in guiding individual choice. Thus, disinterested third parties to conflicts can be expected to apply neutral criteria based on general principles in resolving disputes. A political implication of this deduction is that interested parties will commonly resort strategically to moral appeals in order to entice neutral third parties into political conflicts.

A methodological implication of this result for studies of self-interest is that it can be hazardous to interpret abstract tests of rationality, based on mass surveys, that contrast self-interest with principles and ideological values, because surveys attach no tangible consequences to one's choices. Individuals responding to surveys often express support for group norms or higher principles even at the expense of self-interest. For example, in a national survey asking citizens how they would respond to violations of the rights of individuals they did not know, a surprisingly high percentage claimed (contrary to the logic of collective action) that they would take costly measures to redress the injustice, ranging from writing letters to one's congressmen to organizing protest rallies.[27] We *know* that these responses greatly exaggerate the initiative that people actually take in such predicaments. When costs are low, other-regarding intentions are more common, but it is unclear how much other-regarding behavior will be demonstrated.

Partisan and Ideological Choices

That people often rely on standing values and partisan leanings also follows from the general deduction that rational calculation requires clearly differentiated alternatives. Given the small expected returns from political participation available to the average voter, we would not expect people to pay much attention to politics, and—to the extent that they follow public affairs—we would expect people to be most attentive to domestic issues that are relevant to their lives. Indeed, the hopes and fears of Americans are concentrated on personal matters, such as family finances, children, and personal health and well-being rather than on more remote political issues. Personal contentment is heavily contingent on the quality of one's marriage, friendships, job, health, and neighborhood.[28]

Thus the decision-making process in politics relies more heavily on standing political orientations than on continual calculation. The average person devotes little time to following politics and current affairs and is content to use partisan and ideological cues to form his preferences. People are likely to gather more information when preparing to make a decision with large financial consequences. When there are negligible differences between alternatives or when their consequences are hard to map ($\pi_L = \pi_R$, or π_L and π_R are unknown), we would expect that political orientations and values (a and b) would exert more influence over one's choice.

Berelson, Lazarsfeld, and McPhee were loath to characterize voting as a rational choice, but their description of the division of labor in election campaigns explains how voters use simple rules to determine which candidate serves their interests: "The individual voter may not have a great deal of detailed information, but he usually has picked up the crucial general information as part of his social learning itself. He may not know the parties' positions . . . but he cannot live in an American community without knowing broadly where the parties stand. He has learned that the Republicans are more conservative and the Democrats more liberal—and he can locate his own sentiments and cast his vote accordingly. After all, he must vote for one or the other party, and, if he knows the big thing about the parties, he does not need to know all the little things."[29] In short, every individual is not well informed, but every individual does not need to be well informed, merely to be informed in broad terms about the nature of the party system.

Early Socialization

Socialization could be described as opinion formation in highly impressionable individuals. In general, children pattern their attitudes and behavior after those who have social backgrounds similar to theirs, beginning with their parents and role models in the immediate vicinity. Therefore the kinds of values that people acquire in their formative years are consistently correlated with their socioeconomic backgrounds. Since children do not have the luxury early in life of surveying the range of possible reference groups that they might give allegiance to, their choices are severely constrained by a limited perspective and restricted social networks. The reference groups they encounter are all that they know at the time, so it is unsurprising that the benefits of membership in these groups fosters identification with them.

Early socialization thus occurs without individual biases in favor of L or R and without extensive calculation. Susceptibility to influence translates into $a = b > 0$, meaning that children are open-minded about adopting either L or R. Weak values permit incentive-driven choices. When there are no strong dispositions favoring L or R, the beliefs and values formed tend to mirror the balance of social forces in one's environment; p^* will reflect whether π_L or π_R predominates. Parental messages are likely to carry special weight in the child's limited environment, not only by dominating other messages by their frequency, but also by being coupled with greater incentives.

To be sure, even if we assume that the child begins socialization as a tabula rasa, group identifications are likely to develop readily. The mechanism behind early socialization is probably a combination of such identification with one's reference groups and an intuitive comprehension that one is better off by adopting the views and following the practices of those who are in positions of authority. This process strikes me as being roughly rational in the sense that it is not clear how a rational individual with limited experience and knowledge and highly constrained alternatives might behave otherwise. At the same time, many of the choices made in these circumstances will not involve substantial deliberation and will seem relatively "mindless" in the sense that we often refer to social conformity.

Group Identifications

While in theory individuals can choose the groups best suited for use in achieving their goals, these choices are in practice limited early in life by family and socioeconomic circumstances. Group identities and loyalties grow naturally out of an individual's socialization experience. People become familiar with the customs and values of the groups they belong to and depend upon, and they become comfortable with a particular way of life. But whether group identifications are sustained over time depends on whether they continue to constitute useful bases of coordination for social and political action. People do not use arbitrary reference groups when identifying themselves to others, but rather use reference groups that are in common usage in the society: "It is the institutional definitions of the social structure which may focus the attention of members of a group or occupants of a social status upon certain *common* reference groups."[30]

We can model the formation of dispositions (*a* and *b*) in the same way that we model changes in preference between norms (*L* and *R*). Identification with a group (e.g., a type *a* or a type *b* group) depends on coordination around the symbols and ethos of that group. A political or social identification that fails to continue producing material or social rewards will begin to wane. If group identifications cease to be associated with political outcomes—that is, if the rewards for holding identifications *a* or *b*, π_a and π_b, respectively, approach 0—such identifications will weaken over time and they will become less salient bases of organization. By the same token, group identifications that yield greater benefits over time will be more attractive to individuals. If people with identity *a* tend to give *L* responses in an environment that more frequently rewards *R* responses, there will be an incentive to move from identity *a* toward identity *b*.

Group Norms and Values

The dynamics of the model reproduce the convergence of opinions and beliefs that occurs within reference groups. Social interaction, discussion, and the circulation of ideas within groups will produce shared opinions on matters of common interest such as religion, culture, politics, and morality. Group members develop common evaluations, identifications, and norms as the influence and conformity processes tend toward social equilibria.

Common beliefs and attitudes reduce the transaction costs of social exchange and coordinate individual actions. Individual group members may start out with a heterogeneous set of opinions p_{L0}, but as long as they share an underlying group identification (equivalent *a* and *b* values), their views will converge over time as they interact with each other. Identification with the group makes a person amenable to the group's norms.

The classic laboratory experiment that mimics this process was designed by Muzafer Sherif around the "autokinetic effect," an optical illusion in which a point of light shining in a darkened room appears to move but actually does not.[31] In one version of these experiments, several subjects are brought together and asked individually to judge how far the spot of light moves in a two-second interval when the light is turned on and off. They are then asked to repeat their judgments over a large number of trials. Subjects initially disagree about the degree of movement, each offering his own private assessment. But over the course of the experiment they unconsciously pool their judgments and converge on highly similar estimates of the distance that the light travels.[32] The subjects in effect establish a group norm about how far the light moves that is a compromise among the individual judgments. It is appropriate to characterize the point of convergence as a norm, because the value established by the group continues to influence individual judgments even when subjects are tested alone in follow-up experiments.[33]

What groups do, then, is develop common interpretations of social, and often physical, reality. Our social and political beliefs are developed out of the need to construct some organized way of understanding how society works: "The norms of our culture . . . give the otherwise perplexed individual ready-made attitudes for comprehending his universe."[34] Even though many of these beliefs may be inaccurate or incorrect, it would seem at a minimum true that an individual is better served by acquiring some functional view of his society than to be bereft of any templates for interpreting events and knowing how to respond to social situations.[35]

Cross-Pressures

Some individuals will hold conflicting dispositions and interests that leave them "cross-pressured" between competing alternatives.[36] Working class Protestants, Republican union members, and conservative Democrats are all examples of individuals who possess conflicting group memberships. A portion of the identity of a cross-pressured individual inclines him to support L, while another part of his identity predisposes him toward R. Since he belongs to conflicting groups, he will also be presented with incentives to support both L and R on any given issue; for example, alternative L may offer benefits to his union member self, while alternative R holds promise for the Republican in him. Research on electoral choice has found that cross-pressured voters tend to make their decisions later in the campaign and tend to be more apathetic about politics in general. Both their reluctance to make a decision and their general apathy are easily explained by their indifference between the alternatives before them. If a roughly equals b, and π_L roughly equals π_R, meaning that dispositions and incentives are almost evenly split, then p^* will be close to .50, signifying indifference between L and R. When there is little or nothing to choose between the alternatives, it is harder to make a decision, and easier to make no decision at all.

Conventions

Many norms are conventional in the sense of providing people with an agreed-upon understanding of their social world that spares them the task of individually reconciling heterogeneous opinions. A convention L is a regularity of behavior that is self-enforcing because almost everyone expects almost everyone to conform to L, and almost everyone prefers to conform to L on the condition that others do so.[37] When faced with a choice among potential conventions, individuals prefer the alternative chosen by most other people, and may (at least initially) feel indifferent about alternatives as long as most people agree upon the chosen one. Therefore, individuals will prefer L to R if L is the predominant choice, but will reverse their preference if R is the predominant choice. One is better off speaking English when English is the majority language, but would prefer to learn French if French is the predominant choice of others. An individual who is predisposed toward neither alternative ($a = b$) will tend toward either L or R depending on which is practiced with the greatest frequency. Remember the general rule: if $a = b$, then p^* reduces to $\pi_L/(\pi_L + \pi_R)$. But even if one is predisposed toward R, if practically everyone else chooses L, then $\pi_L \to 1.0$ and $\pi_R \to 0$, and $p^* \to 1.0$; therefore, the model predicts that he or she is also very likely to choose L. By the same token, one will choose R if almost everyone else chooses R, irrespective of one's disposition toward the alternatives.

Cultural Diffusion

The model also represents three main forms of cultural diffusion. The cultural diffusion of ideas, innovations, fashion, taste, and vernacular is another form of social learning that follows much the same dynamics as group conformity to norms.[38] Robert Boyd and Peter Richerson identify three main routes by which a cultural item is diffused.[39] The adoption of a characteristic can be based on:

1. *The frequency with which the characteristic is displayed.* In evaluating the merits of a cultural characteristic, an individual may refer to the frequency with which that attribute is displayed. As the number of models possessing the attribute increases, there is a greater likelihood of exposure to the innovation and there is more security offered to the person who adopts it. In frequency-dependent transmission, "the naive individual does not directly evaluate the merit of the variants to which he is exposed; rather, he simply uses

the frequency of a variant among his models (not the population) as an indirect measure of its merit."[40] All cultural transmission of a characteristic is likely to be dependent on its frequency, so it is useful to contrast biased with unbiased transmission. In unbiased transmission, the likelihood of acquiring a characteristic is simply the proportion of models that display that feature. With frequency-biased transmission, there is a bias in favor of adoption when more than half of the models display the attribute, but there is a corresponding bias against adoption when fewer than half the models display it.

2. *A direct assessment of the merits of alternative cultural items.* Directly biased transmission in contrast requires a more discriminating evaluation of the merits of different cultural characteristics. It is a form of biased transmission because the probability of acquiring the characteristic consistently exceeds the proportion of models bearing that feature; but in contrast to frequency-dependent transmission, the presumed mechanism is that the individual evaluates the various choices and tends to prefer one variant over all others because it has superior qualities. Directly biased and frequency-dependent transmission exact contrasting decision-making costs.

3. *The prestige associated with a characteristic because it is possessed by a role model.* Opinion leaders and innovators do not promote and transmit only those beliefs and attributes that further their own or their group's welfare. Instead, role models advance, through their example, intentionally or inadvertently, a variety of practices and beliefs that have no functional relationship to particular goals and therefore do not directly serve anyone's interests. In this manner, preferences and practices that do not spawn from materialistic individual motivations can nevertheless diffuse through groups and the society as a whole. Leaders can start trends because they are regarded by others as successful role models whose successes attach value—both symbolic and instrumental—to the complex of beliefs and practices they display.

Some traits are seen to be causally related to the role models' success, but there are also unrelated corollary traits that become more desirable or attractive to others merely because the role model displays them. Nike tried to capitalize on the ambiguity between these two kinds of traits when it proclaimed, tongue-in-cheek, that "It must be the shoes" in an advertising campaign featuring experiments trying to find an explanation for Michael Jordan's extraordinary basketball skills. Both the material and immaterial characteristics of role models are emulated because (a) it is easier to copy wholesale rather than to try to ascertain what traits contribute to success and (b) it is desirable to display the symbols of success, even if they are not materially related to achieving success. Celebrity advertising rests on these assumptions.

These three mechanisms of cultural diffusion are parallel to the three interpretations of the social learning mechanism that I have placed at the center of my model. Individuals choose to conform to a norm, belief, or practice due to its popularity, its costs and benefits, or its favored status among opinion leaders. As in the model of cultural diffusion, individuals can either make a direct assessment of the merits of a cultural characteristic or they can rely indirectly on indicators of its popularity and status by following the lead of others.

Stability over Time

The model indicates why we might expect a great deal of attitude stability over an individual's life span and continuity of norms and values across generations. Individual attitudes and values will be stable if people reside in an environment that maintains their dispositions and offers the same incentives over time. The equilibrium, p^*, does not change without a change in the value of a or b, or π_L or π_R. It is to be expected that, throughout the course of one's life, social interaction and communication will be biased by group memberships and social networks. The constancy of one's environment may be partly a function of personal choice, as individuals settle into groups and social networks that are relatively homogeneous in composition and agreeable with their preferences. Consequently, most discussion turns out to be confirming rather than controversial, and typically reinforces existing beliefs and values.

In addition there are elaborate mechanisms in our society that are designed to ensure intergenerational continuity of norms and values. Children are socialized according to the values of their parents; schools are designed to perpetuate the community's prevailing norms; there is social pressure to conform to traditional beliefs, customs, and practices. The political biases of groups persist for the same reasons. There is considerable intergenerational continuity in partisan preferences, as most people vote the way their parents and grandparents voted. Young voters have weak dispositions and are easily influenced by the partisan inclinations of their parents. Furthermore, one is likely to grow up in, marry into, and work and socialize with groups that share the same social strata and partisanship as one's parents.

Changing Values

While there are strong tendencies toward stability in society, the model also provides for the possibility of change in response to new incentives. Value change is initiated by changes in underlying identifications and changes in the incentives for holding one set of values versus another. When group norms change or when individuals change groups, there is pressure on individuals to change their identifications and their opinions and values. The equilibrium value p^* shifts in accordance with changes in identification (a and b) and incentives (π_L and π_R).

Social mobility between groups with contrasting interests will therefore lead to the formation of new political preferences that accord with one's new interests. There may be some asymmetry, depending on the direction of social mobility. In the case of upward mobility, the incentive to identify with one's new group is likely to be greater than in the event of downward mobility. But resistance to conformity to lower-status groups should be more clearly expressed on matters of style than of substance. Similarly, individual reactions to new group norms will vary according to the relative attractiveness of the old and new norms. Those group members who gain from the change in norms will adapt most readily, whereas people who will suffer a loss of utility will be inclined to resist change. Individuals with strong dispositions in favor of the prior norm may display a slower rate of change because they lack the skills or knowledge to adapt completely. Therefore a full transition to the new group norm requires not only incentives but also identification with the new group. Incoming generations, however, will usually adapt readily to the new norms because they do not have strong predispositions to do otherwise. They will simply acquire the norms of their environment (as described above under "Early Socialization.")

Patterns of Opinion and Value Change

Changes in popular preferences follow systematic patterns that depend on the interaction between people's incentives to change and their dispositions either to accept or to resist change. General dispositions affect the individual's flexibility to adapt to change. People do not face issues *de novo;* they have prior beliefs or resilient identifications and traits that are resistant to change. The a and b parameters therefore vary according to the zeal with which the respondent adheres to a particular political viewpoint. True believers are likely to be more dogmatic and resistant to discrepant norms than political moderates, and, irrespective of ideology, better-informed respondents are likely to be more selective about the types of norms they accept. Youths, without strong priors and dependent on their reference groups, will be easily socialized to any set of prevailing norms.

Political appeals will produce patterns of opinion change that vary according to rates of exposure and acceptance. We should consider in this context three basic patterns of opinion formation and change that have been documented in the literature: group polarization, the development of a consensus across groups, and nonlinear patterns of attitude change.[41] Where there are two groups with contrasting norms, group members who are appropriately cued will tend to acquire their respective norms, leading to the formation of distinct cultures. For example, in a heterogeneous environment, with opinion leaders for L and R sending out conflicting messages (so that π_L and π_R are comparable in size), rank-and-file group members who are predisposed toward L or R will become polarized, accepting messages that are consistent with their prior beliefs and identifications and rejecting inconsistent messages (a is large, while b is small, for those inclined toward L; the reverse holds for those inclined toward R).

The model also identifies circumstances when all individuals reach a consensus on a single norm despite beginning at diverse starting points. When there is a uniform stream of messages supporting one side of an issue—say R—support for that position increases with exposure to those messages (the speed of learning is directly related to $\pi_R b$). If partisan opinion leaders on all sides promote the same message, or if there is a theme that is appealing to all partisan perspectives, everyone is motivated to accept the idea because the issue is no longer partisan (a is small and b is large across the board, meaning there is little resistance to the pro-R message). Therefore, any individual factor that increases the probability of receiving those pro-R signals—such as education, interest in politics, attention to the mass media, membership in political organizations—will promote support for the consensus position.

Under certain conditions, rates of attitude change will be nonlinear in relation to personal characteristics. In the public opinion literature, we occasionally observe that rates of opinion change are nonlinearly related to levels of political sophistication. For example, support for liberal (conservative) policy proposals among conservatives (liberals) will be nonlinearly related to information levels. Those with moderate levels of information about politics will show stronger support for the proposal than either those who are well informed or those who are poorly informed. This result can be explained by variations in the degree to which members of each of these groups are exposed to the issue and susceptible to persuasion on it. In order to support a new policy, a person must first hear about it and then must be persuaded to accept it. If either π_L, the likelihood of receiving a pro-L message, or a, the disposition to accept a pro-L message, is close to zero, then the probability of endorsing L will be close to zero.

Levels of political sophistication will be positively related both to the strength of one's dispositions and to the likelihood of receiving a particular message. With respect to a liberal proposal, conservatives of middling sophistication will be more likely than the least sophisticated conservatives to hear an ideologically contrary message (i.e., π_L will be greater in the middle group) and they will be more likely than the most sophisticated to be persuaded by it (i.e., a will be greater in the middle group than in the group of sophisticates).

Because π_L is small in the low information group and a is small in the high information group, the product $\pi_L a$ is small in both groups in comparison to those with moderate levels of information. *The stability of the extremes therefore stems from the failure of the least aware to encounter dissonant messages and the refusal of the most aware to entertain them.*

Competing ideological messages therefore will consolidate the rank-and-file but will not draw much new support. Partisan leaders have to fashion more neutral appeals if they hope to win support beyond the in-group. (I will devote a section in chapter 4 to the strategy underlying apparently impartial principled appeals.) Consensus issues are known in the study of elections as "valence" issues because they are not ideologically cued but instead contain honorific themes—peace, children's welfare, economic good times—for which there is broad-based popular support.[42] Well-informed partisans will probably be able to see through most strategic communications by their opponents, no matter how cleverly they are camouflaged, but for the reasons just given, less-sophisticated individuals may not have such reliable defenses against persuasion attempts. Furthermore it may be possible to take another tack by influencing people's dispositions so that they are more receptive to the message.

CONCLUSION

The model of choice presented in this chapter lays the groundwork for the remainder of the book. According to this model, individual preferences are guided by both dispositions and incentives. This means that, in selecting between any set of alternatives, an individual may, by virtue of his group identifications and values, be predisposed to favor one alternative independently of the current incentives associated with the alternatives. These current incentives are based on the material and social rewards attached, the arguments offered by others, and the distribution of choices that other people make. Dispositions are acquired through socialization over the life course and, in theory, are open to continual change in response to changing incentives, though in practice they tend to stabilize, as people settle into constant social environments that reinforce existing orientations.

In essence, social conformity is a conflict-reduction process, as people with divergent views converge toward a shared norm. People will adopt common beliefs, conventions, and norms if they have incentives to conform. They will develop identification with groups that can provide them with benefits that they cannot obtain on their own. Socialization, opinion leadership, and social pressure all contribute to common norms, identifications, and conventions.

The rationality that characterizes individual behavior is not a global rationality in which people are aware of the full array of life's options and make choices with complete foresight about their implications. Unfortunately, there is no handy formula instructing us on how to develop the values, group identifications, knowledge, and skills that will permit us to live a perfectly integrated life. All we can do is adapt to our circumstances and try to behave rationally in light of the decisions already committed to in an earlier period of our lives. The traits we acquire, the attitudes that result from socialization and conformity, the truths and misconceptions that we come to believe, are all factored into how we try to accomplish what is best for ourselves.

Although norms coordinate expectations and choices and reduce transaction costs *within* social groups, they also increase them *across* groups. The interest one has in a system of norms strengthens over time to the extent that one has made choices based on those norms which constitute investments with long-term implications. A person may not always possess the capacity or wherewithal to alter course when circumstances change and new opportunities arise. As I will explain in chapter 3, this is one of the dynamics that explains increasing attachment to familiar norms and social practices. Past choices condition evaluations of interests and lay the foundation for conflicts over competing norms and social practices.

CHAPTER THREE

Coordination and Conflict

We shape our buildings, then our buildings shape us.

Winston Churchill

Why are new social norms and conventions so often resisted? The model developed in chapter 2 provides us with a compact way to represent how people will choose between competing alternatives, whether those alternatives are policies, norms, opinions, or identifications. As I will show in this chapter, it also offers insight into why people are reluctant to change their norms and values. The answer can be traced to the model's basic premise that individuals react to change depending on their incentives to change and on their personal capacities to change. What is distinctive about cultural conflicts is that they often do not involve straightforward choices between material alternatives; but although the interests underlying social norms are not always transparent, this does not mean that instrumental calculations and interests are not relevant to their formation and defense.

FOUR MECHANISMS OF DEFENSE

A culture consists of shared rules, beliefs, values, and standards of evaluation that provide guidance on how to live. A culture changes when people introduce new rules, beliefs, values, and standards. When old values are supplanted by new values, the norm shifts from L to R or from R to L; similarly, when new groups introduce competing conventions, there is no longer agreement over the choice between L and R—some people choose L, while others choose R. In either case, there is a discrepancy between one's propensity to choose L and the likelihood that L will be rewarded or reciprocated, meaning that one's routines no longer coordinate as well with the choices that others are making, or, even worse, that one's preferences no longer garner the same social and material rewards that they once did.

Several mechanisms sustain people's preference for a familiar norm L over an alternative norm R and make it difficult for them to adjust to social change. Each mechanism relates to a particular reason why people believe they will receive greater benefits by defending the old norm than by shifting their allegiance to the new norm. Although I will discuss these mechanisms separately, it will be evident from the examples used to illustrate them that they are not mutually exclusive, and often work in concert.

1. *L is preferred because others prefer L; changes in the norms therefore create coordination problems.* Coordination problems occur when people's responses are no longer synchronized with the choices of others in the community. One chooses L and hears R in return, or vice versa. There is a disjunction between one's choice and the choices of others when, for example, one's spoken language is not understood or when a norm of social interaction is violated. When there are competing norms, people have difficulty communicating with one another and anticipating one another's actions. The breakdown of conventions weakens group cohesion and solidarity and hinders collective action. Institutional changes instigated by new groups create feelings of disorientation and resentment over the erasure of familiar symbols and social practices.

Various responses to competing norms and conventions are possible, including segregation of the respective groups into their own social circles and institutions and regulation of their behavior through laws designed to maintain conformity to a common set of standards. Those in the majority, with greater political and economic power at their disposal, will tend to have reasonable success in imposing their norms on those who are in the minority; alternatively, they will try to erect barriers that limit their contact with these groups. Those in the minority can try to assimilate by altering their beliefs and behavior; alternatively, they can take collective action to alter the norms or they can exit from the mainstream to form separate communities. The perspectives of the majority and the minority are therefore distinctly asymmetrical, as I will elaborate in the last section of this chapter.

2. *L is preferred because of psychological attachment to L and to groups that practice L.* People attach greater value to familiar bases of coordination, including norms and group identities. Ethnocentrism is a belief in the superiority of the features of one's own culture owing to a variety of cognitive and perceptual biases. People conform to a group's norms because other members of the group conform to them, but a preference that originates in the norm's coordination benefits may turn into a preference that is supported by a belief in the norm's instrumental superiority over alternative norms. Rational choice assumes that people prefer L or R on the basis of *information* that they have gathered about the merits of L and R. But ethnocentrism may bias the values of π_L and π_R by skewing the information that one receives as well as how that information is interpreted. The stronger one's group identification, the more likely it is that one will gather information that reinforces group norms and the less likely that one will gather favorable information about other

groups. Underlying dispositions also affect how information about L and R will be interpreted; if one is predisposed toward L ($a \to 1$, $b \to 0$), then pro-L arguments and evidence will strengthen support for L, but evidence that there is virtue in R, if it is even recognized, will have little effect. These psychological biases make support for L difficult to dislodge, for a person's assessment of the utility of alternatives is no longer independent of his dispositions.

3. *L is preferred because one does better under L and cannot readily adjust to R.* Individuals who have planned their lives around existing conventions and standards of evaluation have vested interests in the status quo, and may not be able to adapt readily to new bases of coordination, including new rules for distributing material benefits and social status. When an individual adapts to his social environment, he learns whatever responses are needed to gain acceptance within his reference groups and to receive the social and material benefits of membership. Group membership leads to identifying with the group and to developing attitudes, traits, and skills that serve the individual in that environment. Some of these investments are portable and can be applied successfully in alternative environments, while other dispositions are tailored for particular contexts. Life decisions are therefore premised on the existence of a certain kind of society. If the norms of that society change, altering the status and prestige associated with various activities, then those people who invested in activities valued under the old system, but not the new system, will be more likely to oppose change.

A person is generally able to capitalize on new opportunities only by acquiring certain capacities. The ability to conform to L or R depends, respectively, on possessing the characteristics a or b that allow one to make the proper response. A way to conceptualize this problem is to observe that an a-type individual will have difficulty adapting to a b-type environment. People are initially neutral with respect to their preference for L or R, and are willing to be guided by whichever alternative is more rewarding to pursue. But they gradually develop dispositions that reinforce the choice they are inclined to make based solely on external incentives. In an environment in which L is rewarded 70 percent of the time, one is better off choosing L consistently rather than alternating probabilistically between L and R. This can be accomplished only by developing stronger dispositions in favor of L. If one is dispositionally neutral with respect to the alternatives, then 70 percent of the time one will choose L, and 30 percent of the time, R. But the stronger one's disposition toward L (i.e., the more a exceeds b) the higher the probability of choosing L and the greater one's likelihood of being rewarded.

When dispositions and incentives reinforce each other in this manner, people have successfully adapted to the reward structure of their environment. If people are flexible and can alter their dispositions in response to changing incentive systems, then they will be less prone to resist change. However, when norms and incentives change, some people may be unable to benefit under the new norm because they do not have the requisite skills and training, or they may be unwilling to conform because of deeply held identifications and values. These people are made worse off by the new norm. For example, as we shall see, traditionally socialized women will enjoy greater success in a society that values traditional sex roles, according to which men are primarily responsible for earning wages and women for raising children. When the social norms shift from R to L—to a culture in which women also pursue higher education and careers—women who have not trained for a profession are ill-equipped to accommodate themselves to these changes. If the characteristic required to accommodate to L is higher education, those who elected to forgo such education earlier in life may find that it is too late to catch up—a b type cannot take sufficient steps to transform into an a type.

4. *L is preferred because collective action is based on common beliefs and values L.* Political leaders are constantly trying to organize and mobilize the mass public around common interests, identifications, and values. To the extent that politicians make appeals to group loyalties and values, those identifications and values are strengthened by the political process. When political power derives from mass coordination around common norms, values, and group identifications, individuals are motivated to embrace those beliefs as long as their conformity to them continues to be rewarded. New norms and values, and the groups that espouse them, threaten to overturn the institutions that benefit defenders of the traditional norms. I will develop this final point in chapter 4.

COORDINATION PROBLEMS

In a letter to the editor, a duffer is disgruntled over the recent popularization of golf among youngsters hoping to emulate the new phenomenon on the professional tour, Tiger Woods: "I find play disrupted by thrown clubs, screaming across fairways, 'playing through' without asking, wild gesturing, and loud, obscene conversations during play. Also, the terrible clothes and inappropriate shoes that are sometimes seen would not be allowed on the better courses."[1]

Whenever groups of individuals develop a common code, the code tends to coordinate social interaction among group members while screening out others who cannot or will not accommodate themselves to the designated conventions. A common denominator of all social groups is that they have barriers to entry. This is true even of low-status groups that people of higher-status typically do not wish to join. These barriers become apparent whenever people (e.g., researchers, informants, and undercover agents) attempt to infiltrate a group and pass for one of its members.[2] Although suburban middle-class youths, for example, typically have no desire to infiltrate urban youth gangs, gang members still have incentives to enforce standards and rules and demand conformity from individuals who are attracted to their group and wish to gain its acceptance. Likewise, the easy and relaxed manner and practiced grace of upper-class members constitute styles that are learned and cultivated and which have the effect of defining members and erecting barriers to class entry.[3] The parvenus of the late nineteenth century made their fortunes on the industrialization and urbanization of America more quickly than they were able to develop social sophistication and learn the manners of the upper class. The traditional upper class used the crude behavior of the parvenus to stigmatize them and to deny them the social status that might normally accompany substantial wealth: "Typically a small-town businessman who struck it rich would move to the city to advance the social fortunes of his wife and children. There he would encounter complexities undreamt of in the snug security of his native hearth."[4]

As I have noted, coordination around group norms provides common knowledge and lends meaning and predictability to one's social environment. It follows that uncoordination makes social exchange more difficult and reduces the predictability of other people's actions, and that the resulting uncertainty creates distrust and conflict. Some opposition to alternative ways of life may be emotional, residing in fear of the unknown, but there also are practical costs associated with the need to accommodate multiple conventions, and it is not easy to weigh the relative effects of the two components.

The interest inherent in many political and social norms lies less in the actual substance of the norm than in the capacity of the norm to coordinate individual actions. With respect to many social choices—such as the language we speak, the currency we use, and the side of the road we drive on—it does not matter which convention we follow so long as we all follow the same one.[5] In such cases, the chosen convention provides a basis for social coordination. A convention created for one situation may be extrapolated to help resolve a coordination problem in another related but novel situation. For example, pedestrians may follow the same conventions on the footpaths as they do on the road, such as keeping to the right when passing oncoming pedestrians (do they keep to the left in Britain?).

Whereas a norm carries social sanctions to deter nonconformity, everyone has an incentive to abide by a convention if other people conform to it. It might therefore appear that explicit norms are superfluous in coordination situations that are self-enforcing. When people are faced with coordination problems, they often develop conventions to solve them. One has to ask, therefore, whether the norm adds anything to the convention that has been formed out of self-interest: "There is sufficient self-interest motivation to adhere to an established convention that there need be no further norm-based motivation. Perhaps the norm could be useful to regulate the behavior of slow learners— but only if the norm could be learned more easily than the self-interest could be comprehended."[6]

However, as David Lewis puts it, there is a sense in which "conventions may be a species of norms: regularities to which we believe one ought to conform."[7] Hence, one's failure to conform to a convention will be met with social disapproval if it is apparent that the violator has intentionally acted against his preferences and the expectations of others. There is a presumption, for example, that one who attends a formal wedding dressed in jeans has done so in order to insult one's hosts. One *ought* to know better; indeed, it is assumed that one *does* know better.

What are the circumstances in which differences over lifestyles and social norms will produce conflict? Contrasting norms are a source of conflict when those in the minority cannot be readily absorbed into the population—saved, reformed, converted, or socialized into the majority. Failure to coordinate has its downside, leading to problems such as an increase in unpredictability and distrust, breakdowns in communication, and the need to make costly institutional changes to accommodate diverse groups.

Minor uncoordination on social norms and conventions can be a welcome feature of society. It creates novelty, change, and excitement. There are benefits, for example, to having small ethnic and religious communities, and trendy neighborhoods in the city. One can visit these alternative establishments for entertainment, enlightenment, or relief from one's usual routines. Even the uncoordination represented by minor criminality and deviant behavior can stir excitement in otherwise sleepy towns. However, people become less tolerant when violations of existing norms reach a level that threatens the maintenance of the norms or imposes substantial costs, or "externalities," on the rest of the community. Groups therefore struggle to preserve their way of life against encroachment from new groups when such groups threaten existing patterns of behavior that are deemed to be beneficial.

Coordination and Trust

Our attitudes, beliefs, and knowledge offer critical clues about how we are likely to behave in the future and in hypothetical circumstances. Coordination around attitudes, identifications, and emotions revealed in ordinary conversation and socializing provides the foundation for possibly more significant collective action in the future. As Allan Gibbard observed, the capacity to contemplate, speculate about, react to, and discuss the hypothetical greatly enhances one's opportunities to cooperate. It is a characteristic that enhances the biological fitness of the species: "Those who can work out together reactions to an absent situation—what to do and what to feel—are ready for like situations. They are better prepared than they would otherwise be to do what is advantageous in a new situation, and they can rely on complex schemes of interpersonal coordination. On general evolutionary grounds, then, we might expect shared evaluation to figure centrally in a complex social life—and in human life it does. Much of our speech fosters shared reactions to absent circumstances."[8] Coordinated attitudes and values therefore help to establish the conditions for reciprocity. One assumes, for example, that a person who does not feel the appropriate indebtedness for a favor will be less likely to reciprocate in kind.

Groups that practice different norms are distrusted and sometimes feared because they are unfamiliar. Trust is built upon shared cultural, social, and physical attributes. People who are manifestly different are assumed to possess different underlying dispositions, and their behavior is believed to be less predictable as a consequence. To the extent that social preferences are believed to be motivated by individual dispositions that vary systematically across groups, group differences will be assumed to extend across issues and be perceived as relatively immutable. In Williamson County (see chapter 5), it was readily assumed that people who were different (e.g., liberal versus conservative, heterosexual versus homosexual) would make opposing social and political choices in a variety of spheres.

The path to respectability and trustworthiness in our society requires that one live up to an entire constellation of norms and conform to a variety of characteristics and traits. For example, in the nineteenth century, nativists continued to treat immigrant groups who lived up to most of the tenets of Victorian culture as aliens because they remained different in crucial regards.[9] Discrepancies signal foreign status and ignorance of cultural rules and conventions. Muslim women in the United States today who choose to wear head scarves, or chadors, in public, in accordance with the teachings of the Koran, are subject not only to stares and harassment but also to attempts by strangers to scam them because they are assumed to be naive.[10]

At the turn of the century, Protestants despised Irish Catholics because they dressed and spoke differently and held different religious ideas. Catholics seemed unpredictable. They ignored the acknowledged rules of fighting—kicking below the belt, beating up on small boys, and loading their snowballs with rocks. They also drank to the point where they lost control; each such act violated the majority's understanding of what constituted normal behavior.[11] Likewise, in Rieder's study of racial conflict in Brooklyn's Canarsie neighborhood in the 1970s, white high school students accused blacks of not adhering to conventions by using knives and guns in fights when there was an unwritten rule against weapons.[12] Residents spoke about the general difficulty they had in assessing the motives and character of blacks, claiming that class markers were less reliable for understanding blacks than whites.[13]

Transaction Costs and Externalities

Conventions smooth over social interaction between groups of individuals. In *The History of Manners,* Norbert Elias argued that increasing population density forces individuals to make adjustments in their personality and emotional structures.[14] When populations were widely dispersed, individuals could act upon their aggressions and impulses more freely. When people began to live in close quarters and engage in regular interaction, however, manners were required to regulate interpersonal relations. In *Morals for Children,* Erasmus promoted widespread adoption of social conventions to reduce the idiosyncrasy of symbols and actions and thereby facilitate communication. He abhorred the use of exclusive conventions by any group, irrespective of class: "Previously, the practices of a particular group or milieu had been held up as norms. By contrast, Erasmus sought to use a common code of manners as a basis for establishing social transparency, which he considered a necessary precondition for broader social intercourse."[15] Civility and common knowledge were intended to foster social exchange.

Colonial Americans were also deeply concerned about the state of manners in their new communities. The new society's preoccupation with establishing rules of social interaction created a market for books on etiquette and manners. Although the settlers imported most of their customs and manners from England, adherence to English conventions gradually weakened in the absence of authoritative enforcement from the mother country and American manners grew increasingly distinctive.[16]

Friction between members of different groups can be traced to the basic inconvenience of living among others who do not abide by the same conventions. At Cornell University, for example, the comfort and appeal of one's own racial and ethnic group conventions have prompted several minority groups to establish separate dormitories on campus, and this has intensified the pattern of voluntary housing segregation that already existed. Gay students who requested their own dorm were denied by university administrators intent on counteracting this trend.[17] The sociological forces giving rise to these desires, however, are hard to resist. The University of Massachusetts, for example, recently approved setting aside an entire floor of a dormitory for gay, lesbian, and bisexual students.[18]

Cornell students outside the mainstream explain repeatedly that they feel more comfortable in familiar social surroundings.[19] There are, so to speak, lower *transaction costs*—the costs of conducting business and social exchange—among those who share the same cultural background.

> Minority students on North [campus] said it is less tense to live among your own. "By the end of the day at a school like this, you're tired," said Ruth Ramos, a Chickasaw Indian who lives in the Akwe:kon house. "This school is so English, so white, day in and day out you're a little more comfortable with your own. I'm the norm in this house."
>
> "I know no one's going to be asking me why I wear my hair this way," says Ms. Myatt, the black freshman who lives in Ujamaa and wears her hair braided. "It gets tiring explaining yourself to white people all the time. Here I can come home and I know it will be music I like to listen to." . . .
>
> It's why Alison Nathan, of the Lesbian Gay and Bisexual Alliance, will continue pushing for a gay dorm. Ms. Nathan said that in a regular dorm, she can't be open about having a woman friend and feel comfortable. "Gays want a place where they can just be students without constantly justifying," she says, "so they can do their homework in peace, too."[20]

Students naturally are attracted to communities in which their preferences are reinforced. Although many minority students consciously choose to live in separate houses, white students often gravitate to the predominantly white West Campus at Cornell for reasons that are not explicitly racially based.[21] Students on West Campus, they understand, are friendly and hold good parties. Or they learned from parents or friends of the family that West Campus is the most desirable place to live. Only as an afterthought do they realize that West Campus, which is located about half a mile away and on opposite sides of a gorge from North Campus, is almost entirely white—like the people who made the recommendation. More than half of the residents on North Campus, on the other hand, are racial minorities. Some white students expect West Campus to be predominantly white, but are shocked by the severe imbalance.[22]

Thus, white students have a higher threshold for racial integration than is revealed by their choices, but individually they cannot do anything to alter the pattern of segregation.[23] The best they can do is reinforce existing tendencies. Any individual might feel worse off in an environment where he was in the minority, and thus sticking with one's own group may not be optimal but is still better than the alternative.[24] This coordination equilibrium therefore remains stable. But the situation has become intolerable to the campus administration, and the university president has mandated that all freshmen live on North Campus, so that they will have more opportunities to interact, and that all thematic houses be located on North Campus, if they wish to house freshmen.[25]

Popular reactions to mass immigration highlight the problems of social un-coordination. Ethnic neighborhoods generally win praise for enriching the larger city, but new groups with the resources to enter majority bastions will almost certainly elicit resentment if they do not conform to standard ways. Immigrants bring their own social conventions to their new country, and they face serious adjustment costs as well as impose costs on native residents by being unfamiliar with existing norms. Those who are in the majority may have difficulty communicating with immigrants and doing business with them. There are also likely to be institutional costs attached to recognizing separate conventions and trying to accommodate them.

Whereas a trickle of immigrants can be readily assimilated into the ways of the community, large-scale immigration often forces development of new social programs and institutions. In Wausau, Wisconsin, for example, an initially small influx of Southeast Asian immigrants in the 1970s was readily absorbed by the town. The first wave of immigration, however, turned Wausau into a magnet for other Southeast Asian immigrants, because it was already home to a large number of them. Subsequent waves, combined with higher than average birth rates in the immigrant population, created new expenses for the community and applied increasing pressure on local resources. Schools have had to offer special language training now that immigrant children make up a quarter of the elementary school population. Imbalances in the residential concentration of immigrants have prompted school busing. New schools have had to be built and additional teachers hired. Immigrants who could not find employment in the local economy have turned to public assistance. Immigrant youth gang activity has been reciprocated by native gang activity. What was once "novel and neat" has turned ugly and conflictual.[26]

Social and Physical Disorientation

In addition to these tangible consequences, there also appears to be a heavy psychic cost to feeling disoriented when one's conventions no longer prevail—as in Henry James's dismay upon returning to New England at the turn of the century to find that the crowds he encountered on the streets sounded entirely foreign to him: "No sound of English, in a single instance, escaped their lips; the greater number spoke a rude form of Italian, and others some outland dialect unknown to me. . . . No note of any shade of American speech struck my ear, . . . the people before me were gross aliens to a man, and they were in serene and triumphant procession."[27] The dominant values provide a social identity to group members; not only does their way of life come naturally to them, but, since they have invested a lifetime learning it, alternatives may strike them as repellent. (These processes are elaborated upon in the next section.)

Conventions therefore acquire strong emotional attachments that do not seem to be explained completely by their utility (although they are related to the feelings of distrust and uncertainty prompted by those who adhere to different social norms). When neighborhoods are transformed, the predictability of one's physical and social environments is disturbed. The people are no longer familiar, the institutional markers provided by stores, businesses, and community centers may be permanently transformed or gone as well.

In Canarsie, older Italian and Jewish residents resented blacks for "destroying" their former neighborhoods in adjacent Brownsville, Crown Heights, and East New York. The old neighborhoods were recalled with fondness and nostalgia, and their dilapidated state intensified white anger and prejudice toward blacks: "When I moved from Brownsville, I left my whole life behind me. That was where I grew up. My parents passed away there, but it wasn't the same place any more. By 1960 you could see the changes on Pitkin Avenue. It makes me nostalgic to think of it. I'd say to myself, 'What happened to that store that used to be here?' The delis were bodegas, there were no Jewish people, it was completely changed. I felt sad. It left me with a depressed feeling."[28] As Rieder observes, "A stage of life, a style of living, or a scrap of culture is associated with the physical stage on which it is enacted."[29]

Why do we wish to preserve our neighborhoods from change even after we have departed? Our wish may depend strongly on the kinds of past associations that we had with those neighborhoods (but our capacity to remember selectively may make even this qualification unnecessary). If our lives progress so that earlier experiences in the neighborhood become less important than more recent accomplishments, or if the earlier experiences were painful rather than pleasant, then we may feel a smaller sense of loss. We derive significant utility from reliving pleasant life experiences—from reenacting old conventions—and our ability to retrieve these memories is aided by revisiting old sites and institutions where these experiences occurred.[30]

An obsessive attachment to the past is considered to be reactionary if not irrational.[31] But it is common for people to wish to see continuity in the line of cultural development in their communities. We can readily expect that neighborhoods and cities will modernize and that old buildings will be replaced by new structures, but the signposts of the neighborhood must not be so altered that they fail to evoke recollections of past experiences. Therefore, one can be pleased upon seeing the remodeling of a familiar church but be disturbed by the intrusion of new religious symbols in the neighborhood. Old institutions can be changed, but they should not be transformed to the point of being unrecognizable. The prodigal sons and daughters should not feel disoriented. A further cost is exacted when the social composition of a neighborhood is overturned. When we return to the old neighborhood, we can speak to people who have direct links to the past, and our conversations with them are a prime source of nostalgia. To the extent that they have been replaced by new residents, we are deprived of the pleasure of old acquaintances.

Thus, opposition to school busing in South Boston in the 1970s was intensified by strong community ties and the fondness with which adults remembered their high school. Many working-class South Boston residents were graduates of the local high school and regarded their school years as the best time of their lives. Because few went on to college, neighborhood residents attached great significance to high school exploits, memories, and experiences. The school reinforced community values and traditions in succeeding generations of students. Consequently, high school status continued to have social currency for those adults who remained in the community following their graduation. School busing, however, threatened to break the continuity between past and present and to transform the meaning of annual traditions that centered on the high school, such as the cross-town football rivalries that brought the neighborhood together.[32]

ETHNOCENTRISM

When we know that two things belong to separate social categories, we tend to compartmentalize them further by accentuating similarities between members of the same category and differences between members of different categories. Moreover, we tend to develop ethnocentric beliefs that sharpen contrasts between our own group and others along those dimensions that reflect favorably on ourselves.[33] Virtuous qualities that distinguish our own group become defining characteristics.

Group norms and values are *believed;* that is, they are internalized as true or right, and can become second nature. Sarah Boyle believed that, because her family was reputedly the most distinguished family in Virginia, this naturally "meant it was the best in the world." She was convinced that her ethnocentrism about the region was supported by historical facts: "We thought our beliefs about her could be reached by pure reason. We would gravely point out that Virginia was settled originally by 'the best class of people—younger sons of the nobility, mostly—from England and Scotland.' . . . Then, too, an abundance of slaves had granted Southern people leisure to accumulate culture, charm, and human understanding. . . . The best people in Virginia tended to meet—and therefore marry—only each other. As a result a wonderful, special breed of people had come into being, as different from other people as grey-hounds are different from other dogs."[34]

Not surprisingly, given her chauvinism about the culture, she felt cross-pressured when, unlike most of her friends and neighbors, she sympathized with the goals of the civil rights movement. Despite her determination to join the fight for racial equality, southern norms defending white supremacy continued to feel natural and proper to her. Although she befriended blacks, she was self-conscious about socializing with them, afraid that her friendliness would be misinterpreted as an invitation for them to become excessively famil-iar with her. She had difficulty thinking of blacks as southerners, because she had always assumed that only white people could be southerners. And try as she might to address blacks formally as "Mr." and "Mrs.," rather than to use the more familiar forms of address that denoted her superior status, she became tongue-tied and unable to speak the proscribed words. But unlike many of her compatriots at the time, Sarah was remarkably determined to defeat her habit-ual conformity to discriminatory southern norms, at one point going so far as to enlist the tutelage of a local black newspaper editor to help her overcome her stereotypes and prejudices about blacks.[35]

The processes maintaining beliefs and values may be different from the processes that created initial adherence. The motivation to resist new ideas is fortified by explanatory theories and normative beliefs—ideologies, religious values, prejudices—consisting of empirical and moral claims that justify cul-tural preferences and group loyalties. Such beliefs defend existing practices and question alternatives. In chapter 1, I discussed how ideological beliefs can serve as the knowledge that a person holds about the consequences of alternative choices. The status of such knowledge, however, is not unproblem-atic, because ideological beliefs need not be grounded in evidence or accurate inferences. Indeed, the connections that people draw between group member-ship, cultural practices, and economic and political outcomes are often spe-cious and reflect psychological biases in the manner in which they gather and interpret information.

Hardened dispositions may cause us to perceive the world in ways that rationalize existing norms and institutions. For example, Christian Science believes in healing with the mind instead of medical science. How could such a doctrine emerge? In the late 1800s, nonscientific cures for illnesses abounded, because there was not yet general acceptance of scientific approaches. It was in this environment that Christian Science founder Mary Baker Eddy's trea-tise on faith healing could compete with other medical practices and find ad-herents among those seeking relief from their ailments and diseases.[36] Because scientific medicine had not established itself as the dominant approach in the treatment of the ill and injured, spiritual remedies were still regarded as a viable alternative.

But in today's environment, maintenance of Christian Science belief depends on the ability of devotees to minimize their cognitive dissonance. Dissonance is reduced, first, simply because Christian Scientists tend to come from families of Christian Scientists and so are less exposed to contrary views. Second, Christian Scientists become adept at ignoring contrary information by denying their illnesses and concealing their maladies from one another. Even manifest ailments are ignored; people do not mention or acknowledge each other's sicknesses. Illness is discussed only in the context of cases in which the illness has supposedly been successfully cured by prayer and faith.[37]

To the extent that dispositions dominate our choices, they limit our social contacts, skew the information that we gather, and bias how we assess evidence. While choices are still based on reasons, a stricter standard of rationality requires more reliable methods of gathering information and greater openness to evidence. Preferences are only nominally contingent on evaluation of the costs and benefits of the available choices if these instrumental calculations are themselves colored by group identifications and values and are merely justifications, rather than independent reasons, for those preferences.

The incentives (π_L and π_R) and dispositions (a and b) in these instances constitute a mutually reinforcing ideological system that is difficult to disentangle. The group identities and values that people carry with them skew their assessment of the instrumental benefits of alternative norms and practices. If they identify with group a rather than group b, then the cultural norms and practices of group a are believed to be better—morally superior, more conducive to collective goals—than the norms and practices that define group b. Consequently, individuals will tend to choose the alternative that is consistent with their underlying dispositions, because the perceived incentive associated with that choice will be greater than the perceived benefit of alternatives.

Chauvinism in favor of one's own group can assume varying degrees of extremism. A life built around L rather than R can encourage beliefs that L is intrinsically superior to R, that it is in the interests of the group to maintain L, and that groups which practice R are unworthy of equal treatment and opportunities. Even those who suffer under L may share in the ideology represented by these beliefs. An ethnocentric belief system is hard to penetrate, because information is filtered through values and group identifications. The most powerful cultural groups believe that their norms and institutions serve both themselves and the larger public good.

The ethnocentrism of the dominant group in a society is likely to be buttressed by real evidence of its higher socioeconomic status. If members of group *a* tend to be more successful than members of group *b,* then people will be more likely to encounter positive images of the higher-status group; therefore, those who already possess a psychological identification with group *a* will have their loyalty reinforced by their experiences with members of *a* and *b.* Racial and ethnic stereotypes can originate in this fashion. Members of outgroups are disparaged and thought to be less fit for leadership and responsibility because they are less successful and are not integrated into the mainstream of society.

Social Theories

Amos Tversky noted that people have greater facility in devising intuitive theories than in testing their propositions. Indeed, they are poor testers *because* they are facile theorizers. Experiments demonstrate that people are quick to infer systematic patterns from data that have been randomly generated; it is difficult for them to step outside the bounds of their theories to inspect the evidence. Actual covariation between two factors—a cause and an effect— may have less influence on one's likelihood of perceiving such covariation than the a priori theory that there is a covariation between two factors.[38]

People use social theories to explain their own behavior and the behavior of others, and they are likely to interpret evidence in a manner that further substantiates the theories.[39] When people are "introspective" about why they did something, or when they reflect upon why someone else did something, they are likely to be evaluating possible causes against plausible theories that fit the situation. Thus we tend to attribute monetary motives to business people because that accords with our preconception about the constitution of business people. In seeking an explanation for our own actions, we may draw upon some relevant theory rather than identify the actual reasons that motivated our behavior. When asked, for example, why we chose the major that we did in college, we might recall a general theory that people tend to go into fields that accord with their aptitudes and overlook the more happenstance route that may actually have been followed. The reasons given may therefore identify the theoretical rather than the actual causes of behavior.[40]

Psychological Explanations

There is much evidence from social psychology that observers tend to provide mistaken dispositional explanations of a person's behavior when situational factors are actually determinant.[41] This bias is known as the "fundamental attribution error."[42] For example, a person who does not come to the assistance of another person is likely to be judged to have stood by because he was callous and unreliable rather than because the situation was fraught with risk and uncertainty.[43]

In general, actors give *intentional* explanations for their behavior that point to features of the situation, while observers give *causal* accounts that center on deep-seated personality characteristics which are assumed to guide behavior consistently across a number of realms. Lee Ross and Craig Anderson note that, "As 'intuitive' psychologists, we seem too often to be nativists, or proponents of individual differences, and too seldom S-R [stimulus-response] behaviorists. We too readily infer broad personal dispositions and expect consistency in behavior or outcomes across widely disparate situations and contexts. We jump to hasty conclusions upon witnessing the behavior of our peers, overlooking the impact of relevant environmental forces and constraints."[44]

Social psychologists make a distinction between "strong" and "weak" situations, referring to the characteristics of the situation and the capacities of the individual that make it more or less likely that situational pressures will be influential. The features of strong situations cause people to "construe the particular events in the same way, induce *uniform* expectancies regarding the most appropriate response pattern, provide adequate incentives for the performance of that response pattern and require skills that everyone has to the same extent. . . . Conversely, situations are weak to the degree that they are not uniformly encoded, do not generate uniform expectancies concerning the desired behavior, do not offer sufficient incentives for its performance, or fail to provide the learning conditions required for successful genesis of the behavior."[45]

The bias toward trait-based explanations prevails even in experimental settings in which the situational forces seem obviously strong. The most plausible explanation for this difference is that the actor and the observer enjoy very different perspectives on the action.[46] While the focus of the observer is on the actor, it tends to be only on the manifest actions of the actor. The context of the actions (at least in these experiments) has less salience for the observer. The observer can only draw inferences about the thoughts and mental processes of the actor; and the observer also may not have a baseline for evaluating the actor's current actions if he is unfamiliar with the actor's past. In contrast, the actor is oriented toward the external situation, specifically to the incentives and deterrents that are before him. The actor also has the advantage of being aware of his own mental processes and of his own past behavior. Therefore he can more readily distinguish between the external and internal causes of his own actions.

It appears that only in extreme cases in which the actor's behavior is obviously controlled by external forces (such as when actions are coerced) does the observer tend to place situational factors ahead of traits and dispositions in his explanation. In a study by Mark Snyder and Edward E. Jones, for example, subjects were asked to copy mechanically an essay written by someone else; under these conditions, observers did not assume that the essays reflected the writers' true feelings and opinions.[47] This result, however, may be the proverbial exception that proves the rule of the fundamental attribution error. One would think, for example, that movie audiences would not attribute the traits of the characters played by an actor to the actor himself, since they are aware that the actor is merely playing a role. But this would belie the care with which Hollywood actors and their agents scrutinize their roles. Indeed, actors are often apprehensive about accepting a particular role (such as playing a homosexual) if they fear that their association with the character will damage their reputations and popularity as a consequence.[48]

Consistent Traits

Finally, given a limited amount of information about someone's traits, people will readily extrapolate to the other traits the person is also likely to possess.[49] This tendency is true in the evaluations of hypothetical people as well as in evaluations of real people. Also, trained clinicians are prone to the same errors as laypeople.[50] Erving Goffman noted that we tend to force all of the facts of a person's life into a single consistent biography, in the process making sense out of any incongruities by showing how they can be derived from the underlying theory that explains his or her actions.[51] We tend to look for—and find—coherence in people's dispositions and behavior where none may exist. People are prone to generalizing about a person's entire character on the basis of a single attribute.[52] Roger Brown concludes that the overwhelming finding in studies of people's impressions of personality is that: "Impressions are *integrated*. . . . Integration means, in the first place, that impressions of persons always go beyond the information given; they strain toward completeness even when the data base is very small. Integration means, in the second place, that each item of information is interpreted in the light of all the others, that each part takes its character from the whole. What is it that guides us in going beyond what we know and in adjusting the parts to one another? It is some kind of implicit personality theory, some unconscious notion, often very simple, of how persons are constituted, how they hang together."[53]

Although these personality theories do not withstand scrutiny, people nevertheless adhere to them and apply them in making judgments about others. Since people operate according to these folk theories, they must also adjust their behavior in a fashion that takes them into account. The objective in-

accuracy of these theories, in other words, does not detract from their social consequences.

Prejudice and Discrimination

In keeping with the tendency for people to build social theories centered on
personal characteristics, members of different social groups are assumed to
possess different traits. People go from observing that different racial and
ethnic groups consistently enjoy varying levels of socioeconomic success to
believing that differential success is explained by the innate characteristics of
the group members. The intuitive behavioral theories that people find persuasive emphasize internal rather than external causes. Groups at the bottom of
the socioeconomic ladder are presumed to suffer from a cluster of negative
traits such as a lack of ability, intelligence, character, desire, and ambition,
whereas groups that are more successful are thought to be blessed with favorable traits and dispositions.[54] The status quo supposedly represents the natural
order of things. Cognitive biases therefore retrace the route and deepen the
path described in the first section between coordination problems and social
conflict.

The socioeconomic status of immigrant populations is a continual source
for speculation about the relationship between group membership and economic outcomes. Henry Seidel Canby recalled that, when he was growing up,
he thought of all Greeks as fruit-stand operators and of Italians as railyard
workers. He did not remember there being much in the way of social mobility within those groups.[55] Sarah Boyle repeatedly attributed deficiencies among
blacks (illiteracy, poor housing conditions, dirty appearances) to inherent shortcomings that she felt were characteristic of blacks as a group rather than to
socioeconomic inequality and racial discrimination in the segregated South.[56]
At the turn of the century, social scientists speculated that the reason Irish
women were more likely than either Italian or Jewish immigrant women to
be employed as servants was that they were more comfortable assuming subservient roles. But this claim overlooked evidence that large numbers of Irish
immigrants were single women who were not constrained by family obligations, which made them more eligible to become domestic servants. In
contrast, Jewish and Italian women were more likely to emigrate with their
husbands and families. Single Irish women were therefore more attracted by
the living quarters and companionship of a family that accompanied domestic employment. It did not hurt that they also had the advantage of speaking English.[57]

It is a slippery slope from wariness about strangers to prejudice and discrimination. Stereotypes foster misunderstanding and influence people's choices in

the social and economic realms. Discrimination in the labor force, for example, stems from assumptions that members of the disfavored group are not equally reliable and capable workers. The favoritism shown toward West Indian immigrants over American blacks among white employers in the Red Hook neighborhood of Brooklyn illustrates how stereotypes filter hiring decisions. American black residents are held responsible for the crime and disorder of the neighborhood and, for that reason, are assumed to be poor risks as employees. Therefore, employers are more likely to hire immigrants from beyond the neighborhood, not necessarily because the employer knows a great deal about these immigrants, but because the immigrants are not associated with the squalor of local neighborhoods and are believed to be harder workers. The unknown is preferable to that which is known.[58] Discriminatory stereotypes not only encourage people to favor members of one group over those of another but also influence how they process information about these groups, so that the underlying prejudices may be difficult to recognize, much less alter. In the worst cases, prejudices are held so steadfastly that contrary information (e.g., positive messages about a group held in low esteem) is not recognized. This cycle therefore has self-reinforcing characteristics: *selective acceptance of information strengthens underlying dispositions; stronger dispositions bias information processing even further.* The end result is an ideology, or theory, that elevates one's own group and perpetuates choices that maintain existing social practices. Here, then, the theory of symbolic values may prevail.

Those who do not conform to conventional ways are stigmatized and treated with suspicion. The stigma detracts from other attributes that might be creditable and becomes embedded in an elaborate theory about why people with the stigma should be discredited: "By definition, of course, we believe the person with a stigma is not quite human. On this assumption we exercise varieties of discrimination, through which we effectively, if often unthinkingly, reduce his life chances. We construct a stigma-theory, an ideology to explain his inferiority and account for the danger he represents, sometimes rationalizing an animosity based on other differences, such as those of social class. . . . We tend to impute a wide range of imperfections on the basis of the original one."[59]

In the mid-nineteenth century, drinking was a stigmatized trait believed to symbolize weak character. Alcohol consumption reflected impulsiveness, recklessness, and unreliability—characteristics associated with failure and ruin. Sobriety, in contrast, connoted self-control, diligence, and seriousness; it was a behavior associated with respectable middle-class standing. A person who sought upward mobility had to abide by this standard: "Prohibition was not seen as an isolated issue but as one which pitted cultures against each other." Abstinence "was one of the ways society could distinguish the industrious from the ne'er-do-well; the steady worker from the unreliable drifter; the good credit risk from the bad gamble; the native American from the immigrant."[60]

Ethnocentrism and discrimination set in motion a variety of processes that harden attitudes and behavior. Prejudice and discrimination reinforce existing networks and reduce social interactions between groups that might contribute to attitude change. In Los Angeles, where blacks and Latinos are disproportionately represented in the unskilled labor force, black-white hostility and conflict between blacks and Latinos are both exacerbated by the favoritism shown toward Latinos by white and Asian employers. There is a widespread presumption among whites and Asians that blacks cannot be trusted; worse, blacks are often feared. However, the employment of Latinos, as day laborers, domestics, gardeners, hotel service workers, and valets, places them into routine contact with whites and Asians, which increases the familiarity between the groups and reinforces the comfort that whites and Asians feel in the company of Latinos compared with blacks. There need be no organized campaign among whites and Asians to exclude blacks from consideration for these jobs. Nevertheless, the consequence of hundreds of separate decisions based on common stereotypes and assumptions about blacks is a collective outcome that widens the racial gulf and at the same time heightens competition between blacks and Latinos.[61]

Those who are stigmatized are disqualified from certain life activities. The task of removing a stigma is made more difficult because those who associate with the stigmatized tend to end up being similarly discredited. Social information is conveyed by the company that people keep: "The social identity of those an individual is with can be used as a source of information concerning his own social identity, the assumption being that he is what the others are."[62] There will therefore be a tendency for those in the mainstream to avoid contact with those who are stigmatized.

Minority groups may feel that they have a stake in policing themselves in order to counteract negative stereotypes and to improve their status. The actions of individual members of minority groups will have a greater effect on their groups' images—both positive and negative—than the effect that the actions of individuals in the majority will have on the majority group's image. Northern blacks resented the influx of southern blacks into their cities earlier in this century because the migrants were typically poorly educated and unskilled and generally ill-equipped to deal with their new environments. Black northerners criticized the bad manners and behavior of the newcomers, but they were victimized nonetheless by the punitive reactions of northern whites against blacks in general: "Black northerners, including the contemporary black newspapers, denounced them as ignorant, vulgar, rowdy, unwashed, and criminal. As these southern-born blacks became a majority of the black population, northern whites began to erect barriers against *all* blacks—in jobs, housing, and social activities."[63]

Recent controversies in Hollywood over who should make films dramatizing the histories of racial and ethnic groups such as Jews and blacks stem from the desire of racial and ethnic leaders to exercise control over how their groups are portrayed to mass audiences.[64] The popular medium of film is assumed to play an important role in reinforcing or breaking racial and ethnic stereotypes. Claims that blacks, Jews, Italians, or Hispanics should have the right of first refusal to make films about their own group imply that group members are superior at representing details of their group's culture and more sympathetic to the group's point of view. (The symbolism to group members of having one of their own with the talent and resources to head up the project also cannot be overlooked.)

Though individuals may reject standards of evaluation that discredit them, stigmatized people often accept that there is something discreditable about themselves, and make efforts to disguise or remove the stigma.[65] Sometimes, to preserve self-esteem, individuals rationalize that they have elected the way of life that has been forced upon them. The cavalier attitudes and values displayed by young black men in southern cities in the late 1800s were psychological defenses against their marginal existence and limited opportunities. Unlike black women, who readily found employment as domestics, black men faced bleak prospects as the country industrialized. Their low expectations gave rise to dissonance-reducing values that promoted promiscuity and hustling over regular employment, marriage, and other elements of a conventional lifestyle that were beyond their reach.[66]

Ethnocentric norms can be inadvertently fortified by the compliance of those who are victimized. By conforming to the customs, whether out of duress or resignation, the disadvantaged party validates the relationship between the majority and the minority. Members of the majority, as a result, do not witness any discontent with the status quo. Southern whites, for example, assumed that blacks preferred segregated institutions because they conformed to them. Following the Civil War, blacks directed their energy toward receiving separate but equal treatment because they assumed that segregation was a fact of life and not realistically worth challenging in most realms of southern society: "Negroes themselves favored this policy over exclusion. . . . Equal access rather than integration was their chief aim, As a result, they convinced any doubting whites that they too wanted segregation. Their decision to form separate churches immediately after the war further strengthened this impression."[67] The overt conformity of blacks to white standards and expectations reinforced white attitudes that their conventions and norms were indeed supported by all members of society from the top to the bottom.

Hortense Powdermaker noted in her 1930s study of the black community in Cottonville (a pseudonym for a city in the deep South) that blacks became highly adept at conforming to white expectations in order to get along, but most whites remained oblivious to this deception, choosing instead to believe that blacks preferred their subservient position: "The average white person in this community seldom realizes the extent to which this group questions his superiority. . . . The prudent colored man keeps his convictions to himself. As long as the White remains ignorant of them, he remains unruffled and unalarmed. Since so much of the Negro's trouble is due to the white man's fears, it pays to keep him feeling safe. With many middle-aged Negroes, the policy of the dual role is deliberate and articulate. . . . Every successful colored landowner can tell a long tale of the small and subtle diplomacies he practices daily in order to 'get by.' The more successful he is, the more tact and flattery he must use to make the white man feel that he is staying in his place."[68]

In the days of segregation, black students at Tuskegee University needed to reconcile the conflicting norms of the black and the white communities. On campus, they tried to live up to Booker T. Washington's dictates of propriety, comportment, and dignity, even though off campus they continued to be discriminated against and treated with disrespect. As he listened to their recollections during his travels through the contemporary South, V. S. Naipaul imagined that the students must have experienced excruciating psychological cross-pressures: "Within the campus, the erect posture, the military correctness. Yet always—and how the irrationality would have twisted people!—it was necessary to make signals to the people outside that you were not getting above yourself."[69] (While also, I would add, making signals to the people inside that one's deference to whites was insincere.)

Do people hold discriminatory social theories *because* they maintain the status quo and undermine disadvantaged groups? It may be that the antipathy—driven by largely psychological motives, such as fear of the unknown or unusual—comes first, followed by prejudice, which subsequently motivates actions that restrict the opportunities of the out-group. People do not form fearful beliefs in order to keep groups down; rather, certain groups are kept down because people truly distrust and are afraid of unaccustomed manners and appearances and act on such beliefs. The failure of disadvantaged groups to achieve socioeconomic equality is ironically taken as evidence supporting the tendencious social theories. When new groups push for greater political and economic equality, beneficiaries of the old order may fight to preserve the inequities of the status quo in order to protect their social and economic position.[70]

The irrational aspects of ethnocentrism and prejudice do not, however, preclude rational political responses (organization, collective action, image enhancement) from those who are stigmatized, as I will show below, nor, as I will elaborate in chapter 4, do they prevent political leaders from mobilizing people around such prejudices for quite rational, instrumental purposes and goals. One effect of the reluctance of others to give individuals their due is to radicalize them and strengthen their minority group identification. The instrumental benefits of embracing a group identification depend on the degree to which individual opportunities are tied to collective action by group members.

VESTED INTERESTS

When the revolutionary clap skates were introduced by a Dutch inventor to the sport of speedskating, they promised to allow skaters to go faster than ever before because the hinged skate blade remains in contact with the ice for a longer period of time than does the old fixed-blade skate. Even so, older skaters were reluctant to learn the new skating mechanics necessary to capitalize on the superior technology, because they were required to change their skating motion in a manner that felt uncomfortable to them. So Dutch trainers put the skates on their younger skaters, who had fewer ingrained physical habits to unlearn. Veteran skaters in the meantime called for a ban on use of the clap skates in the 1998 Winter Olympics, so that there would be no advantage to skaters who were more familiar with the new skates. When the proposed ban failed, practically every top skater, out of necessity, switched over to the new skates, although not every skater maintained the ranking that he or she held when everyone used the fixed-blade skate.[71]

As I discussed in chapters 1 and 2, people sometimes are bound by habit to the point of missing superior opportunities. When the norms change, people have to adapt their behavior to the new system or else they will suffer a loss of benefits. But there are reasons other than psychological rigidity that may slow, deter, or prevent adaptation to institutional changes. Only some individuals may have the requisite knowledge, skills, or values to take advantage of the new norms. People may need to reeducate themselves or switch their group allegiances in order to keep up. In academic fields, for example, resistance to new theoretical and methodological developments may be motivated by the interest that researchers have in maintaining the status of approaches with which they are familiar, given the impracticality of retraining themselves.[72]

A key element of one's response to new norms is whether one has a vested interest in the existing norms. Every individual invests in developing a particular repertoire of skills and values, only some of which have universal appeal and status. The investments that people either make or forgo in their education, training, and social relationships are guided by a given system of norms. As we grow up, we decide how we wish to spend our time and energy in preparation for adulthood. These are typically not uncircumscribed choices, because people's opportunities for personal development, education, and training depend on the availability of resources and knowledge. In addition, class differences in socialization will skew people's values and aspirations. A youngster has a brief time frame as well as limited awareness of alternative courses of action and paths of personal development; for this reason, social pressure from peers is often determinative. Our skill in prognosticating about the future perhaps improves over time. Experience with varied life situations helps our decision making, but the problem of anticipating future desires and circumstances never goes away. Whatever we elect to do, early choices to develop traits and values, and to acquire knowledge and skills, end up binding us in the future. The freedom of individuals to make unfettered choices in pursuit of life opportunities is constrained by earlier decisions that they have made based on limited information.

Once people have made a commitment to a particular way of life, it may be difficult for them to compete in a different venue because these commitments are tailored to a given system of norms and constitute long-term investments. Like the speed skater who has trained on fixed-blade skates, we may have trouble duplicating our success in a system that rewards different behavior and requires new values and capacities. Consequently, there will be individuals and groups who have a stake in protecting the culture they have been raised in because they will suffer a loss of prestige, status, and economic opportunity if people begin to coordinate around new values and standards of evaluation. A person may not be able to receive the same returns for his skills and values in a new market.

In the early 1800s, scientifically trained physicians thought that performing abortions contradicted their belief in the Hippocratic Oath, their image of themselves as protectors and savers of human life, and their feeling that women should fulfill traditional social roles. Nonetheless, there were economic incentives to perform abortions. The scientific doctors' opposition to abortion on moral and ideological grounds forced patients seeking abortions to obtain service from "irregular" doctors who were not trained in modern medical practices. These doctors threatened to take patients away from regular doctors, because a woman who was denied an abortion by her doctor might go elsewhere and never return. To protect their livelihoods, some regulars defected from the ranks and performed abortions. Most regular doctors, however, chose not to compromise their values and instead sought to root out their competition. They lobbied for anti-abortion legislation in order to remove the economic incentive to perform abortions and to undercut competition from unconventionally trained doctors. By changing the incentives on the issue, they could remain true to their values.[73]

In the dynamics of the model, the ability to adapt successfully to changes in norms depends on one's *capacity* to make the proper response to the new incentives. For example, if there is a shift in norms from L to R (π_R grows relative to π_L), those who are receptive (large b) to R will adapt most rapidly. But for those who are locked into making L responses owing to strong dispositions, a shift in norms only produces a disjuncture between one's response and the evolving norm. This would be the case for example if a were large, but b were small or zero, which places an upper limit on the probability of making an R response. In general, in order to make an R response, a person has to possess or develop the requisite capacity, which may be easy or difficult to accomplish. Whether one has the ability to make such a transformation will affect one's stance toward the competing norms. Those who are unable to move from a to b in order to take advantage of R may oppose the change from L to R, or they may retreat into a separate camp that is governed by more compatible norms.

If we think of L as the more liberal norm and R as the more conservative standard, the structure of opposition against either progressive or reactionary social change is identical. Both revolve around the prospect of declining returns given one's prior socialization and training. A person who has been socialized in an environment that promotes and rewards conformity to L will develop stronger a-type characteristics that are well suited to an L-dominated environment but are less successfully adapted to an R-dominated environment. Consequently, a shift in norms from L to R puts one out of step with the social practices that are favored. The same holds true in reverse when the norms shift from R to L, leaving in its wake those who possess a disproportionate share of b-type qualities.

Conflict is worst when dispositions and interests are perfectly aligned, specifically when people have strong dispositions that cause them to favor one system of norms over another to which they are less well suited. But notice that there are, according to the model, inherent dynamic tendencies for this to occur, because value formation and group identification are themselves responsive to incentives. To the extent that dispositions are proxies for the balance of incentives within a community, there will be a natural alignment between dispositions and interests. When two groups with distinct norms conflict, the result is intense opposition between two sides, each vying to establish the norm that complements its members' dispositions.

A system of norms and values affects the status and opportunities of individuals and groups in society. The dominant norms determine which repertoires of behavior will be valued most highly. Individuals will therefore evaluate changing norms in terms of how these norms affect their current group (and consequently themselves) and whether they have the capacity to thrive in a system that is governed by the new norms. Although individuals constantly move between different groups and domains within society (which is the essence of social mobility), individuals whose mobility is restricted also have strong incentives to remain within a particular subsystem and to insulate that system from change and external penetration: "One of the noneconomic benefits of remaining within one's neighborhood ethnic group or organization is precisely the avoidance of a free social market, that is, the avoidance of unremitting and full-scale competition in courtship and marriage, friendship groups, social clubs, and general esteem."[74]

Therefore, the interest that we have in developing *some* group loyalties and in integrating ourselves within *some* system of norms and values becomes transformed into an interest in a *particular* normative system once we make life choices having long-term consequences based on this normative system. We develop a greater attachment to our norms and values perhaps because of psychological rigidity or cultural inertia, but also because of past investments in those norms through education, career plans, financial investments, and social relationships that cannot be reversed. We have a stake in ensuring that the repertoire of beliefs and behavior that we have developed will continue to be rewarded by society.

This means that on the whole we should expect generational differences in the rate at which change is embraced. Aging should be related to increasing conservatism, manifested in greater opposition to new routines and standards of evaluation. Older individuals will wish to retard changes that will produce a lower rate of return on their investments in socialization and training. This is why social change may depend heavily on generational replacement rather than conversion. As Gary Becker explains: "To change their behavior drastically, older persons have to either disinvest their capital that was attuned to the old environment, or invest in capital attuned to the new environment. Their incentive to do so may be quite weak, however, because relatively few years remain for them to collect the returns on new investments, and much human capital can only be disinvested slowly."[75]

We would also expect that those individuals with the least portable skills would be most strongly wedded to the status quo. Those with limited education will be more apprehensive about social change because they have less capacity to adjust. In the wake of Ku Klux Klan attacks on a "Walk for Brotherhood" in Forsyth County, Georgia, for example, Atlanta mayor Andrew Young traced the roots of Klan membership to economic impoverishment and poor future prospects rather than to mere racial hatred: "I don't view the Klan action as just racist. These are the desperate acts of people who find that history is leaving them behind. Basically what we need are some job training programs that help people get into the mainstream."[76]

Limited personal capital might also account for the difficulty in rallying workers behind radical programs. Part of the antipathy of members of the working class to radical ideologies must be due to their being *ideas*—that is, abstractions that are difficult to follow and foreign to their vernacular. Radicals speak of capitalist exploitation, a man's relationship to the means of production, and the like—notions related to bread-and-butter issues, to be sure, but which are not expressed in conventional terms. Moreover, radicals speak of overturning the political system and the economy, events which, if they come to pass, will require individuals to acquire new resources and adapt to a new environment. Those with the smallest investment in education and other portable skills will be the least likely to be able to adapt successfully to such changes. (Another problem with radical doctrines is that they frequently champion the interests of minority groups and other social and economic underdogs who are in direct competition with the white members of the lower and working classes—but that is another matter that will be discussed further in chapter 4.)

While higher-status individuals have greater wherewithal to change, they may derive greater than average benefits from the status quo. They may also possess stronger social ties and reputations, and experience more difficulty altering their views, because their status is anchored by their social networks. Those individuals who are identified with the old norm may find that they cannot credibly change their views and may not be able to reap the rewards of conformity to the new norm.

Some capital serves as baggage from the past that cannot be unloaded— for instance, a political leader's racist reputation or his previous association with organizations now universally despised. John Patterson, Alabama's attorney general in 1954, collaborated with other southern attorneys general in planning the legal strategy for the region's "massive resistance" campaign against integration. It proved to be a turning point in his career: "whatever chance I might have had to play a part in national affairs was diminished as a result of the race issue and because of a stand that I had to take to even be on the scene at all in the South."[77]

Because people are believed to be consistent in their traits and behavior, bad behavior is assumed to reflect an undesirable underlying trait. Consequently, those individuals who are in principle adaptable (who can, for example, shift from disposition b to disposition a in accordance with the change in norm from R to L) may nevertheless still be shunned even if they conform to the new norm, so they may elect instead to maintain their allegiance to the old norm, especially if they can locate a niche where traditional routines continue to be praised.

From a rational choice perspective, people eventually change their values when it is no longer beneficial to continue conforming to them because of changes in social conditions. But, contrary to the assumptions underlying symbolic theories, systematic resistance to changes in social values can constitute evidence that *supports,* rather than contradicts, the rational choice model. The main opponents to changes in social values will be those groups with a vested interest in the traditional ways of doing things. We would therefore anticipate that the strength of one's attachment to an existing norm will be contingent on the relative incentives offered by a competing norm and the ease or difficulty with which one can make an adjustment to that norm. Those who are unable to adapt to the new norm will suffer a decline in the quality of their lives and may join efforts to resist change.

Abortion Rights Activists

It has been noted that women are not significantly more supportive of abortion rights than men, and this observation has been used to challenge any notion that abortion attitudes are self-interested. But the questionable assumption underlying this test is that all women naturally share a greater self-interest in preserving this right for themselves than do men, who supposedly possess no such stake. In fact, the interest underlying abortion rights is likely to depend on the past investments that women have made in education and career training. In her study of pro-life and pro-choice women activists in California, Kristin Luker found that pro-choice activists were much better educated on average, had higher incomes, were more likely to be drawn from the professions, and, when married, tended to be married to professional men. Pro-life activists were more likely to be married, had more children on average, and were more likely to attend church and to say that religion played an important part in their lives.[78]

The abortion attitudes of the activists were therefore consistent with their ability to adjust to the changing role of women in society. Pro-life activists were generally not prepared to pursue a professional life, because they had not obtained sufficient education and were constrained by their marital and child-care responsibilities. Pro-choice women, on the other hand, had a stake in supporting new social values that increased their opportunities as career-oriented women. This is not to say that all women's attitudes toward abortion were based entirely on their current life situations. Rather, these attitudes were the product of a chain of consistent influences, dating from early socialization, that not only affected their views on abortion but also shaped their attitudes toward family, career, marriage, and children. Pro-choice and pro-life women typically grew up in contrasting environments that placed sharply different values on the roles of conventional and career women. By investing in the roles that were upheld as ideals in their communities during the course of their socialization and upbringing, the women limited their options in the future: "Activists on both sides of the issue are women who have a given set of values about what are the most satisfying and appropriate roles for women, and they have made *life commitments that now limit their ability to change their minds.*"[79]

Pro-life and pro-choice women are therefore differentially affected by how women's roles are defined and by which roles are granted the most prestige by society at large. If a woman's reproductive role is given primacy, then women who wish to compete with men in the marketplace for jobs will be harmed by the assumption among employers that they are not as devoted to their careers as men.[80] On the other hand, if a woman's professional role is accorded greater respect, this status undermines how traditional women are likely to be treated in comparison with those women who have invested a greater part of their lives in education and career training. In this regard, both sides in the abortion conflict adopt positions that reflect their respective preparation for a meaningful role in society.

High Culture versus Mass Culture

When people have a differential capacity to adapt to new norms, the institution of those norms will create distinct boundaries between conformists and non-conformists. The norms will not be equally accessible to all parties owing to variations in how much preparation or training is required to become familiarized with them. An example of this kind of self-sorting occurred in the visual and performing arts in the late 1800s when artistic elites imposed professional standards in their fields in order to elevate the status of art, music, and theater in American society. In line with this new perspective on the arts were new norms governing how people should appreciate artistic works and performances.

For much of the nineteenth century, what we now think of as the high culture of theater, opera, and museums attracted mass audiences from a broad cross-section of the American public. Before these realms became professionalized, the boundary separating performers and audiences was fluid, as traveling orchestras and theater groups routinely recruited local amateur musicians and actors. The manners of the audience showed that they did not hold performers in reverence and did not regard them as specially trained professionals. Patrons were unrestrained in shouting their approval and disapproval in the course of the performance.[81] They felt no compunction about disrupting performances by entering and leaving the concert hall or theater as they pleased. Their children were allowed to run and play in the aisles. In the museum, the patrons handled the art pieces and paid little respect to the surroundings.

The campaign to socialize unruly patrons coincided with the gradual professionalization of the arts, which led to the establishment of more elaborate standards and to increased specialization within the art world. Artistic performances became a more highly regulated and less interactive experience: audiences could enter or leave the hall only at the appropriate breaks and intermissions; they were told to remain quiet and to concentrate on the performance; their appreciation of the performance depended on possessing some knowledge of art; they became passive recipients of art, leaving criticism to art critics who had extensive formal training.

The inevitable upshot of imposing prerequisites and behavioral norms in the arts was to skew the audiences toward the upper class. The upper class had the resources to become educated in the arts and thereby to make the arts accessible to themselves. Those without special training felt increasingly intimidated by the new standards. The emergence of alternative venues of mass entertainment—sports, vaudeville, cinema—which offered recreation without the prerequisites demanded by the new "high culture," reduced their incentive either to resist or to accommodate themselves to the new norms. As a world of high culture, in contrast to popular culture, was carved out and protected by the cultural elite, the masses gravitated increasingly to those arenas in which there was no strict code of behavior. The expressive behavior that had once constituted the norm of the playhouse was transferred to other venues.[82] Mass and elite audiences could henceforth choose their separate forms of entertainment and abide by their distinctive norms as they saw fit. It is this subsequent class segregation, resulting from the imposition of norms, that gives the arts—opera, the symphony, museums—their exclusive quality.

A shift in norms from, say, L to R (from idiosyncratic to regulated) therefore required a corresponding dispositional shift from a to b in the sense that the ability to make the proper response required some prior investment. Those unfamiliar with, or unwilling to conform to, the new standards of decorum demanded in the theaters and concert halls naturally began to shy away and seek alternatives with which they were more comfortable. Cultural practices become second nature to people who partake in them regularly while they remain foreign to those who do not. The exclusiveness of any particular venue of entertainment depends partly on the extent to which behavior at that venue is regulated. There are certain forms of contemporary mass entertainment—the rock concert, the major sporting event—that allow for widely idiosyncratic audience responses. Other kinds of activities, however, such as the symphony, the opera, or the theater require spectators to adhere more closely to conventional behavior. Consequently, those who are unsure of their familiarity with these conventions will be apprehensive about visiting such venues.

Contemporary museum directors have recognized that their audiences will be small if the public believes that enjoying art takes special training or greater mental effort than is normally demanded during recreational activity. For this reason they have tried to encourage popular attendance by organizing exhibits that are less arcane and by making the museum more accessible to the public through improved parking facilities, cafes and restaurants, longer hours of operation, and special activities for children. So-called blockbuster exhibits organized around Picasso or Impressionism are marketed like motion pictures and target patrons whose interest is limited essentially to shows that have the stature of a mass event. Going to the museum has therefore become more like an outing than an educational experience: "Much museumgoing is not about art at all. It's simply social, rather like visiting a Barnes & Noble bookstore or meeting friends for a cappuccino. It's entertainment, not enlightenment or inspiration."[83] Already, there are purists who worry that the trend toward deferring to mass audiences, driven by the profit motive, will undermine the role of museums to challenge and uplift the patron, as well as to provide enjoyment in the process. Déja vu.

MAJORITIES AND MINORITIES

Let me close by returning to the original problem of how people contend with the coordination problems that arise when norms are shifting, but now let us adopt the perspective of the minority. The bulk of this chapter has focused on why individuals who are part of the mainstream culture are likely to resist changing their norms or tolerating the introduction of competing conventions into their community. The perspectives of majority and minority populations, not surprisingly, are asymmetrical even if their decision making employs similar calculations.

When multiple conventions are being employed, or when people disagree over which norm should govern their community, the social system described by the model is out of equilibrium. Technically, there are various routes that can be taken to reestablish coordination around a common norm. An ambitious response to heterogeneity is for one to become more *cosmopolitan*—that is, multicultural—so that one can comfortably traverse a variety of environments whether they are governed by L or R. Someone who is well versed in multiple conventions can switch back and forth between one convention and another, in effect thriving equally within either kind of environment. Whereas an inflexible individual (someone for whom either a or $b = 0$) can only make one kind of response, the multicultural individual ($a = b = 1$) readily blends into whatever environment he circulates in. This person can adapt to multiple conventions because he has the knowledge and capacity to do so.

Fashion can be flexible in this way. A recent trend among young people in Japan, for example, is to dye one's hair brown (known as "tea hair") as a symbol of free spiritedness, independence, and style.[84] These traits are valued among students, but the practice is commonly banned by schools and frowned upon by employers because it is regarded as a frivolous distraction. The symbolism extends to personal relationships. Brown-haired dates are seen as more fun, but black-haired partners are believed to make more reliable spouses. So students dye their hair when they are out for a good time and change their hair back to black when they have to go on job interviews.

Short of developing this type of adaptability, there are two major adjustments that can restore group coordination. These are: *conversion* toward a common norm, and *fragmentation* into communities that are governed by different norms. We can always in theory adjust a and b so that p^* shifts toward the more highly regarded alternative, whether L or R. One way to interpret this result is that a person can always in principle adjust his preference or opinion to correspond to the norm of his community. But keep in mind that, substantively, changing a and b means that a person has been resocialized to make a new response that is consistent with the new norm. Therefore, in order for conversion to occur, in practice, people must have the ability to change their attitudes and behavior, and there must be an incentive for them to comply. This is the standard mechanism behind conformity.

One's preferred solution to the problem of competing norms is likely to depend on whether one is a member of the majority or the minority culture. The majority will have less incentive to change and will try to regulate the degree of nonconformity in their environment through a mixture of benefits and sanctions. The majority may try to build barriers between themselves and the minority culture, or they may use inducements to convert the minority to the majority culture. The assumption behind the American melting pot has always been that new immigrants would shed their old country ties and loyalties and conform to Anglo-American culture. While there has been greater recognition of late of the rights of minority groups to preserve certain aspects of their culture, especially in their private lives, and of the value this provides to the dominant culture, there has not been acceptance of the idea that such groups can create parallel political and social institutions across the board.

The majority will try to regulate undesirable behavior using social pressure or legal sanctions that establish either L or R as the only acceptable response. Legal change is sought—that is, the state is resorted to—when informal sanctions become insufficient or when the sanctioning group cannot enforce its solution because it suffers from collective action problems. For example, Prohibition was advocated more vociferously as the dictates of the church became less effective. As Donald Black has observed, the quantity of law will increase as other forms of social control diminish.[85]

Newcomers recognize that they have an interest in adapting to the majority culture. The primary routes to success in society require that one learn the social norms and conventions of the majority population. However, not all members of the minority group will have an equal ability to make the adjustment. The first generation of immigrants will have more difficulty making the transition because they cannot easily learn a new language and are not in a life stage when they would normally pass through the institutions that socialize citizens in a country.

New immigrants may also have weaker incentives to assimilate because they continue to maintain ties with family and friends in the homeland. At the turn of the century, first- and second-generation immigrants who were able to maintain old ties or who anticipated staying briefly in the United States retained their loyalty to their home countries. For example, frequent travel to and from the home country slowed assimilation of Canadian and Mexican immigrants and nurtured divided national loyalties in them beyond the first generation. Significant proportions of southern and eastern European immigrants who arrived at the turn of the century returned home after earning enough money in the United States. Consequently, they established no permanent ties to the community; they moved from one city to another following jobs where they became available and made little effort to learn English and adapt to the American way of life. Some of those who did not eventually return to their homelands nevertheless still formed weaker American identities because the prospect lingered in their minds.[86]

The sons and daughters of immigrants will likely see the advantages of being versed in the majority culture and will readily acquire language skills and conform to mainstream norms through education, exposure to the mass media, and social interaction with members of the majority. Moreover, because they are fluent in the majority language and know the social conventions, they will elicit less prejudice than their ancestors. The educational and occupational attainments of third-generation southern and eastern European Americans, for example, approach the levels achieved by those of British descent. Occupational mobility, residential integration, and ethnic intermarriage have steadily acculturated later generations of white ethnics and blurred ethnic boundaries. Rates of intermarriage have reached such high levels that the term "intermarriage" tends no longer to be used to describe unions between people having different European ancestry but is now reserved for interracial marriages. As a result of these social changes, the continued expression of ethnic identity has assumed a more voluntary, subjective character.[87]

For all of the reasons I have discussed in this chapter, however, the majority will be reluctant to open up competition to newcomers on equal terms because it will not be in their interest to do so. Indeed, they have a vested interest in the status quo. They are also likely to believe that they deserve their superior status in the society and that changes in the culture threaten to undermine their accomplishments. They may also hold ethnocentric beliefs that justify their prejudices and discriminatory behavior. Because the majority do not have an incentive to change the norms, the actions they take may reduce the likelihood of cooperation.

The strategies that people adopt in response to competing norms—whether they change their norms, withdraw into separate communities, or try to convert nonconformists—depend on variations in their capacities and incentives. When either the capacity or incentive to conform is lacking, individuals are more likely to form separate communities with like-minded people. In order to minimize friction, individuals who have a-type (or b-type) dispositions can seek out other a's (or b's) for the purpose of forming a homogeneous community. Voluntary segregation eases tensions, because individuals can elect whether and when they will be exposed to a different culture. This can be accomplished most decisively by segregating oneself within a homogeneous community in which the norms and values promoted in that environment complement one's own socialization.

Creating and sustaining alternative social conventions requires a critical mass of followers. When there are few potential adherents, those in the minority may out of necessity simply conform as best they can to existing conventions. Doing otherwise invites isolation or ostracism. The number of minority group members and their capacity to organize is therefore significant. Any large group potentially has the resources and numerical strength needed to sustain alternative norms. If the minority group members can organize themselves politically, then it is also possible that they will attempt to introduce new standards and conventions into the mainstream.

Recent debate over the racial and ethnic categories that are used in official government classifications and the U.S. census partly reflects the desire of

individuals to coordinate themselves under a common label for political purposes. Arab-American leaders, for example, are lobbying for a Middle Eastern
designation, in place of the present practice of lumping them in the white or
Caucasian category.[88] African-American political leaders fear that a hybrid
"multiracial" category will dilute their group's numerical strength. Strong
group identification, however, can be a two-edged sword. The more an individual identifies with a particular community and makes use of the resources that
it offers, the less likely it is that he will be able to enter into broader social
networks. Opponents of racial classification warn that the practice reifies group
differences and inevitably encourages individuals to think of themselves and
therefore to organize along racial and ethnic lines.

Individuals conform to group norms when they believe that it is worthwhile
for them to pay the price of membership. For reasons of capacity or budget,
some individuals may regard the demands of conformity to be excessive and
may elect instead to change social spheres rather than to comply. Attempts
to convert individuals will therefore produce a degree of group segregation if
there are viable alternatives available for those who choose not to comply.
When capacities are relatively fixed and suited to a particular environment,
or when there are strong incentives to retain existing norms, then personal
change will be resisted. Those who are stigmatized in some manner owing to
physical, behavioral, or ascriptive characteristics will have incentives to separate and form communities that will provide them with status and social and
material benefits.

A disabled group, such as the deaf, will have difficulty fitting into the mainstream hearing society, and their lower capacity to join the mainstream gives
them an incentive to concentrate their resources and build their own support
networks. For example, activists in the deaf community who fervently advocate teaching deaf children American Sign Language rather than English recognize that those children will enjoy less access to the speaking world than
those who master the ability to speak. However, the deaf culture movement's
attempt to encircle the deaf community and create a society that shares a common language may be seen as a rational response to the limited mainstream
alternatives a deaf person faces. Because integration with the speaking world
is difficult to achieve and undermines the deaf community by dispersing its
collective resources, building a deaf culture that consciously rejects efforts to
conform to the mainstream and takes pride in the characteristic that the mainstream treats as a physical handicap becomes an attractive strategy.[89]

The majority would like the minority to fit in, but socialization requires
contact and interaction, so there will need to be a transition period that is
costly. It is incumbent upon the majority to tolerate the disequilibrium that
marks this transition while the level of nonconformity diminishes over time.

Conversely, the expedient solution may be to perpetuate segregation. The final example that I offer in this chapter is interesting because self-sorting and segregation occurred despite the majority group's limited effort to socialize outsiders and bring them into the fold. But carrot-and-stick campaigns to convert nonconformists that are light on incentives—that are, for example, not accompanied by equal-status membership—will not meet with great success unless they are coercive.

Group Dynamics in Steelton

John Bodnar's study of the social and economic order of Steelton, Pennsylvania, in the late nineteenth century illustrates the group dynamics that lead people to invest in ethnic identification, community organization, and countercultural values in response to discrimination. Steelton was a company town whose social hierarchy was based on race and ethnicity. Native whites (Anglo-Saxon Protestants) and Irish and German immigrants dominated the community; from their circles came the politicians, the businessmen and merchants, and the foremen in the local steel mill. Menial and unskilled work was reserved for eastern and southern European immigrants, who had recently arrived in the country, and blacks, who had migrated to Steelton from the South in pursuit of higher industrial wages. Residential neighborhoods were segregated along the same racial and ethnic lines as work groups in the mill.[90]

The native groups in Steelton were characteristically ambivalent about how best to deal with the immigrant groups in their midst. On the one hand, they sought separation from new immigrants; on the other hand, they took measures to change the immigrants' ways. Bodnar writes that "despite the hostility in Steelton, persistent attempts were made to ameliorate the condition of the immigrant. . . . The immigrant could be condemned and segregated but that was not enough to ensure social stability. He also had to be instructed, made to understand 'American ways,' and, occasionally assisted."[91] (Note the parallel here with the transformation of audience norms—in the art world, the elite also wanted to create institutional barriers between themselves and the burgeoning immigrant population but at the same time aspired to educate the masses.)

There is no contradiction here. Members of the dominant group vacillate between compartmentalizing the newcomers, whose ways and habits offend them, and converting them to traditional values and behavior. It is not readily apparent to them which is the wiser strategy. Unfortunately, if both impulses are allowed to express themselves, they can produce self-defeating actions. The impulse to segregate immigrants compromises the majority's best intentions to bring them into the fold of mainstream institutions. Superficial attempts to integrate minority group members do not give them sufficient incentive to adapt their ways to the dominant culture. Steelton's immigrants were encouraged to attend English classes, learn patriotic songs, and attend existing churches, but the majority's attempt to integrate the immigrant was half-hearted in that there was no desire to share status and political power with the new groups. (It is difficult to obtain conformity without providing appropriate benefits for compliance.) Croats and Slovenes attending the Catholic churches in Steelston and nearby Harrisburg had difficulty understanding English priests and experienced a sense of social inferiority because they had to sit in the rear pews of the church while the front pews were rented to wealthier, better established Irish families.[92]

The investment needed to conform was believed to be excessive in relation to the rewards. Steelton's immigrants coped by building separate communities and supporting their own religious and cultural institutions, which provided them with social life, status, and respect.[93] The growth of these separate cultural institutions, however, magnified the differences between the norms and conventions of different ethnic groups. With so little opportunity for social exchange between groups, prejudices and stereotyping flourished. The most common explanations given for the poverty of blacks and new immigrants pointed to lack of discipline and character, inability to save, and other inherent character flaws rather than to structural conditions.

The theoretical point is that limited intergroup cooperation forced new immigrants to withdraw from the mainstream into separate ethnic communities, where mutual cooperation among group members could occur. The resulting standoff between groups is stable; a rational member of one group will not cooperate with a member of an opposing group if by doing so he loses the opportunity to cooperate with members of his own group.[94] Once group members display a propensity to trust only fellow group members and to be hostile toward outsiders, this will set in motion a process leading to the complete polarization of the two groups. When individuals anticipate conflict with members of another group, they best defend themselves by refusing to cooperate right from the start. Thus, there is no opportunity to start a relationship based on mutual exchange, because all evidence suggests a hostile adversary. Innocents within either group will have no choice but to conform to the typical behavior within the group, or else face ostracism.

In Steelton, the separate institutions that minorities created to combat prejudice eventually grew detrimental to their well-being. Individuals persisted in defending cultural values that had once been adaptive but which had begun to limit their opportunities. Low rates of social mobility among immigrant families had created disdain for formal education, while reliance on kinship and ethnic ties for employment had perpetuated working-class status across

generations. Pride in ethnic history and antagonism toward outsiders had reduced the likelihood of intermarriage with members of other groups. Thus,
segregation and discrimination forced the first generation of immigrants to
carve out a separate culture that nurtured distinct group values and practices
but reinforced segregation. The development of this culture out of group interest had the unintended effect of encouraging individuals to lower their aspirations and to make decisions that limited their opportunities and increased their
dependence on ethnic ties.[95] The early life choices made by adolescents and
young adults in conforming to their subculture's norms constrained their future
prospects. Cultural practices that had once facilitated social mobility became
increasingly maladaptive.

This general pattern of conflict repeats itself in many contexts and describes
several of the other cases I have discussed in the chapter—the lobbying of
racial and ethnic minorities and gays and lesbians for separate dormitories,
the coordination of the deaf community for mutual support and collective action, the fragmentation of the artistic culture according to social class. The
common feature of these cases is that a minority group is stigmatized and
denied equal opportunities and benefits within the majority culture. The stigma
may be a physical disability that interferes with one's ability to function in
the majority culture, or a behavioral or ascriptive feature that engenders distrust and discrimination. A lack of communication and trust between groups
results in the minority group's being denied acceptance into the mainstream.
Because their incentive to conform is compromised, members of the minority
seek out a more congenial environment of their own.

CONCLUSION

The socialization of individuals to a system of norms, values, and group affiliations also builds resistance to change and creates the potential for conflict
between competing ways of life. Individuals adapt their opinions and values
to the norms and conventions that are supported in their reference groups.
They develop the dispositions that enable them to capitalize on the incentive
structure of their environment. As long as people continue to be rewarded
adequately for the choices they have grown accustomed to making, they are
content with existing institutional arrangements. So far so good. The difficulty
arises when new or competing norms threaten to reduce the coordination benefits of conventional behavior and shift status and material benefits to groups
other than one's own. Competing norms and conventions create coordination
problems that increase the costs of communication and social exchange. New
groups also impose externalities on the community if institutional changes are

needed to accommodate multiple norms and conventions. New standards of evaluation can potentially undermine one's social and economic standing.

Because the majority have greater resources at their disposal, they will tend to impose their preferences on the minority. The majority would like the minority to adjust to the majority culture—this is the melting pot theme. Those in the minority who have the capacity to adapt and who will be rewarded for doing so will be the most inclined to conform to the mainstream. But minority groups that are unlikely to thrive in the majority culture have less incentive to conform and may be better served by seeking their rewards from alternative subcultures. One of the consequences of heterogeneous conventions is that there is a tendency for groups to seek refuge in separate communities, each defined by distinct social norms and values. Isolated communities in turn strengthen group identifications and nurture ethnocentric beliefs in the essential virtues of one's own culture. Thus the desire that people have for coordination by common norms and conventions has a way of sorting out individuals and keeping them apart.

This turn of events is ironic because conformity is meant to coordinate preferences and facilitate harmonious social exchange, yet coordination within groups also invariably sharpens boundaries between groups, creating conflicts of interest, if not animosities. According to the sociological model, dispositions formed early in life end up controlling choices over the life span, so that conflict over changing norms is due largely to deeply held values and group identifications rather than current calculations. Consistent with this view, I described how rational processes cannot carry the full weight of explaining the transmission of group norms and the animus behind normative conflicts. People have a tendency, as a result of psychological biases, to impute greater value to their own cultural norms and practices.

One might therefore locate the root of group conflicts in contrasting values and identities, but that is only part of the story, and not in my view the essential part. It is not the differences per se between values that create friction between groups, but the real and perceived material and social consequences of those value differences. The distinction is worth elaborating. When the way of life of some individuals is rendered obsolete by social change, we can expect them to prefer the status quo ante because they fared better under the previous system of norms. Conflicts over social norms have their origin in past events only insofar as the path dependency of life socialization and personal development affects people's ability to adapt to current prospects. Socialization of beliefs and values, education, and career training all occur early in life, but the resources acquired in that stage must often be sufficient to last a lifetime. However, the pace of social change, including changes in institutions, knowledge, and technology will often leave individuals at some point unable to maintain their position because their skills have grown outdated. Between the older incentive structure and the newer, the choice will be obvious to those who are constrained by their earlier decisions. As I will explain in the following chapter, preference for the status quo is further reinforced by the political benefits that derive from coordinating collective action around existing group norms and identifications.

CHAPTER FOUR

Cultural Mobilization

And one man in his time plays many parts.
William Shakespeare, *As You Like It*

Early socialization produces attitudes and affinities that are not easily erased by contemporary events, because people develop an interest in maintaining the group identities and values that coordinate their expectations and actions. Those who share common identifications, values, and cultural knowledge can be readily mobilized for social and political goals.

In a prejudiced society, for example, in which choices are made on the basis of race, it can be rational for someone to conform to such prejudices. A person develops an interest in identifying with a particular racial ideology if there is common knowledge that people use racial considerations in choosing their friends and business associates. Loyalties are strengthened when individuals believe that their fate rests on their group memberships. When social relations are conditioned by race, it is difficult for an individual to rise above others' prejudices. The writer Harry Crews reflected that racial considerations in his native Georgia during the 1940s and '50s "had to matter because it mattered to the world I lived in."[1] Once a set of social norms is in place, and these norms are supported by a logic and rationale of their own, it is rational for someone to operate as best as he can within the boundaries of those norms.

But there are also important political supports for ideological and group identifications. Once such affiliations exist, it is rational for group leaders and politicians—or political entrepreneurs, in general—to elicit and reinforce them, and it can be rational for citizens to act strategically in concert with others who hold the same identification. Groups that enjoy high internal cohesion on sociopolitical values and norms are ripe for political mobilization. When there are political advantages to be gained from championing a group's interests, we can usually rest assured that some entrepreneur will move into the void and take up the banner. In some of the examples to be discussed in this chapter, existing social cleavages were inevitably exploited for political gain, and the only mystery was which political leader would be the first to seize upon the opportunity. For better or worse, this is the nature of political mobilization. People who benefit from the status quo will have an interest in maintaining the shared values and practices that made their political coalitions possible in the first place. They will coordinate with other group members to defend social institutions that operate on their behalf.

Leaders may sincerely share the beliefs and values of those they are trying to mobilize, or they may cynically support any values necessary to achieve their goals, subject only to the bounds of personal credibility. Because of their dependence on popular support, politicians may have greater incentive than ordinary citizens to change their attitudes when new circumstances demand. Orval Faubus, a former governor of Arkansas, who is best remembered for his decision in 1957 to oppose a federal court order to integrate Little Rock Central High School, is viewed as a tragic figure because he appears to have championed the cause of segregation for political reasons rather than out of personal conviction: "Indeed, Mr. Faubus, the son of a Socialist, was a relatively liberal figure who had never used race as an issue until fate placed him at the center stage in one of the early defining moments of the civil rights revolution in the South."[2] As racism waned in the 1960s and 1970s, and became less effective as an overt means of political mobilization, conservative politicians readily adapted to the more progressive racial norms and tried to rally the populace around alternative issues.[3]

Successful mobilization calls for the discovery of a common denominator that will unify a multitude of individuals. Politicians who offer the right platform end up as winners, while the losers are motivated to search for new issues to resurrect themselves. Candidates seek themes that appeal to the public but also play to their own strengths. There is thus a marketplace for issues that, akin to an economic market, sifts through issues, discarding some because they have no popular appeal and elevating others because they strike a chord.[4] Ideas might be introduced as offhand notions, but once any notion succeeds in rousing popular support, it will likely be integrated into numerous campaigns. It is in the nature of politics that any contested issue gives rise to a variety of competing claims about the interests that are at stake and the norms and values that are relevant to the debate. These claims are likely to be incompatible in the sense that they provide contrasting analyses of the issue and recommend different solutions. Since all political decisions can be analyzed on numerous grounds, the basis on which people make their choices will affect their preferences among the alternatives.

In arguing for the importance of subjective considerations in individual choice, Herbert Simon notes that we need models that delineate "*what* considerations, out of a host of possible ones, will actually influence the deliberations that precede action." We have to locate "where the frame of reference for the actors' thinking comes from—how it is evoked. An important component of the frame of reference is the set of alternatives that are given consideration in the choice process. We need to understand not only how people reason about alternatives, but where the alternatives come from in the first place. The process whereby alternatives are generated has been somewhat ignored as an object of research."[5]

I take up this agenda in this chapter by offering a theory of how people select their frames of reference and how they arrive at common frames in their evaluations of issues. When someone contemplates an issue, he may randomly sample one of his beliefs about the issue and take a stance based on this belief; another possibility is that he scans all of his beliefs about the issue and gives an average response. Neither process seems entirely realistic, since people learn, in the context of particular issues, to discriminate between important and extraneous, or "relevant" and "irrelevant," aspects of an issue.[6] In any controversy or debate, one learns to focus on certain points while ignoring other arguments in the process of forming an opinion.[7]

An accepted premise in the opinion-formation literature is that, between election campaigns, the structure of attitudes "weakens" in that the intercorrelations between attitudes decline as people pay less attention to politics. Election campaigns bring to the fore key issues for public evaluation and choice: "Thus, what starts as a relatively unstructured mass of diverse opinions with countless cleavages within the electorate is transformed into, or at least represented by, a single basic cleavage between the two sets of partisans . . . disagreements are reduced, simplified and generalized into one big residual difference of opinion."[8] Efforts to change attitudes on an issue therefore do not depend exclusively on changing the balance of beliefs that people hold, but instead can rely on manipulating the priority that people give to different arguments.[9] In such cases, people are "primed" or persuaded to focus attention on certain beliefs rather than to add new beliefs or change existing ones. It may indeed often be easier to change frames of reference than the beliefs underlying one's attitude.[10]

My thesis is that there are systematic influences that cause people to pay attention to certain ideas and arguments and to ignore others. As public opinion leaders—politicians, interest groups, social activists, courts, policy experts, journalists, editors, academics—establish the boundaries of debate, the public learns to think about political issues using *common frames of reference*. A person gradually learns, through exposure to public discussion on a topic, to base his opinion on certain pertinent aspects of the debate, and, at the same time, learns *not* to pay attention to other features of the topic deemed to be irrelevant. When there is general agreement among opinion leaders about how to think about an issue, exposure to their messages narrows one's focus to a smaller number of relevant interpretations. This coordination process is the essence of *public* opinion formation—as opposed to private opinion—and it is a key mechanism of political mobilization.

The terms "relevant" and "irrelevant," I hasten to add, have nothing to do with whether any consideration is more valuable, worthy, or persuasive than another. They simply identify the arguments that people tend either to use or to set aside in their discussions of the issue. One does not necessarily obtain a superior comprehension of the issue by paring down the number of interpretations; rather, one has, for better or worse, a more pat characterization of the issue that results from the political process. Lee Bollinger, for example, in his book on freedom of speech, suggests that we sometimes stand to benefit from counteracting this tendency to economize:

> It would be desirable . . . if those who defend and apply free speech—
> especially, of course, as litigators and judges—viewed it as a central les-
> son of free speech that they themselves be wary of their own tendency
> to oversimplify, or, in effect, to censor, the complexity of the problems
> involved in the cases they deal with. . . . While surely not an easy task,
> it would nevertheless be best if those who work in the free speech area
> tried to remain conscious of the tendency to revert to a more or less close-
> minded posture in free speech disputes. One obvious means of avoiding
> the hazard we are considering is to follow the rule—which, admittedly,
> is as difficult to apply as it is simple to state—of giving genuine consider-
> ation to arguments for allowing suppression.[11]

Indeed, the distilled opinions that individuals express need not even be regarded as more truthful than opinions that are less clearly guided by a coherent rationale. V. S. Naipaul wondered whether the southern leaders he was scheduled to interview had been questioned so frequently in the past about their region that their answers would sound rehearsed and no longer reflect their personal views. It worried him that they "might in fact have been reduced to a certain number of postures and attitudes, might have become their interviews."[12]

CREATING COMMON FRAMES OF REFERENCE

In this section, I elaborate on the formal model developed in chapter 2 to explain how people are coordinated around common frames of reference. To this point, I have not discussed how different kinds of advocacy founded on economic, cultural, moral, or partisan rationales are likely to have differing effects on opinion formation. I will now loosen this restriction by assuming that there can be many kinds of arguments advocating either L or R and that these arguments vary in terms of their frequency and effectiveness. Therefore, let us make the following extensions.

1. Different arguments in favor of L and R create different bases for evaluating an issue and, as such, constitute alternative frames of reference, $f(f = 1, 2, 3, \ldots)$. Changing the frame of reference not only alters the perceived merits of the respective choices, L and R, but also the perspective from which people evaluate their decisions. For example, when politicians try to get their pet issues on the agenda during an election campaign, when pro-life and pro-choice abortion activists invoke different moral and legal principles to support their positions, when opponents of big government use symbolic phrases to suggest that social welfare spending disproportionately benefits blacks, they are all trying to influence people's frames of reference for the purpose of swaying them to their own positions. *A frame of reference therefore refers to any basis for making a decision or taking sides on a controversy.*[13] Rationales drawing upon norms, values, interests, symbols, and group memberships are common frames of reference used to coordinate individual perspectives.

2. The *incentives* to support L and R—π_{Lf} and π_{Rf}—vary according to the frame of reference employed to evaluate the alternatives. Some frames of reference show L in a more favorable light, while others give the edge to R. In the 1996 presidential election, voters gave Bill Clinton and Bob Dole contrasting grades depending on which character traits and issues formed the basis of their preferences. Voters most concerned about taxes and the budget deficit and about the candidates' honesty and trustworthiness favored Dole overwhelmingly, while those who cared most about medicare, education, and jobs and who wanted a candidate who was sympathetic toward others and in touch with the times supported Clinton disproportionately.[14] Since voters' preferences can change as they shift their focus from one issue to another, candidates for public office have reason to promote issues that emphasize their own qualifications. In general, shifting the frame of reference can cast new light on the alternatives.

3. The *disposition* to support L or R depends on which group identifications are used by people as their points of reference. Receptivity to any argument depends on the a and b parameters, but we now index those parameters with a subscript, a_f and b_f, to indicate that people's reactions vary according to the particular orientations and identifications they adopt. The impact of any message depends on people's dispositions to receive those messages. For example, Catholic, union workers who think of themselves primarily as "union workers" will probably be more likely than those who identify primarily as "Catholics" to be responsive to economic appeals that address their conditions of employment and standard of living. Those who place their religious identity first may instead have a keener ear for discussions of school vouchers for parents of children who are attending parochial schools.

In general, individuals will have varying latitudes to modify their reference groups. Those who lack a direct interest in a conflict have the most freedom to adopt any number of perspectives, including a disinterested perspective from which to judge the issue on neutral criteria. But we might also expect that, while those without a strong interest may be impartial, they are not necessarily strongly motivated to act. By contrast, it is reasonable to assume that people with a greater interest will be motivated to defend those interests. Therefore, they are more likely to bring those interests to bear in their evaluations and to reveal less flexibility in their perspectives.

Political persuasion nevertheless can help to transform or modify a person's orientation. Walter Lippmann observed that no one can ever be the same person at all times and under all circumstances. Instead, everyone has many group memberships, and the identity that one assumes in any particular situation will narrow the perspective that one adopts. "And so while it is so true as to be mere tautology that 'self-interest' determines opinion, the statement is not illuminating, until we know which self out of many selects and directs the interests so conceived. . . . For in trying to explain a certain public opinion, it is rarely obvious which of a man's many social relations is effecting a partic- ular opinion. Does Smith's opinion arise from his problems as a landlord, an importer, an owner of railway shares, or an employer? . . . Without special inquiry you cannot tell. The economic determinist cannot tell."[15] There is no simple objective correspondence between a person's socioeconomic character- istics and his interests.[16]

4. Different frames of reference predispose one to take different positions on a subject; that is, if an issue is evaluated along one dimension, a person is likely to draw a different conclusion than if he considers it according to another dimension. More precisely, given two frames of reference, $f = 1$ and $f = 2$, p_1^* does not generally equal p_2^*: the equilibrium opinion that is reached on the basis of the first frame of reference does not equal the equilibrium opinion that is reached on the basis of the second frame. Obviously, without this fourth assumption, the frame of reference concept has no leverage.

5. Political coordination results when people converge on a common inter- pretation and evaluation of an issue. If there are multiple frames of reference, then the "grand" preference P^* is the weighted sum of constituent preferences formed on the basis of each separate frame of reference:

$$P^* = w_1 p_1^* + w_2 p_2^* + \ldots w_n p_n^*. \tag{1}$$

The degree to which people converge on a particular interpretation of the issue depends on whether disproportionate weight is given to a specific frame of reference. A concentration of arguments around a small number of themes that appeal to group interests can potentially coordinate members of the group behind a common position. But if people are exposed to a great number of arguments, and respond to these arguments differently depending on their vantage points—some of which are more conducive to L and some of which are more conducive instead to R—then we would expect that they will be quite labile in their response to the issue. Where people stand depends entirely on the arguments and dispositions that are activated at any given moment.

Whether people converge on a common frame of reference depends on both the characteristics of the discussion surrounding the issue and the characteristics of individual members of the public. If discussion and debate are concentrated around a particular theme, then we might expect that people will tend to construe the issue using common terms of evaluation. Alternatively, if the public is questioned about issues that have not been clarified by political discussion, they are likely to offer more idiosyncratic interpretations.

It seems reasonable to expect that, as a rule, the more informed one is about a subject, the more likely it is that one will be attuned to the common interpretations of the issue established by public opinion and reference group leaders. Individuals who do not actively follow politics will instead offer more diffuse opinions on the same subject because they have not learned to rule out a number of competing interpretations. When people's opinions are unfocused, it is harder to marshal them behind collective action than it is when they share a common perception of the problems they face.

Even if people agree to use a common frame of reference, they may still disagree over whether L or R is superior on that criterion. Or they may share both the same criterion and the same preference between L and R on that dimension. For the reasons discussed in chapter 2, one can well imagine that members of different groups will be motivated to choose competing interpretations of an issue. Therefore, I leave open the possibility that, for example, members of liberal communities, whose main contacts are with like-minded individuals, and whose sources of information are similarly biased, may learn to define an issue differently than do members of conservative social and political networks. The arguments and ideas to which one is exposed may hinge on one's political orientation. There is no reason to expect that liberals and conservatives will frame an issue in the same fashion. Aspects of an issue that are deemed unimportant by liberals in forming an opinion may be critical to conservatives. Furthermore, within each ideological camp, more informed individuals will be more likely to adopt ideologically consistent interpretations and to reject inconsistent frames of reference that they encounter.

DEDUCTIONS

The dynamics of public opinion therefore reflect the strategies employed by opinion leaders to convince people to evaluate political issues according to selected group interests, norms, values, and symbols.[17] We can draw several inferences about the tactics that will be used to coordinate people as well as the kinds of maneuvering that will occur among competing parties in their search for a winning formula. I will first list these implications and then elaborate on them in the remainder of the chapter. All of the strategies discussed below—appeals to group norms and interests, political and cultural symbols, ideological values, and universalistic principles—capitalize on the social divisions of the society. The strategies work by coordinating individuals' expectations and priorities and by creating social pressure on people to conform to these shared expectations.

1. *General framing strategy.* What kinds of appeals will be made by political entrepreneurs? What frames of reference will be chosen by the public? Opinion leaders will try to shape public opinion on an issue by steering people toward frames of reference that are most favorable to the leaders' positions. Supporters of L will choose those frames that maximize $\pi_L a$ (the perceived benefits of L multiplied by the disposition to prefer L) while minimizing $\pi_R b$ (the perceived benefit of R multiplied by the disposition to prefer R). Supporters of R will pursue the opposite goal of locating frames that maximize $\pi_R b$ and minimize $\pi_L a$. In short, opinion leaders will attempt to control the agenda by defining, to their advantage, the relevant parties, groups, interests, and arguments in any debate.

Opinion leaders must find the right formula for engaging and mobilizing the public. But it is far from being a blind search, as the reference groups and dimensions of evaluation most likely to be salient will be those that people use regularly to define their social, political, and economic relations. Members of the public will be inclined to view issues from the perspective of those reference groups and values that have the greatest currency in their lives (e.g., race, ideology, partisanship, social class). Thus a common strategy will be to coordinate mass support for a political issue around widely recognized and broadly supported group identifications, interests, values, and symbols. By artfully translating the issue into a choice between in-group and out-group norms, interests, and values, opinion leaders can build support for the issue upon preexisiting bases of organization. In this way, the new political issue boils down to, say, an economic choice involving class interests, a racial issue dividing blacks and whites, or an ideological issue pitting liberals against conservatives. The current choice becomes a reprise of past choices on which individual preferences have been clearly defined.

2. *The element of surprise.* Some of the frames of reference used by opinion leaders to construe an issue will fail to rouse support, while others will galvanize opinion. We cannot be certain before the fact what frames of reference the public will fasten onto. Owing to the uncertainty associated with predicting

who will take an interest in the issue and how they will respond to alternative political appeals, successful campaigns will often emerge from a trial-and-error strategy of searching for the right political formula.

As Kenneth Boulding noted, the mechanism by which cultural and political symbols are able to elicit strong reactions from the public is not obvious.[18] The symbol "white supremacy" will evoke sharply contrasting evaluations from different audiences as it rallies both support and opposition simultaneously.[19] The intent of a message may change entirely if it unintentionally brings to mind a highly charged symbol. Calls by Jewish radicals on the West Bank to "transfer" Arabs out of Israel received an unexpectedly cool reception from Jews who all too readily associated "transfer" with their memory of Jews being transported to Nazi concentration camps.[20]

While there are systematic tendencies underlying public opinion formation, the effectiveness of any political appeal will be subject to many happenstance characteristics of the campaign. First, there is no guarantee that communicators will be able to get their message across for lack of credentials, credibility, or rhetorical skills. The public response to an event can turn on the communicative talents of a political leader. Whether a foreign policy crisis leads to a rally around the flag depends on whether social divisions that are manifest in other contexts are submerged under a common group identification. The administration's patriotic appeal succeeds if it taps into a reservoir of nationalist sentiment and inspires people to respond favorably to the message as "Americans" rather than, say, as liberals or conservatives, or as members of the working class or upper class. But the same nationalist appeal, if framed less adroitly, instead appears jingoistic and causes people to divide along conventional ideological lines, with liberals rejecting the message and conservatives accepting its recommendation.

Second, it is difficult to control the connotations that are brought to mind by a political appeal. Public opinion research has provided abundant documentation of how small changes in the way that political issues are presented can produce significant shifts in people's stated preferences. Third, political entrepreneurs cannot always keep a tight rein on the parties who will see the conflict as being relevant to their interests. Therefore, messages that skew public opinion in the desired direction when targeted at a small, sympathetic audience may have a contrasting effect when presented to a larger, more heterogeneous audience. Opinion leaders may have difficulty controlling the diffusion of their messages, so that their messages may end up provoking people whom they never intended to reach. A Republican presidential candidate must always take precautions so that what he promises before an audience of Christian fundamentalists may not sound alarms in broader constituencies.

3. *Convergence on a focal point.* Successful strategies remove uncertainty about the kinds of appeals that can coordinate the public. A favorable popular response to an idea generates a predictable sequence of reactions leading to convergence around that frame of reference. People are motivated to choose the dimension of evaluation that they are cued to choose by opinion leaders and other members of their reference groups. The greater the proportion of people who elect a particular dimension, the greater the incentive for others to choose the same dimension. Political entrepreneurs will observe that the public is receptive to a particular message and will be encouraged to make the same appeal in their campaigns. Therefore we have the elements of a *coordination process* in which people will adopt a frame of reference because (1) they are cued by opinion leaders to adopt that perspective, (2) they expect that other people will employ the same frame of reference, and (3) they expect to be rewarded for their choice by the collective action that is made possible by the coordination.

Once a strategy of collective action has been established, it may subsequently be hard to displace. The mobilization process is self-reinforcing because popular coalitions that are built around common norms and values are hardened by their political success. The benefits that flow from collective action reinforce group loyalties. When it is in the interest of a group of individuals to coordinate their actions, the established basis for coordination will be stable unless people have the incentive and capacity to switch bases.

4. *Using principled appeals.* Not all rallying appeals will try to motivate individuals by addressing their self or group interest. Opinion leaders will adjust their messages to the audiences they are trying to mobilize. Parties that do not have a stake in an issue will be approached differently from those that do. Particularistic messages that invoke group interests and values will be replaced by more abstract principled rationales that putatively serve everyone equally. Principled arguments will have more credibility and persuasive power if they do not correlate perfectly with the self-interest of the party making the appeal. Principled rationales may also be used to obtain concessions from self-interested persons who have expressed a prior commitment to those principles.

The broader the popular base that needs to be mobilized, the more universalistic must be the rationale underlying one's message. The decision to widen the spectrum of participants is itself a strategic choice. When the self-interested arguments of group leaders fail to win sufficient support from their own constituencies, it is necessary for them to fashion broader appeals that draw support from disinterested parties. A common strategy therefore is to employ abstract, ostensibly neutral principles that mobilize third parties who reconfigure the balance of power in the conflict.

GENERAL STRATEGIES

In my model, preferences on an issue are based on the relevant arguments and on the reference groups and identifications through which these arguments are filtered. Within any population, certain group identifications and values will be more salient than others and will stand out as being more viable bases for political mobilization. The most effective way to rally individuals around an issue is to offer incentives that coincide with their dispositions on it. Therefore, if there is a marked skew in the ideological identification of the population, it will be easier to mobilize people in the direction of the popular bias. If racial intolerance is widespread, then it is rational for politicians to construe issues in terms of the dominant racial group's interests and anxieties. The practice of mobilizing people for political purposes on the basis of their group identifications has the effect of reinforcing these dispositions.

In contrast to these strategic maneuvers, the theory of symbolic politics offers a mechanical, nonstrategic process in which underlying dispositions are spontaneously activated by the relevant objects:

> Longstanding partisan dispositions or basic values are activated by policy and candidate alternatives, thereby influencing the individual's preferences. Racial predispositions are activated by black candidates and racial issues, and influence attitudes toward them. Other basic values can be activated by symbols of injustice, inequity, or immorality, and thus produce mass protest. Longstanding antagonisms toward such groups as the Communists, Nazi party, and Ku Klux Klan are evoked by debates about their rights, and influence support for extending civil liberties to them. . . . The notion of symbolic politics is that political symbols activate underlying predispositions reflexively. Put another way, such symbols automatically activate relevant and accessible social constructs.[21]

My model minimizes any spontaneous activation of underlying dispositions. Instead, people's evaluations are systematically coordinated around group identifications and values, and these identifications and values are renewed and strengthened by virtue of their being politically instrumental. Racial attitudes, patriotism, partisanship, nationalism, anticommunism, and political ideology are made relevant through communications that highlight how an issue affects these values. It is not automatic what frame of reference will be used by the public to evaluate an issue. Because most people are to some extent cross-pressured by several group memberships—meaning that some of their dispositions incline them toward L while others incline them toward R—the challenge faced by political leaders in trying to mobilize the public is to coordinate the frames of reference that people adopt. Individual choice depends on which reference group is given priority.

Therefore, even if we accept the strong thesis that symbolic values override short term self-interest, the symbolic dispositions still have to be cued by opinion leaders and coordinated by a political strategy (in the same manner that self-interest can be cued). Any number of evaluative dimensions can be played up or played down. Just as union members or farmers have to gather information to recognize their interests on an issue, so do partisans, ideologues, and racially prejudiced individuals have to be organized around their interests and values.

When contemplated in these terms, symbolic politics are laden with strategic actions that go beyond the psychological mechanisms that lie at the core of the theory of symbolic politics. In the general strategy of political mobilization I am describing, symbols are simply coordinating mechanisms. Their effectiveness depends on the degree to which they convey, and are generally recognized to convey, common knowledge among group members. Cultural symbols are used to convey information about the group stakes and the social divisions underlying a conflict: "The powerful symbol is that which condenses an enormous mass of information and experience in a single bit—there or not there, for me or against me, right or wrong."[22] Symbols elicit hopes and fears by suggesting values, norms, group interests, and honorific ideals. In order to coordinate around symbols, people must share a common understanding of their meaning and significance, and of the proper response to them.

After Boston School Committee chairwoman Louise Day Hicks became the acknowledged champion of the hardliners opposed to integrating the city's schools in the 1970s, she began to speak in a transparently coded language that appealed to the group interests of her constituents. Like all contemporary symbolic racial appeals that play on anxieties and apprehensions, Hicks's campaign was able to elicit these fears with catchphrases that were racially neutral in appearance. She became a one-issue candidate who vowed to protect the "neighborhood school" from legislative and judicial onslaught. As Anthony Lukas explains, "By then, of course, the phrase 'neighborhood school' had accumulated layers of other meanings—it was not just a school to which one's children could walk, a school which enshrined one's own values and attitudes, but a white school safe from black inundation. It had become a potent political slogan, loaded with subliminal connotations."[23]

Calls for "neighborhood schools" encouraged whites to think along racial lines and to act on their common interest with other whites in opposing school busing. This tactic succeeds if members of the community are persuaded to view their interests in terms of their racial group membership. The racially coded message is especially effective for this purpose because it serves, in Kenneth Burke's phrase, "to sharpen up the pointless and to blunt the too sharply pointed."[24] Overtly prejudiced individuals will have no qualms about responding favorably to an explicitly racist argument opposing school busing, but others who are also racially motivated may prefer to justify their opposition on nonracial grounds, such as the safety or proximity of the schools their children attend. Therefore a blunt racist appeal will draft prejudiced individuals, but deter those who also oppose busing, yet do not wish to appear racist. The trick is to devise an appeal that symbolizes the underlying racial divisions while offering everyone cover for their true motivations.

Candidates for political office routinely use symbols to convey information about the groups in society that would be hurt or benefited by their election to office. When former Virginia governor Douglas Wilder made a run for the presidency in 1992, he referred more explicitly to his African-American heritage than he ever did in his Virginia campaigns. In Virginia, Wilder won the Democratic party nomination for both Lieutenant Governor and Governor without having to compete in a primary against a white Democrat. This allowed Wilder to emphasize issues other than race in order to broaden his support among white voters. In the presidential primary race, however, Wilder brought racial concerns to the foreground by describing himself as the grandson of slaves, recalling his experiences under Jim Crow and claiming that his parents had named him after the black abolitionist Frederick Douglass.[25] The veracity of the last claim was questioned by a reporter who noted that Mr. Wilder's first name was actually Lawrence while his middle name was spelled with one *s* rather than two. Thus it was not clear whether Wilder's desire to associate himself with an African-American icon symbolized his values or merely his political ambitions.

Representing a person, institution, or idea in symbolic terms is a way to transfer the connotations of the symbol to the associated object. In 1988, George Bush retrieved a symbol of disloyalty from the Cold War when he accused his Democratic opponent Michael Dukakis of being a "card-carrying member" of the American Civil Liberties Union. The obvious allusion to Communist party membership was not meant to suggest that Dukakis was literally a Communist, but to symbolize that his views were radical relative to the American public's. Bush also linked Dukakis's liberal policies to his "ivory tower" Harvard University advisers (even though Bush himself was a Yale alumnus). The Republicans played on racial prejudice by creating the infamous "Willie Horton" commercial depicting a black convict in Massachusetts who had raped a white woman while released on a furlough program that Dukakis had supported as governor. These attacks suggested that the Democrats were out of touch with the mainstream, more interested in preserving abstract rights and protecting peripheral groups through government intervention than in serving the interests of (middle) America.[26]

The motivating force of a symbol depends on its status as a convention.

There must be a collective awareness that the symbol has a common meaning among individuals. A symbol "works" when people are confident that they are drawing the same lesson from the symbol as others and are emboldened by this knowledge to take action on the expectation that others will follow suit.

> People respond to key terms in the way they think specific other groups expect them to respond. The worker, spending much of his life in a factory working with other employees, is likely to choose these other employees as his "significant others." In their role as employees (rather than as Catholics, Poles, whites, or high school graduates) he expects them to respond favorably to the symbol "higher wages," and he does so himself, thereby reinforcing their expectations and being reinforced in his own. A white southerner is likely to choose as his reference group other white southerners; and in their role as white southerners (rather than workers, church members, etc.) he expects them, and cues them to expect him, to respond favorably to the symbol "white supremacy."[27]

Therefore, the symbol is able to coordinate people's responses because people know they share a group identification that gives them a common frame of reference for evaluating messages.

Existing norms, values, symbols, and group identifications become more salient as a result of political organization. Group identifications are psychological predispositions that are converted into political resources. The more people are rallied around a cultural identification or value, and the more they see that others share the same orientation, the more likely they are to adopt that orientation themselves. As I discussed in chapter 2, a disposition is maintained only to the extent that it continues to be instrumentally useful. There is no self-explanatory, reflexive reaction to a new political issue; instead, there are always many possible reactions that might be forthcoming and it is through the political process that individual expectations and actions are coordinated.

The historical continuity of symbols rests on the persistence of features of the environment that gave rise to them in the first place. If political institutions and economic and social relationships remain stable, the symbols that have currency in that environment are likely to be perpetuated. The meaning of the term "southern," for example, has changed as a result of increased integration. Southern blacks have become more comfortable with southern identification and, although southern whites may still think that the term "southerner" refers primarily to southern white natives, they now are more likely to concede that blacks also are southerners.[28] Thus the connotations evoked by symbols can be altered by social change: as a symbol takes on new meanings, it no longer brings to mind the same images or calls forth the same emotional reactions as it did under past institutions.[29] When southerners include both blacks and whites in their immediate conception of what a southerner is, the color line is truly blurred, and new political coalitions become possible.

THE ELEMENT OF SURPRISE

Which frames of reference will work? It seems implausible that political elites can arbitrarily guide public discussion toward any dimension of an issue. Nevertheless, some models of opinion formation imply that the partisan, or ideological, faction that expends sufficient resources on propaganda and manipulation can always prevail in defining the terms of debate merely by saturating the airwaves with its loud signals. In practice, opinion leaders have less control than this suggests; their influence in policy debates is constrained by the public's tendency to favor certain frames of reference. Common frames of reference emerge from the byplay between opinion leaders and the public. Some views are easier to promote because the public is already predisposed to give priority to those concerns over others. Opinion leaders must account for these predispositions by making arguments that take into consideration the interests and identifications of their constituents.

There is considerable uncertainty built into the framing process if we allow that individuals have their own priorities on political issues while also being subject to persuasion and coordination by political entrepreneurs. The effectiveness of a message will depend on who is sending it and on whether competing messages are sent by opposing parties. The message may prove to be more popular than the messenger. After briefly shining in the 1992 presidential primary race, David Duke disappeared just as quickly into obscurity because Patrick Buchanan usurped his central themes on race, Christian values, affirmative action, and protectionist trade policies. Duke objected that he was the first to embrace the far right platform and that it was Buchanan who was sounding increasingly like him rather than vice versa. Be that as it may, Buchanan was evidently the messenger preferred by conservative voters. Therefore, "Political analysts and some of his own supporters . . . say Mr. Duke's foray into Presidential politics may be proving that his racially charged ideas have a political future but that he does not."[30]

Further complications, as I noted in the last section, are created when there are different audiences that can potentially be targeted by a political appeal or that might subsequently be drawn into the conflict. A message that works in one constituency may play less well if the constituency is broadened. In the Williamson County, Texas controversy over health-care benefits for unmarried domestic partners described below in chapter 5, the county commissioners inadvertently added moral overtones to an otherwise conventional economic decision and spent the next few weeks trying to prevent outside parties from intervening on the issue.

Therefore, even though they have ample incentive to be able to gauge popular preferences, politicians are frequently surprised when their proposals strike a chord in the mass public. Although the research literature is replete with examples of how public preferences are susceptible to framing effects and heresthetic, or agenda-setting, maneuvers, these discoveries tend to be made after the fact. We cannot speak confidently about when attempts to manipulate the public will succeed and when they will be ignored. Race baiting might prove remarkably effective in one campaign but backfire in another. Candidates forced to rely on incomplete information to make educated guesses about what kinds of issues will appeal to the electorate can end up taking distinct positions in campaigns instead of converging on the median.

In his 1974 race for reelection to the U.S. Senate, Bob Dole trailed his opponent, Dr. William R. Roy, an obstetrician, in the polls. Dole was hobbled by his close association with the Nixon administration; he had been the Republican party chairman at the time of the Watergate break-in. Moreover, because of his role in the national party, he was criticized for neglecting his home state of Kansas. Dole also was on the defensive for having opposed the legislation that created the Medicare program.

Roy successfully kept Dole in retreat on these issues for much of the early campaign. In September, during a candidates' debate on agricultural issues, a frustrated Dole lashed out at the doctor by asking about his position on abortion and demanding to know how many abortions he had performed. The questioning was entirely out of order given the subject of the debate, and some of Dole's assistants were sure that the tactic had backfired. But following the debate, anti-abortion activists began rallying in opposition to "the abortioner" doctor. Dole's "outburst turned out to yield unexpected political benefits."[31] Ironically, Dole capitalized on an issue on which he did not have strong views. But this is not surprising, because the abortion issue was not on the radar screen at the start of the campaign: "It was not a major point of conviction for him. It's just that it turned out to be a significant point of vulnerability for his opponent."[32]

This story is emblematic of many political tales in which a politician discovers an issue that captivates the electorate and suddenly becomes its greatest champion. The Williamson County controversy was similarly sparked by an inadvertent remark about homosexuality. It was known that moral attitudes were generally conservative among county residents, but it was not possible to predict that concerns about homosexuality would become one of the focal points of discussion on a routine tax-abatement issue.

In January 1950, Joseph McCarthy was fishing for a campaign issue to advocate in his 1952 senate reelection run. During a dinner McCarthy had with his advisers, three proposals surfaced. The first two were quickly rejected—promoting the St. Lawrence Seaway (insufficient interest) and updating the Townsend Plan (too inflammatory)—before Father Edmund A. Walsh, a priest and educator, suggested that taking up the cause against communism had potential (although he also admonished McCarthy to champion the issue in a responsible manner). McCarthy warmed to the idea and immediately prepared to deliver some speeches on the communist threat. Still McCarthy was caught completely by surprise by the furor that grew out of his infamous Wheeling, West Virginia speech, in which he claimed that he possessed a list containing the names of 205 Communist party members currently employed in the State Department. He was so unprepared for the attention he received that he later had to hunt for a transcript of his remarks to make sure of what he had said.[33]

Similarly, the intensity of the Boston school busing controversy in the mid-1970s caught School Committee Chair Louise Day Hicks off guard before she ultimately rode the issue to electoral victory. Hicks had campaigned for a seat on the Boston School Committee as a reformer dedicated to putting an end to the cronyism and political favoritism that had plagued the committee for decades. There was no reason to expect that she would make her reputation as the leader of reactionary forces opposed to legislative and judicial efforts to correct the racial imbalance in Boston's public schools. Despite her legacy, there is evidence that Hicks's actions were driven significantly by community pressure and political incentives rather than by heartfelt bigotry and racism. Her classmates in college never witnessed a trace of racial prejudice, and Hicks had earlier shown concern over the separate and unequal state of Boston schools. But, ultimately, the prospect of political gain motivated Hicks to take the side of the racial hardliners. As it became apparent to her that conciliation on the busing issue was politically costly, she forswore her moderate stance, and her conversion was richly rewarded at the polls, especially in white working-class neighborhoods: "She had found her issue or, more accurately, it had found her."[34]

Because there is uncertainty about the elements of a winning formula, past evidence of successful coordination around particular values and identifications will give that strategy considerable inertia. George Wallace, for example, toughened his stand against integration following his failure to win the 1958 governor's race after his opponent, John Patterson, outflanked him in garnering white racist support. The contrasts in their positions were not large, but they proved sufficient in that racially volatile environment. The critical development in the campaign that crystallized perceptions of the difference between the two candidates occurred when Wallace repudiated the Ku Klux Klan after Patterson had accepted its endorsement of his candidacy. Thus "Patterson . . .

established himself as the stridently irreconcilable segregationist, while Wallace, more by default than anything else, became the muted and circumspect segregationist."[35]

By 1962, Wallace had learned his lesson and was adept at giving the electorate what it wanted. He had simplified his oratory and developed a rhetoric that played to the Alabama public's racial fears. He used trial and error to determine what symbols most reliably evoked and coordinated racial identifications. His aides took note of the phrases that got the biggest response from his audiences; the ones that worked were adopted into the permanent repertoire: "I remember the time he first called [federal district judge] Frank Johnson a low-down, carpetbaggin', scalawaggin', race-mixin' liar. The crowd liked to went wild. People started advising him he ought not to be talking about a federal judge thataway, it wasn't dignified, but we told him to stay with it. Got to where, later in the campaign, ever time he started coming up on that line, the folks'd start punching and poking each other and grinning and all, waiting for him to get to it. Once he put in 'pool-mixin' just to see how that would sound. He liked to work around with things like that, and we'd watch the crowd reaction."[36] According to an aide, the best litmus test of a proposal was whether it could get a rise out of the farmers in attendance at his campaign stops: "You knew he'd scored with something when you saw them just kinda quietly nod their heads. Or even better, when you'd see those hands coming out of those coverall pockets to clap, out from behind those coverall bibs, you knew he'd reached them. Those folks don't take their hands out from behind them bibs for much they hear. It's got to be something special. So when we'd get back in the car with George and start out for the next place, we'd tell him where the hands had come out of the pockets and say, 'You wanna stick with that one, now.'"[37]

A successful campaign reveals what kinds of arguments people are disposed to accept and what kinds of coalitions can be formed. When a party ideology proves its success in an election, it tends to be banked on until it has clearly run its course.[38] Thus, we witness the paradoxical reaction of both Democrats and Republicans at the onset of the Depression—the kind of crisis that according to analysts would inevitably have forced either or both parties to adopt a more activist stance in providing relief and assistance to the unemployed. In the deterministic view, President Franklin Delano Roosevelt merely carried out policies that virtually any politician so situated would have felt compelled to promote: "At a time of suffering beyond all precedent, the policies of the government could not have remained forever frozen. An activist government would have been installed somehow; if not through Roosevelt, then through someone else; if not through the Democratic party, then through some other party; if not in 1932, then assuredly in 1936. And realignment would have come about in any case. The key variable in the 1930s was not leadership but the overwhelming intrinsic power of the Great Depression as a realigning issue."[39]

But the "inevitable" took time because President Herbert Hoover's conservatism made him reluctant to endorse massive government intervention. Hoover firmly believed in limited government; Republican resistance to government assistance to the needy was based on the rationale that government intervention merely rewarded those who lacked effort ("slackers") and reduced the initiative behind philanthropy and private charities. More importantly, the party's laissez-faire philosophy was the source of its mass appeal and the reason for its majority status in the electorate. Instead of proposing government action, Hoover placed his trust in "voluntary cooperation in the community."[40] Republicans were also faithful to the principle of self-government in recommending that local and state governments, rather than the federal government, should take the lead in providing relief to citizens.

While the Democrats, as the party out of power, were eager to exploit the crisis for political gain, they too remained timid initially about recommending governmental intervention. The Democrats were understandably enamored of the Republicans' electoral success, and thus were prone to emulate the Republicans. It was not until after the 1932 election that the political realignment of the parties occurred, when the Democratic party behind FDR finally moved away from its centrist position and posed itself as a distinct alternative to Hoover's Republican conservatism.[41]

In the aftermath of the Democratic landslide of 1936, the behavior of the two major parties followed a predictable line. The old guard of the Republican party became obsolete and were overtaken by younger more moderate Republicans such as Henry Cabot Lodge Jr., who had learned the lessons of the New Deal revolution. The Democratic party, on the other hand, maintained an activist orthodoxy that would eventually undermine its electoral prospects in the 1970s.

CONVERGENCE ON A FOCAL POINT

Evidence of success will bring out of the closet imitators of the same basic ideas. A box office hit in Hollywood spawns a series of sequels and "prequels" and copycat movies that are putatively in the same genre as the original success. In like fashion, a heterogeneous political environment can quickly become aligned once it is proved that the public can be readily coordinated along a particular dimension. If, for example, it is apparent that certain group identifications are given priority by the mass public, and that such identifications can be readily invoked by opportunistic entrepreneurs, then alternative frames of reference for political mobilization will be eliminated from the agenda.

Louise Day Hicks could not retain a monopoly on the busing controversy, and eventually the racist rhetoric surrounding the issue reached proportions that took her aback. By catering to prejudice and racial group loyalties, she and other political opportunists inflamed mass opinion and created a hospitable climate for political extremism. Politicians converge on a popular issue like moths to light. ("A successful alignment accumulates a tremendous body of hangerson.")[42] Once an issue is selected for its popularity, ambitious politicians will compete among themselves to become its leading advocate. In Boston, a number of unreconstructed racists in local politics fought for their share of the limelight and in the process exacerbated racial divisions in the city.[43] The extremist shift of the issue ultimately repelled the very person—Louise Day Hicks—who had earlier exploited it to its fullest potential.

Coordination on Jim Crow Norms

A similar runaway dynamic coordinating elite and mass opinion brought Jim Crow norms to full force in the South by the turn of the twentieth century following three decades in which race relations had attained a modest degree of integration. During Reconstruction, white southerners began to reconcile themselves to the idea that blacks would remain a significant presence in their society. The South would not inevitably revert at the conclusion of Reconstruction to a racially segregated society in which blacks were totally subordinated.

At this juncture, there was a range of political ideologies on race, and many potential resolutions of the issue of race relations. In the minority were liberals who advocated racial integration and equality and attacked theories of racial superiority. The most virulent racism was embodied in Radicalism, an ideology which deemed that the elimination of slavery removed the institutions that lifted blacks out of a primitive, bestial state. Elements of Radicalism had always existed in prewar, proslavery arguments that blacks could not survive without slavery. Radicalism claimed that new generations of blacks born in freedom would return to a savage state of nature and threaten civilized white society.[44]

The majority position was staked out by conservatives who argued that blacks and whites had to respect and support a natural social order in which each class and group in society had a rightful place: "Like other conservatives of the period, the Southern conservatives believed that every properly regulated society had superiors and subordinates, that each class should acknowledge its responsibilities and obligations, and that each should be guaranteed its status and protected in its rights. The conservatives acknowledged that the Negroes belonged in a subordinate role, but denied that subordinates had to be ostracized; they believed that the Negro was inferior, but denied that it followed that inferiors must be segregated or publicly humiliated. Negro degradation was not a necessary corollary of white supremacy in the conservative philosophy."[45]

In the eyes of conservatives, opposition to all forms of racial contact was prevalent only among unrefined, lower-class whites. Southern conservative racial doctrine tried to walk a fine line between appeasing more extreme racist sentiment and attracting black support through paternalistic inducements. Blacks recognized that, between conservative paternalism and lower-class racism, their interests were better safeguarded in an imperfect alliance with the conservatives. Conservatives had their own interest in attracting and maintaining the political support of blacks in the face of challenges in the 1880s from third parties defending agricultural interests in the South.[46] Conservative southern Democrats even had aspirations of attracting black support away from the Republican party by supplying patronage to blacks and offering blacks greater respect and status in society.

This accommodation between the races began to disintegrate when populist appeals to blacks and poor whites gained ground during the recession and depression in the 1890s. With their political dominance threatened, conservative Democrats resorted to blatant racial appeals to undermine the populist coalition. The Populists campaigned for black and white support on economic grounds. Tom Watson, the Populist leader, trusted that self-interest would bring together white and black farmers, sharecroppers, and laborers.[47] Since blacks experienced the same economic hardships as poor whites, populists challenged racism on rational, materialist grounds and sought to fashion a racially mixed coalition based on common economic grievances and interests. But this was a monumental undertaking, because the most promising source of white support for the Populist program—poor, lower-class whites—was the same segment of the population that harbored the strongest racial animosities.

The modest success enjoyed by the Populist platform was therefore no small achievement, but it rested on a precarious coalition between blacks, Populists, and Republicans. Populism was soon countered by a Democratic propaganda campaign that pointed to continuing federal interference in southern elections and public education as evidence of the beginning of a second Reconstruction era that would further integrate blacks into white southern society. Press stories played up themes of racial conflict, reported sensationally on crimes committed by blacks against whites—especially the rape of white women—and made claims about growing black disrespect and insubordination toward whites. The Democratic offensive was intended to ensure that the topic of discussion would no longer be economics, as the Populists wished, but race: the message was that blacks were winning political power, and white society—white women especially—was in peril. This campaign of words was reinforced by physical intimidation and economic reprisals against Populist leaders and their supporters.[48]

As a result of this campaign, extreme variants of racism quickly gained widespread currency in the South. Radicalism trumped conservative and liberal racial ideologies in the black belt southern states in areas in which blacks constituted a third or more of the population.[49] In every region of the South, whites and blacks had previously established racial conventions that had made social order and harmony possible. But Radicalism overturned these conventions of race relations wherever it was introduced. Using an ecological metaphor, Joel Williamson describes the competition of racial ideologies in this way: "In and after 1889, a new organism, Radicalism, appeared. Whenever white encountered black, in body or in mind, Radicalism strove to dominate that contact, to feed upon it. As Radicalism grew rapidly stronger it engrossed the available food supply. Every thought, every act in race relations tended to become Radical. Other organisms, other patterns of interracial thought, Conservative or Liberal, deprived of food, withered and wasted away. Once Radicalism won dominance in the social ecosphere, it jealously denied the breath of life to any alternative."[50]

Ideological variation in this political environment was thus eliminated by a powerful and politically popular idea. Political parties offer diverse platforms so long as there is some uncertainty about the distribution of popular preferences, but they rapidly converge on similar platforms if it becomes apparent that there is a clear winning electoral formula.[51] This is what happened in the black-belt South and in parts of surrounding states, as politicians readily converted to Radical views. "To be a Mississippian or a South Carolinian was ipso facto to be a Radical or else to be alone in one's racial views."[52]

As occurred much later in the Boston school busing conflict, Radicalism quickly overtook the politicians who were trying to exploit the idea for political advantage. Populists and Republicans saw the same potential for making hay of the putative racial threat, yet failed to take the initiative. But the political and social forces behind the issue eventually proved irresistible, so that even more moderate politicians rallied beneath the Radical banner. Progressive and paternalistic racial views lost ground in the competition against extreme racism, and politicians who would normally have been voices of moderation instead threw their support behind the most racist alternatives: "Representatives of the old conservative school, such as Senator John T. Morgan of Alabama, gave aid and comfort to the racists; or like Hoke Smith went over to them lock, stock, and barrel, and became one of their leaders. Younger men whose background, associations, and ideas would have normally drawn them to the conservative, Hamptonian position on race in earlier days . . . were swept up in the tide of racist sentiment and gave voice to it."[53]

Elites coordinated the masses and themselves around racist propaganda: "Even so, it was not a world they ever made. If white supremacy politicians in some shape had not existed in North Carolina in 1898, they would have been created by the Radical hysteria. And they would have been molded from any clay—Democratic, Populist, or even Republican. Each of these parties had a very large and important lily-white faction, and each was poised for a flight into Radicalism. In North Carolina, the Democrats took flight first. For a time they grounded the rest, in part simply because whatever a Democrat was, a Populist or a Republican ought not be. The young Democrats who opted for Radicalism chose to ride the wave of the future. They thus assured themselves of possessing high power in their state in the formative decades of the twentieth century."[54] The entire South yielded increasingly to the most racist sentiments as the forces tempering extremism receded. Northern liberals made matters worse when they sought reconciliation with the South by agreeing to pay less attention to the racial issue and to support conservative views on race. Neutral third parties outside the South therefore offered little further assistance to blacks.

The Power of Coordination

The failure of populism demonstrated that racial divisions were hard to dislodge with new political or economic alignments because racial identifications were supported by social and political institutions. Blacks and whites not only occupied different economic and political strata, but they also practiced separate conventions of language, music, religion, and education.[55] Racial extremism was not merely a political platform but a broad sociopolitical ideology: "Ideas about race began to fuse with ideas about other things—the nature of man, economics, politics—to form a world-view."[56] A racially based coalition, deeply rooted in the history of southern white supremacy, proved more viable politically and socially than a class-based one. When Ben Tillman, the governor and later senator for South Carolina, stumped the lecture circuit at the turn of the century, he routinely offered his audience a choice between his two prepared lectures, "The Race Question" and "Railroads, Trusts, and Monopolies," and found that race, far more often than not, was the subject on people's minds.[57]

In general, to the extent that there is common knowledge that a certain dimension of evaluation is preeminent, it will be difficult for political debate to move away from that dimension because political power hinges on its continued use as the basis of coordination, and those who benefit from the current political alignment will act to preserve it. Attempts to shift the frame of reference may therefore prove futile to the extent that people's dispositions to view events from a particular vantage point may leave them inured to the influence of alternative views. When racial group interests and identifications governed southern politics, it was a nearly impossible challenge for any politician to deviate from that premise. "It seems reasonable to suppose," Schattschneider observed, "that the more intense conflicts are likely to displace the less intense. What follows is a system of domination and subordination of conflicts."[58]

In a community in which people are coordinated around a particular value or norm, it is risky for individuals to violate the norm without exposing themselves to retribution by way of social pressure, ostracism, or electoral defeat at the polls. Consequently, there is little debate over such dominant cultural values and norms when the institutions of society do not provide any incentives to challenge the status quo. For example, the disfranchisement of blacks diminished any incentive that the political parties had to promote racial equality.[59]

Focusing attention in a campaign on a particular dimension of evaluation has the natural effect of strengthening beliefs along that dimension and of further increasing the weight given to that dimension in political evaluations. As the importance of the dimension increases in the determination of public opinion, entrepreneurs have even greater incentive to play to those concerns; to avoid joining in on the issue or to try to change the agenda places one at risk of being irrelevant to the debate. A lonely voice addressing alternative issues will be insufficient to raise their salience.

Suppose, for example, that the proportion of individuals who support L is greater than half. It therefore will be advantageous for leaders to argue in favor of L. But the success of such appeals will lead to similar appeals by most competitors, which will have the effect of further increasing individual and collective support for L (the disproportionate number of messages promoting one side increases support for that side, since there was a propensity to accept such messages in the first place). As the bias favoring L grows, political entrepreneurs have little choice but to appeal to community sentiment. The preponderance of messages promoting L therefore makes it fruitless for any leader to go against the grain. Quickly, unintentionally (in the sense that no single leader planned to bring about this extreme outcome), one viewpoint comes to dominate all others.

According to these dynamics, initial group inclinations—toward certain social norms and values or opposed to certain groups and practices—can become exaggerated in short order as a consensus develops, among constituents and entrepreneurs alike, over the priorities and perspectives they bring to the issues. McCarthyism built on the anticommunist suspicions of the mass public and was nurtured in the Cold War climate of international instability, but the explanation for McCarthy's popularity resided in his support among Republican party elites and in the reluctance of his opponents to curb him. The Korean War, international tensions, Communist party activities, breaches of national security, domestic spying, government expansion, and liberalizing social changes created a cluster of political discontents that the Republicans sought to exploit among voters. McCarthyism was typical politics, in which the party out of power tried to tar the party in power by questioning the patriotism and loyalty of its leaders: "The animus of McCarthyism had little to do with any less political or more developed popular anxieties. . . . Leaders of the GOP saw in McCarthy a way back to national power after twenty years in the political wilderness."[60]

Consequently the most powerful explanatory factor for popular attitudes toward McCarthy was party affiliation: Democrats predominantly opposed him, while Republicans lent their support. Nevertheless, McCarthy was able to hammer away on the issue of domestic communism because his opponents were afraid to fight popular sentiment. The hold of McCarthy was therefore hard to break, because his success caused opposing politicians to refrain from criticizing him.

McCarthy's elite support was strongest within the midwestern faction of the Republican party, which had become its staunchest conservative wing. Moderate Republicans, including those in the Eisenhower administration, backed away from attacking McCarthy for partisan reasons. Eisenhower was interested in maintaining the unity of the party, and McCarthy had obviously struck a raw nerve in the Democrats. Even liberal Democrats checked their opposition because they were apprehensive about McCarthy's ability to hurt their reelection chances. A civil liberties counterattack against McCarthy carried the risk of being construed as sympathy for communism.[61]

The irony here is that the elites' support of McCarthy combined with the reluctance of opponents to denounce him skewed the debate in his favor and contributed mightily to McCarthy's ability to coordinate mass opinion to his side. The public took its cues from the political leaders they respected. Even though it is likely that the public was primed for McCarthy's pitch because of the political issues of war and general international tension and insecurity following World War II, elite acquiescence in McCarthy's charges undoubtedly steered the mass response toward the intolerant direction in which it veered.[62] Therefore, the elite's apprehension over being punished at the polls was exaggerated and, to the extent that it was real, was a product of their own aversion to challenging McCarthy's accusations.

Arguing with Principles

A political appeal that addresses the self-interest of members of a particular group may not have much attraction outside that group. In contrast, principles are not particularistic, which means they can be inclusive. During the 1997 United Parcel Service strike, the Teamsters Union demanded that management transform part-time positions into full-time slots. In its effort to generate popular support for its position, the union claimed to be doing its share in the larger battle being fought by labor against a trend in the economy to hire part-time workers and to pay them unsatisfactory wages. A self-interested bargaining position thus became a defense of a more noble principle.

People have a strong desire to employ, as frames of reference in bargaining and arguing, impartial norms or principles to justify their position and persuade other parties to their side.[63] Principles are general rules that are applied neutrally in specific cases without reference to the identities of the parties involved. In this section, I will discuss five facets behind the strategy of employing principled rationales. First, principles will often be used to cover for self-interest because they are neutral bases of evaluation that, in the abstract, enjoy widespread popular support. Political leaders hope to convert the abstract support for a principle into concrete support for their side in the dispute. Second, even if appeals to principles are ruses, they may not be transparently so, because there are more and less effective ways to make one's case with principled arguments. The uncertainty over whether a principled appeal is sincere may be sufficient to lend it persuasive power. Third, even when self-interest underlies principled appeals, principled rationales may nevertheless strengthen the resolve of individuals who have an interest in the conflict and need to rationalize their actions. Fourth, principled appeals also may be effective when directed at rational actors who place value on maintaining their capacity to claim to be principled. Finally, there are circumstances under which principles will be persuasive (even if they are also self-serving). If a party does not have a large stake in the issue, self- or group-interested appeals lose their relevance. Because neutral parties by definition do not have a stake in the outcome, they are more likely to be attracted to a principled position. Therefore, principled arguments may be influential with those who have committed themselves to the principle and with neutral or third parties who have the potential to join the fray.

The Advantage of Principled Arguments

Among rational actors, the mere attribution of one's motives to impartial principles may not, and perhaps should not, be accepted at face value. Principled arguments can be offered strategically as a means to furthering self-interest, or they can be made sincerely without regard to self-interest. Principled appeals that emanate from self-interest will tend to overlap, partially or entirely, with self-interest, while sincere principled arguments will only coincidentally correlate with self-interest.

Someone who proposes a principled resolution to a conflict should accept the same resolution if he were on either side of the dispute. To the extent that people can be persuaded in conflicts of interest, they are more likely to be persuaded by a party that is believed to be principled; research on persuasion verifies our intuition that people are more influential when they argue positions that appear to be objective rather than motivated by self-interest.[64] A person who takes a position that appears to run counter to his self-interest can be especially influential. Curiously, we seem to rely on principled debate even when there is a strong presumption that the principles being bandied about are self-serving fronts for one's own interests.

Part of the inclination for couching one's advocacy in terms of principles is due to the social norm against overt selfishness. In general, principled behavior is valued by others precisely because it is unselfishly motivated. Principled individuals are credited for making occasional sacrifices on behalf of abstract rules. Childless residents of neighborhoods undergoing school busing may be more likely to stave off pressure from parents to become involved by offering a principled excuse than by pointing to their lack of a stake in the issue. This is merely the flip side of a principled appeal by interested parties to recruit other members of the group who are less vested in the particular dispute. By construing the issue in terms of threats to group norms, and not merely to individual self-interest, people apply pressure on those on the sidelines to contribute to the defense of group values. In this regard, a principled appeal that trades on common group identification is a more refined means of persuasion than is coercion and arm twisting.

Egoism is expected in our society, but it is not highly prized as a character trait, which explains the admiration showered upon those who act altruistically. Even principled choices that produce undesirable outcomes may still elicit grudging admiration for the motive that is the wellspring of choice. One becomes known as a person who is capable of acting out of principle rather than merely out of personal interest. For these reasons, it may be in one's self-interest to adhere to a principle if that shores up one's reputation as a principled individual, even if such adherence compromises immediate self-interest.

Because of the ostensible neutrality of principled rationales, a debate carried out at the level of principles can also have the effect of elevating discussion above direct conflicts of interest. Principled rationales can represent or at least give the appearance of constituting impersonal bases of choices. Mediators choosing on principle preserve civility between themselves and the disputing parties by removing the personal element from their choices. Consequently, the rhetoric of principles may take the edge off of the conflict of interest.

Nevertheless, we would expect that actual sacrifices on behalf of principles by rational actors are likely to be small and to follow systematic patterns. Principles are more likely to be applied wholeheartedly when self-interest is not significantly compromised. So people are more likely to talk principles, to profess support for principles in the abstract, to insist upon principles in the actions of others than they are to make large sacrifices themselves for the sake of upholding principles. To the extent that individuals occupy a disinterested role, we can expect greater evidence from them of sincerely principled decisions. And we may expect some instances of principled behavior that sacrifices immediate gain when calculations of self-interest are placed within a longer time frame. But we should also anticipate frequent attempts to conceal self-interest behind principles.

Principles as Shields for Self-Interest

There are ways to have one's cake and eat it too—that is, to reap self-interested benefits by appearing to be driven by principles. A reason why principles often do not undercut self-interest is that there can be a surfeit of applicable principles in any one case, so that the principle a person finds apposite may correspond rather closely to his own self-interest. Many principled appeals are therefore simply rhetorical strategies that serve to coordinate and give cover to self-interested actors. We have reason to expect interested parties to adopt a self-serving interpretation of what principle applies to their particular case. For tactical reasons during the slavery debate, for example, politicians could side with abolitionists without openly opposing slavery if they couched their support in terms of democratic principles (such as the right to petition government) that they wished to preserve. Northern Whigs gave such a rationale when they voted against the gag rule in 1836. They may or may not have sincerely sympathized with the abolitionist cause; we do know, however, that the Whigs "were a new party looking for issues with which to challenge the incumbents. The antislavery cause was a promising one, especially if pressed in the context of the right to petition. They could be against slavery, which most northerners disliked or even detested in the abstract, and for freedom of speech but still avoid the stigma of abolitionism."[65] In effect, one principle was substituted for another because it better served underlying political interests.

In the late 1800s, supporters of restricted immigration sought an ostensibly neutral principle that would have the effect of reducing the influx from non–Anglo Saxon countries. They proposed that prospective immigrants require certification of their good character from the overseas American consulate. An alternative plan called for a twenty-dollar head tax for every immigrant. Neither of these proposals, however, passed muster. Consular approval would not discriminate clearly between old and new immigrant stock, whereas a head tax was criticized for its unegalitarian spirit. Eventually, nativists found the perfect measure in the literacy test, which would deny entry to any immigrant who was illiterate in his native language: "The literacy test . . . provided a highly 'respectable' cultural determinant which would also minister to Anglo-Saxon sensibilities. 'No one,' said Senator Chandler in 1892, 'has suggested a race distinction. We are confronted with the fact, however, that the poorest immigrants do come from certain races.'"[66] Still, the literacy test failed to receive passage four times between 1897 and 1906.

Reasonable suspicions that principles are merely fronts for self-interest may nonetheless be difficult to prove, which makes such deceptions worthwhile to continue. Even when principles are suspected of being used disingenuously, it still requires some cognitive work to make the case, and sometimes there will only be a preponderance of evidence supporting that conclusion. When self-interest and principle coincide, we can only speculate about the predominant motivation. When state bar associations fight the growing trend toward lawyers' advertising their services, they contend that poorer, less well-educated clients are most likely to be taken in by such practices and to wind up with inferior representation. At the same time, advertising stiffens competition and threatens to lower fees, so that established members of the bar have the most to lose.[67]

In Cicero, Illinois, a largely white Chicago suburb, city officials explained that a housing ordinance restricting the number of people who could live in a single unit was meant to equalize property tax burdens and was not targeted at Hispanic residents, the group that was most affected by the measure. If taxes were an insufficient reason, a city spokeman added, for good measure, that there was also "a safety reason and a school overcrowding issue."[68] Students of racial attitudes debate whether opponents of racially progressive policies are closet racists or believers in individualism. Individualists argue that disadvantaged people, including blacks and the poor, should raise themselves through their own hard work rather than through government assistance. Because the same racial policy positions can be explained by either racial animosity or belief in individualism, it is difficult to disentangle the true motivations. Those who are motivated by racial prejudice, however, do better by explaining their position in terms of support for individualism, because there is a much larger alliance of believers in individualism (sincere and insincere) than there is of individuals who are willing to admit to racial prejudice.

There nevertheless still are rules that must be adhered to in using principles, so that abiding by these rules may require occasional sacrifices of self-interest. To avoid the scrutiny of skeptics, one may do better to argue a principled position that does not coincide perfectly with one's self-interest. If a coincidental argument is made that can be viewed as self-serving, the argument may be sapped of its persuasive power. Thus it may be instrumental to increase one's credibility by arguing for a principled outcome that departs marginally from self-interest. Or it may simply be necessary to compromise on a principle that sacrifices a measure of self-interest in return for broader support from other parties. The best principle for gaining additional support may not quite be the ideal principle to serve self-interest.[69]

Self-Justification through Principles

Principles offer a shield, a socially acceptable defense, for behavior that may otherwise appear illegitimate or morally repugnant. The defense is sometimes for external consumption, but it may also be the case that believing one's behavior is driven by a principle, such as justice, for example, makes one more determined to stay the course. In addition to people wanting others to regard them favorably, they also need to maintain their own self-esteem. For this reason, they may engage in self-deception by believing that their actions are motivated by principle rather than self-interest, such as when individuals insist that their behavior (e.g., litigation) is motivated by principle and not by self-interest (money).

Action that is justified by principles may exact greater effort and determination born of self-righteousness than action that is motivated solely by interest. This "transmutation" of motives, as Elster puts it, may be further assisted because there is less social pressure to desist when one professes socially approved motives. Vigilantes will go through the motions of carrying out a "fair trial," complete with judge and jury, in a feeble effort to show that their actions were not arbitrary before they dispensed their summary justice.[70] One wonders why they would bother to go through the motions, but even lynch mobs apparently feel a need to bow to fair procedures even if by so doing they make a mockery of them.

It is not clear whether such gestures are made to remove residual cognitive dissonance, or whether they are carried out in the event that there might be other people who subsequently challenge the legitimacy of their actions. Slaveholders, for example, felt compelled to develop an ideological defense for slavery only after being confronted with the egalitarian arguments of abolitionists. Opponents of slavery contended that the condition of blacks was due to the institution of slavery rather than to any innate inferiority of blacks. Defenders of slavery counterattacked by arguing not only that blacks were naturally inferior, but also that their natural standing in society should be that of a servent or slave, since they were incapable of independence and citizenship.[71] Defenders of slavery also argued that the institution of slavery had divine support and that abolitionist tactics encouraged insurrection and were therefore unconstitutional.

The proslavery side was therefore drawn into the debate by abolitionists who managed to place slavery under the light of democratic and religious values. Even ardent supporters of slavery could not ignore the potential contradictions between the values they subscribed to and their behavior toward blacks: "The abolitionist contention that Christianity and the Declaration of Independence not only affirmed equality in theory but cried out for its immediate implementation could not go . . . unanswered by the defenders of black subordination."[72] But advocates of slavery resolved this tension between their beliefs and actions by arguing that the same high principles and values were never meant to apply to blacks; in this manner, the treatment of blacks was not held to egalitarian standards. This was probably no more than a calculated reconfiguration of the issue: "To understand this conflict, one must recognize that southerners could mean two different things when they questioned the applicability of the Declaration of Independence. They could reject the idea of equality in general, . . . or they could reject simply the interpretation of it which included the Negro as a man created equal to the whites. Those who embraced the second option saw themselves as preserving the egalitarian philosophy as a white racial prerogative."[73]

White southerners thus eliminated any conflict between their treatment of blacks and the abstract values that define a democratic society. Democratic values never weighed heavily in how southerners thought they should deal with blacks because they never believed that blacks qualified for membership in this democracy: "In fact, southerners felt that blacks were in their appointed place, and that they, the Southern whites themselves, were the most democratic of Americans."[74]

The Premium Placed on Consistency

Of course, there are telltale ways to smoke out the self-interest that underlies ostensibly principled or non-self-interested claims. For example, principled arguments lose credibility when they are not backed with consistent action. When a tabloid newspaper claims that it wants to see justice served by offering a big reward for information leading to the capture of a child killer, it gets less credit if it does so only after it has been roundly criticized for earlier publishing photographs of the crime scene that might undermine the prosecution.[75] In general, any newspaper's motive for offering a reward is always suspect, because it receives publicity for doing so, and it gets an exclusive story if anyone happens to come forward with valuable information.

South Boston residents in the 1970s doubted the sincerity of those who argued in favor of school busing using abstract principles of racial equality. Both black and white residents felt that racial tolerance and idealism among white liberals was mainly due to their remoteness from the consequences of their values. In contrast, they felt trapped by the busing plan, and their lack of alternatives stiffened their opposition. Alice McGoff, whose family's experiences were traced in *Common Ground,* was skeptical from the beginning of President Johnson's speech supporting the use of affirmative action to achieve equality: "She knew full well which whites would pay the price for all of this. It wouldn't be those who worked in the big corporate and law offices downtown, the ones who dined in those Back Bay clubs and lived in the comfortable, all-white suburbs. No, as usual it would be the working-class whites who shared the inner city with blacks, competed with them for schools and jobs and housing, and jostled with them on the street corners."[76] (This case, however, might just as easily illustrate how people are more likely to support principles when they occupy a neutral vantage point.)

If principles are going to be invoked, then it is important that they are invoked consistently right from the start rather than as an afterthought following failure of other arguments; such inconsistency undermines the sincerity of principled appeals. In Wilmette, a suburb north of Chicago, officials recently lodged a complaint against neighboring Evanston's practice of sounding an alarm in the early morning hours to warn residents to move their cars or have them towed in order for the streets to be cleaned. Wilmette residents, awakened by the sirens, had been unsuccessfully pressing Evanston officials for two years to cease this practice. Then, Wilmette officials expressed concern that the sirens constituted a possible public hazard because they bear some resemblance to tornado warning signals. One Wilmette official said that, if Evanston continued to sound its sirens, Wilmette residents might become confused and not pay attention to a real tornado warning. Why does this argument sound hollow to us?

Because of the premium placed on consistency, principled arguments may prevail against parties who are constrained to act consistently with those principles because they have endorsed them in the past on behalf of issues that served their interest. A person cannot support his position with a principle, but then refuse to adhere to that principle in another context when it no longer serves his interest. Doing so would eliminate any credibility he had for being impartial.

Claiming to be motivated by a principle amounts to a commitment to actions that are consistent with that principle (or, at a minimum, commits one to providing an explanation for why that principle is not relevant in a particular instance). Hence a person's wish to maintain credibility with others may require sacrifices in order to remain faithful to principles that he or she has previously avowed. In this fashion, self-interested individuals may develop commitments to principles that were once employed in their self-interest, but now work against them. A rational person may have to conform to a principle in order to retain credibility in making principled arguments in the future. People may feel bound to live up to principles that no longer serve their interests because we impose demands on others to believe and act with relative consistency. Individuals are expected to be motivated by a consistent core of values and to make choices that are consistent with those values. Not to do so creates an impression of unreliability and unpredictability, which may be more costly in some instances than following a principle that is not in one's self-interest.

The backlash suffered by the so-called Redeemer administrations in the South following Reconstruction illustrates how people are held to their own principles. The Redeemers triumphed over the carpetbaggers partly on the strength of accusations of corruption by the incumbents, a charge that made them especially vulnerable to retribution from the voters after some financial scandals of their own in the 1880s.[77] One consequence of the New Deal's focus on the underprivileged was that it raised discussion of principles and values that could easily be extended to the treatment of blacks. The force of the Constitution rests on abstract principles that are applied to new cases. But, as critics of the courts realize, principles may be applied in ways unanticipated by those who enunciated the principles originally, causing debate over the proper extrapolation of those principles.

Principled Appeals to Neutral Parties

The history of collective action in this country comprises efforts by groups to change social and political institutions in order to enlarge and enhance the opportunities available to their members. But there still is an issue of how groups that strive to transform the norms are able to overcome opposition from those who benefit from maintaining the status quo. A critical element in this process is that, although self-interest may preclude concessions by dominant groups to minority interests, the challengers may have allies beyond the immediate sphere of the conflict, and appeals to higher jurisdictions may yield more favorable results. Weak challengers who fare poorly under an existing alignment of political forces therefore have an incentive to change the boundaries of the debate by using various tactics, including invoking abstract principles, in hopes of activating and winning over third parties to their side.

The key element that makes viable the use of principles for political mobilization or self-defense is the presence of third parties who have the power to intervene and tip the balance in conflicts rather than remain neutral. Strategic calculations have to allow for change over time in the scope of the conflict. A tactic that succeeds at the local level when the conflict is contained may be trumped by a competing strategy at the national level of politics once additional participants are drawn into action. Blatantly nativist appeals that work well in solidifying a local majority may have the self-defeating effect of drawing in external parties sympathetic to the underdog. Those who are losing a conflict can try to reframe the issues or they can attempt to enlarge the number of relevant parties to it. The main disputants must worry about third parties to the extent that they may hold some leverage and are willing to exercise it. As the sphere of the conflict expands, the side that currently enjoys the upper hand may see its advantage slip away.

Principles are used either in defensive maneuvers as justifications to prevent third parties from interfering or, alternatively, to draw them into the dispute through moral persuasion. Third parties whose interests are not compromised by enforcing these principles will be amenable to impartial appeals. Nonviolent demonstrations in the civil rights movement were calculated to provoke southern police brutality in the hope of generating national public outrage and federal government intervention. Some southern police chiefs tried to undermine this tactic by instructing their officers to leave the protesters alone, but the police chiefs often found that, in the heat of the moment, they could not reliably hold their officers in check.[78] In retrospect, the civil rights movement succeeded in large part because the struggle for racial equality was primarily a southern regional conflict until the mid-1960s, which allowed white northerners to support the cause without substantial consequence. During a brief but significant two-year interval between 1963 and 1965, the civil rights movement turned race relations into what the public perceived to be the most important issue facing the country. It was in this period that the civil rights agenda in the South dealing with public accommodations, voting rights, and job discrimination was written into national legislation by a Congress dominated by a Democratic party that was fresh from its 1964 electoral landslide.

As the focus of the conflict shifted and the movement increasingly impinged on life in northern cities, divisions emerged between blacks and their northern liberal allies. Support from white northerners tapered off, and the liberal Congress began to retreat from its civil rights measures. C. Vann Woodward observed:

> So long as it was considered a "Southern" problem, the heat was on, and we have seen the striking progress made under pressure in the Southern states. Once it appeared that the courts were going to move against de

facto school segregation in Northern cities, however, the commitment to
integration quickly cooled. Many of the old Southern arguments re-
emerged, this time from Northern mouths, those of liberals included: desegregation promoted racial conflict and disorder in schools; it was of
doubtful benefit to black students anyway and blacks did not want it; it
destroyed neighborhood schools and neighborhoods; it was impossible in
cities with growing black majorities in schools without busing, and that
was too costly, counter-productive, and politically disastrous.[79]

Disadvantaged groups seek inclusion under generally accepted norms of
equality, and their success often depends critically on swaying public opinion
and persuading higher authorities to intervene. Numerous jurisdictions and
layers of authority in the United States create many opportunities and avenues
to alter the configuration of relevant parties: "To a great extent, the whole
discussion of the role of government in modern society is at root a question
of the scale [of] conflict. Democratic government is the single greatest instrument for the socialization of conflict in the American community. . . . Government is never far away when conflict breaks out."[80]

Many debates in American public life are therefore carried out with an eye
toward obtaining support from public authorities (legislatures, courts, executives) that can make enforceable rulings. These third parties may be drawn
into the dispute out of consideration for their own interests in containing the
conflict, but they also may be responding to the force of principles or to public
pressure that emanates from sympathy for such principles. Appeals to such
abstract principles as equality and liberty may of course garner more sympathy
than action. People have incentives to be moral and to have reputations for
upholding principles, though these incentives may be insufficient to spur significant protest. Yet public sympathy may be a powerful ally if it is followed
up minimally by voting behavior that acts on these sympathies and creates
incentives for legislatures to intervene. As long as the public is also willing
to act on its moral sentiments at the ballot box, politicians will have a direct
interest in addressing moral issues. The involvement of the masses may not
be narrowly rational to the degree that they are injecting themselves into a
dispute that may have little direct bearing on their lives, but this lack of self-
interest puts them in an ideal position to express moral outrage at a relatively
low cost.

CONCLUSION

An important tactic of political debate is to shape the interests, symbolic
associations, principles, and group identifications that people bring to bear in
evaluating political issues. By manipulating frames of reference, opinion lead-

ers influence people's criteria for evaluating issues. People can be made more receptive to ideas not only by changing their beliefs, but also by influencing their frames of reference. The concept of framing assumes that some representations of an issue are more persuasive than others, so that attitudes and opinions will be swayed in predictable ways if attention can be concentrated on those representations.

My model tries to capture the process by which public opinion converges on common frames of reference as people make sense of the issues and establish where their interests lie. Coordination on a frame of reference is readily achieved when opinion leaders are able to synchronize their messages with people's dispositions to receive those messages. In practice, opinion leaders will often try to frame issues around group norms, interests, values, and symbols that already enjoy widespread support among those who are being mobilized. Coordinating people for political purposes on the basis of their group memberships tends to strengthen those identifications and to reinforce existing social divisions. If the goal is to bridge different constituencies, then appeals to specific group interests must yield to more abstract arguments based on general values, norms, and principles that reach across socioeconomic groups. Along these lines, we ought to distinguish between the intensity of an ideology and its appeal. Intense ideologies require considerable devotion from their followers, including the holding of beliefs that are not widely shared and large investments of time in the group, which limits their overall reach. Any ideology that is targeted more widely has to become more accessible and less demanding.[81]

An effective strategy of political mobilization must not only coordinate individuals, but should also establish the population for whom an issue is relevant. A strategy must account for, as well as influence, the breadth of the "public" that will become engaged by an issue. It may be the case, for example, that an in-group appeal rounds up support from members of that group, but elicits strong opposition beyond the group, so that the net effect is mixed. If this is so, organizers may wish to tailor their messages to suit the respective audiences, or argue that the issue's relevance is limited to the in-group. They might also seek an alternative campaign formula that still coordinates group members, but does not antagonize outsiders. A successful strategy must therefore also take account of potential third-party intervention, as the arguments put forth in any debate can either forestall or encourage intervention by neutral parties. The advantage of using a symbolic or principled argument, for example, may be to camouflage a socially unacceptable motivation (such as racism or naked self-interest) that would ignite opposition if it were overtly pursued. In sum, strategies of political mobilization must consider how a particular tactic will affect not only interested parties, but also currently neutral third parties that might be provoked by the terms of the debate to intervene on behalf of one side.

Political conflict therefore raises the stakes of opinion holding and opens a window into the process by which values, norms, and group memberships are related to political and economic interests. In case studies of communities in turmoil over divisive social issues or pressing economic concerns, researchers invariably find that people possess clear, often emotionally charged opinions.[82] There is no inconsistency between these findings and those derived from abstract public opinion surveys that reveal an uninformed and apathetic citizenry. Schattschneider recognized that "there is no more certain way to destroy the meaning of politics than to treat all issues as if they were free and equal. The inequality of issues simplifies the interpretation of politics. Politics becomes meaningful when we establish our priorities."[83] The mass public is not deeply engaged in politics under normal circumstances, but intense conflicts over values can arise when people are aroused and mobilized on issues that are salient to them. Opinions are readily formed under circumstances in which people have an incentive to hold them.

Economics Meets Morality
in a Texas Community

*When we start deceiving ourselves into thinking not that we want
something or need something, not that it is a pragmatic necessity
for us to have it, but that it is a moral imperative that we have it,
then is when we join the fashionable madmen, and then is when
the thin whine of hysteria is heard in the land, and then is when
we are in bad trouble.*

Joan Didion, "On Morality"

There are only two forces that unite men—fear and interest.

Napoleon I

What happens when individuals and communities are forced to choose between preserving their moral standards and lifestyles or pursuing their economic interests? Recently, citizens in conservative Williamson County, Texas,
faced this question in debating whether to grant tax breaks to attract Apple
Computer Company, even though Apple maintained a locally unpopular policy of extending health-care benefits to the unmarried domestic partners of
employees. The dilemma concerned whether tax benefits should be granted
to a company that was seen by many to promote values contrary to community
norms. A panel of county commissioners first refused the tax breaks, by a three
to two vote. The vote created a firestorm of controversy and was subsequently
reversed, but not before the cultural and economic divisions in the community
were brought to the surface.

The commissioners who originally voted against the tax break were swayed
by public criticism that Apple's policy welcomed homosexual and unmarried
heterosexual couples into the county. Economic growth and new employment
opportunities would therefore be gained at the expense of conservative community norms and values. The commissioner who cast the deciding vote, after earlier stating that Apple's policy was its own business, explained that
"all I have is my integrity and my values and my strong belief in traditional
values."[1]

The analysis in this chapter rests on interviews with local citizens and the main participants in the imbroglio about how they resolved their dilemma. It also draws on examinations of correspondence sent to politicians during the controversy and county survey data collected shortly after the first vote.[2] While the poll gives the more accurate snapshot of where people in the county stand on the issue, in-depth interviews are better for probing people's reasons and explanations for their actions, their conception of what is in their self-interest and the interest of the community, and their motives for protecting social and religious values against rival beliefs.

Although the opinions voiced in these interviews are not necessarily representative of the entire community, the focus here is less on making precise inferences about the population than on delving into how citizens make decisions in disputes over values and interests, and on identifying characteristic mechanisms through which values and interests are able to motivate individual action. The purpose of this chapter is to analyze how people evaluated the costs and benefits associated with the Apple plan and to investigate, more generally, the connections in people's minds between morality, community, politics, and economics. Why are some people more prepared than others to sacrifice material gain in order to preserve their social and moral values? And can actions aimed at preserving a community consensus on particular moral beliefs and lifestyles be construed as rational and, if so, in what sense?

What the Apple case reveals is that the development and maintenance of a value system is imbued with interests. Cultural values coordinate political coalitions and social activities, counsel people on how to live their lives, and constitute a simple folk theory that lends coherence to their lives and their understanding of how other people live. People do the best they can within the priorities established and the biases and constraints imposed by their value system.

BACKGROUND

Williamson County began as a farming community in the the mid-nineteenth century. There are still many small farms and ranches in the countryside today. Georgetown, the seat of Williamson County, has the look and feel of many small towns across the country. Its domed courthouse sits in the middle of the town square, surrounded by a hardware store, an ice cream parlor, small shops, and the offices of the local newspaper. Town residents can still run up a tab at the local cafe. In Georgetown and the other communities of Williamson County—Round Rock, Leander, Cedar Park, and Taylor—the people are friendly and the pace is deliberate. But there are signs that life is changing in the county: new strip malls and corporate parks are sprouting up along

Interstate 35, the highway joining Williamson County to Austin, twenty miles to the south.

In the 1970s, the towns along the highway, particularly Round Rock and Georgetown, became suburbs of Austin, the state capital and home of the main campus of the University of Texas. Austin is generally considered to be the most liberal city in the state. While it has all the amenities of city living, it also has many of the problems associated with contemporary urban life, including a high crime rate and troubled public schools. Williamson County residents pride themselves on having a family atmosphere that contrasts with the more cosmopolitan lifestyle of neighboring Austin.

Williamson County has lately become more active in pursuing economic development. *Texas Business* recently named Round Rock the most attractive city in Texas for corporate relocation and expansion. According to its findings, "No other city, large or small, can match its combination of pro-business attitude, quality of life, infrastructure, and low costs."[3] The county uses hefty tax abatements to attract business from other parts of Texas and the rest of the country. The tax abatements are politically controversial but generally popular among most of the Williamson County business community. As a result of this commitment to economic growth, Williamson County enjoyed an unemployment rate that was barely half the state rate at the time of the controversy.[4]

Economic development has been accompanied by population growth. The population doubled in the 1970s, and nearly doubled again in the following decade, so that now almost 160,000 people reside in the county. Eighty-seven percent of the population is white, and only about 5 percent is black. Hispanics constitute 14 percent of the residents. Average family income and years of education have increased significantly in the past twenty years. Like many parts of the South, the county has shifted politically to the Republican party. While county voters backed Hubert Humphrey in 1968, George Bush carried the county in 1992 with 42.8 percent of the vote compared with Bill Clinton's 31.7 percent; 25.2 percent preferred Ross Perot.

Apple and Williamson County

In September 1991, Apple announced plans to relocate its customer service center to an Austin business development zone located in Williamson County. The company planned to build an $80 million facility, including nine large office buildings, on a 129-acre corporate campus.

Apple formally asked the five-member Williamson County Commissioners Court for tax abatements for its facility in the autumn of 1993. The tax abatement was valued at about $750,000.[5] An economic analysis prepared by Ray Perryman of Baylor University, commissioned by the court, predicted that the facility would result in a $200 million boost to the local economy and would eventually support 1,700 jobs. Phase One of the project would employ 700 people and, in each of the two subsequent phases, 500 additional workers would be hired or transferred to the facility.

At a commissioners' meeting to consider the tax abatement in early November 1993, Commissioner Jerry Mehevec casually mentioned that Apple had a domestic partners benefits policy which covered workers' same-sex partners. Mehevec warned that "these companies are destroying families as we know them in America."[6] Commissioner Greg Boatright also said that Apple's policy troubled him.

Two other commissioners supported the tax abatements. Mike Heiligenstein, a member of the Round Rock Chamber of Commerce Economic Development Committee, was Apple's chief supporter on the court. He believed that it was inappropriate for government to get involved in corporate policy.[7] Initially, David Hays also publicly supported the tax abatements, citing the economic growth that would accompany Apple—namely, more jobs, more services, and more companies following in Apple's footsteps.[8] In a letter to the editor of the *Round Rock Leader,* he wrote: "The majority opinion around here believes government doesn't have any business telling companies how to run their operations."[9] Young and inexperienced in politics, Hays was the most recently elected commissioner. Before his election, he worked for his family's title company and, as a result, he had many connections to Williamson County's real estate community.

The fifth member of the Commissioners Court, Judge John Doerfler, remained publicly undecided, although his past voting record suggested that he would support Apple. Before the vote, he told the press: "I am strongly opposed to homosexuality and same-sex marriages. But how far should county government go in interfering with a company and its policies? Does government of any kind have the right to regulate morality?"[10]

The Vote and Its Aftermath

The Commissioners Court met on November 30, 1993, to vote on the question of tax abatements for Apple. The meeting was unusually crowded with constituents; some accounts reported that seventy people were in the small meeting room. During the period reserved for public comment, many of those attending the meeting expressed their opposition to Apple and condemned homosexuality.[11]

Following the public discussion, the commissioners voted three to two against granting tax abatements to Apple, with Heiligenstein and Doerfler in the minority. David Hays reversed his earlier position and voted against the abatements. He had received scores of phone calls the week before the vote from constituents who argued that Apple's policy undermined the family and the community's moral values.[12] Christian activists posed a credible threat: they had recently forged a majority coalition on the Round Rock school board and, in a bitter dispute, had managed to dismiss the school superintendent after he decided to ban public prayers at high school football games. Following the vote, newspaper accounts widely quoted Hays's explaining, "If I had voted 'yes,' I would have had to walk into my church with people saying 'There is the man who brought homosexuality into Williamson County.' "[13]

Apple executives were shocked at the outcome. Bill Keegan, who attended the meeting, said that Apple would be looking to locate elsewhere. He suggested that Apple might even leave Texas.[14] Apple's public relations representative in California, Lisa Byrne, said that Apple would not go forward with its plans in Williamson County and would not back down from its benefits policy.

The vote set off a week of intense political activity. The commissioners' offices were deluged with phone calls, letters, and faxes from both angry and supportive residents. The day after the vote, Hays defended his decision on a Christian radio talk show hosted by Mike East, a local far-right activist. Many members of the local Christian community were ecstatic about the commissioners' vote and praised David Hays as a hero. On the other hand, other residents were infuriated by the commissioners' decision. Members of the business community mobilized to persuade the commissioners to change their vote. Organizations like the Round Rock Chamber of Commerce and the Williamson County Board of Realtors urged their members to contact the commissioners who opposed the tax abatements, especially Hays. Politicians across Texas weighed in on both sides of the debate. The vote also drew heavy national attention, as all the major networks and many major newspapers sent reporters to cover the story. As a result of this attention, the commissioners received mail from across Texas and around the country either admiring or ridiculing the decision.

Behind the scenes, Apple's supporters, including Governor Ann Richards, tried to salvage the deal. Richards, and other business and political leaders, contacted Apple and urged them not to abandon the Williamson County site. Several days after the vote, Hays began to waver under pressure from constituents and members of the business community. Heiligenstein, Hays, and lawyers for Williamson County worked with Apple representatives to repackage the tax abatements. In the new proposal they drafted, Apple would no longer receive "tax abatements." Instead, it would pay taxes to the county, but be reimbursed $750,000 over seven years, roughly the same amount as the original abatements.[15]

On December 7, 1993, nearly 200 people, including dozens of television and print reporters, attended the Commissioners Court for the vote on the revised proposal. On one side of the aisle, people wore badges that said "Keep Apple in Williamson County." On the other side of the aisle, Apple opponents sported badges that said "Just Say No! An Apple Today Will Take Family Values Away."[16] As was expected, Hays changed his vote, and the motion carried three to two, with Mehevec and Boatright remaining steadfast against the proposal.[17]

SETTING THE AGENDA

Tax-abatement issues tend to pass without notice in Williamson County, and it appeared initially that the Apple decision would be no exception. Why did it turn out otherwise? In the abstract, some leaders in the community would seem to have had an incentive to turn the Apple issue into a controversy for their own benefit. Political entrepreneurs have an interest in seeking out advantageous issues around which to build and consolidate their constituencies.[18] One common method is to champion an issue that enjoys clear majority support; in so doing, one advances a collective interest that simultaneously promotes one's own political fortunes as a community leader. For this reason, enterprising individuals might have been expected to try to exploit the Apple decision by raising fears about homosexuality.

But, in fact, there is little evidence that anyone sought to drive a wedge through the middle of the community on social issues. Although they have their differences, political, business, and religious leaders are in agreement about their plans for Williamson County. In general, practically everyone believes in economic growth and traditional values; business interests and conservative morality are seen to go hand in hand and people are loath to tamper with this consensus.

For example, Phil Brewer, executive director of the Round Rock Chamber of Commerce, and an ardent supporter of economic development in the region, including the Apple project, sounds just like Apple's opponents when he explains what he finds appealing in Williamson County: "Living in a neighborhood where your children can go out and play in the front yard. Knowing who your neighbor is halfway down the block. Going to church on weekends and seeing your neighbors in church with you. And not having to feel that if somebody . . . wants your little boy or little girl to come down to their house and play with their children, that . . . you've got to do a background check on this person to make sure that they're not going to molest your child. Those are the kinds of values that we have in our community. . . . We've been trying to market this community as having very strong values, a very low crime rate. It's just a very good place to live."

By the same token, opponents of Apple are in general very sympathetic to economic growth, as long as moral standards are not compromised. The pastor of the Heritage Baptist Church in Georgetown, the Reverend Donald Ledbetter, said that when he first heard about Apple's plans to move into the community, he was pleased by the news: "We welcomed that because it means more industry and hiring more people, and more people come in, and that gives us more prospects for the church." A local businessman who opposed Apple agreed: "My business thrives on growth. The more new construction that's in the county, the better off I am financially. And so I'm *for* growth. And normally it would be something that would be exciting to me to see a company the size of Apple."

The Apple conflict therefore arose largely by accident. It was not orchestrated but was the unintended result of a series of uncoordinated individual actions. Clark Thurmond, publisher of the *Williamson County Sun-Times,* surmises that "all it takes is a few loony people" to run with an issue and stir up controversy. The commissioners who voted against the abatements did not seem to have ulterior motives for raising the issue, nor did they plot strategy together. In fact, they had only a vague idea of each other's intentions. Thurmond believes that Jerry Mehevec himself was surprised by the intensity of feeling that he aroused by his off-the-cuff remark in early November disparaging Apple's policy.

Mehevec confirms that he may have been the most shocked commissioner at the first vote, when Hays turned against Apple. He claims that, at the meeting, he was not even sure how Boatright would vote. Boatright also did not expect the motion to fail. Mehevec said: "It really caught us by surprise. The audience, they [could have] died, flipped over, especially the Apple people and the people promoting the abatement. The judge called a recess. Hays just took off immediately. He left. He made this big spiel for about five or ten minutes about how great it was, and then he just turned around and voted the opposite way."

Despite Mehevec's pivotal role, he makes no effort to claim credit for the resulting conflict. Indeed, he confesses that he would not have been disappointed if the first vote had instead been 3 to 2 in *favor* of Apple. Mehevec insists that he did not cause the controversy, but rather points the finger at Hays. He is adamant that he did not lobby Hays at any time.

David Hays also takes no pride in splitting the community, and claims that he did not intend to pander to his religious constituents. In retrospect, Hays says that if he had forseen the controversy he would have made sure he had the flu. To be sure, Hays received an unusually large number of telephone calls before the first vote that, by his recollection, were all opposed to granting the abatement to Apple. Still, there was no evidence of substantial organized mobilization against Apple. Phil Brewer was so confident about the outcome of the first vote that he did not even attend the meeting. He was dismayed when he heard the news the next morning: "It was a very small and vocal group that caused this problem. It is not the mind-set of the majority."

Once the commissioners voted against Apple, the fallout in the ensuing days made the issue salient to everyone. One of Hays's constituents, John Warden, recalls: "The commissioners themselves, I think, made this an issue. If they hadn't made it an issue, I probably wouldn't have known about it. I probably wouldn't have become involved. When the commissioners made this an issue, then the news media picked it up, and it was spread all over the United States that this was an issue because homosexuality is a hot item politically. So they—the commissioners themselves—made it an issue."

As we will see in the next section, many in Williamson County did not want to choose sides in a dispute between economics and morals, and they were appalled that the issue was being defined so crudely. From the vantage point of business-professional interests, religion is an important stabilizing force in the community; it should guide school board decisions and help maintain conformity and harmony in the community. Good schools, safe streets, and stable communities are attractive to families and corporations. But business interests do not want religion to become a divisive element in community politics, as it was threatening to become in connection with the Apple matter.

FRAMING STRATEGIES FOLLOWING THE FIRST VOTE

Although little strategic maneuvering was evident before the first vote, the vote taken against Apple highlighted concerns about homosexuality and overturned what had previously been a straightforward business issue. Consequently, the outcome of the following debate depended heavily on the result of political jockeying over how the issue should be defined or framed.[19] The pro-Apple side argued that the county should concentrate on the economic dimension and not interfere with Apple's internal corporate policies, whereas the anti-Apple forces fixed attention on their opposition to homosexuality. (All of the political leaders, it should be noted, wanted to minimize community turmoil and find a way to put the issue behind them.)

Both sides had the right intuition about their political strategy. Apprehension about homosexuality was evident in the letters sent by those who wanted Apple to locate there. Many echoed a local real estate developer's views: "Personally, I do not condone homosexuality; and I'm not sure that I understand it." Another businessman wrote: "I too believe in family values; I believe it is time (actually, far past time) for good, moral Christians to take a stand, draw a line in the sand, on the ever-growing attacks on the fiber of our society by liberal socialists. But, clearly, in my mind, this is not the issue on which to make this stand."

In the only Williamson County area survey of public opinion taken during the controversy, 50 percent of the respondents indicated shortly after the first commissioners' vote that they disapproved of the decision, versus 37 percent who supported the decision to deny tax abatements to Apple. On the other hand, the survey registered a deep reservoir of opposition in Williamson County to homosexual relationships: 47 percent disapproved of gay or lesbian couples living together against only 5 percent who said they approved of such relationships; 42 percent claimed to have no strong feelings one way or another. Similarly, 42 percent disapproved of unmarried heterosexual couples who cohabit (the other major group covered by Apple's policy), and only 9 percent approved; 43 percent of the respondents remained neutral.

One interesting note in this context is that, although community leaders accurately perceived the extent to which county residents disapproved of homosexuality (and therefore the importance of keeping it on or off the agenda, depending on one's purpose), they tended to magnify regional differences of opinion on the Apple issue. Moreover, they tended to overestimate the amount of agreement in their constituencies with their own opinions. Boatright and Mehevec believed that there was overwhelming support for their positions in their precincts (centered in Cedar Park and Taylor), whereas Heiligenstein, Doerfler, and Hays (after the second vote) thought that they represented the majority position, with the opposition being concentrated in the less commercial, more rural regions of the county outside Round Rock and Georgetown.

The sharp regional differences described by the commissioners are not borne out by the public opinion data. Regarding the first vote, disapproval-approval margins by town were similar: 51-34 in Georgetown; 50-39 in Round Rock; 54-32 in Austin; 54-38 in Leander; 53-32 in Taylor; and 51-38 in Cedar Park. However, the strongest opposition did come from rural residents, who approved the first vote by a 57 to 33 margin. With respect to homosexuality, disapproval-approval margins by town varied only slightly: 51-3 in Georgetown; 49-6 in Round Rock; 43-7 in Austin; 38-4 in Leander; 53-0 in Taylor; and 46-8 in Cedar Park.

Citizens' perceptions about the community were also skewed in the direction that reinforced their attitudes and made their decisions easier, a tendency that repeats itself (as we will see later) in their assessments of costs and benefits.[20] Regardless of their position, residents of the community believed that they were in the majority and imagined the other side to be an insignificant minority. Many of those who wrote to Hays before the second vote tried to impress upon him that most others felt as they did: "The 'moral majority' has kept quiet long enough, and has allowed a small number of unthinking radicals to ruin the moral fabric of our society." "I feel that the majority of the constituents are against homosexuality as a life style and applaud the message that the Commissioners have sent out by their vote." "I trust if you desire any future in politics you will reverse your decision and work diligently for the remainder of your term to convince me that you are representing Georgetown and not just the people sitting next to you in church." "We feel the majority of Precinct #3 support the principle of separation of government and religious viewpoints." "You were elected to represent the entire community instead of a vocal minority."

Supporters of Apple were unprepared to complicate the original issue by factoring in moral concerns. David Hays reinforced this point by commenting that, until Mehevec mentioned Apple's domestic partners policy, it was not normal practice to raise social concerns in conjunction with tax issues. When asked for his reaction to Mehevec's comments, Hays said, "Shock, mainly. . . Not so much that the policy was there, but that it was brought up in regards to the corporate location. *[So you thought it was not relevant?]* It was not relevant initially, but the fact that it was brought up. It was immediately something that the press seizes upon and [makes] into an issue." Hays explained that it was important to set the homosexuality issue aside: "Most people don't condone the gay lifestyle. They're against that. . . . I think that's the way most of my friends felt. Then it gets down to why did you vote the way you did. Then you get down to secondary issues and there may be some difference in that."

Likewise, Phil Brewer thought that the decision rules were settled on issues like the Apple plan: "I don't think it's . . . a governmental entity's business to be dictating corporate policy. That is a company's own business, I think, and if you're going to lay down some guidelines and not do abatements because of things like that, you need to have that established, and you need to have that down pat before a company comes. . . . I mean, you are going to have to give some thought to that kind of stuff." Brewer's comment reveals how decision-making conventions guide choices. The county had no prior experience factoring moral considerations into economic issues; the presumption therefore was that those considerations were out of bounds. If people had thought about the Apple issue along prescribed economic lines, their decision would have been easy to predict.

Some Apple supporters felt not only that the debate was unwinnable if it were structured in terms of gay rights but also that they themselves would have had difficulty supporting the issue on that basis. They were concerned not only with the final decision—whether a deal was struck with Apple—but with how their vote would be construed by others in their community. It was important that they be seen pursuing economically advantageous outcomes for economic reasons; it was not enough to receive those same economic benefits indirectly if it appeared that they were motivated by an unpopular social cause.

This concern is most evident in the construction of the final compromise agreement, which provided essentially the same financial benefits to Apple as the original proposal, but appeared to make a concession to those opposed to Apple. The revised proposal allowed supporters—primary among them, David Hays—to claim that the government would not be subsidizing Apple's domestic partners policy because Apple would be paying property taxes, even though it would eventually receive tax rebates in roughly the same amount granted in the original proposal. Beyond window dressing, there was no real difference, as leaders on both sides were willing to admit during the interviews.

The desire to frame the issue in economic terms also appears to have been motivated by psychological reasons as much as by political goals. When Greg Boatright was asked if there were differences on the court on the homosexuality issue, he replied candidly: "No, everyone on the court thinks that homosexuality is wrong. I mean they said they did." Therefore, by thinking about the issue strictly as a business decision, Apple supporters did not have to wrestle with their consciences and reconcile moral and economic arguments.

In an effort to control damage, Mike Heiligenstein specifically advised homosexual rights activists to stay out of the fight so that the issue would not be seen to be about gay rights: "The best thing you can do is keep out of the argument right now." He feared that if the issue were a gay rights debate, there would be majority opposition in Williamson County:

> If it had become a gay rights kind of thing, then it would not have been turned around. Because there were a lot people that I was dealing with that don't buy into a separate set of rights for the gay community. I don't think the business community would ever have come around. It wouldn't have supported the issue if it wasn't an economic issue. Keeping that out was real important. It was one of the most subtle things that happened, but it was incredibly important to it. Because it would have folded if there had been a [gay rights] demonstration at the courthouse. *[What about the business community, the realtors?]* They would not have supported it. *[Do you think you could have?]* I think I would have had problems. . . . Obviously from a political standpoint—but not so much that, as I very narrowly define what I think are constitutional rights. I probably wouldn't be so broad as to include some of the rights that the gay community is proposing.

Heiligenstein was asked, "If the issue had been redefined as a gay rights issue, the basic outcome would have stayed the same—Apple would still bring jobs and improve the tax base—then why does it change things if the issue is framed differently?"

"Because then it would have been drawn into the purely social realm. It would have become part of a movement. We would have been forced to become part of a discussion that we had very little to do with, very little exposure to, which we really didn't know all the arguments of. It would have been corrected, if at all, over a period of several weeks while we structured new arguments that would come into it—the more national arguments, so to speak. I think if that had occurred, it would have been a whole new ballgame."

An Apple supporter made a similar observation in her letter encouraging Hays to reverse his vote: "I personally regret that this issue has provided a forum for the religious right to spread their judgmental propaganda, as well as a forum for the most vocal spokespersons for gay rights. The public is thrown into black and white thinking."

A different frame of reference throws a wrench into the discussion, because people have not previously sorted out the new arguments. People tend to have pat resolutions of certain questions, which they can no longer depend upon if the issues are restructured along different lines. Heiligenstein admits that the framing strategy might be seen as cowardly:

> It kind of sounds like we're trying to avoid the big questions: are gay rights right or wrong? But I think it would have been pulling it outside of what was truly the core question and that question dealt with Apple Computer, the corporation, and its policies, and do we have a right to amend our policy because of a policy that they had. And that was the issue, really. Socially there are many other issues involved, but I don't think we were prepared to go through that. . . . Those issues are still being debated. Those are substantive social agenda issues that we were not prepared to deal with, and I knew that if it got to that realm, then that boat was sunk. Now we can debate those issues in our churches and in our congregations, our homes, our classrooms, our roundtables, but that was the forum for that debate. That's really where I justified my position— that that was not the correct forum. And I thought the coalition groups [the opposition] picked the wrong forum for that debate.

Naturally the opposition begged to differ, and wanted to debate the issue right then and there in the Commissioners Court and on its own terms. Dorothy Duckett, mayor of Cedar Park, was convinced that the Apple decision was a moral issue, and she resented the efforts of those who tried to frame it differently: "I felt like what happened is it was very cleverly staged and that it wasn't really an issue of economics, it was an issue of the gay groups being accepted, but they very cleverly make it into an economic thing because most people are going to oppose those lifestyles, but if you can get the focus off of the lifestyle and put it on jobs, and get people to think in that vein rather than that other vein, then it becomes a whole different ballgame." Greg Boatright thought it was transparent why people could not keep homosexuality off the agenda: "Because the homosexual issue is such a controversial issue. It's like abortion. . . . I really think that people, their emotions really get stirred when you start talking about those issues. Most people have a very definite feeling and opinion about it, just like abortion. . . . You're not halfway for or against abortion; you're either for it or against it. The same thing is true about homosexuality. You're either for it or against it. There's really no place to stand in the middle on that issue."[21]

When asked more generally whether morality can be balanced against economic considerations, Boatright's answer is revealing, because he says that morality is something that people either have convictions about or they do not. Introducing a moral concern, by implication, pushes that dimension to the forefront of the debate. Other dimensions permit tradeoffs and pragmatic considerations, but morality is absolute. What distinguishes moral concerns is that they are principled and do not allow compromises. Boatright asks rhetorically: "How can you set morality apart from the economic issue?" As the analysis in the remainder of the chapter will show, the two may be inseparably fused in people's assessments of causes and consequences and costs and benefits.

COMPETING WORLDVIEWS

How an issue is framed, how we evaluate information, how we diagnose social ills, and how we assess the consequences of public policy are all wrapped up in the more general ideologies, belief systems, and theories that structure our perceptions and give coherence to our lives. Such belief systems comprise assumptions and propositions that often cannot be proved or disproved. However, whether they have the status of scientific facts, moral principles, maxims, prejudices, or superstitions, these beliefs are often accorded the same respect as facts and are factored into our calculations when making decisions.

Through religious training, for example, people acquire the view that morality and strong character are prerequisites for community and prosperity. The element of faith that underlies this belief may not be significantly different from the confidence (or faith) that secular individuals place in the marketplace to generate efficient outcomes. Most of our beliefs are accepted originally because they have been communicated to us by credible sources, or because they are the conventional wisdom in our families and social circles; seldom will these beliefs be subjected to empirical analysis or other kinds of close scrutiny.

People can be surprisingly introspective about how their perceptions are shaped by their political ideologies or religious beliefs. For example, Glen Vanlandingham, minister of music at the First Baptist Church in Round Rock, acknowledges that his perspective on the Apple issue derives from his religious convictions. He even makes the counterfactual observation that if he did not hold the religious beliefs that he does, then he supposes that he would be willing to tolerate a much broader range of lifestyles and behavior. In other words, he thinks the way that he does because of the way in which he was raised, but admits that if he had been raised differently he would be able to support different positions.

Similarly, Randy Staudt, a member of Leander's city council, acknowledges that his analysis of causes and consequences on a host of matters stems from his worldview: "The effects [homosexuality] has on the community have to go back to an understanding of what your worldview is of the community, what your understanding is of how law and order is born and how communities are formed. I have a Christian worldview, and that tells me that the basic foundation of the community is the family." Not surprisingly, people's worldviews are not easily amended.[22] For example, a recurring theme among opponents of Apple is that homosexuality is a chosen behavior rather than a genetic disposition. It is action that is under the control of the homosexual, so the homosexual can be held responsible. Commissioner Boatright, who held such an attitude, had nevertheless come across studies that suggest that homosexuality is genetic, but when asked if his attitude would change if future studies *proved* that homosexuality had a biological cause, he replied candidly that he would never believe such studies. They would forever be "theories" in his view, just like the theory of evolution, which he also disregards, since he believes in Creation.

Contrasting beliefs about the connection between economics and morality are at the nub of the Apple dispute. Ironically, Boatright and Phil Brewer, standing on opposite sides of the controversy, use an identical metaphor to depict their worldviews about the relationship between these two major spheres of society. Brewer claims that: "There are only—of course, spoken like a true [economic development] person—there are only two directions that the community can go—and that's either you grow or you die. And if you're not growing, you're stagnating, and eventually you're going to lose your banks, and people are going to move away. One of our long-run strategic goals is to create jobs in this community not only for the people who are already living here, but hopefully for our children. . . . So that when my little boy grows up and goes away to college and graduates from college, and if he wants to come back to Round Rock, he can come back to Round Rock and find himself a job in this community."

The "grow or die" theme also emerges in Boatright's discussion of why a community needs to sustain common moral values. Boatright argues that "controversy is what tears things apart. If [people] are constantly embroiled in controversy [over moral issues], then they're not going to grow as a nation; they're not going to prosper. . . . I think that a society has to get along, because if they don't, the society will, as a whole, be oppressed and not allowed to grow. Anything that doesn't grow finally withers away."

From one perspective, Brewer and Boatright have an identical goal—they want to establish the conditions for a strong, productive community in which social divisions and problems are minor or nonexistent. And, despite recommending different routes to this common goal, they employ the same metaphor to capture their vision of the dynamic that drives societies. For Brewer, however, the key to achieving this goal is in sustaining the economy; for Boatright, it is in maintaining strong moral values.

Brewer believes (as Commissioner Heiligenstein does) that strong communities and families and social order stem from economic prosperity. Economic security keeps families stable; stable families lead to reduced crime. With employment comes purchasing power and collective goods: "That's where quality of life starts—in having a job. We want to be able to provide jobs for everybody in this community. . . . At the present time, I think that's the consensus of this community."[23] Following the first vote, David Hays received forty-two form letters from members of the business community echoing the same theme: "There is nothing more important to maintaining strong families than a good steady job. It is absolutely undisputed that areas where unemployment is the highest are also the areas where families suffer the most. Unemployment increases the rate of divorce, child abuse, alcoholism, etc."

For Boatright and other members of the opposition, the causal arrow is reversed: economic growth can only be built on a solid moral foundation. His ally, Randy Staudt, echoes these sentiments: "It's crucial that the family unit be maintained. . . . We must propagate or we'll die. If you get your values straight, if you get your families strong, if you keep your streets safe, if you keep the crooks in jail, make people pay time and restitution for what they've done. . . . you'll have a good economy. And indeed, I think that's why the United States has the economy that it has, why we've become what we've become in the world, because we started off with our value system straight. We gave honor to God."

The Brewer-Boatright debate symbolizes the tension, in spite of the broad conservative economic and moral consensus in Williamson County, between the newer, more urban, secular, educated professional and business class and the older, more rural, traditional, fundamentalist community over which group best represents present-day Williamson County's values and its priorities for the future. Whereas the traditionalists worry about newcomers' disrupting the community, their more cosmopolitan counterparts feel that the major threat to harmony is more likely to emanate from internal intolerance than from external contamination.

One sign of this tension is how the professional and business community resented the way some media portrayed county residents as backward and rural during the controversy. David Hays complained that "ABC, they came down and did a little clip on Georgetown. They go find a woman that has no teeth, shoot a picture of cactus, and show a jackrabbit, one building standing out there with a windmill behind it, and say Apple Computer wants to come to this town. I think that was ridiculous."

Similarly, Phil Brewer feared damage to Round Rock's reputation immediately after the first vote. According to Brewer, the national news made it appear that reactionary groups were dominant in the community: "It was frustrating that evening . . . to see the national news playing an angle on this issue, and picking literally ranchers and farmers who had just come into town, when, in reality, they're a minority. . . . There are a lot more folks wearing coats and ties and dressed up than there are driving pick-up trucks with a gun in the back of the pick-up truck, and wearing boots with their blue jeans stuck in, and their cowboy hats. But that's the image that the national media was going to play up on this deal, and they were going to make us look like a bunch of country bumpkins and rednecks, and that is not the case."

Such comments focusing on dress, education, and lifestyle betray some of the Apple supporters' stereotypes of the differences between them and their opponents. Although representatives of the business community, like Brewer, generally share the same conservative social values as those who resisted Apple, they part company in not wanting religious and social issues to dominate political and economic decision making. In discussing what separated themselves from the most vociferous opponents of Apple, Brewer, Thurmond, Heiligenstein, Hays, and Doerfler all zeroed in on their opponents' uncompromising style. That style, which Brewer characterized as "Bible totin' and Bible gloatin'," will in their view have to be restrained if the county is going to keep its standing as one of the fastest growing regions in the country.

Brewer nevertheless is confident that his reference group represents the majority and that business priorities and values will prevail over the "old-timers' mentality." He paints an unclouded vision of the future, such as we might anticipate from the leader of the chamber of commerce: "Round Rock, when you compare it to the other communities in Williamson County, is probably the community that has changed the most in the last twenty years. . . . You don't have this old-timers' mentality of 'We don't want to grow. We want to stay small. We like it just the way we are. We don't like these new folks coming into the community.' Round Rock has a different attitude than that, and I think that's why we have been successful at bringing companies into this community. . . . And with that comes, I think, new ideas and a changing, not necessarily of morals but, in some cases, values or the expansion of those values."

Clark Thurmond, however, worries that these new ideas might cause some growing pains in the county:

> The old-fashioned cultural conservatism that the county has enjoyed over the years is going to change. I don't know that we're going to get flaming liberals . . . but we'll get a lot of middle of the road people. But it will be interesting. One thing that some of the merchants have complained to me about: they're accustomed to everybody kind of knowing each other and getting along. But now they're seeing more transactions that are arm's length, suspicious transactions. It's big city buying and selling. Here you go into a store, you know the guy, you go to the same church, maybe his kid's on the same softball team as your kid, so you bring something back if it's not what you want. Now they're seeing people who go and buy a prom dress, wear it, and bring it back, say they didn't like it, and want their money back. Now that's not happening a lot. But we're beginning to see that kind of harshness, that arm's length, anonymous economic transactions. Big city stuff. Abusing something and then complaining and wanting your money back. That didn't happen around here before. If you got the jeans and put 'em on and they didn't fit, then your kids spill choco- late milk on it, you didn't take 'em back. It was too bad. Now people will take it back. It's not extreme; it may sound like it's a big deal, but it's just something I've heard a couple of people mention. So it is chang- ing, with that kind of consumerism developing here.

But the central question remains: As communities experience economic and population growth, and the resulting clash of new ideas and foreign ways, why do people insist that others live like themselves?

THE ROLE OF SOCIAL AND MORAL BELIEFS IN SOLVING COORDINATION PROBLEMS

Apple's opponents argue that the company's domestic partners policy will attract people who threaten to disrupt the homogeneous Williamson County community. Sometimes these arguments are made in broad, unspecific terms that reflect an uncomplicated religious proscription against homosexuality ("We've rejected God"; "That's one of the things that is pretty much outlined [in the Bible] as taboo"). Other times, people reveal that they are simply afraid of homosexuals and do not want them as neighbors in their community ("I think homosexuality is an abomination"). People also justify their position by saying that homosexuality is immoral ("Fornication outside of marriage is wrong, whether it's with a man and a woman or two men or two women"). These comments suggest that once the issue is defined in terms of homosexual- ity the decision becomes automatic, so that further reasoning becomes super- fluous in light of the repulsion or moral dictum.

In general, there may be symbolic and psychological motives for enforcing conformity to a way of life stemming from prejudice, habit, socialization, psychological needs, or personality traits.[24] No reasons beyond convention, for example, are given by Judge Doerfler when asked his reaction to disputes in the Round Rock school district over whether "Christmas" should be renamed "Winter Break": "As far as changing the name of the holidays like Christmas to Winter Vacation, or something, I personally think that's B.S. It's always been known as Christmas, it should be known as Christmas, we should recognize it as when Christ was born, at least that's what the Christians think. And if the Jews or the Moslems don't tend to believe that, well that is fine, but that was originally set up as Christmas, and that's the way it should stay."

There would appear to be, however, a more elaborate logic behind why people invest so much effort maintaining community norms than is suggested by habit and emotion. For what sustains habit and emotion? The interviews reveal that, beyond psychological aversion and moral prescriptions, there are tangible social, political, and economic reasons why people desire cultural harmony. On the Apple issue, opponents tend not to rest their case simply on the argument that homosexuality is abominable, morally wrong, or contrary to the teachings of the Bible. Rather they associate homosexuality with a breakdown of the moral consensus that is required for social order, material growth, and human progress. People justify their moral beliefs by referring to the functional consequences of those beliefs: a moral consensus makes possible social coordination and creates the necessary conditions for political and economic cooperation.

In exploring with our subjects *why* they felt so strongly about maintaining their way of life, a number of themes emerged: in communities that share a consensus on social and moral values, there is more trust and familiarity, people can predict what others will do, there is less friction in social interaction, people come to one another's assistance, communication is facilitated, and social coordination is possible. In turn, coordination around common social and moral values not only increases trust and smooths social interaction but also lays the foundation for harmonious business relationships, unified political action, and collective action on behalf of community goals.[25] In general, there are much higher transaction costs living in a community in which people with different values are regularly at odds. Achieving cultural harmony therefore simultaneously improves group and individual well-being. The group is better off when everyone coordinates around the same values, because, as a result, it is able to act for collective ends; at the same time, individuals are better off conforming to community norms, because they can then enjoy the fruits of social coordination.

The next section discusses how people relate social and moral disunity to coordination problems; the analysis in the subsequent section examines how political coalitions and public policies are seen to follow from common social and moral values.

MORALITY, TRUST, AND SOCIAL ORDER

There is real concern in Williamson County, especially among Christian fundamentalists, that the social and moral consensus, and its attendant benefits, are being threatened, if it has not already been lost. Mike East argues that "multiculturalism is being ushered in at a pace faster than we can keep up with." East laments that the mutual assistance that used to be common in communities has now disappeared: "There are no community relationships anymore. Everything is now built around money." He recalls: "It used to be communities stood together, but that's not the case anymore. Why, nowadays in America, your neighbor hardly knows you, knows what you stand for, or anything about you. It did not used to be that way. As a result of that loss of communication and that loss of friendship . . . we've lost that bond, and now we're haphazard, and consequently, we're a mess. Nobody believes the same thing. So we're losing it. We've got too many cultures in this country. We're allowing other cultures to come in and do away with the culture this country was founded on."

According to East, contrasting views bring rancor and disagreement and are a barrier to friendships: "I think it's hard to have a good relationship with anybody when you don't share most of your ideas; when most of your ideas are not in common, it's hard to become friends. . . . I heard a guy say one day, 'I have a lot of friends that are gay.' I said, 'That's funny, I don't have any.' Because they don't embrace the same ideas. So, why would I have a friendship with someone that I consider my enemy? Does that make sense? Why would I want to develop a relationship with something that is totally against what I stand for? That makes no sense. I'm a Christian. Why do I want to run around with an agnostic? I'm a conservative, why would I want to sit at the table everyday with a liberal? . . . I don't just want to go around and spend my life in argument. It makes no sense."

Greg Boatright elaborates on the connection between opinions and friendship by noting that shared values promote communication and signify deeper characteristics that permit trust: "Are you going to spend time with someone that has a complete different viewpoint than you do? I don't enjoy being in an environment where you're uncomfortable . . . where you have to be careful what you say. No one likes to be put in that situation. People tend to spend time with folks who have the same viewpoints and the same lifestyles, and you have things in common. That's just natural. If you don't speak the same language as someone . . . you're not going to spend much time with them because you can't ever establish a relationship. If you have totally different viewpoints on issues, then how do you establish a common ground for a relationship? There's no way. There are probably exceptions to that rule. There are people that you find interesting that hold different viewpoints than you do. You have respect for them, but yet you still don't have that same closeness as you do with family and the friends who you feel comfortable with and you share ideologies with."

Why are shared views so important? "Because I think human nature is to want to trust people. We all want to trust people, and to be able to believe what people tell you, and be able to depend on people. That's the very basis of a relationship—is being able to trust someone. If you are around someone that you don't have anything in common with, then you're not going to trust them."

Boatright also mentions that when he knows what people believe, their actions become more predictable: "If you don't ever take a stand for anything, then what's the purpose of being there? It's very difficult to deal with people like that because you can't count on them. They'll tell you one thing, and do another thing. They have no conviction. If you know a person's a liberal, you know where they're coming from. If you know they're a conservative, you know where they're coming from. . . . I'd rather deal with one side or another. . . . A liberal . . . has more faith in society and in man's wisdom than someone who puts their faith in God and has a more Christian view on things. I think people that have some conviction are going to look at things a lot different than people who believe what man says. If you believe in evolution, then . . . you believe that the things that man has discovered and that man has researched is the gospel, it's the truth."

For Boatright, trust paves the way for doing business: "If you know that people hold the same viewpoint or have the same convictions as you do, then you're going to do business with them. . . . For instance, the folks that I go to church with. If they are in a business that I need services from, I'll go to them first. So I guess that's an example of utilizing people that have the same viewpoint or belief that you have. My CPA, I go to church with him. And anybody that has a product or something that I use, if at all possible, [I'll turn to] someone that I know [because] I know something about them."

Randy Staudt sees pervasive repercussions when the bonds of trust and moral consensus are weakened. People are less free and more fearful when they can no longer be confident about others' intentions: "People are starting to lock their doors. They have to have burglar alarms on their cars. They put the Club [an antitheft device for automobiles] on their steering wheel. They don't want their wives to jog around the street because they're afraid she'll be mugged. They don't want their kids walking to school in the daytime. It matters a lot to these people. Our freedom is being lost . . . to the decadence that's going on around us."

When newcomers bring customs into the community that are at odds with the majority, social externalities are created. Staudt has an elaborate scenario about how one vice leads to another once the process is set in motion. According to Staudt, homosexuals are attracted to vice—strip parlors and adult bookstores: "Not every homosexual is a troublemaker, a brawler, and all that kind of stuff. But there's a significant number of them who are and the lifestyle that's involved with pornography and promiscuous sexual behavior is one that requires a higher level of titillation to maintain the buzz, so to speak. I've been there, I've done that. Now I want to go here to do this. That's the kind of thinking that goes on." There is fear, therefore, that once the camel's nose gets in the tent, troubles will quickly magnify.

To illustrate how a free society depends on conformity to the same norms, conventions, and rules, Staudt offers a metaphor of a stunt pilot in the sky, whose routines appear to be totally free, but in fact are highly choreographed: "He has almost no freedom . . . because everything that he does is a coordinated, practiced, planned maneuver. It looks very fluid and very free, but it's not. . . . Our culture is that way, also. We don't have a free culture unless we have individuals in that culture who are self-restrained. They walk in known paths that are accepted by the general culture and they stay there. Then we can have freedom. I can have freedom. A hundred years ago, I had the freedom to go out here and make a deal with somebody on the street or a word of mouth deal. . . . Because they had a culture and a moral understanding that would not allow it to be otherwise. And that was lost, we had to write everything down. . . . Well, what have we got from that? . . . Our lives are constantly being squeezed further and further 'til we're no longer free. You can't be free unless we're moral."

POLITICAL REPERCUSSIONS OF CULTURAL DIVERSITY

Cultural differences not only foster distrust and a breakdown of communication; they also foreshadow political conflict. In explaining why they reject Apple, opponents employ the following logic: homosexuals have immoral lifestyles and therefore cannot be trusted in positions of responsibility and leadership in the community. In addition, they are typically politically liberal, so they introduce conflict when they form political organizations and field candidates to contest local political offices. And because they hold different moral and political beliefs, homosexuals are likely to express different preferences in elections and on collective issues that affect the community at large.

Glen Vanlandingham, for example, lays out the dynamics of attracting gays to the community. The ramifications will be felt in a variety of spheres: "There's the financial issue; there's the community overcrowding issue. There's the idea that stems from the moral issue—the type of people you're bringing into the community. They're going to be coaching softball, baseball, volleyball. They're going to be attending school board meetings, voting on school board issues, voting on city council, running for city council. There are all kinds of dynamics to this thing. Williamson County has been a very conservative community."

The Reverend Donald Ledbetter adds that immorality affects "commerce, education, politics, all the way through" because immoral people will inevitably divide the community by supporting the wrong kinds of political leaders. "If it's a real pluralistic community, you really have a hard time bringing the community together for just about anything." A morally united community, on the other hand, has the cohesion and solidarity to achieve collective goals.[26]

An important concern in the minds of those opposed to homosexuality is that many moral controversies will be settled through the political process. Greg Boatright commented that he does not want the homosexual community to get a foothold in Williamson County. He worries about the implications of allowing morality to slide. If a society makes too many wrong choices, he argues, then that society will cease to exist. Therefore, according to Boatright, it is essential to keep an eye on the growth of opposing coalitions: "I don't think that the government can be all things to all people. There are choices that will have to be made. . . . It all depends on who's making the decisions. I mean, your school board, your principal—if they have religious convictions, then you're going to get a favorable decision. If not, then religion will be removed from the school activities. People elect people based on the things that they believe in. . . . If religion is a big issue, which it is in Round Rock, then if people feel passionate about it, then they'll elect people who represent their views."

Even though he supported Apple, John Doerfler concurs with the view that majority rule should prevail in moral conflicts. He feels that these cultural disputes should be settled at the ballot box. He says, "Beat me at the polls," if you believe something different. "That's democracy. Life is basically unfair, but in a democratic society that we supposedly espouse, that's the way it's got to go. . . . The only answer I see is move to another community that's more inclined to think as you do." Mike East harks back to a period in childhood when people who embraced conservative ideas were in a distinct majority and community standards and values were sufficiently homogeneous that there was broad consensus on how to punish wrongdoers.

Randy Staudt derides the notion that politics should be kept out of moral

issues. In fact, he feels that politics are essentially about settling moral disputes: "It's a basic philosophical, moral debate, and it's the only thing that
we do discuss in politics. When some politician jumps up and says, 'Well,
I'd just like to take the politics out of this'—well, that's as stupid to me as
saying that you can't legislate morality. Why do we have political systems?
Because people have moral understandings that are different. That's why you
have two different political parties. . . . To say that you want to depoliticize
something is to state a profound misunderstanding about what politics is all
about—because it is a discussion of moral principles. And to talk about sex
is a political effort. To say we want to depoliticize it really means, 'We don't
want you to talk about what you believe. Accept my views and we'll all be
happy.' "

Although he disagrees with the anti-Apple forces, Clark Thurmond agrees
that their views are bound up in a more elaborate ideology that is concerned
about political consequences. Thurmond offers a revealing theory about the
ideological motivations behind the anti-Apple forces. On the one hand, he
appreciates that they share a strong visceral objection to homosexuality. At
the same time, homosexuals are seen to be part of a coalition of cultural
elites—liberals, feminists, easterners, etc.—who represent different political
points of view and who threaten the tranquility of the community: "It may
also be that homosexuality is seen by those people as one of the units of the
elite, so to speak, the cultural elite that everybody talked about for awhile. I
believe that they see, maybe not a conspiracy, but at least a coalition of all
these, what they believe are strange, very narrow interests coming together
and running the political show. The homosexuals can't do it by themselves;
the media can't do it by themselves; feminists can't do it by themselves. But
homosexuals are part of that group."

Thus, lifestyle and moral beliefs serve as two cues for people. They indicate
whether someone has the same dispositions, sensibilities, and intentions as
oneself, and they give important clues to one's political inclinations. Agreement on beliefs is not only pleasurable in itself but also increases mutual trust
and establishes a foundation for political and economic exchange.

To use the classic Weberian distinctions, the moral actions of the residents
were not purely affective or habitual, but value-rational in the sense that their
actions were calculated to defend their values; furthermore, their actions were
not merely value-rational, but arguably motivated by self-interested reasons.
While defense of social values sometimes took the form of moral absolutes
without regard to worldly benefits, they were also frequently couched in instrumental terms. Moreover, the logic behind preserving cultural values drew
heavily on tangible material and social implications. In this sense, there was
not a stark contrast between the moral opposition of the anti-Apple side and

the more explicit economic rationales used by the pro-Apple forces. Those who opposed Apple employed conventional instrumental reasoning, rooted in social and material interests, to justify maintenance of the norms and values of their community.

EVALUATING INFORMATION AND REASONING ABOUT MEANS AND ENDS

Judging from news accounts, one would assume that many Williamson County residents were torn by the Apple issue once it was broadened to encompass both economic and social dimensions. The media invariably reported that residents were choosing morality over economic benefits on the assumption that people passed up obvious economic benefits in order to hold the line against homosexuality. Greg Boatright explained after the first vote that "it boiled down to weighing economics against moral and family issues. Common sense tells you homosexuality is a perverted lifestyle; it just goes against nature completely. I'm not going to vote for something that violates my conscience."[27]

Actual psychological turmoil, however, appears to have been less common than was suggested by media accounts. One reason, as we have seen, is that people had a tendency to limit their attention to either the economic or moral dimension. Consistent with what we know about public opinion formation, people deliberately set aside certain considerations while giving priority to other aspects of the issue that were of higher priority to them.[28] But an equally significant factor is that few opponents of Apple felt that they would actually fare worse economically if their side prevailed. Likewise, few supporters believed in the dire social and moral consequences of accepting Apple. Not everyone, in other words, agreed to the same stipulations of fact.

Owing in part to their competing belief systems, there were sharp disparities in how people assessed the costs and benefits of the Apple project, with people emphasizing the benefits associated with their position and downplaying the costs. Observations that people were severely conflicted between morality and economics therefore may be overdrawn, since there may have been few instances in which people were torn by the issue. The image of a community divided remains accurate even though perhaps not many individuals were cross-pressured by the decision.

Through either of two routes—framing of choices and selective interpretation of information—people simplified their decisions. By using these shortcuts, people tended to make up their minds early and to stick with their views—David Hays being the most striking exception. But Hays was a public figure whose views were subject to scrutiny and who was targeted for public pressure because of his pivotal political role. Left to his own devices, before feeling the weight of social pressure, he thought that Apple should receive the abatement and that moral concerns were irrelevant.

Ironically, it was Hays—widely criticized for blowing in the wind—who offered one of the better examples of someone who open-mindedly weighed the arguments and evidence as best he could before making his decision. The only problem he had was that the arguments on *both* sides sounded so persuasive. According to Hays, other citizens had talked exclusively with their small circles of friends. Hays feels that if they had shared his vantage point and heard all the arguments, then they would have drawn the same conclusion that he did: "Of course, they don't have that luxury of hearing everything and seeing everything. . . . All they know is what they're reading in such and such paper."

In retrospect, Hays feels that it is very important to explore whether a company has any controversial elements and, if it does, to address them. He believes that companies need to devote resources to inform the public and to build good public relations in the community. Hays is a champion of the idea that people make decisions based on the facts they have about their alternatives; in his view, the same input of facts leads to the identical conclusion: "A lot of times, [the people] don't have enough facts to really know what's right. If they had the facts that you had, then they would understand, and would probably vote the same way you did."

Ideology and Information

In practice, *pace* Hays, there appears to be a strong relationship between people's prior beliefs and values and the kinds of information that they find credible. Prior values and ideological beliefs also affected people's inferences about the likely effects of different policies. Proponents therefore envisioned very different scenarios regarding economic and social costs and benefits than did opponents. Even the county commissioners, who had access to much the same information, saw the issue in markedly different terms, depending on their inclination.

Apple supporter Phil Brewer, for example, offered a detailed description of how Apple dollars brought into the community would have a substantial multiplier effect: the tax base is broadened, schools are helped, payrolls are increased, money is funneled to stores in the community, other retail outlets will be attracted to the area, leading to further improvements in the tax base. He cannot see any costs to the county.

Commercial developer and realtor Frank Warzetha similarly had no difficulty assessing costs and benefits, because they were so lopsided in his mind:

"The cost is actually nil. Anything that the county gives up in tax abatements, you're making back so many times over in taxes on property, taxes on the goods and services that the people who are employed by any company purchase, property taxes on the houses that they own or on the apartments that are built for them. They purchase cars; they purchase gas; they purchase groceries. Any abatements are actually quite nil, when you figure it out."

Many Apple supporters were worried about the long-range impact of denying the abatement. Besides losing Apple, they feared that the county would also lose future businesses, which might decide to locate elsewhere rather than face community opposition. One letter writer advised Hays: "Hire a public relations firm that can begin to dig Williamson County out of the hole you have put us in."

Warzetha was unpersuaded by the opposition's position: "There was only one [counterargument]—it was their policy toward domestic partners. That's something that just isn't widely tolerated in this area. There were just two arguments; one for and one against; very cut and dried. As long as there are no harmful side effects to having this particular company here—I don't consider their domestic partner insurance policy to be a harmful side effect."

Like Warzetha, Judge John Doerfler downplayed any claims that Apple's entry would cause the size of the homosexual population to increase significantly in the county: "I think people were lying to themselves if they were saying that we don't have homosexuals in Williamson County already. If they think also that if you get Apple Computer in here that has a domestic partner policy, that we're just going to be inundated with same-sex partners. . . . Those who were denying that we had same-sex partners in Williamson County anyway were just lying to themselves and to other people. Apple Computer had about 14,000 employees worldwide, the way I understand it. And of that 14,000, less than 1 percent were same-sex partners that were in that policy."

Opponents of Apple, who searched the issue for its moral implications, did not feature economic considerations in their decision making. Those who did downplayed the number of new jobs that would be created by the Apple development. They argued that, because Apple would be moving from a temporary customer service facility in Austin, many of the jobs in the permanent facility would already be occupied by current employees who now lived in the area. Few opponents mentioned that money spent on the Apple complex would benefit the region indirectly by increasing spending in the local economy, adding construction jobs, stimulating housing construction, and so forth. The opposition discounted any benefits they did acknowledge because they felt these benefits would be more than offset by Apple's receiving tax relief for several years. Lastly, they rejected arguments that losing Apple would discourage other businesses from coming to Williamson County

A good illustration of the discrepancy between the two sides is how different commissioners viewed the Perryman Report, which estimated that the Apple complex would bring substantial primary and secondary economic benefits to the community. Whereas Heiligenstein, Doerfler, and Hays gave considerable credence to the report, Commissioner Mehevec discounted its findings: "I've seen [Perryman's] studies before and, you know, basically, . . . [it's] just like an expert witness. You can get an expert witness to say whatever you want. I didn't give a whole lot of credit to his study."

Similarly, Mayor Dorothy Duckett could not fathom what the benefits were: "It had no benefits whatsoever to us, the county. It's in Austin city limits. Even though there may have been fiscal benefits, I felt like the issue involved would not be worth what we would be giving up. Because again, I saw what was driving this thing and that got lost in all of this jobs thing."

The opposition foresaw a variety of economic costs that the pro-Apple side rarely mentioned. They identified the added burden on social services—schools, emergency medical service, law and order—that they believed would accompany the Apple development. Hence, the costs of growth would exceed its benefits. Commissioner Mehevec expounded that companies like Apple attract a "transit" population that brings troubles to a community: "We had a boom in the early eighties and it kind of busted out in 1984. . . . Well, after the boom busted, these people were without jobs; they hung around and pretty soon they became lawbreakers. It really puts this county in a bind because we were stuck now with a bunch of lawbreakers. . . . A transit population moves a lot between jobs. . . . They have a tendency to have a higher degree of divorce in families, there'll be children from more than one marriage, there might be two marriages or three marriages, with my kids, your kids, and our kids. That starts causing a lot of problems in . . . our juvenile justice system. . . . Too much growth is bad, and the people—this transit group that moves around—they come in here, and they demand too many services for the amount of weight that they carry in their [taxes]. And so, over the years, I saw that growth doesn't pay for itself."

Another recurring theme is that Apple will attract homosexuals who will bring AIDS to the community and saddle it with astronomical health-care costs. Dorothy Duckett drew this scenario: "As an elected official, I am charged with the safety and the welfare and the health of the community. And I could not in good conscience see bringing anything in here, be it Apple or any group whatever, that was going to or that might in any way endanger the safety, health and welfare of the community. The whole issue was the gay community. Why would you want to do anything—grant any abatements, give any incentive to bring people in here that you knew carried the HIV infectious diseases. Why would you want to attract that group of people into your community? So any monetary benefit you might gain to me would be more than offset with this possible aspect."

Commissioner Mehevec drew a similarly dire implication: "Our city got ten people over here living an honest life and so you create four jobs, but these four or five contaminate these ten. So what do you get?" Therefore, even in terms of simple economic costs and benefits, many opponents of Apple denied that the decision to bring Apple to Williamson County was good business.

ARE THE CITIZENS OF WILLIAMSON COUNTY ACTING IN THEIR SELF-INTEREST?

Whether people's choices in the Apple controversy were rational or, more narrowly, in their self-interest depends on several conceptual issues.[29] First, do we make an objective analysis of the costs and benefits of different alternatives or use people's subjective assessments? Second, can it be in one's self-interest to pursue social goals such as cultural values, lifestyle, and community harmony in addition to material benefits? And third, are people required to use information optimally in reasoning from means to ends, or does rational choice merely refer to making decisions based on the information that one possesses, even if one's information and inferential processes are flawed?

In objective terms, it appears from a distance that the residents of Williamson County stood to benefit from the decision to attract Apple into the county. New employment created by the proposed customer service center would only be the most apparent direct benefit. The Apple development would also bring additional county tax revenues, stimulate the construction industry, increase consumer spending in local stores, and create various other indirect benefits. The Perryman Report predicted an overall economic stimulus of $200 million.

While everyone stood to benefit from the general economic stimulus to the region, some people—realtors, developers, contractors, shop owners, and others in the business community—were undoubtedly in a better position to profit from the development. According to rational choice theory, we would expect those people with the largest economic interest to be Apple's strongest backers. Certainly people in Williamson County perceived that the business community supported Apple more strongly than did any other group (though, as we have seen, local perceptions have to be taken with a grain of salt). Phil Brewer, who is probably a more reliable source on this point, recalls that there was almost unanimous support in the Round Rock Chamber of Commerce:

"Our Chamber membership had over 400 members. I think that's a pretty good random sample of the community. . . . The majority of the folks wanted Apple to be here. . . . Nine-tenths of my board wanted Apple Computer here. Ninety-eight percent plus of my Century Club wanted it—from the presidents of banks, to the CEO's and manufacturers in this community, to the insurance salesman down the street. I think that's a pretty good cross-section of the community; and they're all saying 'Yeah, we agree Apple needs to be here.' "

Therefore, of the substantial minority in the county who opposed granting tax breaks to Apple, it could be argued that on objective grounds—if we accept the terms of the Perryman Report—they were not acting in their best economic interests. However, in subjective terms, as our interviews brought out, Apple's detractors tended not to accept the same economic analysis as those supporting Apple. They saw fewer benefits, and they identified a host of economic repercussions that were not recognized by the other side.

The opposition was also driven by religious and moral concerns that outweighed any economic benefits they did acknowledge. Regular church attenders approved the first vote by a 45 to 43 margin in contrast to a 25 to 64 margin among those who rarely attend church. Many Apple opponents framed the issue exclusively in moral terms and relegated economic considerations to the background. Prominent in their minds were the threats and dangers associated with allowing disruptive elements into the community.

As was noted earlier, there are differences in the degree to which people think strategically about religious matters. Some individuals automatically translate their religious beliefs into political stances without engaging in broader calculation. They have been socialized to adhere to their values and have developed a deep emotional attachment to them. Consequently, they may think their values are superior without being able to provide elaborate reasons other than that they believe what they believe.

But what underlies such moral and religious values? What is the role of religion in political decision making and political participation, and what is the mechanism that explains how religious values affect political behavior? While the business side's economic interests tend not to require explanation— we naturally assume that people with a monetary stake in a policy will be more likely to support it—analysis of the anti-Apple side's motives is more complicated, because religious motives are not as straightforwardly explained as are economic interests.

Studies comparing the effects of self-interest and so-called symbolic motives on policy positions have not focused specifically on how religious values are traded off against self-interest; however, they have interpreted how similar kinds of general values (such as ideology, nationalism, political partisanship, and racial prejudice) affect policy preferences. These studies do not give substantial weight to the instrumental reasoning that people use when they connect these values to policies. Instead the mechanism is purported to be emotional and affective.[30]

Concerns about protecting a moral or religious consensus and way of life are typically placed outside the purview of self-interested action on the grounds that self-interested behavior is materially rather than expressively oriented and is epitomized by means-ends instrumentality.[31] Investigation of the Apple controversy, however, shows us that many people also readily connect their moral and psychological motives to tangible social, political, and economic consequences. Those who are attuned to politics are especially likely to appreciate that conflicts over social and moral norms are laden with strategic implications. Political activism on moral issues therefore emanates partly from recognition of the real political consequences of those issues.

We should consider two complementary answers to the question of why people are attracted to and defend religious beliefs. First, as I discussed in chapters 2 and 3, people have an interest in coordinating around an agreed upon system of beliefs. Ideologies, political and national identifications, racial identities, and religious belief systems all serve this goal. Values define people's intentions and reveal their preferences and goals to others. A value consensus in a community provides the basis for social coordination, coalition formation, communication, and collective action.

Second, a religious belief system contains special kinds of rewards that are unavailable through alternative secular belief systems, namely promises of rewards in the hereafter. People invest in religious activity in return for the benefits of an afterlife and insight into the meaning of their lives and other metaphysical matters. Church membership is also a route to friendship and leisure activities.[32] In Williamson County, the nonsecular rewards that accrue from battling immorality are augmented by other more mundane secular, political, and social rewards that result from, say, going to church picnics and controlling school board elections.

Although many of Apple's opponents remark that money is not everything (thus implying that they are giving up some) and defend their position on moral grounds, it is hard to interpret their actions as making a personal sacrifice. They were not taking actions on behalf of others that were contrary to their own desires, nor, given their understanding of the ramifications of their choice, were they doing anything but what they thought was best for themselves. In this respect, they are not so different from the proponents of Apple. Nevertheless, rational choice models of decision making cannot be successfully applied to these cases unless they factor in social goals, like group coordination and social harmony, that people pursue in conjunction with their economic interests. Social goals also figure in the decisions of Apple supporters.

Many people were willing to support Apple only so long as their decision was interpreted as a business decision rather than as a vote—against the majority view—for broadening homosexual rights.

Cultural politics therefore follow interests very much as economic politics do. Intolerance of diversity may stem partly from an aversive emotional reaction to foreign ways, but people also want their cultural practices and beliefs to predominate over other views.[33] Majority groups insist that others live like themselves because they do not wish to relinquish either political power or cultural sovereignty—the two are seen to go hand in hand. In the end, the Apple case is not especially mysterious; it does not require any elaborate stretching of the concept of self-interest. People do what is best for themselves given their beliefs about the bases of social order and material prosperity. The collective interest and the individual interest are in harmony in Williamson County: keeping nonconformity to a minimum ensures that political and economic aspirations can be pursued unhindered.

An essential question remains: How important are the reasons that people give for their decisions? The reasons that people offer for their own actions can enter into decision making in a variety of ways, with each possibility leading to a different interpretation of the balance between affect and cognition in political choice. In the conventional view of attitudes, the reasons that people cite give rise to their affective reactions; attitudes and policy choices are the product of beliefs and arguments.[34] Accordingly, perceptions of social and economic costs and benefits are the reasons why people supported or opposed Apple in Williamson County.

On the other hand, beliefs may follow rather than precede affective reactions. Aversion to homosexuals, for example, may stimulate production of reasons for those feelings (just as people who have their attitudes manipulated under hypnosis will create reasons justifying their new attitudes). Even if the beliefs are generated after the fact, the rationalizations may still intensify the affective reaction and thereby influence attitudes. Beliefs can strengthen attitudes and reinforce actions without necessarily being the reason for the attitudes in the first place. Consequently, people may choose among alternatives based on the beliefs they hold about those alternatives in a manner that mimics rational decision making, but the beliefs themselves may be immune to counterevidence, or they may be based on interpretations of evidence that do not follow the rules of probability.

Both sides in the Apple dispute showed the kinds of perceptual biases that are well documented in the psychological literature on social cognition.[35] Opponents of Apple perceived a correlation between homosexuality and AIDS, crime, pornography, and licentiousness. They believed that Christianity was a necessary condition for economic growth and social order. They saw few economic benefits in the Apple project. Proponents of Apple, on the other hand, did not commonly measure costs associated with economic and population growth such as pressure on the school system, crowding, and a weakening of community bonds. They dismissed what they considered to be a small, vocal minority that resisted development, even though evidence suggested that almost 40 percent of the population opposed abatements for Apple and an even larger percentage condemned homosexuality.[36]

Such beliefs nevertheless have an effect on attitudes regardless of whether they are held on faith. Beliefs about the consequences of homosexuals' moving into the community are analogous to beliefs about the effects of immigration or school busing. Such beliefs augment and intensify any purely aversive reaction that people might have to those who are different. The religious, political, and economic ideologies that people hold describe and explain how society works. People rarely have an incentive to change these beliefs, because they ease decision making and facilitate social relationships and harmonious communication.

Whether we choose to call ideologically driven decision making rational is a conceptual matter. At some point, sociological and economic explanations of political choice begin to merge.[37] If people act on their perceptions of consequences and follow the path that they believe to be in their self-interest, but their perceptions are biased and reflect prejudice as much as learning, then the two explanatory models complement each other. None of this suggests that people are employing especially good methods for pursuing their goals. Good decision making is best served by taking account of all of one's goals and recognizing the various alternatives that are available to meet those goals. Good decision making also implies openness to information and evidence about the available alternatives.[38]

In Williamson County, calling people's motives "symbolic" shortchanges the reasoning underlying their choices, yet calling their decisions "rational," in the textbook sense, overstates the objectivity with which they interpret information. Prior values strongly predispose individuals both to favor supporting evidence and to pursue favored courses of action.

CONCLUSION

There is an old joke about a husband and wife explaining their division of labor. She makes all the small routine decisions—plans each night's dinner, chooses the family doctor, picks their church, finds the house they buy, decides on their children's school—whereas she leaves the big decisions up to him, such as whether the United States should recognize Red China.

As ordinary citizens, we have almost no opportunity to influence foreign policy, but the more routine choices and decisions that we make regarding neighborhoods, schools, and religion can markedly affect the quality of our lives. It should come as no surprise, then, that social conflicts in these realms are recurrent. What is surprising, however, is that there has been a tendency to view such conflicts over ways of life, social norms, and religious values as involving essentially symbolic issues and to separate them analytically from economic conflicts over material outcomes. On the contrary, these kinds of conflict, with Williamson County being a prime example, are far from being purely symbolic.

Consensual values may stem from a variety of sources—arbitrary conventions, group specialization, political entrepreneurship, individual and group interest—but all such values, once diffused, become signifiers of group membership and have to be adopted by individuals in the pursuit of their self-interest. Conflict over values is never confined to meddling in other people's beliefs but reflects more worrisome concerns about the implications of those beliefs in the social and political life of the community. Existing social institutions are vulnerable to the influx of new ideas and values. As new behaviors and social customs are manifest in everyday life, the economic and political balance is likely to be upset. The Williamson County controversy offers a contemporary perspective on how such tensions develop.

CHAPTER SIX

Mass Adjustment to New Norms

Every new adjustment is a crisis in self-esteem.
Eric Hoffer, *The Ordeal of Change*

Many citizens of Williamson County frown upon nearby Austin's tolerant culture, but they are content to live and let live, since they are not forced to adopt that lifestyle and they have Austin's amenities at their disposal when they choose to take advantage of them. But when that culture threatens to be transported northward, they worry that their social norms and conventions will be disrupted and that their control over the community's values and priorities may be challenged.

People are inclined to defend norms that operate on their behalf. For example, the extension of the norm of equality to include formerly excluded groups is due mainly to those groups' acquiring sufficient political power to challenge the old order. Rather than voluntarily concede power, dominant groups lose their capacity to maintain existing social institutions in the face of pressure applied by new political forces.

The transition to new norms can be made with relative ease, or it can be marked with conflict and social division. In this chapter, I will examine the factors that affect compliance with new social norms, focusing especially on perhaps the quintessential case of social change in American society in this century—the transformation of social and legal norms governing race relations. When the Supreme Court invalidated segregated schools in 1954 and when Congress passed landmark civil rights legislation in the 1960s, there was a great hue and cry in many parts of the country, as well as active defiance of the new laws. What is striking, therefore—given the vehemence of those who opposed reform at the time—is the degree to which these changes promoting racial equality have, over the course of two to three decades, become accepted throughout American society.

Public opinion polls conducted in the early 1940s showed that a majority of Americans backed racial segregation in schools, restaurants, and on streetcars and buses. In the South, there was practically unanimous support among whites for segregation in these and other realms.[1] Over the next twenty years, however, both northern and southern white opinion was transformed dramatically. By 1963, a majority of white northerners supported racial integration in schools, neighborhoods, and in public transportation. Support for integration in schools among white southerners increased over this time span from 2 percent to over 30 percent; support for integrated public transportation rose from 4 percent to 52 percent; and support for integrated neighborhoods grew from 12 percent to close to 50 percent. Given the southern consensus on segregation in the 1940s, Hyman and Sheatsley concluded that "the greatly increased support for integration must have come mainly from segregationists who switched to the opposite camp."[2]

By the mid-1970s, a scant twenty years after *Brown v. Board of Education of Topeka,* support for integration of public schools had reached 85 percent, and today it approaches unanimity. Add to this the abundant evidence showing that the "social distance" separating whites and blacks diminished significantly in the same time frame, as substantially larger proportions of whites claimed to be comfortable with racial integration in restaurants, churches, residential neighborhoods, and hotels.[3]

Many of the questions asked in postwar surveys to gauge racial tolerance deal with how whites *feel* about blacks as much as with their views about equal rights. The answers reflect people's underlying racial attitudes and not simply their willingness to comply with new legal and social norms of racial equality. For example, whites are asked whether blacks should have the right to do certain things (to move into any neighborhood, to share the same buses and trains, etc.) as well as whether they "mind" or "object to" racial integration. So what some of their responses appear to indicate is not only that they are more willing to *comply* with changing norms than they were formerly but that their *attitudes toward the norms* have also been transformed in the process.[4]

A change in racial attitudes has therefore occurred in little more than a generation that is larger in magnitude than could have been produced by generational replacement or migration of northerners into the South; the transformation of the South clearly reflects individual level change by "former segregationists whose senses and consciences have been touched by the Negro protest, or who have simply changed their opinions as segregation appears increasingly to be a lost cause."[5] As Americans have grown older, their attitudes on racial matters have progressed with the times. In their report on the status of racial attitudes in the late 1970s, Taylor, Sheatsley, and Greeley reiterate Hyman and Sheatsley's earlier conclusion that a sizable portion of the increase in support for racial integration "represents actual modification of attitudes on the part of older people."[6]

To be sure, there is still much room for improvement in racial tolerance. The color line collapsed most rapidly in the most impersonal and abstract realm of society involving public spaces and legal rights for black citizens, such as the right to vote and to have equal access to public accommodations. The color line has proved more resistant on matters of employment and housing and in interpersonal relations between blacks and whites.

There is also evidence that the expression of racial prejudice has been diverted underground. In place of openly racist views, people now substitute code words and other symbols to signal their racial antipathies.[7] A team of researchers led by Patricia Devine has written that "many people appear to be in the process of prejudice reduction. A necessary first step is the adoption of nonprejudicial standards. Fully overcoming the 'prejudice habit' presents a more formidable task and is likely to entail a great deal of internal conflict over a protracted period of time."[8] But Devine and her coauthers are confident that the public renunciation of prejudice is an important advance even if many people still harbor lingering prejudicial feelings. Therefore, while part of the increase in racial tolerance may be discounted because some respondents are only capitulating to social pressures—saying what is socially acceptable while concealing prejudices—the balance of the evidence indicates that many Americans have at least partly adjusted to the idea of a more integrated society. Opposition to the idea of racial integration has eroded while acceptance of the new norms and legal standards has strengthened.

INCENTIVES AND DISPOSITIONS (REPRISED)

Despite the enduring problems of race relations that remain in this country, the transformations that have occurred demonstrate the potential to change entrenched values and routines of social interaction. These changes are all-the-more remarkable given the pessimism that plagues discussions of race in American society. Nicholas Lemann reflects that "thinking about the history of American race relations can easily give rise to bitterness and fatalism, but it is encouraging to remember how often in the past a hopeless situation, which appeared to be completely impervious to change, finally did change for the better. The framers of the Constitution, idealists though they were, couldn't imagine an American nation without slavery—but in the long run slavery was ended. In this century legal segregation looked like an unfortunate given, impossible to eliminate, until well after the end of World War II. That black America could become predominantly middle class, non-Southern, and non-agrarian would have seemed inconceivable until a bare two generations ago."[9]

It is worth detailing the basic individual and social elements affecting the outcome of this tug of war between old and new norms of race relations. The pursuit of racial equality struck at the heart of the southern identity and belief system, so we would not expect native white southerners to convert readily to a new racial orthodoxy.[10] Opposition to change, however, reflects not merely habitual resistance but also the investment embodied in socialization to a particular repertoire of beliefs, values, and behaviors that permit successful adjustment to society. This investment, unfortunately, cannot be easily shifted, the way a financial investment can be taken out of an existing account and reinvested in a more profitable instrument. Instead, the learning that occurs in political socialization is deep-seated and resistant to change precisely because it shapes investments in personal development and social relationships that may be difficult to redirect under a new system of norms.

It may also be true, however, as was emphasized in the symbolic politics research, that socialization teaches a person to draw associations and to respond to stimuli in ways that cannot be easily erased or extinguished by contemporary events. To unlearn and relearn something may be much more difficult than to learn something new, since old habits and tendencies have to be suppressed even though they have proved functional for long periods of one's life. A model of social change therefore should be able to accommodate both this sort of *psychological resistance* to social and cultural change, and the *economic responsiveness* of individuals to changes in incentive. Whereas the first factor adds friction to the process of change, the other acts as a kind of lubricant by easing adjustment and adaptation to new ways of living. By taking both motivations into account, we can get a handle on why values are often stubbornly resistant to modification and when they are likely to change.

The extraordinary effort mounted by diehard segregationists to prevent defection from the ranks of the traditional South is, ipso facto, evidence that at least some southerners were inclined to shift their views in line with the more progressive norms. If attitudes are a function of deep-seated racial resentment rather than social and political calculations, and if racial resentment is stable and does not respond readily to the social and political environment, then why was it necessary to exert such extraordinary pressure on people to remain true to the old ways? It must have been because some southerners saw that it was no longer worthwhile to defend the old norms, that there were reasons to change, not least of which that it would be extremely disruptive to southern communities to continue resisting social protest and federal laws promoting greater racial equality. Social change, on this view, depends on altering the normative incentives and conventions of southern society so that individuals are rewarded for racially tolerant as opposed to intolerant values and actions.

The model developed in this chapter to explain such transformations builds on the model developed in chapter 2 to show how new norms and values gain popular support. The premise of the model is that norms not only alter the costs and benefits of different options but also change people's preferences by shaping their feelings and beliefs about the substance of the norm and their expectations about other people's reactions.[11] Norms affect behavior directly by changing incentives, but they also instigate social and psychological adjustment to social change by causing people to adapt their social relations and tastes to the prevailing norms. Normative pressures can therefore offset countervailing social and psychological dispositions favoring the old norm.

SOCIAL ADJUSTMENT TO NEW NORMS AND PRACTICES

In the early 1980s, in the New England fishing town of Gloucester, Massachusetts, members of the Unification Church—known pejoratively as Moonies—purchased prime waterfront property in what appeared to be an effort to take over the local fishing industry. The townspeople were alarmed: they professed that they feared for their livelihoods, but they also undoubtedly felt threatened by the arrival of what they considered to be a weird religious group. The mayor, Leo Alpert, said, "I felt we were being invaded," and town leaders took steps to preserve the status quo by restricting church activities. A drawn-out legal battle followed, which was finally resolved when the church agreed to pay the town for municipal services and to follow town regulations concerning the use of property it had bought. In reasonably short order, the settlement normalized the relationship and left the two sides fairly amicable: "Now the town seems to have accepted the Unification Church members, however grudgingly, and many local lobstermen bring their catch to the International Seafood Company, owned and operated by Unification Church members."

In the meantime, day-to-day contact between the church members and the townspeople also appears to have helped. Greg Dishman, sales manager at the lobster plant, explained that "people are getting to know that we're not robots or zombies. We're real people like anyone else." This recognition has made Gloucester "calmer on Moon's followers." Whereas only a few years earlier the town had been up in arms over the prospect of "Moonies" in their midst, "in a recent mayoral election the subject never came up."[12]

The Gloucester story illustrates an important *adjustment process* in society that is central to the transformation of social norms and practices. People change their attitudes in response to changes in social relations and institutions. They change not only their attitudes but also their moral reactions and emotional sensitivities to the behavior in question. Changes in the norm can alter *both* social relations and how people feel about the behavior prescribed by the norm. Evidently, this occurred in Gloucester, where the citizens gradually adapted to the presence of the church members in their town until they were hardly bothered by them. The town recognized the agreement that civic leaders negotiated with the church, accepted—albeit reluctantly—members of the Unification Church into their community, and gradually relaxed when, contrary to expectations and fears, church members did not overrun the town and did not prove to be as strange as they were first made out to be.

The adjustment process is similar to cognitive dissonance reduction, as well as to the notion of "sour grapes," but I intend it to be more inclusive than either of these ideas.[13] Dissonance reduction and rationalization are among the many (not particularly rational) ways in which people adapt to new circumstances. When it became apparent there was nothing they could do, some of Gloucester's citizens probably resigned themselves to the idea of having Unification Church members for neighbors and tried to make the best of a bad situation. They might have looked for evidence that the church members were good and decent people, not too different from themselves, or they might have denied being upset about the issue in the first place.

Yet it appears there was more to the adjustment process than can be explained by either dissonance reduction or rationalization. People's attitudes about what is right and normal are shaped by the prevailing norms and conventions of society. New social norms are rendered less strange and threatening in the course of people's experiences with them. The norms prompt new patterns of social interaction that change attitudes. In Gloucester, the townspeople seem to have corrected a number of misconceptions they once held about Unification Church members and to have developed a measure of regard for them. Revised assessment therefore seems to have contributed as much to the change in Gloucester as rationalization. This has left Gloucester's citizens less aggrieved, "calmer."[14]

What happened in Gloucester happens in varying degree all the time in our society as new social and legal norms lead people to accept arrangements they once opposed. The essential idea behind social adjustment is that changes in the norms alter behavior as well as popular sentiments. People regard their current norms and conventions as being normal, right, and superior to alternatives. But if they are reoriented to an alternative set of conventions and norms, they have a tendency to see those new standards to be proper and normal also. When smoking in restaurants and public buildings used to be the norm, people did not think twice when someone lit a cigarette in their presence. Now that smoking in public buildings is widely prohibited, people are more likely to regard such restrictions as being appropriate. When metal detectors were first implemented in airports, they struck passengers as an unusual intrusion—the ACLU argued that they violated a traveler's right to privacy—now they are taken for granted as an essential component of airport security.

As marches, rallies, demonstrations, sit-ins, pickets, and other less conventional forms of political participation became commonplace in the 1960s and

1970s and were placed under the umbrella of the First Amendment, they also became less controversial to the public. Public familarity with these tactics combined with the new norms associated with them removed much of their power to shock and outrage the public. By no means have the groups behind these activities been embraced by the public, but, as Erskine and Siegel aptly remarked, even though "broad hostility toward particular groups of protesters has often been manifest, the questioning of authority has become a more integral part of the political process."[15] People therefore tolerate more diverse types of political protest than in the past because they have come to regard such activities as a legitimate component of democratic politics. As Anthony Lewis noted in a commentary on the establishment of new rights and liberties, "Doctrines seen as radical when they first appear have a way of turning out to feel familiar and right."[16]

Perhaps no subject more vividly demonstrates the capacity of people to adapt psychologically to new standards and norms than on matters related to sex and morality. Whether the issue is sex education, the availability of birth control, censorship, premarital sex, homosexuality, prostitution, nudity, or simple candor, as social standards and practices have become more permissive and lenient, the public has adjusted its own moral sensibilities.[17] In every generation, there have been sexual taboos and customs that cause great consternation when they are violated (e.g., teaching about sex to schoolchildren, using foul language in public, cohabiting out of wedlock, wearing skimpy bathing suits, residing in coed dormitories). But to the extent that these taboos are widely ignored in practice, or contravened by new laws or policies that relax sanctions and prohibitions, as occurred in the course of the "sexual revolution" in this country, then each violation becomes less noteworthy and less shocking to the observer. Tolerance increases, and shock decreases, with the proliferation of a phenomenon that once flabbergasted the public but is now taken for granted.

One of the best illustrations of this process is the manner in which the public has adapted to increasingly lenient standards of censorship. In every era, there are materials that society considers to be so offensive that they are banned from public circulation. However, the words and images that raised the hackles of the public at the turn of the century, or in the 1950s and 1960s, do not have the same emotional impact today. For this reason, the types of material subject to censorship in different periods are an excellent indicator of how moral sensibilities regarding sex and sexuality have been radically transformed.[18] Both the legal and popular definitions of obscenity have changed to such an extent that, as Lawrence Tribe put it, "What was once beyond the pale rests comfortably on today's living-room end table."[19] With only slight exaggeration, we might say that, currently, "anything goes." Today's sexual attitudes make prosecutions on obscenity charges exceedingly difficult to obtain.[20]

Obviously, a sexual revolution in tastes and sensibilities has occurred as the permissiveness of American society has increased as a whole. Our reactions to the same ideas, words, images, and pictures have not remained constant.[21] People have, to varying degrees, accommodated themselves to these new sexual and moral standards and are not simply grudgingly conforming to more liberal norms. Norms have been relaxed, accompanied by changes in behavior and sentiments. Much of today's tolerance of the "new morality" therefore is a product of social-psychological adjustment rather than self-restraint.[22]

A MODEL OF SOCIAL ADJUSTMENT

The general case of social change that I want to discuss in this chapter involves the introduction of a new norm that is endorsed by some, but not all, groups in society, so that there are problems of compliance. For example, in the transition from racial segregation to racial desegregation in schools and public accommodations, new legal norms did not result immediately in compliance, nor did the compliance revealed necessarily reflect attitudinal support for the new norm.

Imagine that, in some initial state, there is a close correspondence between the norm R guiding choices and behavior in a given realm and actual choices and behavior, and that attitudes toward R are favorable. This is therefore a relatively harmonious arrangement in which people are conforming closely to the norm and they are comfortable doing so. What if there is a disturbance to the system that shifts the norm from R to L? Behavior may follow in quick succession once information diffuses that L is the new norm that everyone is now coordinating around. Revised expectations about how people are supposed to act alter behavior accordingly.

By the same token, attitude change may correspond to behavioral change, so that favorable attitudes are developed toward L, just as attitudes toward R were favorable when R rather than L constituted the norm. When there is no inherent attachment to one norm or the other—that is, when there is no underlying disposition that resists change—the only hitch in making the transition from R to L is in the efficiency with which people recognize that L is the new norm; but this difficulty may be eased if there is some central coordination provided by an opinion leader or a trend setter.[23]

But many of the transformations in social norms that have been discussed are not easily accomplished, because people develop an attachment to an existing system of norms. They make decisions based on this system of norms that may subsequently make it difficult for them to take advantage of the new norms. They envision that their norms are instrumental to economic growth and social order. The new norms call for a change in behavior that may require retraining or resocialization, or the old norms may simply be biased in their favor. Any transition to a new norm will run into opposition as long as people feel they will suffer a loss of opportunity or welfare under the new system. The magnitude of opposition depends not only on the stakes at hand but also on the extent to which those inclined to resist change can coordinate their opposition.

However, to the extent that new norms have causal force, through sanctions or through coordination of choices, then people may find it in their interest to comply with the new norms. As compliance increases, people engage in new social and economic relations; if those relations are beneficial, people will develop more favorable attitudes toward the new institutions and have less incentive to resist them. Whether attitudes change depends critically on whether individuals are persuaded that the new norm will prevail and whether they can take advantage of the opportunities made available to them by the new system. If we suppose that attitudes cannot change—in the sense of psychological inflexibility or constraints in personal resources and investments— then the only path to compliance is through increasing sanctions. People will have to be dragged reluctantly to a new equilibrium. My point is that such resistance to the new norm diminishes as people adjust their behavior and their attitudes to the new standard.

The process by which society adapts to new social norms and practices can be represented by a series of formal equations. Once again I will evaluate a dynamic system centering on three factors—the state of the norm, N; the state of people's attitudes or dispositions toward the norm, A; and C, their compliance with, or choices with respect to, the norm, given the incentives they face. The new feature I have added to the model is a set of parameters to take account of factors affecting changes in each of these three elements. Also, in contrast to the discussion of the model in earlier chapters, which focused on individual decision making, I will now be referring to the average, or mean, states of groups and communities.

The model assumes that N, C, and A can all be located in relation to one another on the same underlying continuum. This is an abstraction, but a reasonable assumption if we consider that norms, attitudes, and behavior in any particular realm can often be characterized as being more or less permissive, more or less tolerant, more or less liberal or conservative. To be sure, some realms may require more than one dimension to represent the competing normative positions, and some realms may be more accurately characterized by several discrete alternatives rather than by a continuum of positions, so we are exercising a degree of abstraction as well as licence in the mathematical model.

Because there is no natural metric in the model, I have arbitrarily selected parameter values that keep the system values bounded between 0 and $+1.0$ or, in one illustration below, between 0 and -1.0. Substantively, it might be easier to follow the dynamics of the model if we think of increasing values as indicating change in the liberal direction and decreasing values as change in the conservative direction; but the reader may choose the reverse designation if he or she finds that easier to remember. All of the analysis of the model will focus on whether attitudes and behavior adapt to the norm.

Suppose we set the value of the current norm, N, equal to 0 in period n. Assume further that compliance, C, with the norm is perfect (i.e., $C_n = 0$) and that people have a favorable disposition or attitude, A, toward the norm (i.e., $A_n = 0$). Current behavior is therefore in harmony with both the norm and underlying dispositions. As before, dispositions reflect how people would prefer to behave if there were no external incentives.

Next, let us assume that there is pressure to change the norm, N, from 0 to 1 according to the process represented by the following equation:

$$N_{n+1} - N_n = s + m(C_n - N_n). \tag{1}$$

Equation (1) states that there is pressure to move N away from its current value. The value of the norm is not constant but varies across time periods, depending on two factors. The constant term, s, stands for *social forces* pushing for a change in the norm—opinion leaders and political entrepreneurs, social movements, court rulings. These are various kinds of exogenous forces that influence the direction in which the norms change. Efforts to change the norm, however, are tempered by the degree to which people comply with the norm. To the extent that there is a discrepancy between the new norm and popular practice, there is countervailing *mass pressure*, corresponding to the size of m, to rein in the new norm by bringing N in line with C.

Equation (1) therefore states that popular behavior places a constraint on movement of the norm. On the other hand, equation (2) assumes that popular behavior will, in turn, be cross-pressured by the conflicting incentives (e and r, respectively) to follow either the new norm or the old norm:

$$C_{n+1} - C_n = e(N_n - C_n) - r(C_n - A_n). \tag{2}$$

A new norm might be enforced by legal sanctions as well as by social pressure, or its power may reside in the information embodied in the norm about what people can expect others to do. To the extent that people deviate from the new norm ($C < N$), there is pressure on them, represented by the coefficient e (for *enforcement*), to change their behavior.

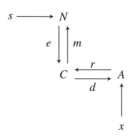

Figure 6.1. Dynamics of norms, compliance, and attitudes

The second component of equation (2) indicates that people have opposing incentives, r, to behave consistently with their original preference for the old norm. Underlying attitudes must change in the direction of the norm, or else compliance will be coerced. When $A = C$, compliance is given without reservation, but when $C > A$, there is a discrepancy between people's attitudes and their behavior, which causes them to resist conformity to the norm, with the magnitude of that resistance being indexed by the coefficient r. The intensity of resistance to the norm will depend on the strength of competing social forces working against it. The size of r will therefore vary according to the extent to which people develop the means to coordinate around and enforce conformity to the alternative (old) norm.

Finally, equation (3) completes the dynamic system by stating that people's attitudes change in conjunction with behavioral changes that have been prompted by the new norm.

$$A_n = dC_n + x. \tag{3}$$

The coefficient d captures the rate at which people *adapt* their attitudes to new norms and social practices. Changing the norms therefore changes behavior and shapes public sentiments and feelings. Adjustment reflects increasing comfort and familiarity with a new standard of behavior.

I have also left room for *exogenous* factors, x, to change attitudes. For example, generational replacement is an exogenous factor that increases the adaptability of the population; if we replace resistant older individuals with more flexible younger ones, adaptation to a new system of norms will be accomplished more readily.

Equilibrium

The three equations constitute a dynamic system that is represented by figure 6.1. The norm guides behavior, but behavior in turn can force reconfiguration of the norm. Likewise, attitudes are in a reciprocal relationship with behavior.

Because attitudes respond to behavior (as specified by equation 3), normative changes also influence attitudes depending on the magnitude of the adjustment parameter d. The course that this system takes over time is determined by the relative strengths of the coefficients marking each of the arrows in the path diagram. The values of the coefficients represent the strength of social forces influencing the state of the norm and the incentives and deterrents for people to adjust their attitudes and behavior in response to changing norms. We can gain a better idea of how these coefficients combine to establish the eventual state of the system by examining the properties of the system's equilibrium. Then we can make a comparative static analysis to explore how the system behaves when we perturb the values of the coefficients.

An important issue in the analysis of dynamic systems is whether the system, in the limit, will attain *equilibrium.* There are really two questions involved here: (1) What are the equilibrium values of the system? and (2) Under what conditions or circumstances will the system actually reach those values? Here I will deal only with the first and leave discussion of the second in a note.[24]

The system will be in equilibrium when both $N_{n+1} - N_n$ and $C_{n+1} - C_n$ are equal to 0—when, in other words, the norm and behavior are stable over time. Therefore, to determine the equilibrium values of the system, we simply have to set equations (1) and (2) equal to zero and solve for the values of N and C (which we will designate N^* and C^*) that will satisfy the two equation system:

$$0 = -mN^* + mC^* + s ; \tag{4}$$

$$0 = eN^* + (rd - e - r)C^* + rx. \tag{5}$$

The equilibrium values for N and C bear a close relationship to each other. First,

$$C^* = se/[rm(1 - d)] + x/(1 - d). \tag{6}$$

Then, by substituting C^* into equation (4), rearranging, and canceling terms, we obtain the value of N^*, which is simply

$$N^* = C^* + s/m. \tag{7}$$

These values can be interpreted as follows. Consider first the equilibrium value for the level of compliance. If we assume that $d < 1$ (less than perfect adjustment), and $r, m > 0$ (some incentive to resist and some responsiveness to mass resistance), then $rm(1 - d) > 0$. As a result, the size of C^* will be directly related to the size of the numerators of each component, se and x, and inversely related to the size of the denominators, $rm(1 - d)$ and $(1 - d)$. The numerator of the second component of C^*, x, represents the effect of exogenous factors on the attitudes of the public. The product term, se, is the magnitude of the change in the norms initiated by political entrepreneurs, opinion leaders, collective action, and other agents of social change, multiplied by the degree to which the norms are enforced. Therefore, ceteris paribus, the greater the change initiated by entrepreneurs, and the more vigorously the norms are enforced, the greater the change in behavior. Keep in mind, however, that it is a two-way street and that entrepreneurs can move the norms in either direction, from 0 to $+1$ (when s is positive) or from 0 to -1 (when s is negative).

The denominator of the first component of C^* equals the product of three important factors: r, the incentive to resist the new norm and to abide by the old norm; m, the countervailing pressure that the targets of the norm exert on the norm when their behavior deviates from the norm; and $(1 - d)$, the extent to which the public adjusts its attitudes in conjunction with changes in its compliance with the norm.

The denominator of the second component of C^* is simply $(1 - d)$. Therefore, as the targets of the new norm have greater incentive to defend the old norm (higher r), become more influential (higher m), and are less adaptive to change (lower d), the denominator increases in size and the equilibrium level of compliance is lowered (if $s > 0$), or raised (if $s < 0$).

The equilibrium level of the norms, N^*, is identical to C^* but for the addition of one extra term, s/m. Therefore, the difference between N^* and C^* reflects both the strength of exogenous forces to change the norms and the degree to which the norms are constrained by the extent to which people are willing to comply with the norms.

As people develop new expectations about social behavior, they accommodate themselves in varying degrees to the new norm; their behavior, however, may remain at odds with their underlying attitudes toward the norm. In some realms, it is reasonable to expect that attitudes go hand in hand with conformity in the sense that people are acting in a manner that is consistent with their attitudes. But people sometimes conform reluctantly, capitulating to external pressure despite being ill-disposed toward the norm.

Start with the case in which people have no vested interest in the old norm ($d \to 1$). Consequently, there are no strong incentives to resist conforming or strong pressures to repeal the new norm (r and m are small). Since the only force in the system pushes in the direction of the new norm, people readily comply. For example, what is fashionable changes continually. People with the means and the desire to stay in style will follow the trendsetters in whichever direction they are taken. If s is positive, the norm shifts from 0 toward $+1$ (fig. 6.2); if s is negative, the norm shifts from 0 toward -1 (fig. 6.3); either way, compliance follows.

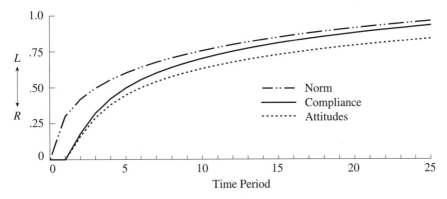

Figure 6.2. Voluntary compliance with a normative change from 0 to 1.0

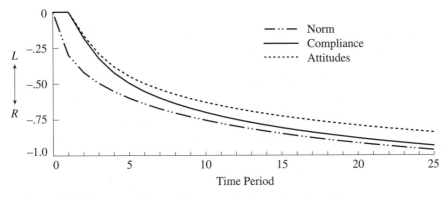

Figure 6.3. Voluntary compliance with a normative change from 0 to −1.0

However, if A is less malleable because the new norm requires some reso-cialization, then the change in the norm will meet with a measure of resistance (fig. 6.4). The United States, for example, has encountered difficulty making the transition from the old British units of measurement to the metric system. Businesses are reluctant to absorb the cost of adopting the new convention; individuals accustomed to thinking in terms of pounds and yards have diffi-culty recalibrating to kilos and meters. As usual, some will have a greater incentive or easier time changing, but unless the pressure to change is suffi-cient, the conversion is partial—and a partial convention is generally an unsuc-cessful convention.

Although the model of adjustment is based on constant system parameters, we can easily add more complexity to the system by allowing the coefficients to vary, either over time or in conjunction with one another. Such variation may be a more realistic approximation of the forces operating in many cases.

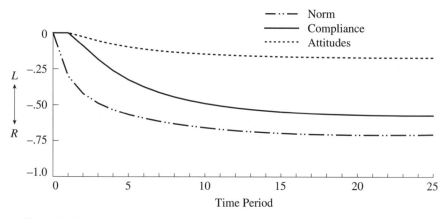

Figure 6.4. Resistance to a new norm

For example, if the *s* coefficient in equation (1) represents the pressure applied by a social movement, the magnitude of this pressure might be assumed to vary over time, depending on the ability of the organizers to keep the movement on track. Similarly, the value of incentives to adhere to the old norm or to switch to the new norm may not remain constant. It may take time for proponents to shore up monitoring and enforcement or for opponents to organize themselves in defense of the old norm. We could also allow the adjustment parameter to vary over time on the assumption that people refrain from changing their attitudes until after they have been exposed to debate over the competing norms.

   In addition to varying over time, there are likely to be circumstances when the parameters are correlated with one another. The cluster of parameters that dampen rates of change might be expected to cohere systematically. The more people are invested in the old norm, the lower the rate of adjustment, the greater the pressure to conform to the old norm, and the greater the reaction against the new norm. The strategy for enforcement must be gauged according to how strongly the new norm is being resisted. Strong opposition may prompt even stronger enforcement measures. Or, alternatively, an accommodation may be reached. For example, the Supreme Court's published guidelines for implementing *Brown* anticipated southern resistance to a speedy desegregation plan.[25] Of course, stronger sanctions may be reciprocated with stepped-up countermobilization (or it may cause the opposition to relent), so that the *e* and *r* parameters may be correlated in practice, positively or negatively. I will not be exploring all of these possibilities but mention them to indicate the flexibility of the model to accommodate a variety of more elaborate parameter specifications.

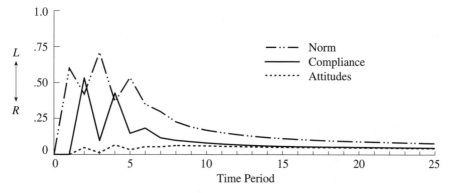

Figure 6.5. Compliance with the norm when adjustment increases over time but enforcement is relaxed

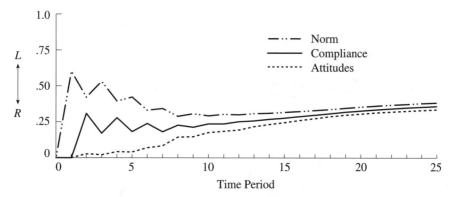

Figure 6.6. Compliance with the norm when both enforcement and adjustment increase over time

If the parameters vary systematically over time, then the outcome of competing efforts to change or defend a norm will depend on whether the right combinations of forces come together at the right time. The importance of concordant forces is evident in the two simulations illustrated by figures 6.5 and 6.6. In both simulations, r and m are set at high levels, while the value of d increases over time from an initially low level to a subsequently high level. The differences between the two simulations are due to fluctuations in e, the level of enforcement. Figure 6.5 depicts the dynamics of the system when e moves inversely to d—that is, when d is high, e is low; but when d is low, e is high. Because r and m reflect strong countervailing pressure in favor of the old norm, behavior does not respond readily to enforcement of the new norm early on when social adjustment is slow, nor does behavior conform later when the rate of adjustment has increased because enforcement is now too lax. In contrast, the simulation represented by figure 6.6 shows

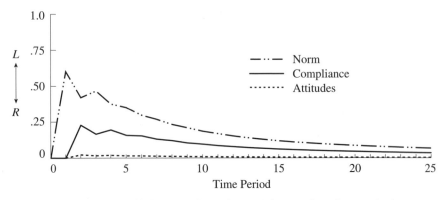

Figure 6.7. Compliance with the norm when enforcement is strong but adjustment is slow

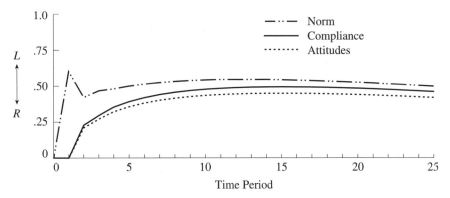

Figure 6.8. Compliance with the norm when enforcement is strong and adjustment is rapid

what happens when the level of enforcement increases alongside the rate of adjustment. When both enforcement and adjustment operate in concert, the forces of resistance, r and m, are eventually overcome and both attitudes and behavior shift markedly in the direction of the new norm.

Some degree of adjustment is critical to change. Otherwise compliance to the new norm is coerced and any reduction in incentives to conform to the new norm results in a reversion of behavior to the previous standard. This point is brought out by the two simulations illustrated in figures 6.7 and 6.8. As before, both simulations assume that there is a tug of war between efforts to enforce the new norm, e, on one side, and incentives and pressure to resist change, r and m, on the other. The outcome of this contest depends on the rate of social adjustment. If the rate of adjustment is low, the system unfolds according to figure 6.7: the new norm changes behavior initially, but because attitudes do not change, there is strong downward pressure in favor of the old norm, making the new norm impossible to maintain. Conversely, as figure 6.8 shows, if the rate of adjustment is high, enforcement of the new norm changes both behavior and attitudes enough to undercut counterpressure against it. The values of N, C, and A all turn upward before eventually stabilizing.

MECHANISMS OF SOCIAL CHANGE

The model indicates that effective organized countermobilization against social change must be forthright; otherwise, compliance with the new norm sets in motion a process of social adjustment to the new standard. According to the model, to produce mass noncompliance, the incentive to resist, r, needs to be maximized at the same time that adjustment, d, is minimized. In addition, m must be large, meaning that mass resistance to sanctions is rewarded by a relaxation of the norms.

On the other hand, compliance with the norm is gained by enforcing sanctions and withstanding counterpressure against the norm. Weak compliance with a legal norm (reflected in a large discrepancy between N and C) produces demands on public officials for a relaxation of the standard. The responsiveness of the system to counterpressure is indexed by the coefficient m. A small m means that officials hold the line against such pressure, and buy enough time for people to accommodate themselves to the new norm. This interlude is critical, as I noted above, if people are not amenable to change until they realize that the new norm will be strictly enforced. If m is sufficiently large, the norm reverts so quickly that people have no reason to change their attitudes and behavior. Therefore, only sustained enforcement of the new norm can eventually produce a sufficiently high rate of attitudinal adjustment to support higher levels of compliance.

The South was especially difficult to change because of the political and social homogeneity of the region on the subject of race. All of the major socializing institutions supported and reinforced segregation, and all social and economic relationships between blacks and whites were premised on racial inequality. Those who did not abide by the norms were harassed and pressured to conform, or they were driven out of the region.[26]

Although prejudice was widespread, the intensity with which southerners supported discriminatory norms varied. Many white southerners undoubtedly conformed to such norms simply because they were customary. They followed the norms without giving them a great deal of thought, as there was no debate over alternative conventions. Among such individuals, a new norm could potentially win converts because there may be inadequate self-interest for them to resist the new norm. However, those who have a greater stake in the old norms can take measures that alter the incentives facing moderates and make it in their interest not to change their attitudes and behavior. As I noted in chapter 2, a person's interest in defending a social norm depends partly on the choices of other group members; these issues, by nature, raise considerations of social coordination. Norms cannot be sustained by individuals acting alone, so they are seldom supported by individuals acting unconditionally; instead, one's willingness to conform to a norm usually depends on there being a sufficient amount of group conformity.

For this reason, those with a stake in the outcome have an interest in ensuring that others resist change, even if this requires coercion and social pressure. The massive resistance movement in the South following the *Brown* decision, for example, used social pressure, economic sanctions, and coercion and violence to ensure strict and universal conformity to racial traditions. The campaign was organized at all levels—neighborhood, community, town, county, and state—in united opposition to school desegregation. The building block of the movement was the Citizens Council chapter.[27] In their role as "guardians of the community," the councils were dedicated to rooting out and punishing any sign of nonconformity; there was no tolerance for ambivalence: "If you're a white man, then it's time to stand up with us, or black your face and get on the other side." Nonconformity on the race issue resulted in general social ostracism in personal and business relationships. There was no such thing as friends and neighbors agreeing to disagree. Georgia governor Herman Talmadge recommended that "anyone who sells the South down the river, don't let him eat at your table, don't let him trade at your filling station and don't let him trade at your store." Blacks who petitioned for school desegregation were also threatened with the loss of their jobs, the withholding of credit, and eviction from their homes.[28]

By clamping down on any sign of nonconformity, the South appeared more homogeneous than it was in fact, because those who were inclined to favor desegregation tended to be less vocal than those who opposed it. While the leaders of southern institutions like the church, trade unions, businesses, and schools and universities may have privately questioned the wisdom of resisting social change, they did little to restrain the massive resistance movement because they feared the consequences of a popular backlash.

Whether the old norm or the new norm prevails in this environment depends again on a combination of people's underlying attitudes and dispositions and the comparative strengths of the incentives attached to the norms. The critical dynamic behind change is that the advantage of continuing to coordinate around the old norm has to be undermined and people have to be reoriented toward alternative social practices. The interest in the old norm has to be counteracted with sanctions and new incentives. Sustained enforcement of the new norm creates an alternate basis for social coordination that outweighs the incentives to continue to organize and mobilize around the old norm. As the political advantages of the original norm diminish, people's attitudes adjust to the new norm.

Several conditions affect the ability of normative change to produce social change. The norm must be clear about the value or goal that it is promoting, and it must indicate to the public which value, among competing alternatives, has greater priority and legitimacy and which kinds of behavior are unacceptable. There must also be effective monitoring of behavior to ensure that people are complying with the norm.[29]

Effective enforcement of the norm depends on whether the targets of the norm are accessible to monitoring and regulation. Monitoring needs to be coupled with sanctions that make it costly to fail to comply with the norm. To the extent that people cannot be detected and punished for violating the norm, the magnitude of e diminishes, and, therefore, compliance with the norm declines. The effect of a norm against racial discrimination will therefore vary according to the realm in which it is applied. For example, it is easier to bring about enforcement of voting rights by monitoring public officials than it is to monitor real estate agents who might be discriminating against minorities in the sale of homes.

Some people may be able to sidestep sanctions by leaving those institutions in the social system that are governed by the new standards. Thus the pressure represented by the e coefficient can be avoided by removing oneself from the authority of the system. If e equals 0 (and if there are no exogenous forces changing attitudes), C will not budge from its current value. Some southerners chose to avoid integrated schools by placing their children in newly created private schools. (This option was, however, closed to poorer white parents, who could not afford the tuition fees.) Some teachers likewise chose not to teach in the public schools even if this meant a lower salary.[30] (Recall from chapter 3 that the decision to exit also describes the reaction of working-class patrons in the nineteenth century to changes in the norms governing how the arts were to be viewed and received. With the proliferation of popular entertainment venues, these customers chose different forms of recreation rather than conform to the new standards imposed on them by the emerging professional artistic class and their upper-class benefactors. Similarly, in Steelton, as newer ethnic groups ascended in the political and economic structure and began to alter community norms and values, those of Western European descent increasingly relocated to new municipalities.)

The effect of the norm will be undermined if there are rival values that support behavior that is contrary to the norm. Competing norms, each justified by its own principle, leave open the possibility that people will comply with the norm that maintains their interests.[31] Southerners pursued a version of this strategy by trying to undermine the legitimacy of federal laws and judicial decisions—in effect, to reduce the enforcement power, e, of the new norms of equality by invoking states' rights. Social norms against desegregation were backed by new, impromptu state laws that punished dissent while legitimizing actions taken in opposition to *Brown*. In the areas of voting, education, and economic opportunity, segregationists countered abstract arguments for racial equality by advancing their own traditional values—the right of states to set criteria for voting rights, the right of communities to decide education policy, the right of free enterprise and private property.[32] "Legal" means, based on ostensibly neutral principles, were used to eliminate thousands of blacks from voter registration lists and to divert public funds to private schools.

Law acquires its force from the sanctions that it provides for noncompliance but also from the justification that law gives to a course of action. Social and legal norms instruct citizens about how they should conduct their lives and respond to controversial social issues. People prefer to believe that they are not only doing what is best for themselves or their community but also that what they are doing abides by the law and has the endorsement of the state. The interposition of states' rights was intended to negate the normative influence of federal law by substituting an alternative law that was compatible with popular values. Oppositional tactics such as these slowed the acceptance of racial integration, but they could not be sustained against the pressure of federal action and civil rights protest. For example, the South's improvised laws were transparently self-serving, and while they fortified southern resistance, the principles underlying them did not gain support outside the groups that originated them.

How the South Was Won

Despite a fortress of entrenched interests and institutions, the South did eventually relent to popular and federal government pressure to alter its norms and behavior. Without doubt, changes in racial tolerance were accelerated by the social and legal enforcement of laws and by the adaptation of mass attitudes to the new norms.

First, *social, economic, and legal penalties for continuing to adhere to the old norms proved excessive to white southerners.* Businesses saw that federal funds would dry up and that investment in the region would decline without compliance; federal enforcement of voting and public accommodations laws made noncompliance too costly; court orders deterred school boards from shutting down schools. Expressed opposition to desegregation and racial equality was easier and less costly than behavioral opposition: it was one thing to oppose vocally and in print and another to back up these threats. To the extent that threats were followed with violence against integrationist forces, the violence often proved counterproductive, as it increased federal intervention in the region, intensified black protest, and further destabilized communities.[33] White southerners realized that "the price of maintaining complete segregation—the cost of preserving the undiluted traditional culture—was prohibitive. To insist on total segregation in the face of escalating black protest and increasing federal intervention meant that other valued goods—public schools, economic development, an orderly and peaceful society—might be denied white southerners."[34]

Second, *the revolution in race relations cannot be understood without also recognizing that society adapted with remarkable speed to new standards of racial interaction, thereby undercutting the coordination power of white supremacy.* If social adjustment is negligible, transformation of the norm produces a precarious tension between social practices and underlying attitudes. Behavior is held in check by institutional pressures without being supplemented by voluntary compliance, so that a relaxation of those constraints will cause a sharp reversion to past form. When there is a large gap between norms and attitudes, this creates opportunities for political entrepreneurs to organize opposition to unpopular norms. On the other hand, if attitudes are flexible, then people adapt to the new norm and the social pressure to maintain the old norm is alleviated accordingly—if people are complying and they are comfortable with complying, then there is no incentive for political entrepreneurs to try to organize around the old norm or exploit it for political gain. Given a high rate of attitude adjustment, resistance to the new norm can be maintained only by increasing r and m. But there is little profit in rallying opposition or in yielding to its demands if popular attitudes are rapidly adapting to the new norm. If attitudes change readily in the new environment, the advantage of the old norm is undermined.

The social adjustment parameter is therefore critical to reducing the strain of normative change. New norms alter behavior patterns, thus resulting in new experiences and changes in beliefs and emotional sentiments. In changing behavior, the law also changes appearances about what is right and normal and, with that, the entire configuration of social pressures that operate on the individual: "The civil rights laws have forced hotels and restaurants to open their doors to people of all races. . . . The fact that these hotels and restaurants must not discriminate does not in itself change bigots to nonbigots; the owners may still feel the same way about race. But coercion creates a new situation— it changes public behavior—and when this happens, real or imagined peer pressure may start to work on people's minds. A segregated restaurant first becomes illegal, then impossible, and finally unthinkable. At that point, the battle against Jim Crow restaurants is over for good."[35]

As Jim Crow was defeated in the South, mass attitudes became more tolerant of limited forms of integration and southern politicians backed off from advocating segregation. Increasing mass compliance with more egalitarian racial norms reduced political incentives to mobilize around racially intolerant attitudes and group identifications. In turn, the reorientation of political mobilization around issues other than white supremacy and segregation reduced the salience of racial identifications and symbols in the public.[36] Laws promoting racial equality helped to coordinate those individuals in the region who were sympathetic or at least indifferent to integration but who were afraid to speak out because they could not be sure if they had allies in the community.

A new generation of Americans has grown up and been socialized in a radically transformed political environment which no longer promotes and legitimates old-fashioned racist appeals. As blacks have acquired equal rights in this country, they have been able to compete on a more equal footing with whites. New racial norms are reinforced by blacks' becoming politicians, business leaders, teachers, work associates, neighbors, friends, and family members by marriage. The experience of seeing blacks occupy higher-status positions contradicts negative stereotypes and causes prejudices to diminish.[37] As older, less flexible individuals die off, they are replaced by people who have not had to adapt psychologically to a new social order, because they never built their lives around the old order. This newer generation increasingly accepts what older generations find (or once found) problematic. The consequence of these two developments is a population which, in the aggregate, harbors significantly less racial prejudice.[38]

We may describe equation (3) as the "stateways changes folkways" assumption: norms have the ability not only to produce mere compliance but also to alter underlying sentiments. Evaluations and preferences on political issues are shaped by social and legal prescriptions and prohibitions. Recently, in Noblesville, Indiana, a building contractor accidently discovered an old local membership roster of the Ku Klux Klan dating back to the 1920s that contained the names of many prominent community members from that era. Some of the descendants of Klan members still lived in the area, and the discovery was an occasion for all residents to contemplate their own racial attitudes. A local lawyer, in his sixties, was deeply troubled in retrospect by his own obliviousness to racist practices that were the norm when he was growing up in the 1940s and 1950s: "I look back and ask myself, 'Why wasn't I upset as a kid when black kids couldn't sit with us in the movie theater? Why wasn't I upset when they could not swim at the public swimming pool?'"[39]

This man's disappointment in himself underestimates the extent to which people take for granted their social norms and hold them up to scrutiny only when they are challenged by groups that find them unjust or inappropriate.[40] Given that there often is no objective analysis or correct interpretation of political and social practices, people look to the prevailing social or legal norm for guidance. Law and public policy teach people how to think as well as feel about social issues, so that as law evolves and is rewritten, it can just as easily alter people's "natural" reactions to these matters.

The vicissitudes of racial sentiments and feelings demonstrate how attitudes can adapt to existing standards of race relations to produce either greater or lesser consternation over integration, depending on political circumstances. When Jim Crow norms ruled, even remote forms of social contact with blacks made whites uncomfortable, whereas, in today's climate, public expression of racial prejudice is virtually universally condemned, and racial discrimination by businesses is economically costly when exposed.[41] Each political era in the South has been defined by the position of blacks in society. Every new social order, however, appeared to those living within its confines to be a proper, natural, and intrinsically sensible arrangement: "Few stopped to reflect that previous systems had also been regarded as final, sane, and permanent by their supporters."[42]

Throughout the late 1800s, blacks voted in great numbers; they were encouraged to do so by the white leaders of the major parties, and their votes were hotly contested. "Qualified and acknowledged leaders of Southern white opinion," C. Vann Woodward emphasizes, "were on record as saying that it was proper, inevitable, and desirable that they should vote." Nonetheless, around 1900, blacks were disenfranchised and prevented from voting. When this happened, "qualified and acknowledged leaders of white opinion" suddenly had a change of heart and "said it was unthinkable that they should ever be permitted to vote."[43]

Similar changes in public sentiment followed the imposition of Jim Crow norms on the trains and other public accommodations. Again, Woodward takes pains to draw out the contrasts in attitudes and feelings before and after segregation was enforced:

> It has also been seen that their presence on trains upon equal terms with white men was once regarded in some states as normal, acceptable, and unobjectionable. Whether railways qualify as folkways or stateways, black man and white man once rode them together and without a partition between them. Later on the stateways apparently changed the folkways— or at any rate the railways—for the partitions and Jim Crow cars became universal. And the new seating arrangement came to seem as normal, unchangeable, and inevitable as the old ways. And so it was with the soda fountains, bars, waiting rooms, street cars, and circuses. And so it

probably was with the parks in Atlanta, and with cemetaries in Mississippi. There must even have been a time in Oklahoma when a colored
man could walk into any old telephone booth he took a notion to and
pick up the receiver.[44]

But Jim Crow laws defined for white southerners the proper bounds of racial
interaction; therefore, they also established what types of behavior should be
deemed improper and offensive. This led to the proscription of behavior that
previously had troubled few whites but that, once outlawed, was cause for
considerable consternation and outrage.

CONCLUSION

Introduction of a new norm disrupts existing ways of life and creates a period
of transition in which people can choose to side either with the old norm or
with the new one. At issue is whether people can be given sufficient motivation
to conform to the new norm. A person's behavior will change if the incentives
provided for compliance are adequate to induce him to change his ways rather
than to resist. If popular support tips in favor of the new norm, the new norm
becomes naturally comfortable to succeeding generations that are unfamiliar
with past ways. Old stalwarts may successfully dodge the new norm by maintaining their traditional reference groups, but only at the cost of isolating themselves from the mainstream and denying themselves the benefits that are available from engaging with the rest of society.

Some normative changes are relatively frictionless. Changes in fashion, for
example, are largely changes in convention and require only that people learn
about the latest trends and conform to them; no deep-seated attachment to
current styles needs to be overcome because what is considered fashionable
is essentially arbitrary and established by clothing designers, role models, and
trendsetters in the society.

But normative transitions that have consequences for those adhering either
to the old or to the new norm will not proceed as smoothly, especially if it is
difficult for people to take full advantage of the new norms owing to previous
decisions that limit their future flexibility. And normative standards that have
also become so ingrained over time that believers feel that these standards are
superior to alternatives and essential to the well-being of their community will
obviously acquire staunch defenders. As I have noted, such beliefs are not
simply psychological rationalizations or symbolic attachments; on the contrary, social and economic relationships are built upon the common knowledge
and expectations embodied in social norms and values. When existing norms
are reinforced by social and political institutions and patterns of social interaction, legal sanctions may provide the necessary motivation to overcome popu-

lar resistance to change. Such legal measures, however, are most effective when they can instigate changes in social relations and underlying sentiments, so that people reorient themselves to the incentives offered by the new system of social norms and relinquish efforts to restore the status quo ante. Interests and institutions have to be realigned to create support for the new norms. Sometimes this can only be accomplished through legal changes and sanctions for noncompliance.

The propensity to change can therefore be regarded as both a psychological disposition and a motivation that depends on one's circumstances. Some individuals may be ruled by inflexible traits, but they may also be restricted by limited resources and past investments that reduce the return that they can expect under the new norm. As I noted in chapter 3, some individuals may be saddled by reputations that make it difficult for them to reap the benefits of conformity under the new norms. For example, a politician who has built a career out of defending R may not be able to switch credibly to L and may therefore have stronger incentives to be an entrepreneur for supporters of R. Resistance to change may have less to do with inflexible psychological dispositions than with the respective opportunities made available by the competing norms.

The period marking the transition from old to new norms is therefore often a tug of war between competing social and individual forces. Prejudicial beliefs and group loyalties supporting old social norms have to be undermined in order to create willing support for new norms, but this can sometimes be accomplished only by enforcing the new norm against popular opposition and demonstrating that the dire consequences predicted are not an inevitable consequence of changing the norms.[45] In due course, defenders of the traditional culture adjust to the new reality, while newer generations without vested interests in previous ways of life more readily adapt to the new regime, because they have known no alternative.

CHAPTER SEVEN

Culture and Strategy

Everything should be made as simple as possible, but not simpler.
Albert Einstein

It would be odd to say that we choose the lives we live or the beliefs we hold in the same way that we choose the things we buy from a store. Or that our attachment to familiar social norms and resistance to changing our values are based on deliberate calculation of their consequences. We do not appear to maximize our choices of cultural beliefs and ways of life in the same manner that we make economic decisions.

Political conflicts over cultural values often elicit stronger visceral reactions than economic disputes and seem to be driven by psychic and symbolic gratification rather than rational political choice. Whereas people can negotiate over and accept differences of opinion rooted in competing material interests, they are more emotionally invested in moral disagreements that betray their values. Normative disputes tend to be especially hard fought and to bring forth great personal animus because they involve contests over outcomes that do not lend themselves easily to tradeoffs. Unlike a dispute over pending tax legislation, in which both sides may compromise on a settlement, it is difficult to split the difference in normative conflicts when the competing alternatives represent absolute moral positions.

But, as we have seen throughout this book, there are also many similarities in decision making in both social and economic realms. Cultural values constitute priorities, goals, and social facts that people make plans, organize, and form their lives around. People view culture as an important determinant of economic outcomes and therefore draw material implications from cultural alternatives. In the end, to say that we live rational lives is to say that we make practically rational decisions throughout our lives in the way we form our beliefs and values, coordinate our choices with others, and defend our cultural preferences against alternative ways of life.

Whether the issues are social or economic, individuals must still establish their interests, and they must still be coordinated or mobilized for collective action to protect those interests. And this process is not necessarily accomplished more efficiently in the economic realm. Both economic and cultural choices will be motivated by a combination of values, group identifications, and social and material incentives. It would be a mistake therefore to assume that there are two different realms of decision making with different models required for each. Regardless of the policy domain, we can understand people's positions only by analyzing their values, reference groups, and sociological and economic beliefs about the choices they face.

A Unifying Theory

Two commonly cited shortcomings of rational choice explanations are that they stop short of addressing where beliefs and preferences come from and that they underestimate ideological and normative commitments and loyalties based on social identification.[1] The model of choice that I have presented fills this void by assuming that preferences are a function of both dispositions and incentives. Dispositions are traits, knowledge, values, and group identifications that are formed over the life span. They are shaped by social influences in one's reference groups and respond to changing material and social incentives. Incentives are costs and benefits calculated on the basis of people's desires for material goals and acceptance in their social groups. The model thus tries to make sense of a number of dualisms that counterpose culture and economics, self-interest and group interest, social and material benefits, values and interests, and instrumental and noninstrumental action.

The model assumes that individual choice cannot be divorced from social contexts. A culture comprises an array of social and political institutions and shared values and traditions that allow people to enjoy a meaningful life. People define their conception of the good life and pursue their interests within the bounds of their cultural institutions; they have limited perspectives, which means that their choices do not take account of the set of all possible cultures. Culture not only exists in people's heads in the form of shared understandings and meanings but is also manifest more concretely in the most important institutions of society—in the government, school system, churches, and marketplace.[2]

Society is organized by class, religion, race, ethnicity, gender, ideology, occupation, and other salient social categories. One pursues some interests on an individualistic basis, but many interests are pursued in collectivities and depend on cooperation with other group members. Therefore, interests will be affected by group affiliations that are based on ascriptive characteristics as well as socioeconomic factors. Group identifications and social values are assumed to be developed much like other attitudes and beliefs. People embrace the norms and values of a group in exchange for the esteem of other group members; they coordinate with other individuals around a social identification when there are benefits to holding common affiliations. Individuals make their decisions by assessing the relative merits of the available alternatives as well as the preferences of other people in their reference groups.

Through these assumptions, I have adopted factors that are central to sociological explanations but given them an economic cast by conceptualizing them as a product of past decisions and subjecting them to strategic calculations. In effect, individuals look both backward and forward before making their choices by taking into consideration their histories and their prospects. Social and material interests have a hand in shaping values, which in combination with assessments of the costs and benefits of the available alternatives, determine choices. The model therefore reduces, without eliminating, the scope of purely noninstrumental action by supplying a rational mechanism for group-based and value-based motivation. The result is a more dynamic model that yields deductions about the circumstances under which preferences, beliefs, values, and social identifications are formed and are likely to change over time.

VALUE FORMATION

The model that I have developed is a fluid one that examines individual choices made over the life course. People do the best they can to acquire a coherent view of the world, develop attitudes and values that are favored within their reference groups, and display traits and characteristics that produce material benefits and social status for themselves. They have to develop the right dispositions in order to take advantage of opportunities in their environment. Socialization is tailored according to the requisite demands for success in the particular environment in which one circulates.

During early socialization, children are not predisposed to favor any particular norms or way of life but are inclined to accept the norms and values of their immediate reference groups. When vistas are narrow and alternatives are few, ideas and values are readily transmitted from parents to their children. Group norms establish the types of values and behavior that are most highly regarded among one's peers. The utility of many group norms lies in their ability to coordinate the expectations and actions of group members. People have an interest in establishing with others a coherent understanding of society that allows them to make choices more readily, and they have an interest in developing a common basis for collective action. Nevertheless, we would also expect that group leaders tend to identify and promote norms and values that provide greater benefits to themselves and other group members. Conformity by the rank and file therefore furthers individual interests even though many individuals have not made their own calculations but have instead followed the lead of higher-status individuals in their midst.

The model's processes tend toward equilibrium values that factor in the relative strengths of dispositions and incentives. There are powerful social forces leading to convergence of views and subscription to common norms and conventions. Coordination around common identifications and norms creates collective power that benefits individual group members.

But, at the same time, the relations between individuals and groups and between different groups are dynamic. Neither group membership nor group status is constant. Groups vary in the amount of status and resources they enjoy in the society. People prefer to belong to more prestigious groups and will seek membership in them if they have the ability and opportunity to join. Individuals remain in or move out of their groups (resist or conform to a new system of norms) on the basis of their assessment of their ability to thrive under competing normative systems.

We develop broad strategies for living that are embodied in the traits and skills we cultivate, the values and ideologies we internalize, and the reputations that we carve out for ourselves. It is in the nature of dispositions that they will not lead to an optimal decision in every life situation in which we find ourselves. An integrated life is hard to achieve because dispositions that are useful for some purposes can be detrimental in other respects. Moreover, dispositions are to some extent internalized, so that they cannot be readily turned off or fine tuned. No one, for example, would doubt that bravado is a disposition that is well-suited to a boxer. But a fighter's bravado may be the reason why he does not deign to study the strengths and weaknesses of his upcoming opponents. While such tactics help to bolster self-confidence, ignoring one's homework may ultimately prove detrimental, as when a boxer is befuddled in the ring upon discovering that his opponent is a southpaw. Great track runners have to develop an obsession for running, but the dedication that makes them successful may also be their downfall if it leads them to train excessively to the point of injury. Middle distance runner Mary Decker Slaney's training regimen has been compared to an addiction because she has repeatedly run herself to the breaking point. One of the main tasks facing her coach, former marathon champion Alberto Salazar, is finding a way to keep her healthy by limiting her workouts: "It's a two-edged sword. The greatest athletes want it so much, they run themselves to death. You've got to have an obsession, but if unchecked, it's destructive. That's what it is with her. She'll kill herself off unless you pull the reins back."[3]

Although dispositions are not fixed entities, neither are they easy to change once we have made the effort to invest in them. There comes a time when it is, for practical purposes, difficult to change one's stock of personal capital in education and career skills. One is also understandably reluctant to change a political ideology that was intended to economize on decision making until it becomes obviously mismatched with one's current interests.

It can furthermore be difficult for social reasons to change one's personal traits and values. The symbolic politics literature emphasizes how psychological mechanisms can restrict one's ability to respond to new influences. But social expectations can also limit a person's adaptability to change. A person's reputation for possessing certain personal characteristics affects what others expect of him and how they will treat him. Reputations therefore constrain a person's ability to define and redefine himself. People tend to assume that others are guided by a consistent core of attitudes and dispositions that can account for their behavior, so that excessive changes in beliefs and attitudes raise uncertainty about one's personality and character in addition to questions about one's reliability and stability.

The dispositions we display constitute a major element of our reputations. Since we are expected by others to live up to the personal characteristics that we wish to be known for, this often requires that we uphold our reputations by behaving consistently across situations. We may not only protect our reputations in specific relationships with individuals we see on a regular basis, but we also may adhere to a consistent line of behavior as a general rule in our social interactions. More fine-tuned strategies may be self-defeating, since we are unlikely to receive credit for having certain attributes (e.g., cooperativeness) unless we display them consistently across a range of contexts, occasionally at the expense of our self-interest. In defending our reputations, we typically have to bend to the intuitive assumptions that people have about the connectedness of an individual's character and personality.[4]

Competing norms and social conventions create coordination problems in the form of higher transaction costs. Heterogeneous conventions make it more difficult for people to communicate with one another and to engage in smooth social interaction. New norms become especially problematic when they threaten the investments that people have made in the existing value system. The skills and values a person acquires in order to adapt to one environment may not be equally valuable in an alternative environment marked by different social norms.

Early life decisions especially, made with limited knowledge and insight into the future, may close off future opportunities and restrict our capacity to adapt to new environments. Long-term investment in group norms can create a vested interest in defending those norms when group members do not have, or do not wish to expend, the resources necessary to adapt to new norms. For this reason, individuals who cannot prosper under new social norms, because they cannot or are unwilling to reinvent themselves, are likely to resist change and to apply social pressure and coercion on other group members to do the same.

Individual attachment to cultural norms, however, goes even deeper than personal investments embodied in past decisions. Adherence to cultural values is, in addition, reinforced by social theories that provide intellectual and moral rationales and defenses for existing norms. Economic models have difficulty accounting for social-psychological biases in the way that people draw causal inferences relating their traditions and norms to economic and political goals. Resistance to changing existing norms is strengthened by ethnocentric beliefs in the superiority of the characteristics that define members of one's own group. The tendency to attribute intrinsic differences to members of different groups and to assign greater value to the attributes of one's own way of life provides a rationale for the defense of the status quo and may be an essential source of the peculiar animus that often accompanies social conflict over norms. These beliefs are derived from observation, rationalization, and ideological values, and, while not necessarily true and sometimes obviously false, they are not readily amenable to refutation.

Cultural values are further reinforced by political coalitions that are organized around these values. It is both rational for politicians to tailor their messages in order to coordinate people around existing group identifications and values and rational for citizens to conform to such identifications if they are vehicles for obtaining their political goals. Group identifications and values need to be made continually salient, or else they will lose their relevance as points of reference for decision making. Political coordination around group identifications, values, and symbols ensures that these markers will retain their instrumental value. When a coalition of individuals unites around a common understanding of their predicament, the political power that is created gives them an incentive to adhere to that consensus. A successful basis for coordinating expectations and actions around group identifications will be difficult to dislodge as long as it continues to provide political benefits.

To counteract the social processes that foster intolerance and group conflict, it is necessary for a society to provide its members with equality of opportunity. When mobility between groups is possible, individuals have less incentive to invest in any particular group. To the extent that individuals find themselves restricted by their group membership and unable to transfer to alternative groups that provide greater opportunities (e.g., due to earlier decisions that limit their capacities or to discrimination by other more powerful groups), they have an incentive to strengthen their current identification and to engage in collective action on behalf of their own group.

High rates of social mobility reduce the correlation between group membership and socioeconomic status. When unequal opportunity restricts the achievement of certain groups, this encourages people to believe that the low status of members of those groups is due to individual deficiencies. Prejudicial beliefs and stereotypes are likely to confirm and indeed justify continued discrimination. Negative stereotypes based on ascriptive characteristics such as race, ethnicity, and gender are best counteracted by real evidence of group accomplishments. This was of course the thesis of Kenneth Clark's classic research on the effects of institutionalized segregation.[5] As long as blacks were segregated in the worst sections of the community, forced to attend inferior schools, allowed to hold only menial jobs, depicted in unflattering terms in popular culture, people—blacks as well as whites—would develop the belief that blacks were in fact inferior to whites and that they were incapable of similar achievements and not worthy of equal treatment.

SOCIAL CHANGE

The norms that govern society establish the talents, accomplishments, and kinds of individuals that earn status. These norms therefore are seldom neutral but tend to favor some groups at the expense of others, so that changing the norms of society changes the allocation of rewards. Low-status groups will try to overturn social and legal norms that place them at a disadvantage and prevent them from receiving the benefits of full membership in the society. On the other hand, those who are threatened by the introduction of new norms will want to defend the status quo against change. Higher-status groups may choose defensive political action rather than expand opportunities for members of subordinate groups at the expense of their own social and economic standing.

A norm will be followed only if it is based in groups that reinforce the norm and make it rational for individuals to follow the norm.[6] A person's attitudes and values will change if the social and material incentives provided by his reference groups make it more advantageous for him to change his views than to adhere to tradition. When norms support group interests, group members will conform to the norms until those interests are undercut.[7] Advocates of political change must therefore find a way to reduce the incentives for conforming to the existing norms. In a tug of war between competing norms, there is a transition period in which people can choose to side either with the old or the new norm. Their choices depend on the incentives they have either to resist or to shift allegiance to the new norm.

People are more likely to be converted if they have the ability and opportunity to thrive under the new system of norms. The sharpest conflicts therefore occur when people are confronted with social change that threatens their status and livelihoods. If they are unable to opt out of the changes, their only choices are to suffer the consequences or to mount an active resistance by organizing themselves for collective action.

The social incentive to follow a norm depends on the number of people who are conforming to it. As more people adopt a new norm, social pressure mounts on those who continue to hold out. If conformity tips in favor of the new norm, psychological and social mechanisms have a way of making the new norm feel comfortable to converts and to succeeding generations of believers, who have firsthand experience only with the current standard. Of course, both supporters and opponents of the new norm are aware of the same social dynamics and will take measures to win over a critical mass of believers to their side of the conflict. For the old norms to survive, there must be communities of believers who are able to maintain their group norms in the face of external pressure. Diehards can sometimes successfully ward off acceptance of the new norm by maintaining their traditional support groups, but they will have to pay the price of staying outside the mainstream of society.

Community interaction may therefore weaken correlations between narrowly personal interests and policy preferences. Groups apply social pressure on individuals to consider their long-term relationships with others when estimating their self-interest. Public opinion research does not generally consider how rational individuals resolve conflicts between their social commitments and obligations and their personal interests, but chooses to exclude social concerns from the province of rational calculation. Studies of symbolic politics, for example, confine self-interest to a narrow set of personal concerns divorced from an individual's group obligations and social networks. This slim articulation of self-interest, operationalized using comparatively weak objective measures, combined with subjective measures of symbolic factors that bear a close family resemblance to the indicators of policy preferences, tips the equation heavily in favor of symbolic explanations.

In recognizing the power of groups to coordinate individual behavior, we should be careful about extolling the virtues of strong communities in the abstract, for strong communities can foster exclusion and intolerance as easily as they can unite behind noble causes. Because of our tendency to think of collective action problems as problems requiring solutions, we are likely to forget that social capital in the form of in-group bonds and trusting relationships can be marshaled for exclusive goals that are achieved at the expense of individuals who are not part of the inner circle. The Williamson County, Texas, community that I visited has considerable social capital, which has facilitated cooperation among community members. But the wistfulness with which people speak of days gone by, when the community was safer and more trustworthy, unfortunately carries an undertone of intolerance toward the new groups that have moved into the area and are imputed to have eroded community bonds because they do not share the same social values.

Sometimes the institution of new norms can be accomplished only through legal changes, sanctions for noncompliance, and resocialization of individuals. Compliance is won by enforcing the new norm and demonstrating that the new arrangements are workable if given a chance. Law forces changes in behavior, which alters the balance of social pressures and creates favorable conditions for adaptation of underlying sentiments.

Let us not, therefore, overestimate the power of early socialization to limit the capacity for individuals to change by assuming that attitudes and values learned early in life will not yield to changes in social and political institutions. In practice, what often counts is behavior and not underlying sentiments, and behavior can often lead sentiment rather than the other way around. Behavior can be changed despite resistant attitudes by offering the right balance of incentives and sanctions.

Southern prejudice, for example, was deep but was not the dominating factor in dictating white southerners' response to racial equality. Prejudice was only one motive among many, and it was often trumped by competing goals that required accommodation to change, including "monetary profit, political power, staying out of jail, the approval of one's immediate peers, conforming to the dominant decision of the community."[8] White southern bus drivers who claimed they would quit rather than work alongside black bus drivers ultimately chose to accept integration rather than sacrifice their jobs: "It was not that the white drivers deliberately lied. They were probably convinced that this is what they would do. But when they faced the actual—rather than the verbal—choice of working along with Negroes or being without a job, they chose what to them was a lesser evil."[9]

People can therefore appear to change their allegiances quickly from one norm to another, as in the case of racial discrimination and racial equality. Intense identifiers with a norm can force compliance from those in the group who are indifferent or who have weak allegiances in the opposite direction. But when the consensus around the old norm breaks, it becomes possible for this swing group to express support for the new norm: "The Civil Rights movement finally enabled these people to join blacks to attempt a new coordination on a norm of racial equality."[10]

Newer generations, who are unburdened by past decisions and vested interests in previous ways of life, will have less reason to resist—aside from having to deal with social pressure exerted by the older generation. Therefore, the socialization of children is often crucial to the transformation, which explains why school and language policies are recurring battle grounds for cultural conflict. Social and psychological adjustment is a central mechanism that softens and eventually erodes resistance to social change. Adjustment can occur either through dissonance reduction—because one must face up to the inevitability of change—or through learning and experience.

THE LIMITS OF RATIONALITY

The model that I have proposed in this book is developed to integrate sociological and economic mechanisms. But is everything rational by this model? How can the model be falsified? There is perhaps an inevitable trade-off between making rational choice assumptions more realistic and making a model that is straightforwardly falsifiable. Modifications to rational choice theory that relax its assumptions about the nature of interests are at risk of being post-hoc explanations. In any research program, the basic assumptions of the model are reworked when the implications of the model do not accord with the evidence. Ad hoc revisions are rightly avoided when they create conceptual tangles within the theory that reduce its problem-solving capacity. For instance, when Anthony Downs tried to save his economic model of voting by arguing that people go to the polls in order to do their share in preserving a democratic system, he violated his main assumption that one chooses among alternative actions solely on the basis of the relative advantage of each action to oneself alone.[11] Some critics of rational choice theory, however, appear to distrust ad hoc modifications merely because they seem too easy to construct.[12] Leaving aside whether they are easy or difficult to devise—I think the latter is more accurate—ad hoc modifications are not necessarily ill-advised. By definition, an ad hoc modification increases the empirical power of a theory and therefore is a progressive development. Avoiding ad hoc modifications by restricting the domain of a theory shrinks the theory's empirical reach. While an ad hoc modification should generate additional tests of the theory, it is debatable whether those additional tests need to be identified immediately, as opposed to being developed later.[13]

The model presented here broadens the scope of rational calculation. One might claim that a more static model, such as the self-interest model that is paired against the theory of symbolic attitudes, has the virtue of establishing clear boundaries for rational behavior. Studies that use a narrow operationalization of self-interest rule out rational choice if objective, material indicators of self-interest are uncorrelated with policy preferences. Indeed, the rational choice model often falters based on these assumptions.

If, on the other hand, rational choice is based on subjective beliefs and is conditional upon an individual's past investments as well as his social networks, then interests will be susceptible to information, persuasion, and social influences. The rational choice, under these assumptions, may not always be so transparent. If it is in an individual's interests to coordinate around common norms and conventions and if the motive for social conformity is to gain a share of group benefits, then the values and group identifications that a person develops have been shaped in part by his interests. Motivation by norms and identifications therefore cannot be treated as purely noninstrumental causes of action. At a minimum the model that I offer forces us to explain the values themselves and not to assume that they are the (nonrational) bedrock of the explanation.

Falsification is still possible even in this dynamic context. The strength of group identifications, for example, might not be related to calculations of political relevance. Individual support for group norms may occur independently of the capacity of the group to serve as a vehicle for furthering individual interests. Changing incentives might fail to budge choices because of rigid dispositions and habitual tendencies. Social pressure and monitoring may be unnecessary to securing individual contributions to collective goods if actions are sufficiently explained by expressive and moral motives. People may sometimes engage in activities for the intrinsic pleasure of those actions rather than their tangible consequences.

Yet another form of irrationality stems from biased methods of gathering information. For example, people are prone to allow their ideological values to distort their evaluation of evidence. Because the model assumes that decisions are based on beliefs and arguments that one has acquired, it does not technically distinguish between choices that are based on thorough information gathering and decisions that are based on gross misperceptions. As I discussed in chapter 3, biased belief formation contributes to the development of ethnocentrism and prejudice.

People do not always draw the right conclusions from the information they possess, or they may acquire inaccurate beliefs about the situations they face. Information that would lead to a better decision is sometimes not processed because of personal impediments. Perhaps Saddam Hussein blundered into the 1991 Gulf War because, as U.S. envoy April Glaspie explained, "He was too 'stupid' to understand how the United States would react" to Iraq's incursion into Kuwait.[14] Indeed, Glaspie observed that if American decision makers might be faulted retrospectively, it was that they did not "realize that he was stupid—that he did not believe our clear and repeated warnings that we would support our vital interests."[15]

EXPRESSIVE AND MORAL ACTION

The model can be and, indeed, is falsified in some cases to the extent that choices are based exclusively on noninstrumental dispositions reflected in ideological values, moral commitments, and expressive desires rather than incentives. "When I use the term 'instrumental,'" Robert Abelson writes, "I refer to deliberate, rational planning and choice in self-interested pursuit of the prospect of future material benefit. By contrast, I intend 'expressive' to refer to spontaneous enjoyment or value-expressive action, performed for its own sake, with no apparent rational consideration of material consequences for the actor."[16]

Current incentives are irrelevant if individual choice depends solely on the value of the a and b parameters, which means that the choice is unaffected by external pressures or inducements. The hallmark of expressive action is that the benefits of taking such action are inseparable from the process of taking the action. The benefits are in effect consumed in the course of the activity. Playing a sport or mastering a musical instrument provides intrinsic pleasure. An instrumental action, by contrast, is taken with an eye toward bringing about an outcome that is distinguishable from the act itself.

Whether actions are taken for intrinsic or extrinsic reasons will not always be clear to the actor, let alone the analyst, and may be susceptible to manipulation. Work is defined by compensation, while play is activity that is engaged in for its own rewards. We are delighted if we happen to be doing something that we love, but for which we also earn a living. The professional athlete marvels at being paid millions for playing a child's game.

But it appears that one of the dangers of receiving remuneration for child's play is that it creates ambiguities in one's own mind about the motives behind one's actions. Studies indicate that paying people to do something that they initially enjoyed doing for free diminishes enthusiasm for that behavior when the external rewards are removed.[17] It is as if the compensation causes people to think that they must be motivated more by the promise of a reward than by the pleasure of the activity. When behavior is overdetermined in this fashion, people will tend to give greater weight to external incentives.

Moral behavior may share some similarity with expressive activity to the extent that a feeling of satisfaction is achieved by virtue of behaving morally even if the action produces little external effect. The most obvious intrinsic effect of moral choices is a feeling of self-esteem. Sarah Boyle confessed that her efforts on behalf of blacks and the gratitude she received from them in return boosted her own sense of worth.[18] Her moral actions benefited herself as well as those she wanted to assist.

In some cases, the intrinsic personal effects accompanying sympathetic actions are foreseen. Many volunteers choose to help others as a way to treat shortcomings in themselves. Volunteering gives them a reason to leave their houses and meet other people. It allows those weighed down by personal problems to take their minds off their troubles by taking responsibility for others.[19]

It may, however, be too stringent to deduct these psychic benefits and social gratifications from the altruism of their actions.

Society reserves high praise for moral actions taken at great personal expense. There are occasions when personal commitment to moral values overcomes what would constitute, for most people, dispositive counterincentives. We marvel at the heroic actions of those who place their own lives in jeopardy in order to save others—the men and women who operated the underground railroad that spirited slaves out of the South, who gave safe harbor to Jews fleeing Nazism, or the everyman hero who repeatedly leaped into the frigid Potomac River to rescue drowning passengers following an airline accident.[20] The unlikely gift of $150,000 to the University of Southern Mississippi— amassed over a lifetime of frugal living and careful savings—by an eighty-eight-year-old Mississippi washerwoman was met with extraordinary fanfare. She became an instant celebrity, featured in the *New York Times, Ebony, Jet, People,* and other national publications, was named one of Barbara Walters's ten most interesting people of 1995, and was given an honorary doctorate by Harvard University. She has traveled throughout the country to receptions in her honor.[21] Even though we give these heroes our esteem, it is not the prospect of such rewards that motivates their action in the first place. Good works may therefore benefit the good samaritan only as a by-product.

There are, in my view, two weaknesses in discussions of noninstrumental behavior. First, there is an inclination to be overly generous in classifying political action as being noninstrumental, partly in reaction, I suspect, to an opposing trend of seeing almost all behavior as a product of rational choice. Second, there is a tendency to assume that, because moral and expressive behavior by definition carries its own reward, it is unconditional upon either future consequences or the actions of others. The nature of expressive and symbolic theories encourages this type of inference. By tracing action to personal orientations (symbolic or status-based) these theories effectively truncate our inquiry by abbrieviating discussion of collective action problems and thereby ignoring the internal social dynamics of political activism.

As examples of quintessentially expressive action, Abelson cites demonstrations against abortion clinics, protests over the continued display of Confederate symbols in the South, and the gloved "Black Power" salute on the medal podium by American athletes Tommie Smith and John Carlos at the 1968 Olympic Games.[22] These are all questionable examples of noninstrumental action from my perspective, because each of these cases involves political action addressed to real grievances that is not simply "performed for its own sake." Anti-abortion demonstrators are attacking transformations in the culture that they believe to be eroding the moral foundations of the society in which they live. Are they merely intent on voicing their outrage as opposed to deterring patients and doctors? The black athletes chose the Olympic stage to protest racial inequality in the United States in order to garner maximum news media coverage for their message; they sought to galvanize supporters as well as marshal domestic and international pressure on the U.S. government.

Similarly, blacks are offended by Southern symbols that, from their perspective, continue to perpetuate the attitudes and values of an an era defined by slavery, racism, and oppression. The Confederate symbols are not merely symbolic affronts; they retain the power to reinforce anachronistic beliefs and values and coordinate groups of individuals. While some students derive no political significance from the symbols, others take pride that the symbols reflect the university's heritage and feel that those who are uncomfortable with the past should choose another university. No wonder, therefore, that opponents of these symbols believe that they contribute to a hostile environment for African-American students.

The irony here is that such "expressive" actions can be—indeed have been—highly successful in producing social change. The University of Mississippi's administration has become sufficiently concerned that the Confederate symbols hurt fundraising and student recruitment that they have commissioned outside consultants to study how the image of the university can be improved.[23] Anti-abortion protesters who have blocked clinic entrances have intimidated patients and doctors. Moreover the actions of these protesters are affected by cost-benefit concerns. Passage of legislation increasing penalties for blocking clinics has finally deterred some of the most aggressive anti-abortion activists from employing this tactic.[24]

How do we separate rational action from nonrational or noninstrumental status and symbolic pursuits? A purely symbolic action is an action that persists in response to a problem despite a lack of evidence showing that there is a causal connection between the action and ameliorating the problem. The symbolic meaning of the action augments the normal utility of that action.[25] A critical methodological problem is that people are often socialized to give instrumental rationales for their actions and proposals. Therefore behavior may be explained instrumentally by the participants as addressing a grievance even though their actions are more realistically viewed as being symbolic. For example, some people feel that calls to increase prison terms are merely a symbolic gesture rather than a serious proposal to combat crime; all the same, those who defend such measures offer causal claims to support their views— such as if prisons were run more strictly, then longer sentences would deter criminals.[26] We encountered the same problem to some extent in chapter 5 in interpreting Williamson County residents' rationales for their opinions and actions with respect to the Apple controversy. So, on the one hand, we might have what Robert Nozick refers to as a private "network of meanings,"[27] which explains the nature of the symbolic utility behind a symbolic act that may appear strange and foreign to us; on the other hand, we have the instrumental rationales that people are inclined to give because they are more socially acceptable.

We should be less likely to relegate action to the symbolic realm if it affects the opportunities of the winning and losing sides, changes attitudes that affect people's choices, communicates information that coordinates mass audiences, or improves personal or group welfare. If we cannot make the link between political action and one or more of these consequences, then it is more plausible that the actions are essentially noninstrumental. But these are neither necessary nor sufficient conditions, merely clues to underlying motives. Whether or not we can establish any of these connections, we still have to provide additional evidence that these were the reasons behind individuals' taking the actions that they did. Otherwise we fall into the trap of reasoning backward from the consequences of action to its causes. By this logic, expressive action would merely be unsuccessful collective action while successful collective action would qualify as being instrumental. In reality, political action that appears to be futile can nevertheless be instrumentally driven.

What is debatable in many cases of collective action, such as those described by Abelson, is not whether the activists have instrumental goals, but whether their efforts to change social and legal norms can be construed as self-interested action. The issue, to be clear, is not whether alternative social norms make a difference, but whether the difference is sufficient to motivate individuals to join in collective action. The goals in these cases are certainly more abstract than narrow material interests; they often concern broad social change, the preservation of cultural institutions, removal of stigmas, and the betterment of conditions for groups that suffer discrimination. Sometimes, the most effective way to achieve these collective goods is by pressuring the government to pass new laws.

Therefore, while we may question why rational individuals would participate in such campaigns rather than free-ride on the efforts of others, this is different from saying that there are no tangible goals that might be achieved by the collective action and that the individuals participating do not have those goals in mind. The puzzle surrounding such "symbolic" acts is not that they seem to be taken without consequences in mind but that it is unclear why individuals are not foiled by collective action problems. Their actions are directed toward obtaining public goods that will benefit *all* group members, not simply those who contributed.

Many collective action problems may not be solvable among narrowly rational actors. Collective action may require some intrinsically or morally motivated individuals to apply pressure on others to participate. In so doing, they change the incentive structure facing nonparticipants who are more instrumentally oriented. The successful initiation of collective action therefore can depend on combining the intrinsically motivated choices of some individuals with the strategic choices of others, with motivations varying according to the stage of collective action. Early and late joiners are different, just as the actor Dustin Hoffman described the difference between theater audiences at the beginning and at the end of a play's run: "The real audience comes at the beginning and then they're gone. Then you get the theater parties, the husbands who are dragged by their wives and the people who are disappointed, and probably should be, because it's too much money for a ticket."[28]

In studying the modern civil rights movement and other social movements, I came away thinking that essential elements of extrarationality—in the form of moral initiative taken by group leaders—might be crucial to sparking collective action. I emphasized at the same time, however, that these individuals do not seem to emerge randomly out of the group but instead tend to be those already occupying positions of leadership, having strong community connections and resources at their disposal, and responding to obligations and social pressures to marshal those resources for the greater good of the group. Moreover, it would seem that to grant some element of moral autonomy and intrinsic motivation to some individuals does not commit one to ascribe similar motives to all individuals who contribute, and that any model relying exclusively on dispositional explanations will invariably omit most of the interesting strategic interactions that occur within groups. Even in social movements infused with moral and religious conviction, such as the modern civil rights movement, there is evidence both of free-ridership and of social mechanisms, like monitoring and social pressure, that were instituted to minimize it. The expressive or moral benefits of participation are not doing all of the work.

A model combining dispositions and incentives pushes us to look more closely at the circumstances in which expressive and moral behavior are likely to be manifest. Even when participants in collective action are motivated by extrarational considerations, they tend not to act unconditionally. Rather, their choices tend to reflect strategic considerations. One does not necessarily act upon a moral disposition to choose L, for example, if everyone else elects to choose R. The decision to engage in moral action will therefore be influenced by the collective choices of others.

Because people draw information from the choices of others, any value-based motive will be more likely to inspire a person to action when it coordinates with other people's preferences. It is worth distinguishing, therefore, between unconditional moral or expressive behavior and moral or expressive behavior that is coordinated with the choices of others. When expressive and moral motives are present, the actions they give rise to can typically be understood only if due consideration is given to more systematic strategic processes. Expressive and moral behavior will often not be autonomous behavior, but behavior that is generated and encouraged by social coordination and community pressures. This is understandable: moral outrage is more effective when it is expressed collectively than when it is an isolated individual action. The altruist may rationally allocate his efforts and resources so that they will have the greatest impact.[29]

Thus, when we factor in the kinds of irrational or extrarational incentives that may sometimes be crucial to the initiation of collective action, we are still typically left with problems of coordination or "assurance." Expressive motivations, such as zeal and moral outrage, are not sufficient to explain how collective action in favor of civil rights originated. Acts of altruism and compliance with norms tend not to occur unconditionally but to depend on feelings of social obligation that are contingent upon the choices of others. For this reason, the strategic choices faced by political activists are sometimes better represented by coordination games than by the prisoner's dilemma game. In assurance games, for instance, people will remain inactive so long as few people are active, but they will weigh in when the movement grows beyond a certain point. Therefore, while collective action may struggle to get off the ground, people may rush to join after a critical mass is achieved.[30]

My point is that rational choice analysis of strategic behavior is likely to be important in any examination of collective action, whether we make simple or complex assumptions about motives. Social norms, expressive and symbolic actions, and even habitual behavior tend to have strategic components that are amenable to rational choice analysis, even if instrumental rationality does not appear to be the whole story. Groups must have mechanisms to extract individual conformity to group norms and to elicit participation in collective defense of those norms. Individuals must have reasons originally to join groups and to coordinate with other group members around common beliefs, values, and social norms. They must have social and material incentives to maintain their norms and values against efforts to change them. In large measure, the details of these processes have been the story of the book.

A FINAL WORD

Competing theoretical models make their contribution by highlighting certain explanatory mechanisms at the expense of others, usually overstating the case for their universality. Sociological and economic theories of social action are no exception. They emphasize values or group identifications and instrumental calculations, respectively, as the prime motivators of individual action.

The economic model, however, underestimates the extent to which group loyalties and values can trump material incentives. People do not always modify their preferences and behavior in response to new conditions and opportunities. Indeed, they are often prone to defend their way of life against social change. At the same time, the sociological model explains stability better than change because it assumes that values acquired early in life resist contemporary influences; this model pays only passing attention to the instrumental nature of norms and values and the circumstances in which people will either maintain or change their values. Contrary to the sociological model, changes in beliefs and values and, more broadly, changes in the culture, often are the product of intentional actions. The intentional manipulation of cultural resources occurs, for example, when groups redefine their own identity in order to manufacture solidarity and facilitate collective action.[31] "To speak of cultural inertia," warned Barrington Moore, "is to overlook the concrete interests and privileges that are served by indoctrination, education, and the entire complicated process of transmitting culture from one generation to the next."[32]

The model of individual choice that I have developed and applied in this book is primarily an instrumental model that tries to integrate the two contrasting approaches. The resulting model possesses several desirable properties, which I would like to emphasize in this final section. First, it has a simple structure, consisting essentially of two pairs of parameters representing dispositions (group identification, ideology, traits) and incentives (social pressures and rewards, legal sanctions, material benefits) that determine choices over time.

Second, despite its simplicity, the model yields a variety of interesting deductions about individual decision making and group dynamics. Because the model abstractly represents any kind of choice between alternative group identifications, beliefs, opinions, values, and policies, it can be applied to socialization, identity formation, conformity to norms and values, coordination and conventions, political mobilization, public opinion formation, and social adjustment to new norms and practices.

By contrast, theoretical explanations centering on cultural values encourage abbrieviated explanations that lead us away from studying group dynamics. As I argued in chapter 1, rational choice theory raises interesting additional questions about the nature of status, the origin of beliefs, the common social processes that give rise to norms and conventions, the instrumental role of social norms and values, and the sources of value change that are not elaborated by these other theories. Therefore, a rational choice model of the reasons why people invest in their way of life leads naturally to a series of more fundamental issues.

Third, the model also has the virtue of being explicitly dynamic, which corresponds to how social processes actually unfold over time. For example,

public opinion converges on conventional interpretations of issues, acculturation to norms is a gradual process, the accuracy with which people make the
rational decision increases with repeated choice, and normative and social
pressures produce compliance and social adjustment to new norms and practices. The model thus turns our attention away from fixed states and encourages us to think about social processes—change, social interaction, group dynamics, flows of ideas and people, and mobility between groups. Individuals
are products of their society and culture, but they are also agents trying to
transform their environment and their institutions, seeking better opportunities
and improvements in the quality of their lives.

Preferences and choices embody the past as well as look to the future. We
are who we are because of our history of choices, but our choices can reinforce
our past decisions as well as take us in new directions. Our beliefs about the
world and our priorities and goals emerge from these past experiences. Still,
the identifications and values acquired through socialization are sustained only
if they continue to be relevant in our contemporary environment. Individuals
are socially mobile and wish to move to groups that provide them with superior
opportunities and benefits. Psychological constructs such as identities and values are fluid rather than fixed, permanent entities. People intentionally try to
change social norms and institutions; they do not merely pass along their culture to succeeding generations. Groups do not merely reproduce themselves.
The content of socialization changes over time.

Fourth, the model in my view upholds what Charles Lave and James March
prescribed as the third principle (after truth and beauty) of model building,
that, all else being equal, our models should be just. They should recommend
policies and solutions that "contribute to making better, not worse, worlds."[33]
To illustrate, they provide two models explaining why there are group differences in intelligence test scores. The first model emphasizes genetic determi-
nants of intelligence, while the second model focuses on differences in socioeconomic conditions and educational opportunities. It may be difficult to
differentiate between the models using the available evidence. But the two
models yield sharply contrasting policy implications—the genetic explanation
is fatalistic and suggests that ameliorative policies may produce little benefit
for the disadvantaged group, while the socioeconomic explanation prescribes
greater investment in postnatal care and educational facilities.

Between psychological traits and rational choice, a model that focuses on
the incentives behind the development of dispositions and preferences directs
our efforts toward understanding the social and economic motives for people's
beliefs and actions. Because the model guides us to consider both dispositional
and incentive-based explanations of action, and to evaluate the sources of
support for underlying values and dispositions rather than to assume that they

are constant, it helps counteract the tendency to explain behavior strictly in terms of personal characteristics.

The model encourages us to examine the social pressures on people to conform, the effect of norms and values on people's opportunities, the social and material investments made in these values, and the reasons that people give for defending their norms, values, and social institutions. Such understanding of the lives and communities of others is critical to the development of greater tolerance for those who are different from ourselves. People's lives are assumed to have an underlying rationality, but it is not a simple rationality rooted exclusively in material goals. The effort to untangle that rationality implies a respect for people's motives, a recognition that they have reasons for their actions and that their actions are aimed at achieving outcomes and are not simply manifestations of habit, anxiety, frustration, anger, or other reflexive impulses.

We ought generally to distrust explanations for behavior based on cultural values or attitudes until we have taken stock of social and economic constraints and incentives. Otherwise we are likely to assume that cultural inertia—rooted in prior socialization, individual dispositions, and group memberships—rules out individual change. The premise of the model is that the effects of past social influences endure in the present only if they continue to be reinforced. Prejudices, group identities, ideological values, and partisan beliefs have to be continually stoked and coordinated behind group interests or else they lose their relevance. The constancy of personal dispositions is fostered by a corresponding constancy of social circumstances and social expectations.

The model thus protects us against parochial judgments that behavior which is different and difficult to explain is irrational, without reason, and not aimed at fulfilling goals. People's actions are guided by their beliefs about how other people are constituted and their cultural theories about what holds society together. This does not mean that we cannot or should not judge people's actions, only that we should try to understand the motives behind those actions before we evaluate them. We uncover in the process the structure of beliefs and desires that lend coherence to people's actions. Their life decisions have been made in the context of a set of norms; social relations of trust and cooperation and political coalitions have been forged upon these values. In this manner, people have not only developed an attachment to a way of life but they may also be less well served by different conventions and values.

Exploration of the constellation of beliefs and incentives underlying behavior is based on the charitable principle that actions have reasons and that beliefs, goals, and actions are coherent.[34] By making sense of the social and psychological processes underlying formation of beliefs, values, and preferences, and tracing the benefits of conforming to conventions of knowledge and morality, we begin to understand why people invest so heavily in preserving their versions of the neighborhood, community, or nation in which they live. And to understand is to open up channels of communication, to appreciate what is important to others, and to know why they embrace the positions that they do.

NOTES

INTRODUCTION

1. Richard Hofstadter, *The Paranoid Style in American Politics* (Chicago: University of Chicago Press, 1955), 87.

2. See Brian Barry, *Sociologists, Economists, and Democracy* (Chicago: University of Chicago Press, 1978); Jon Elster, *The Cement of Society* (Cambridge: Cambridge University Press, 1989). I should emphasize, as have others who have employed the sociological-economic distinction, that the "sociological approach" is an ideal type, not a characterization of all sociological research. Prominent use of economic reasoning in sociological theory can be found, for example in James S. Coleman, *Foundations of Social Theory* (Cambridge, MA: Harvard University Press, 1990), and Michael Hechter, *Principles of Group Solidarity* (Berkeley: University of California Press, 1987).

3. Bernard R. Berelson, Paul F. Lazarsfeld, and William N. McPhee, *Voting* (Chicago: University of Chicago Press, 1954), 311.

4. Sarah Patton Boyle, *The Desegregated Heart* (New York: William Morrow, 1962), 3–4.

5. "Honesty is more important than anything that can happen to you. Never forget that!" (ibid., 184); "If you run from anything, it will pursue you" (186); the proverbial "George" is not "as hard-working or reliable as most people think. Besides, who is this George anyhow? *You* are. I want you always to remember that" (94).

6. See Nicholas D. Kristof, "Lamas Seek the Holy Child, but Politics Intrude," *New York Times,* 1 October 1990, p. A4.

7. See Elster, *Cement of Society,* 97.

8. See Norval D. Glenn, "Values, Attitudes and Beliefs," in Orville G. Brim Jr. and Jerome Kagan, eds., *Constancy and Change in Human Development* (Cambridge, MA, Harvard University Press, 1980); David. O. Sears, "On the Persistence of Early Political Predispositions: The Roles of Attitude Object and Life Stage," in Ladd Wheeler, ed., *Review of Personality and Social Psychology* (Beverly Hills, CA: Sage, 1983).

9. Grady McWhiney, *Cracker Culture* (Tuscaloosa: University of Alabama Press, 1988), 7.

10. Oscar Lewis, *La Vida* (New York: Random House, 1966), xlv; see also his *Five Families* (New York: Basic Books, 1959). On the culture of poverty, see also Charles A. Valentine, *Culture and Poverty* (Chicago: University of Chicago Press, 1968).

11. See Donald R. Kinder and David O. Sears, "Public Opinion and Political Action," in Gardner Lindzey and Elliot Aronson, eds., *The Handbook of Social Psychology* (New York: Random House, 1985), 2:659; David O. Sears and Carolyn L. Funk, "Self-Interest in Americans' Political Opinions," in Jane J. Mansbridge, ed., *Beyond*

Self-Interest (Chicago: University of Chicago Press, 1990) and "The Role of Self-Interest in Social and Political Attitudes," *Advances in Experimental Social Psychology* 24 (1991): 1–91; Jack Citrin and Donald Philip Green, "The Self-Interest Motive in American Public Opinion," *Research in Micropolitics* 3 (1990): 1–28; Leif Lewin, *Self-Interest and Public Interest in Western Politics* (Oxford: Oxford University Press, 1991); and Dale T. Miller and Rebecca K. Ratner, "The Power of the Myth of Self-Interest," in Leo Montada and Melvin J. Lerner, eds., *Current Societal Concerns about Justice* (New York: Plenum Press, 1996).

12. For surveys of the literature at different stages of political science, sociology, and social psychology, see Seymour M. Lipset et al., "The Psychology of Voting: An Analysis of Political Behavior," in Gardner Lindzey, ed., *The Handbook of Social Psychology,* vol. 2 (Reading, MA: Addison-Wesley, 1954); David O. Sears, "Political Behavior," in Gardner Lindzey and Elliot Aronson, *The Handbook of Social Psychology,* 2d ed., vol. 5 (Reading, MA: Addison-Wesley, 1969); Jeanne Knutson, ed., *Handbook of Political Psychology* (San Francisco: Jossey-Bass, 1973); Kinder and Sears, "Public Opinion"; William J. McGuire, "The Poly-Psy Relationship: Three Phases of a Long Affair," in Shanto Iyengar and William J. McGuire, eds., *Explorations in Political Psychology* (Durham: Duke University Press, 1993); Donald Kinder, "Opinion and Action in the Realm of Politics," in Daniel T. Gilbert, Susan T. Fiske, and Gardner Lindzey, eds., *The Handbook of Social Psychology,* 4th ed. (Boston: McGraw-Hill, 1998); James H. Kuklinski, ed., *Thinking about Political Psychology* (Cambridge: Cambridge University Press), forthcoming.

13. Donald Black, *The Behavior of Law* (New York: Academic Press, 1976). For general discussions of social norms, see Edna Ullmann-Margalit, *The Emergence of Norms* (Oxford: Clarendon Press, 1977); Elster, *Cement of Society;* Coleman, *Foundations of Social Theory;* Robert Ellickson, *Order without Law* (Cambridge, MA: Harvard University Press, 1991); Jack Knight, *Institutions and Social Conflict* (Cambridge: Cambridge University Press, 1992); Russell Hardin, *One for All* (Princeton: Princeton University Press, 1995); John Finley Scott, *Internalization of Norms* (Englewood Cliffs, NJ: Prentice-Hall, 1971); Erving Goffman, *Relations in Public* (New York: Basic Books, 1971); Robert B. Edgerton, *Rules, Exceptions, and Social Order* (Berkeley: University of California Press, 1985); Richard H. McAdams, "The Origin, Development, and Regulation of Norms," *Michigan Law Review* 96 (1997): 338–433; Cristina Bicchieri, Richard Jeffrey, and Brian Skyrms, eds., *The Dynamics of Norms* (Cambridge: Cambridge University Press, 1997); and H. Peyton Young, *Individual Strategy and Social Structure* (Princeton: Princeton University Press, 1998).

14. Dennis Chong, "Rational Choice Theory's Mysterious Rivals," *Critical Review* 9 (1995): 37–58.

15. E. E. Schattschneider, *The Semisovereign People* (New York: Holt, Rinehart and Winston, 1960), 68.

CHAPTER ONE

1. Donald Davidson, *Actions and Events* (Oxford: Oxford University Press, 1986); Brian Fay, *Contemporary Philosophy of Social Science* (Oxford: Blackwell, 1996).

2. Karl Popper, *The Poverty of Historicism* (New York: Harper and Row, 1961). Popper proposes the "zero method," which is "the method of constructing a model on the assumption of complete rationality (and perhaps also on the assumption of the

possession of complete information) on the part of all individuals concerned, and of estimating the deviation of the actual behavior of people from the model behavior, using the latter as a kind of zero co-ordinate" (141). See also Garrett Hardin, *The Limits of Altruism* (Bloomington: Indiana University Press, 1977). On the plausibility of rationality, Hardin asks, "The assumption of pure egoism may not be enough to explain all human actions. If so, will we not discover this sooner by presuming that it is?" (3).

3. Procedural rationality is consistent with Simon's notion of "bounded rationality." See Herbert Simon, "Human Nature in Politics: The Dialogue of Psychology with Political Science," *American Political Science Review* 79 (1985): 293–304. On the subjectivity of rationality, see also Jon Elster, "Rationality, Emotions, and Social Norms," *Synthese* 98 (1994): 21–49, and Jon Elster, ed., *Rational Choice* (New York: New York University Press, 1986).

4. Barry, *Sociologists, Economists, and Democracy,* 174–77.

5. Hardin, *One for All,* 46.

6. Robert Nozick, *The Nature of Rationality* (Princeton: Princeton University Press, 1993), 64. Nozick contends that: "Rationality involves some degree of self-consciousness. Not only reasons are evaluated, but also the processes by which information arrives, is stored, and is recalled. A rational person will try to be alert to biases in these processes and will take steps to correct those biases he knows of. In assessing the import of the information he has, he also will consider what different information could have arrived and how likely it is that it would have arrived, given various facts" (74–75).

7. Some took as strong causal evidence of sorcery a correlation between an angry action taken by a suspected witch toward someone and actual harm falling upon that person. But reasonable doubts were raised by Mather about whether there was adequate proof that the angry action caused the outcome rather than a supernatural force that was independent of the person committing the angry act. Consequently, the proximity between the angry act and the harmful event was a crucial detail. Another type of evidence used in witchcraft trials was spectral evidence. Some accusers testified that they had been visited by a specter that had assumed the form of the accused person. Once again, the difficulty of such testimony was that it was not intersubjectively verifiable. There were cases in which the accuser claimed to be seeing such a specter, but another party present detected nothing. The admission of spectral evidence raised concerns that the devil might deviously assume the form of an innocent person rather than a guilty party who had made a deal allowing the devil to use his or her form. Fortunately, the then-prevailing theory of the supernatural simplified matters by specifying that such deception lay beyond the devil's power. Because physical evidence was hard to obtain, confessions were prized. See Paul Boyer and Stephen Nissenbaum, *Salem Possessed* (Cambridge, MA: Harvard University Press, 1974), 10–18.

8. At this point, I will only outline these assumptions, as their significance will become more evident in the following section, when I discuss competing noninstrumental theories, and in chapter 2, when I present a formal model of individual choice.

9. John C. Harsanyi, "Rational Choice Theories of Politics vs. Functionalist and Conformist Theories," *World Politics* 21 (1969): 513–28.

10. Gary Becker, *Accounting for Tastes* (Cambridge, MA: Harvard University Press, 1996).

11. Mancur Olson, *The Logic of Collective Action* (Cambridge, MA: Harvard University Press, 1971).

12. See, e.g., Stanley I. Benn, "The Problematic Rationality of Political Participation," in Peter Laslett and James Fishkin, eds., *Philosophy, Politics and Society,* 5th series (Oxford: Blackwell, 1979); Albert O. Hirschman, *Shifting Involvements* (Princeton: Princeton University Press, 1982), and "Against Parsimony: Three Easy Ways of Complicating Some Categories of Economic Discourse," in *Rival Views of Market Society, and Other Recent Essays* (New York: Viking, 1986); Howard Margolis, *Selfishness, Altruism, and Rationality* (Chicago: University of Chicago Press, 1982); Tibor Scitovsky, *The Joyless Economy* (New York: Oxford University Press, 1976); Amartya K. Sen, "Rational Fools: A Critique of the Behavioral Foundations of Economic Theory" *Philosophy and Public Affairs* 6 (1977): 317–44; Harvey Liebenstein, *Beyond Economic Man* (Cambridge, MA: Harvard University Press, 1980); George Akerlof, *An Economic Theorist's Book of Tales* (Cambridge: Cambridge University Press, 1984); Amitai Etzioni, *The Moral Dimension* (New York: Free Press, 1988); Karen Schweers Cook and Margaret Levi, eds., *The Limits of Rationality* (Chicago: University of Chicago Press, 1990); Jane Mansbridge, ed., *Beyond Self-Interest* (Chicago: University of Chicago Press, 1990); and Kristin Monroe, ed., *The Economic Approach to Politics* (New York: Harper/Collins, 1991).

13. Lipset et al., "The Psychology of Voting," 1128–34.

14. Larry Laudan, *Progress and Its Problems* (Berkeley: University of California Press, 1977), 17.

15. These issues are elaborated on in Chong, "Rational Choice Theory's Mysterious Rivals."

16. Elster, *Cement of Society;* Daniel Little, *Varieties of Social Explanation* (Boulder, CO: Westview Press, 1991).

17. Doug McAdam, "Social Movements," in Neil J. Smelser, ed., *Handbook of Sociology* (Beverly Hills, CA: Sage, 1988); Aldon Morris, *The Origin of the Civil Rights Movement* (New York: Free Press, 1984).

18. Russell Hardin, *Collective Action* (Baltimore: Johns Hopkins University Press, 1982).

19. Dennis Chong, *Collective Action and the Civil Rights Movement* (Chicago: University of Chicago Press, 1991).

20. Arthur Stinchcombe, "The Conditions of Fruitfulness of Theorizing about Mechanisms in Social Science" *Philosophy of the Social Sciences* 21 (1991): 367–88.

21. Doug McAdam, *Political Process and the Development of Black Insurgency, 1930–1970* (Chicago: University of Chicago Press, 1982), and "Social Movements."

22. Theda Skocpol, *States and Social Revolutions* (Cambridge: Cambridge University Press, 1979); Michael Taylor, "Structure, Culture and Action in the Explanation of Social Change," *Politics and Society* 17 (1989): 115–62.

23. Kingsley Davis and Wilbert Moore, "Some Principles of Stratification" *American Sociological Review* 10 (1945): 242–49.

24. John C. Harsanyi, "A Bargaining Model for Social Status in Informal Groups and Formal Organizations," *Behavioral Science* 11 (1966): 357–69, at 358.

25. Peter J. Boyer, "The Ogre's Tale," *New Yorker,* 4 April 1994, pp. 36–48, at 36, 45.

26. Elijah Anderson, "The Code of the Streets," *Atlantic Monthly,* May 1994, pp. 81–83, 86–89, 92–94, at 80, 88. See also Anderson, *Streetwise* (Chicago: University of Chicago Press, 1990).

27. Forrest McDonald, prologue to Grady McWhiney, *Cracker Culture* (Tuscaloosa: University of Alabama Press, 1988), p. xxii.

28. These observations about the evolution of goaltending styles were made by former Montreal Canadiens goaltender, Ken Dryden, in an interview that I heard on the ESPN radio network on 29 May 1999.

29. Jon Elster, *Ulysses and the Sirens: Studies in Rationality and Irrationality* (Cambridge: Cambridge University Press, 1984), 139.

30. See, e.g., Theodor Adorno et al., *The Authoritarian Personality* (New York: Norton, 1950); Herbert McClosky, "Conservatism and Personality," *American Political Science Review* 52 (1958): 27–45; William Kornhauser, *The Politics of Mass Society* (Glencoe: Free Press, 1959); Seymour Martin Lipset, *Political Man* (Garden City, NY: Doubleday,1960); David McClelland, *The Achieving Society* (New York: Free Press, 1961); Neil J. Smelser, *Theory of Collective Behavior* (New York: Free Press, 1962); Gabriel Almond and Sidney Verba, *The Civic Culture* (Princeton: Princeton University Press, 1963); Daniel Bell, ed., *The Radical Right* (New York: Anchor Books, 1964); David Easton and Jack Dennis, *Children in the Political System* (New York: McGraw-Hill, 1969); Richard Christie, *Studies in Machiavellianism* (New York: Academic Press, 1970); Ted Robert Gurr, *Why Men Rebel* (Princeton: Princeton University Press, 1970); Fred I. Greenstein and Michael Lerner, eds., *A Sourcebook for the Study of Personality and Politics* (Chicago: Markham, 1971); Alex Inkeles, *Becoming Modern* (Cambridge, MA: Harvard University Press, 1974).

31. Joseph R. Gusfield, *Symbolic Crusade,* 2d ed. (Urbana: University of Illinois Press, 1986); Hofstadter, *Paranoid Style;* Seymour Martin Lipset and Earl Raab, *The Politics of Unreason* (New York: Harper, 1970); Murray Edelman, *The Symbolic Uses of Politics* (Urbana: University of Illinois Press, 1964) and *Politics as Symbolic Action* (Chicago: Markham, 1971); Louis A. Zurcher and R. George Kirkpatrick, *Citizens for Decency* (Austin: University of Texas Press, 1976); Joseph R. Gusfield, *The Culture of Public Problems* (Chicago: University of Chicago Press, 1981); Steve Bruce, *The Rise and Fall of the New Christian Right* (Oxford: Clarendon Press, 1990).

32. See the references above in the introduction, n. 11.

33. The classic source is Adorno et al., *Authoritarian Personality.*

34. Gusfield, *Symbolic Crusade,* 166, 173.

35. Ibid., 148.

36. Ibid., 116.

37. Hofstadter, *Paranoid Style,* 91–92.

38. Ibid., 49.

39. Ibid., 53–54.

40. Ibid., 78.

41. Ibid.

42. Gusfield, *Symbolic Crusade,* 195–96.

43. Kermit Hall, *The Magic Mirror* (New York: Oxford University Press, 1989), 251.

44. Gusfield, *Symbolic Crusade,* 123.

45. See, e.g., Alan Crawford, *Thunder on the Right* (New York: Pantheon, 1980); Joseph R. Gusfield, *Culture of Public Problems;* Samuel P. Huntington, *American Politics: The Promise of Disharmony* (Cambridge, MA: Harvard University Press. 1981); Michael Wood and Michael Hughes, "The Moral Basis of Moral Reform," *Amer-*

ican Sociological Review 49 (1984): 86–99; Bruce, *Rise and Fall;* James Davison Hunter, *Culture Wars* (New York: Basic Books, 1991); Erich Goode and Nachman Ben-Yehuda, *Moral Panics* (Oxford: Blackwell, 1994); Citrin and Green, "The Self-Interest Motive"; Michael Kazin, *The Populist Persuasion* (New York: Basic Books, 1995); Sara Diamond, *Roads to Dominion* (New York: The Guilford Press, 1995); Robert Abelson, "The Secret Existence of Expressive Behavior," *Critical Review* 9 (1995): 25–36; Michael Taylor, "Battering RAMS," *Critical Review* 9 (1995): 223–34; William Martin, *With God on Our Side* (New York: Broadway Books, 1996).

46. Citrin and Green, "The Self-Interest Motive"; Abelson, "Secret Existence."

47. For surveys, see Sears and Funk, "The Role of Self-Interest" and "Self-Interest in Americans' Political Opinions"; Citrin and Green, "The Self-Interest Motive"; and David O. Sears, "Symbolic Politics: A Socio-psychological Theory," in Shanto Iyengar and William J. McGuire, eds., *Explorations in Political Psychology* (Durham, NC: Duke University Press, 1993).

48. Donald R. Kinder and Lynn M. Sanders, *Divided by Color* (Chicago: University of Chicago Press, 1996). Kinder and Sanders treat racial resentment as an endogenous variable, capable of influencing and being influenced by perceptions of threat.

49. Ibid., 84, 89.

50. "Among the learned elements of personality in certain respects the stablest and most enduring are the major value-orientation patterns and there is much evidence that these are 'laid down' in childhood and are not on a large scale subject to drastic alteration during adult life" (Talcott Parsons, *The Social System* [Glencoe, IL: The Free Press, 1951], 208).

51. Kinder and Sears,"Public Opinion and Political Action." Elsewhere, Kinder and Sanders write that "in American race relations, interests appear to be less an alternative to the passions than their instrument" (*Divided by Color,* 90).

52. David O. Sears, Carl P. Hensler, and Leslie K. Speer, "Whites' Opposition to 'Busing': Self-Interest or Symbolic Politics?" *American Political Science Review* 73 (1979): 369–84 , at 371.

53. Kinder's and Sanders' examination of perceived threat is an exception in this respect.

54. Tom R. Tyler and Renee Weber, "Support for the Death Penalty: Instrumental Response to Crime, or Symbolic Attitude?" *Law and Society Review* 17 (1982): 21–45.

55. M. A. Lotwis, "The Gun Toter and the Gun Controller: Self Interest and Ideology in Political Attitudes about Gun Control." Paper presented at the annual meeting of the Midwest Political Science Association, Chicago, IL, 1989.

56. Sears and Funk, "The Role of Self-Interest," 72.

57. See David O. Sears and Jack Citrin, *Tax Revolt* (Cambridge, MA: Harvard University Press, 1982), 45–46.

58. Sears and Funk, "The Role of Self-Interest," 59.

59. Ibid., 69.

60. M. Sudit, "Ideology or Self-Interest? Medical Students' Attitudes toward National Health Insurance," *Journal of Health and Social Behavior* 20 (1988): 376–84.

61. Stanley Feldman, "Economic Self-Interest and Political Behavior," *American Journal of Political Science* 26 (1982): 446–66, at 449. See also Richard A. Brody and Paul M. Sniderman, "From Life Space to Polling Place: The Relevance of Personal

Concerns for Voting Behavior," *British Journal of Political Science* 7 (1977): 337–60.

62. See Dennis Chong, "Social Incentives and the Preservation of Reputation in Public-Spirited Collective Action," *International Political Science Review* 13 (1992): 171–98.

63. J. Anthony Lukas, *Common Ground* (New York: Vintage, 1985), 27; see also Ronald P. Formisano, *Boston against Busing* (Chapel Hill: University of North Carolina Press, 1991).

64. Jonathan Rieder, *Canarsie* (Cambridge, MA: Harvard University Press, 1985).

65. Ibid., 198.

66. Ibid., 199.

67. Ibid., 87.

68. Donald Philip Green and Jonathan A. Cowden, "Who Protests: Self-Interest and White Opposition to Busing," *Journal of Politics* 54 (1992): 471–96.

69. "People tend not to reflect on their personal interests when making political decisions in the context of a survey interview, but are stimulated to think about their interests when faced with the choice of whether to take action" (ibid., 475).

70. See, e.g., Chong, *Collective Action,* 31–72; Hardin, *Collective Action,* 173–87; David Hirshleifer and Eric Rasmusen, "Cooperation in a Repeated Prisoners' Dilemma with Ostracism," *Journal of Economic Behavior and Organization* 12 (1989): 87–106.

71. Samuel Popkin et al., "What Have You Done for Me Lately? Toward an Investment Theory of Voting," *American Political Science Review* 70 (1976): 787; see also Morris Fiorina, *Retrospective Voting* (New Haven: Yale University Press, 1981); Christopher H. Achen, "Social Psychology, Demographic Variables, and Linear Regression: Breaking the Iron Triangle in Voting Research," *Political Behavior* 14 (1992): 195–211.

72. See Barry, *Sociologists, Economists, and Democracy,* 89–96.

73. See Herbert McClosky and John Zaller, *The American Ethos: Public Attitudes toward Capitalism and Democracy* (Cambridge, MA: Harvard University Press, 1984), 189–233.

74. See Duane F. Alwin, Ronald L. Cohen, and Theodore M. Newcomb, *Political Attitudes over the Life Span* (Madison: University of Wisconsin Press, 1991), 20: "One typically finds a great deal of similarity between the [ideological and partisan] orientations of parents and children."

75. See Hirschman, *Shifting Involvements,* 70–71; Harry G. Frankfurt, "Freedom of the Will and the Concept of a Person," *Journal of Philosophy* 68 (1971): 5–20, at 6–7 ("Besides wanting and choosing and being moved to do this or that, men may also want to have [or not to have] certain desires and motives.").

76. See Lipset and Raab, *Politics of Unreason,* 452–82; see also Herbert McClosky and Alida Brill, *Dimensions of Tolerance* (New York: Russell Sage Foundation, 1983), 336–414; Dennis Chong, Herbert McClosky, and John Zaller, "Patterns of Support for Democratic and Capitalist Values in the United States," *British Journal of Political Science* 13 (1983): 401–40.

77. Ben Wattenberg, *Values Matter Most* (New York: Free Press, 1995), 92.

78. "This is one of those issues (lowering the capital gains tax is another) where economists know what they believe and often use research and statistics not so much to answer questions as to document what they are sure they already know. They view

the same data through completely different lenses" (David E. Rosenbaum, "90-Cent Dose of Bluster," *New York Times,* 30 April 1996, pp. A1, A12, at A12).

79. David O. Sears. Richard R. Lau, Tom R. Tyler, and H. M. Allen Jr., "Self-Interest vs. Symbolic Politics in Policy Attitudes and Presidential Voting," *American Political Science Review* 74 (1980), 682–83. In the text, I have placed quotation marks around the authors' summaries of the items used in this analysis to indicate the similarity between independent and dependent variables.

80. Kinder and Sanders, *Divided by Color,* 124. In the appendix to this work, Kinder and Sanders explain that racial resentment is essentially the same concept as symbolic racism; the new label better describes the combination of racial animosity and support for individualism embodied in racial resentment. Racial resentment is found to be coherent and stable, to be correlated with a variety of conservative policy positions, to be connected to derogatory racial stereotypes, and to have a statistically significant relationship with racial policy positions.

81. Sears and Funk, "The Role of Self-Interest," 162; see also Jon A. Krosnick, "The Stability of Political Preferences: Comparisons of Symbolic and Nonsymbolic Attitudes." *American Journal of Political Science* 35 (1991): 547–76.

82. Paul H. Mussen and Norma Haan, "A Longitudinal Study of Patterns of Personality and Political Ideologies," in Dorothy H. Eichorn, John A. Clausen, Norma Haan, Marjorie P. Honzik, and Paul H. Mussen, eds., *Present and Past in Middle Life* (New York: Academic Press, 1981), 391–409. See also Herbert McClosky and Dennis Chong, "Similarities and Differences between Left-Wing and Right-Wing Radicals," *British Journal of Political Science* 15 (1985): 329–63.

83. Mussen and Haan, "Longitudinal Study," 404–5.

84. Barry, *Sociologists, Economists, and Democracy,* 97–98.

85. Donald T. Campbell, "On the Conflicts between Biological and Social Evolution and between Psychology and Moral Tradition," *American Psychologist* 30 (1975): 1103–26.

86. Mussen and Haan, "Longitudinal Study," 409.

87. Glenn D. Wilson, *The Psychology of Conservatism* (New York: Academic Press, 1973).

88. Alwin, Cohen, and Newcomb, *Political Attitudes,* 275–76.

89. Ibid., 264.

90. See Donald D. Searing, Gerald Wright, and George Rabinowitz, "The Primary Principle: Attitude Change and Political Socialization," *British Journal of Political Science* 6 (1976): 83–113; Donald D. Searing, Joel J. Schwartz, and Alden E. Lind, "The Structuring Principle: Political Socialization and Belief Systems," *American Political Science Review* 67 (1973): 415–32.

91. Janie S. Steckenrider and Neal E. Cutler, "Aging and Adult Political Socialization: The Importance of Roles and Transitions," in Roberta S. Sigel, ed., *Political Learning in Adulthood* (Chicago: University of Chicago Press, 1989).

92. M. Kent Jennings and Richard G. Niemi, *The Political Character of Adolescence* (Princeton: Princeton University Press, 1974), and *Generations and Politics* (Princeton: Princeton University Press, 1981).

93. John A. Clausen, "The Life Course of Individuals," in Matilda W. Riley and Anne Foner, eds., *Aging and Society* (New York: Russell Sage Foundation, 1972).

94. Bernice L. Neugarten, "Age Groups in American Society and the Rise of the

Young-Old," *Annals of the American Academy of Political and Social Sciences* 415 (1974): 187–98.

95. According to Norval D. Glenn, "Values, Attitudes, and Beliefs," in Orville G. Brim Jr. and Jerome Kagan, eds., *Constancy and Change in Human Development* (Cambridge, MA: Harvard University Press,1980).

96. Theodore M. Newcomb, "Some Patterned Consequences of Membership in a College Community," in Theodore M. Newcomb et al., eds., *Readings in Social Psychology* (New York: Henry Holt, 1947), 345–57.

97. Theodore M. Newcomb, Kathryn E. Koenig, Richard Flacks, and Donald P. Warwick, *Persistence and Change* (New York: Wiley, 1967); Alwin, Cohen, and Newcomb, *Political Attitudes.*

98. Alwin, Cohen, and Newcomb, *Political Attitudes,* 173–74.

99. Ibid., 215–16.

100. Ibid., 249.

101. John Dollard, *Caste and Class in a Southern Town* (New York: Harper, 1937), 47.

102. Ibid., 47–48.

103. Dennis Chong and Melissa Kary Miller, "Racial Attitudes and Identifications over the Life Span," paper presented to the Annual Meeting of the American Political Science Association, Washington, DC, 1997.

104. Robert W. Hodge and Donald J. Treiman, "Occupational Mobility and Attitudes toward Negroes," *American Sociological Review* 31 (1966): 93–102. See also Seymour Martin Lipset and Hans Zetterberg, "A Theory of Social Mobility," *Transactions of the Third World Congress of Sociology* 3 (1956): 155–77; Seymour Martin Lipset and Reinhard Bendix, *Social Mobility in Industrial Society* (Berkeley: University of California Press, 1959); Nan Dirk De Graaf, Paul Nieuwbeerta, and Anthony Heath, "Class Mobility and Political Preferences: Individual and Contextual Effects," *American Journal of Sociology* 100 (1995): 997–1027.

105. Verner M. Sims and James R. Patrick, "Attitude toward the Negro of Northern and Southern College Students," *Journal of Social Psychology* 7 (1936): 192–204.

106. Herbert H. Hyman and Paul B. Sheatsley, Attitudes toward Desegregation," *Scientific American* 211 (1964): 16–23.

107. Martin Gilens and James Glaser, "Interregional Migration and Political Resocialization," *Public Opinion Quarterly* 61 (1997): 72–86.

108. As is suggested by Kinder and Sanders, *Divided by Color,* 274.

Chapter Two

1. All mathematical prerequisites arc covered in Samuel Goldberg, *Introduction to Difference Equations* (New York: John Wiley and Sons, 1958), and David Luenberger, *Introduction to Dynamic Systems* (New York: Wiley, 1979).

2. Philip Shenon, "Admiral, in Suicide Note, Apologized to 'My Sailors,'" *New York Times,* 18 May 1996, p. A9.

3. Berelson, Lazarsfeld, and McPhee, *Voting,* 54–76.

4. Elihu Katz and Paul F. Lazarsfeld, *Personal Influence* (New York: Free Press, 1954), 53. Among the classic and contemporary works on group dynamics, see Charles H. Cooley, *Social Organization* (New York: Charles Scribner's Sons, 1909); George

Herbert Mead, *Mind, Self, and Society* (Chicago: University of Chicago Press, 1934); Georg Simmel, *The Sociology of Georg Simmel*, trans. Kurt H. Wolff (Glencoe: Free Press, 1950); George C. Homans, *The Human Group* (New York: Harcourt, Brace, 1950); Leon Festinger, Stanley Schachter, and Kurt Back, *Social Pressure in Informal Groups* (New York: Harper & Brothers, 1950); A. Paul Hare, Edgar F. Borgatta, and Robert F. Bales, eds., *Small Groups* (New York: Alfred A. Knopf, 1955); Herbert McClosky and Harold E. Dahlgren, "Primary Group Influence on Party Loyalty," *American Political Science Review* 53 (1959): 757–76; Sidney Verba, *Small Groups and Political Behavior* (Princeton: Princeton University Press, 1961); Muzafer Sherif and Carolyn W. Sherif, *Reference Groups* (Chicago: Henry Regnery, 1964); Henri Tajfel, *Human Groups and Social Categories* (Cambridge: Cambridge University Press, 1981); Robert Huckfeldt and John Sprague, *Citizens, Politics, and Social Communication: Information and Influence in an Election Campaign* (Cambridge: Cambridge University Press, 1995).

5. See Robert K. Merton, *Social Theory and Social Structure*, enl. ed. (New York: Free Press, 1968), 140–41.

6. Perhaps with the exception of the small number of people who are the innovators of new trends. See the discussion below on opinion leaders and cultural diffusion.

7. Merton, *Social Theory*, 359–60.

8. Lawrence Friedman, *History of American Law* (New York: Touchstone, 1973), 536. The development of a standard curriculum also provided a basis for regulating the increasing proliferation of law schools. Vocationally oriented law schools catered to those from disadvantaged backgrounds. These schools widened access to the legal profession, thus raising concern among the legal elite over the maintenance of their occupational status and exclusivity, as well as their income. Bar examinations helped stem the flow into the profession (537–38); see also Duncan Kennedy, "Legal Education as Training for Hierarchy," in David Kairys, ed., *The Politics of Law* (New York: Pantheon, 1982).

9. Harsanyi, "Rational Choice Models."

10. Solomon Asch, "Effects of Group Pressure upon the Modification and Distortion of Judgment," in Harold Guetzkow, ed., *Groups, Leadership, and Men* (Pittsburgh: Carnegie, 1951), "Opinions and Social Pressure," *Scientific American* 193 (1955): 31–35, and "Studies of Independence and Conformity: A Minority of One against a Unanimous Majority," *Psychological Monographs* 70 (1956): no. 9, whole no. 416.

11. See Sherif and Sherif, *Reference Groups*, 169.

12. See Campbell, "Conflicts," 1103, 1107.

13. Bill Berkeley, "The Warlords of Natal," *Atlantic Monthly*, March 1994, p. 91.

14. Liang Heng and Judith Shapiro, *Son of the Revolution* (New York: Vintage, 1983), 76.

15. Alexis de Tocqueville, *Democracy in America* (New York: Vintage, 1945), 2:9.

16. Campbell ("Conflicts," 1107), notes that social evolution, like natural selection, describes a process by which "stupid, blind, unforesightful processes can produce adaptive wisdom" without any of the innovators, transmitters, or participants properly understanding the traditions being transmitted and that "a universal tendency for conformity to the opinions of others may be essential to an adaptive social custom cumulation."

17. R. Duncan Luce, "Analyzing the Social Process Underlying Group Voting

Patterns," in Eugene Burdick and Arthur J. Brodbeck, eds., *American Voting Behavior* (New York: Free Press, 1959).

18. See Harsanyi, "A Bargaining Model for Social Status"; William J. Goode, *The Celebration of Heroes* (Berkeley: University of California Press, 1978); Pierre Bourdieu, *Distinction,* trans. Richard Nice (Cambridge, MA: Harvard University Press, 1984); Robert H. Frank, *Choosing the Right Pond* (New York: Oxford University Press, 1985).

19. James B. Stewart, "Moby Dick in Manhattan," *New Yorker,* 27 June and 4 July 1994, pp. 46–66, at 64.

20. See Harsanyi, "A Bargaining Model for Social Status," 357, 359.

21. W. J. Cash, *The Mind of the South* (New York: Vintage, 1941), 93.

22. Experiments also show that individuals who are insecure about their group standing are more likely to conform than those who are securely ensconced in a group. Those who are more valuable to a group are given—and take—greater latitude. See James Dittes and Harold Kelley, "Effects of Different Conditions of Acceptance upon Conformity to Group Norms," *Journal of Abnormal and Social Psychology* 53 (1956): 100–107.

23. Dollard, *Caste and Class,* 45.

24. This assumption makes matters simpler but is not necessary.

25. To be precise, when dispositions refer to subjective states, such as group identifications, they will vary across issues and over time; on the other hand, skills and knowledge are not manipulable through persuasion.

26. These deductions are supported by Taylor, "Structure, Culture and Action"; Citrin and Green, "The Self-Interest Motive"; and John Aldrich,"Rational Choice and Turnout," *American Journal of Political Science* 37 (1993): 246–78.

27. Unpublished data from the 1978–79 Civil Liberties Survey, conducted by Herbert McClosky. For a general report on the results of this survey, see McClosky and Brill, *Dimensions of Tolerance.*

28. Kinder and Sears, "Public Opinion and Political Action." The classic text on the role of party identification in U.S. elections is Angus Campbell, Philip E. Converse, Warren E. Miller, and Donald E. Stokes, *The American Voter* (New York: John Wiley and Sons, 1960). See, more recently, Warren E. Miller and J. Merrill Shanks, *The New American Voter* (Cambridge, MA: Harvard University Press, 1996).

29. Berelson, Lazarsfeld, and McPhee, *Voting,* 321. See also Samuel Popkin, *The Reasoning Voter* (Chicago: University of Chicago Press, 1991). Popkin's thesis is that voters rely on their intuitions and feelings when evaluating political figures and issues, but that these intuitions are founded on experience and information, however fragmentary and fleeting. Much of this information is acquired incidentally and at low cost. People have everyday experiences—such as buying groceries, purchasing a house, obtaining a car loan, being laid off from work, and preparing for their children's education—which inform them about the state of the economy. They get a sense of the state of international relations and the condition of towns and cities from occasionally watching the news and glimpsing periodicals and other publications or talking to their friends and co-workers. In similar fashion, they can easily discern political controversies and conflicts that are at the top of the political agenda.

However, Popkin probably exaggerates in attributing reasonable inference processes to voters who make decisions on the basis of superficial impressions of candidates. Voters use a variety of psychological shortcuts—such as cognitive balancing, generalizing, and extrapolating from given information—to fill in details about candidates where it is deficient. Voter decisions that are based solely on the demographic characteristics of candidates or on suspect tabloid information about them are examples of inferential leaps that may be hard to justify as "reasonable."

30. Merton, *Social Theory and Social Structure,* 246.

31. See Muzafer Sherif, *The Psychology of Social Norms* (New York: Harper, 1936).

32. See Sherif, "Group Influences upon the Formation of Norms and Attitudes," in Guy E. Swanson, Theodore M. Newcomb, and Eleanor L. Hartley, eds., *Readings in Social Psychology,* rev. ed. (New York: Henry Holt 1952).

33. For a similar demonstration of group norm formation on social issues in a small housing community, see Festinger, Schachter, and Back, *Social Pressures,* 73–100.

34. Daniel Katz, "The Functions of Attitudes," in Fred I. Greenstein and Michael Lerner, eds., *A Sourcebook for the Study of Personality and Politics* (Chicago: Markham, 1971), 206–7.

35. See Hardin, *One for All,* 62–63.

36. Berelson, Lazarsfeld, and McPhee, *Voting,* 27, 130–31.

37. Among the basic sources on conventions are Thomas C. Schelling, *The Strategy of Conflict* (Cambridge, MA: Harvard University Press, 1960); David K. Lewis, *Convention* (Cambridge, MA: Harvard University Press, 1969); Hardin, *Collective Action;* Robert Sugden, *The Economics of Rights, Co-operation and Welfare* (Oxford: Basil Blackwell, 1986). See also Robert J. Aumann, "Agreeing to Disagree," *Annals of Statistics* 4 (1976): 1236–39; Cristina Bicchieri,"Methodological Rules as Conventions," *Philosophy of Social Science* 18 (1988): 477–95; Ariel Rubinstein,"The Electronic Mail Game: Strategic Behavior Under 'Almost Common Knowledge,'" *American Economic Review* 79 (1989): 385–91; Vincent P. Crawford and Hans Haller, "Learning How to Cooperate: Optimal Play in Repeated Coordination Games," *Econometrica* 58 (1990): 571–95; David D. Laitin,"The Tower of Babel as a Coordination Game," *American Political Science Review* 88 (1994): 622–34; Randall Calvert,"The Rational Choice Theory of Social Institutions: Cooperation, Coordination, and Communication," in Jeffrey S. Banks and Eric A. Hanushek, eds., *Modern Political Economy* (Cambridge: Cambridge University Press, 1995); Young, *Individual Strategy.*

38. Neil Miller and John Dollard, *Social Learning and Imitation* (New Haven: Yale University Press, 1941), 253–73.

39. Robert Boyd and Peter J. Richerson, *Culture and the Evolutionary Process* (Chicago: University of Chicago Press, 1985), 135. For popular discussions of the diffusion of fashion trends and the growing use of trend spotters in industry, see Malcolm Gladwell, "The Coolhunt," *New Yorker,* 17 March 1997, pp. 78–88; Roy Furchgott,"For Coolhunters, Tomorrow's Trend is the Trophy," *New York Times,* 28 June 1998, Business Section, p. 10.

40. Boyd and Richerson, *Culture and the Evolutionary Process,* 207.

41. See William McGuire, "Personality and Susceptibility to Social Influence," in E. E. Borgatta and W. W. Lambert, eds., *Handbook of Personality Theory and Research* (New York: Rand-McNally, 1968); Philip E. Converse, "Information Flow and the Stability of Partisan Attitudes," *Public Opinion Quarterly* 26 (1962): 578–99; John R. Zaller, *The Nature and Origins of Mass Opinion* (Cambridge: Cambridge University Press, 1992); Chong, McClosky, and Zaller, "Patterns of Support"; Dennis Chong, Herbert McClosky, and John Zaller, "Social Learning and the Acquisition of Political

Norms," chapter 8 in Herbert McClosky and John Zaller, *The American Ethos* (Cambridge: Harvard University Press, 1984).

42. Donald Stokes, "Spatial Models of Party Competition," in Angus Campbell, Philip E. Converse, Warren E. Miller, and Donald E. Stokes, eds., *Elections and the Political Order* (New York: John Wiley and Sons, 1966).

CHAPTER THREE

1. *New York Times,* 18 November 1997, p. A22.

2. Thus, it is wrong to assume that barriers to entry into low-status groups are unnecessary simply because no person wants to join these groups. Jon Elster makes this assumption in *The Cement of Society,* 140.

3. Nelson W. Aldrich, *Old Money* (New York:Vintage Books, 1988), 82. On upper class norms, see also Stephen Birmingham, *America's Secret Aristocracy* (Boston: Little, Brown and Co., 1987).

4. Neil Harris, "American Manners," in Luther S. Luedtke, ed., *Making America* (Chapel Hill: University of North Carolina Press, 1992), 153.

5. See, generally, Lewis, *Convention;* Sugden, *Economics of Rights.*

6. Russell Hardin, "The Emergence of Norms," *Ethics* 90 (1980): 575–87, at 579.

7. Lewis, *Convention,* 97.

8. Allan Gibbard, *Wise Choices, Apt Feelings: A Theory of Normative Judgment* (Cambridge, MA: Harvard University Press, 1990), 72.

9. Stanley Coben, *Rebellion against Victorianism* (New York: Oxford University Press, 1991), 4.

10. Laurie Goodstein, "Women in Islamic Headdress Find Faith and Prejudice, Too," *New York Times,* 3 November 1997, pp. A1, A14.

11. Coben, *Rebellion,* 29–30.

12. Rieder, *Canarsie,* 74.

13. Ibid., 85.

14. Norbert Elias, *The History of Manners,* trans. Edmund Jephcott (New York: Pantheon, 1978).

15. Roger Chartier, *A History of Private Life,* vol. 3: *Passions of the Renaissance* (Cambridge, MA: Harvard University Press, 1989), 171–72.

16. John Casson, *Rudeness and Civility* (New York: Hill and Wang, 1990).

17. Michael Winerip, "In School," *New York Times,* 20 April 1994, p. B13.

18. Ben Gose, "Gay Students Have Their Own Floor in a U. of Massachusetts Dormitory," *Chronicle of Higher Education,* 21 February 1997, pp. A37, A38.

19. Winerip, "In School," p. B13. Students voted by an 80 percent majority to reject an administrative proposal to adopt random housing assignments for freshmen in an effort to improve integration.

20. Ibid.

21. Ibid.

22. Ibid.

23. Thomas C. Schelling, *Micromotives and Macrobehavior* (New York: Norton, 1978), 137–66.

24. Winerip, "In School," p. B13: "'It's a sad commentary, the way we're all separated here,' said Gabe Jacobson, a Jewish sophomore who lives at . . . a mainly Jewish fraternity. 'But it's funny, because we like this, I think Cornell's a happier place.'"

25. Ben Gose, "Cornell President Seeks Racial Integration in Campus Housing Areas," *Chronicle of Higher Education,* 17 October 1997, p. A52.

26. See Roy Beck, "The Ordeal of Immigration in Wasau," *Atlantic Monthly,* April 1994, pp. 84–86.

27. Henry James, *The American Scene* [1907] (New York: Horizon Press, 1967), 231.

28. Rieder, *Canarsie,* 91.

29. Ibid.

30. In a similar vein, the sportswriter Robert Lipsyte suggested that we should have to pay a royalty to an athlete every time we call up and enjoy a memory of a great play that he once made in the field: "Think of the dollar as a kind of residual, a royalty for a repeat performance, even if it is only in my mind's eye" (*New York Times,* 26 October 1997, p. 29).

31. Lipset and Raab, *The Politics of Unreason,* 488–91.

32. Lukas, *Common Ground,* 282–84.

33. See Tajfel, *Human Groups;* Henri Tajfel, ed., *Social Identity and Intergroup Relations* (Cambridge: Cambridge University Press, 1982); Michael A. Hogg and Dominic Abrams, *Social Identifications* (London: Routledge, 1988); John C. Turner, *Rediscovering the Social Group* (Oxford: Basil Blackwell, 1987); Robert A. LeVine, and Donald T. Campbell, *Ethnocentrism* (New York: Wiley, 1972).

34. Boyle, *The Desegregated Heart,* 4, 8.

35. Ibid., 98, 104, 112. On the etiquette and symbolism of forms of address between whites and blacks, see also Edward L. Ayers, *The Promise of the New South* (New York: Oxford University Press, 1992), 132–34.

36. Mary Baker Eddy, *Science and Health* (Boston: Published by the Trustees under the will of Mary Baker G. Eddy, 1906); Caroline Fraser, "Suffering Children and the Christian Science Church," *Atlantic Monthly,* April 1995, pp. 105–8, 110–20, at 107. See also David L. Weddle, "The Christian Science Textbook: An Analysis of the Religious Authority of *Science and Health,* by Mary Baker Eddy," *Harvard Theological Review* 84, no. 3 (1991): 273–97.

37. Fraser, "Suffering Children," 110. See also Thomas Johnsen,"Healing and Conscience in Christian Science," *The Christian Century,* 29 June 1994, pp. 640–41.

38. The literature on psychological biases is large. See, e.g., Daniel Kahneman, Paul Slovic, and Amos Tversky, eds., *Judgment under Uncertainty: Heuristics and Biases* (Cambridge: Cambridge University Press, 1982); Hazel Markus and R. B. Zajonc, "The Cognitive Perspective in Social Psychology," in Gardner Lindzey and Elliot Aronson, eds., *The Handbook of Social Psychology,* 3d rev. ed., vol. 2 (New York: Random House, 1985); Charles Lord, Lee Ross, and Mark Lepper, "Biased Assimilation and Attitude Polarization: The Effects of Prior Theories on Subsequently Considered Evidence," *Journal of Personality and Social Psychology* 37 (1979): 2098–2109; Richard E. Nisbett and Lee Ross, *Human Inference* (Englewood Cliffs, NJ: Prentice-Hall, 1980); David J. Schneider, "Social Cognition," in Mark R. Rosenzweig and Lyman N. Porter, eds., *Annual Review of Psychology* (Palo Alto, CA: Annual Reviews, 1991).

39. Richard E. Nisbett and Timothy DeCamp Wilson, "Telling More than We Know: Verbal Reports on Mental Processes," *Psychological Review* 84 (1977): 231–59.

40. However, to the extent that people actually follow the prescriptions of their

cultural theories, their retrospective assessments of the causes of behavior may well be accurate. If one judges the quality of a party according to generally accepted criteria (quality of food, people, music), then the retrospective answer to the question of why one liked the party (because of the food, people, music) may well be the true answer. Moreover, if other people rely on partially substantiated theories in judging others, then it is prudent for people to factor in those theories in calculating how to act.

41. See, e.g., Fritz Heider, *The Psychology of Interpersonal Relations* (New York: Wiley, 1958); Edward E. Jones and Richard E. Nisbett, "The Actor and the Observer: Divergent Perceptions of the Causes of Behavior," in Edward. E. Jones et al., eds., *Attribution: Perceiving the Causes of Behavior* (Morristown, NJ: General Learning Press, 1971); Lee Ross, "The Intuitive Psychologist and His Shortcomings: Distortions in the Attribution Process," in Leonard Berkowitz, ed., *Advances in Experimental Social Psychology,* vol. 10 (New York: Academic Press, 1977); Edward E. Jones, "The Rocky Road from Acts to Dispositions," *American Psychologist* 34 (1979): 107–17.

42. Lee Ross and Craig A. Anderson, "Shortcomings in the Attribution Process," in Kahneman, Slovic, and Tversky, *Judgment under Uncertainty,* 135.

43. Bibb Latané and John M. Darley, *The Unresponsive Bystander* (New York: Appleton-Century-Crofts, 1970).

44. "Shortcomings in the Attribution Process," in Kahneman, Slovic, and Tversky, *Judgment Under Uncertainty,* 135.

45. Walter Mischel, "The Interaction of Person and Situation." In David Magnusson and Norman S. Endler, eds., *Personality at the Crossroads* (Hillsdale, NJ: Erlbaum, 1977), 347.

46. Jones and Nisbett, "The Actor and the Observer," 79–94.

47. Mark Snyder and Edward E. Jones, "Attitude Attribution When Behavior is Constrained," *Journal of Experimental Social Psychology* 10 (1974): 585–600.

48. This stigma, however, appears to be fading with the increasing number of gay characters in movies and television.

49. Solomon E. Asch, "Forming Impressions of Personality," *Journal of Abnormal and Social Psychology* 41 (1946): 258–90; Solomon E. Asch and Hans Zukier, "Thinking About Persons," *Journal of Personality and Social Psychology* 46 (1984): 1230–40.

50. Roger Brown, *Social Psychology,* 2d ed. (New York: Free Press, 1986), 378–431. See also Richard E. Nisbett,"The Trait Construct in Lay and Professional Psychology," in Leon Festinger, ed., *Retrospections on Social Psychology* (New York: Oxford University Press, 1980).

51. Erving Goffman, *Stigma* (Englewood Cliffs, NJ: Prentice-Hall, 1963), 62–63.

52. Everything about a person has to fit, or that is what we like to think. This is as true with celebrities as with ordinary people whose actions transform them into celebrities. When Joel Rifkin was caught in New York and confessed to killing 17 women, there were the usual professions of disbelief. "Dr. Kleinman [a professor of psychiatry] dismissed as 'meaningless' the protestations of neighbors, who described Mr. Rifkin as a kind-hearted soul who would open a window to let a spider out rather than kill it. 'Some people can project a certain appearance in one aspect, and do awful, obscene behavior in another aspect of their lives,' said Dr. Kleinman. 'Quite frankly, there's sometimes no way of knowing'" (Diana Jean Schemo, "'Victim' Tokens Illuminate a Suspect," *New York Times,* 1 July 1993, p. A9). For research on the actual consistency of behavior across situations, see Walter Mischel, *Personality and Assessment* (New

York: Wiley, 1968); Walter Mischel and Philip K. Peake, "Analyzing the Construction of Consistency in Personality," in Monte M. Page, ed., *Personality: Current Theory and Research* (Lincoln: University of Nebraska Press, 1983); Daryl J. Bem and A. Allen, "On Predicting Some of the People Some of the Time: The Search for Cross-Situational Consistencies in Behavior," *Psychological Review* 81 (1974): 505–520; Daryl J. Bem and D. C. Funder, "Predicting More of the People More of the Time: Assessing the Personality of Situations," *Psychological Review* 85 (1978): 485–501; Daryl J. Bem,"Toward A Response Style Theory of Persons in Situations," in Monte M. Page, ed., *Personality: Current Theory and Research* (Lincoln: University of Nebraska Press, 1983).

53. *Social Psychology,* 383. As an antidote to the biases of impression formation, Brown proposes an "anything goes" rule. By this he means that personalities need not be consistent and that it is possible for people to display any of a number of possible combinations of traits. This would help explain some so-called enigmatic personalities, such as Wagner, who were virtuous in some respects but despicable in others. It would remove some of the irony from Michael Fortier's remark that his friend Timothy McVeigh was actually a pretty good fellow if you could set aside his blowing up the Murrah federal building in Oklahoma City. People are enigmatic only insofar as we expect them to be consistently good or bad. Once we overcome this bias, then we are no longer surprised that most, if not all, people have "peculiar" or unanticipated combinations of traits. As Brown explains: "There is no real enigma in the fact that the Nazis who executed millions in concentration camps loved their own small children and pet dogs and that mafia Godfathers cherish their own families" (396).

54. On the mental processes leading from stereotyping to ideological beliefs, see Hogg and Abrams, *Social Identifications,* 64–91. On predicting behavior using personal traits, see John Sabini and Maury Silver, *Moralities of Everyday Life* (New York: Oxford University Press, 1982).

55. Coben, *Rebellion,* 30.

56. Boyle, *The Desegregated Heart,* 17–18.

57. Stephen Steinberg, *The Ethnic Myth* (Boston: Beacon Press, 1989), 163–64.

58. Malcolm Gladwell, "Black Like Them," *New Yorker,* 29 April and 6 May 1996, pp. 74–81, at 76–77. By championing the virtuous West Indian worker, the employer can also argue that he is not selecting against American blacks because of the color of their skin, but because they have characteristics that make them unreliable employees. The employer uses the West Indian as evidence that he is willing to hire blacks with the appropriate qualifications.

59. Goffman, *Stigma,* 5.

60. Gusfield, *Symbolic Crusade,* 146, 124, 5–6.

61. Jack Miles, "Blacks vs. Browns," *Atlantic Monthly,* October 1992, pp. 41–68.

62. Goffman, *Stigma,* 47.

63. Thomas Sowell, *The Economics of Politics and Race* (New York: William Morrow and Co., 1983), 129.

64. William Grimes, "Should Only Blacks Make Movies about Blacks?" *New York Times,* 28 March 1994, pp. B1, B2.

65. On the subject of minorities' accepting society's judgment about them, and the harm that results, see Charles Taylor, "The Politics of Recognition," in Amy Gutmann, ed., *Multiculturalism and "The Politics of Recognition"* (Princeton: Princeton University Press, 1992). For a discussion of how discredited and discreditable individuals manage information about themselves, see Goffman, *Stigma,* 41–104.

66. Joel Williamson, *A Rage for Order* (New York: Oxford University Press, 1986), 59.

67. Howard N. Rabinowitz, *Race Relations in the Urban South, 1865–1890* (Urbana: University of Illinois Press, 1980), 127.

68. Hortense Powdermaker, *After Freedom: A Cultural Study in the Deep South* (New York: Russell and Russell, 1939), 329–30. Coincidentally, "Cottonville" was the same town as "Southerntown," the subject of John Dollard's study, *Caste and Class in a Southern Town*. Dollard and Powdermaker also happened to conduct their field work in the same period, although independently of each other.

69. V. S. Naipaul, *A Turn in the South* (New York: Vintage Books, 1990), 146.

70. On racial and ethnic group conflict see Lawrence Bobo, "Whites' Opposition to Busing: Symbolic Racism or Realistic Group Conflict," *Journal of Personality and Social Psychology* 45 (1983): 1196–1210; James Sidanius,"The Psychology of Group Conflict and the Dynamics of Oppression," in Shanto Iyengar and William J. McGuire, eds., *Explorations in Political Psychology* (Durham: Duke University Press, 1993); Walker Connor, *Ethnonationalism* (Princeton: Princeton University Press, 1994); Ted Robert Gurr and Barbara Harff, *Ethnic Conflict in World Politics* (Boulder, CO: Westview Press, 1994); H. D. Forbes, *Ethnic Conflict* (New Haven: Yale University Press, 1997).

71. Frank Litsky, "Gerrit Jan van Ingen Schenau, Clap Skate Creator, Dies at 53," *New York Times,* 7 April 1998, p. C28.

72. Those fields that experience a rapid turnover of knowledge—in which new ideas replace older ideas at a high rate—produce careers with shorter half-lives; consequently, the average age at which researchers make their mark is youngest in fields that have the greatest generational changes in training.

73. James C. Mohr, *Abortion in America* (Oxford: Oxford University Press, 1978).

74. Goode, *Celebration of Heroes,* 112.

75. Becker, *Accounting for Tastes,* 37.

76. Quoted in Naipaul, *A Turn in the South,* 54.

77. Quoted in Howell Raines, *My Soul Is Rested* (New York: Penguin, 1977), 304.

78. Kristin Luker, *Abortion and the Politics of Motherhood* (Berkeley: University of California Press, 1982), 194–97.

79. Ibid.

80. Ibid., 201: "Employers might choose to discriminate against women because they might require maternity leave and thus be unavailable at critical times."

81. Lawrence Levine, *Highbrow, Lowbrow* (Cambridge, MA: Harvard University Press, 1988), 192. On the development of high culture, see also Paul Dimaggio, "Cultural Entrepreneurship in Nineteenth-Century Boston: The Creation of an Organizational Base for High Culture in America," *Media, Culture, and Society* 4 (1982): 33–50. On contrasts between mass culture and high culture, see Herbert J. Gans, *Popular Culture and High Culture* (New York: Basic Books, 1974).

82. Levine, *Highbrow, Lowbrow,* 77.

83. Judith H. Dobrzynski, "Glory Days for the Art Museum," *New York Times,* 5 October 1997, sect. 2, pp. 1, 44, at 44.

84. Nicholas D. Kristof, "Chic Japan is Dyeing (Natural It Is Not)," *New York Times,* 29 April 1996, p. A4.

85. Black, *The Behavior of Law,* 107.

86. Michael Walzer et al., *The Politics of Ethnicity* (Cambridge, MA: Harvard University Press, 1980).

87. Richard D. Alba, *Ethnic Identity* (New Haven: Yale University Press, 1990), 20–21.

88. Michael Omi, "Racial Identity and the State: Dilemmas of Classification, *Law and Inequality* 15 (1997): 7–23.

89. Edward Dolnick, "Deafness as Culture," *Atlantic Monthly,* September 1993, pp. 37–40, 46–48, 50–53.

90. John Bodnar, *Steelton* (Pittsburgh: University of Pittsburgh Press, 1977), xv, xvi.

91. Ibid., 83.

92. Ibid., 114.

93. "Steelton's immigrants turned inward and formed ethnic communities as did most other newcomers to urban American in the early decades of this century" (ibid., xviii).

94. See Robert Axelrod, *The Evolution of Cooperation* (New York: Basic Books, 1984), 146–50.

95. Bodnar, *Steelton,* 127, 129–30, 135–36, 144.

CHAPTER FOUR

1. Quoted in Ayers, *Promise of the New South,* 132. See Harry Crews, *A Childhood: The Biography of a Place* (New York: Harper and Row, 1978).

2. Peter Applebome, "Orval Faubus, Segregation's Champion, Dies at 84," *New York Times,* 15 December 1994, pp. A1, C19, at A1.

3. See Earl Black and Merle Black, *The Vital South* (Cambridge, MA: Harvard University Press, 1992).

4. See William Riker, *Liberalism against Populism* (San Francisco: Freeman, 1982).

5. Simon, "Human Nature in Politics," 302.

6. Frank Restle, "A Theory of Discrimination Learning," *Psychological Review* 62 (1955): 11–19.

7. For example, in analyzing how people evaluate controversies over free speech and other civil liberties, I found that individuals whose opinions were framed by Constitutional norms tended to be more tolerant than those who conjured up images of dangerous radicals and nonconformists. See Dennis Chong, "How People Think, Reason, and Feel about Rights and Liberties," *American Journal of Political Science* 37 (1993): 867–99, and "Creating Common Frames of Reference on Political Issues," in Diana Mutz, Richard Brody, and Paul Sniderman, eds., *Political Persuasion and Attitude Change* (Ann Arbor: University of Michigan Press, 1996). The same type of framing effect occurs widely in politics. A key part of the electoral process is deciding on the agenda of issues that deserve special consideration and attention. See William Riker, *The Art of Political Manipulation* (New Haven: Yale University Press, 1986). More recently, the social movements literature has also emphasized that grievances, solutions, and political opportunities are framed strategically by political entrepreneurs: "Movements and countermovements not only are involved in mobilization contests to demonstrate who has the most support and resources at their command, they are involved in framing contests attempting to persuade authorities and bystanders of the rightness of their cause" (Mayer Zald, "Culture, Ideology, and Strategic Framing," in Doug McAdam, John D. McCarthy, and Mayer N. Zald, eds., *Comparative Perspectives on Social Movements* [Cambridge: Cambridge University Press, 1996], 269). See

also David A. Snow and Robert D. Benford, "Ideology, Frame Resonance, and Participant Mobilization," *International Social Movement Research* 1 (1988): 197–217; David A. Snow, E. Burke Rochford Jr., Steven K. Worden, and Robert D. Benford, "Frame Alignment Processes, Micro-Mobilization, and Movement Participation," *American Sociological Review* 51 (1986): 464–81; Sidney Tarrow, *Power in Movement* (Cambridge: Cambridge University Press, 1994).

8. Berelson, Lazarsfeld, and McPhee, *Voting,* 183.

9. Zaller, *Origins of Mass Opinion,* discusses framing effects but explains attitude change as "a change in the balance of positive and negative considerations relating to a given issue. To model it, one must represent the process by which new considerations are added to the pool of existing considerations in the person's mind, thereby permanently altering long-term response probabilities on the issue" (118). His mathematical model of attitude change therefore does not include framing effects. See also Stanley Feldman and John R. Zaller, "The Political Culture of Ambivalence: Ideological Responses to the Welfare State," *American Journal of Political Science* 36 (1992): 268–307; John R. Zaller and Stanley Feldman, "A Simple Theory of the Survey Response: Answering Questions Means Revealing Preferences," *American Journal of Political Science* 36 (1992): 579–618.

10. The priming literature has grown rapidly in recent years. See, e.g., William A. Gamson and Kathryn E. Lasch, "The Political Culture of Social Welfare Policy," in Shimon E. Spiro and Ephraim Yuchtman-Yaar, eds., *Evaluating the Welfare State: Social and Political Perspectives* (New York: Academic Press, 1983); Shanto Iyengar and Donald R. Kinder, *News That Matters* (Chicago: University of Chicago Press, 1987); Donald R. Kinder and Lynn M. Sanders, "Mimicking Political Debate with Survey Questions: The Case of White Opinion on Affirmative Action for Blacks," *Social Cognition* 8 (1990): 73–103; Jon Krosnick and Donald Kinder, "Altering the Foundations of Support for the President through Priming," *American Political Science Review* 84 (1990): 497–512; Lawrence R. Jacobs and Robert Y. Shapiro, "Issues, Candidate Image, and Priming: The Use of Private Polls in Kennedy's 1960 Presidential Campaign," *American Political Science Review* 88 (1994): 527–40; and Chong, "Creating Common Frames of Reference."

11. Lee Bollinger, *The Tolerant Society* (New York: Oxford University Press, 1986), 222–23.

12. Naipaul, *A Turn in the South,* 57.

13. A frame of reference might refer to different issues (as in framing the most important problems facing the electorate) or to different ways of construing a single issue.

14. Gerald Pomper, *The Election of 1996* (Chatham, NJ: Chatham Press, 1996), 197.

15. Walter Lippmann, *Public Opinion* (New York: Free Press, 1922), 173, 183.

16. Compare this assumption to the premise underlying currently popular public opinion formation models in which all of the weight is placed on the likelihood of receiving new information and the disposition to accept or resist this new information. The disposition is treated as a purely individualistic psychological propensity (a symbolic attitude, for example, using Sears's conceptualization) that is not subject to manipulation or transformation. It is most commonly operationalized as an ideological predisposition that might be further specified by the subject's political awareness (e.g., informed ideologues are the most resistant to discrepant claims). Therefore, in the case

of persuasive communications, these predispositions condition how an individual responds to the particular message that he receives. See, e.g., Zaller, *Origins of Mass Opinion.*

17. Edelman, *Symbolic Uses of Politics;* see, more recently, Jacobs and Shapiro, "Issues, Candidate Image, and Priming."

18. Kenneth Boulding, *Conflict and Defense* (New York: Harper, 1962), 281: "What it is, however, that gives this power to some symbols but not to others I believe we do not understand." On the nature of symbols, see also Clifford Geertz, *The Interpretation of Culture* (New York: Basic Books, 1973); Dan Sperber, *Rethinking Symbolism,* trans. by Alice L. Morton (Cambridge: Cambridge University Press, 1975).

19. Edelman noted that potent phrases like "white supremacy" or "starvation pay" connote "ideals or threats, or, more accurately, a combination of the two, with either the ideal or the threat a possibility, depending upon the course of governmental action.
. . . What is desirable for one social cross-section may, however, be the undesirable pole for another. White supremacy may be seen instead as exploitation, starvation pay as low labor costs, and so on. The same dimensions are involved, but they evoke opposite responses, depending on the reference group to which the respondent looks" (*Symbolic Uses of Politics,* 160).

20. Robert I. Friedman, "An Unholy Rage," *New Yorker,* 7 March 1994, pp. 54–56, at 55.

21. Sears and Funk, "The Role of Self-Interest," 13–14.

22. Boulding, *Conflict and Defense,* 281.

23. Lukas, *Common Ground,* 134.

24. Quoted in Edelman, *Symbolic Uses of Politics,* 33.

25. Steven A. Holmes, "Wilder Seeks to Mix Black Support with Middle-Class Votes," *New York Times,* 30 December 1991, p. A10.

26. Thomas Byrne Edsall with Mary D. Edsall, *Chain Reaction* (New York: Norton, 1991).

27.'Edelman, *Symbolic Uses of Politics,* 166. According to Edelman, certain charged phrases and terms can stimulate numerous connotations, but within particular reference groups, the term will tend to have a narrower meaning. He does not explicitly discuss how this agreement comes about, but presumably it is a result of common experience and social exchange. Different reference groups develop their own conventional interpretations of the phrase or term.

28. Earl Black and Merle Black, *Politics and Society in the South* (Cambridge, MA: Harvard University Press, 1987), 211–12.

29. The now venerable symbol of the Constitution did not always enjoy hallowed status. In a letter to John Adams in 1808, Benjamin Rush speculated about what might rally Americans in the event of war against Britain or France: "Which shall we fight for? For our Constitution? I cannot meet with a man who loves it. It is considered as too weak by one half of our citizens and too strong by the other half." Today, the content of the Constitution remains vague to most Americans, but its valence is unambiguously positive to practically all Americans. There are controversies about the interpretation of the Constitution, but not about its significance to the political system. Nonetheless, it required the better part of a century for the Constitution to develop into a national symbol. In the process, the Constitution came to reflect the strength of the people as well as the maturity, heritage, and core values of the nation. See Michael Kammen,

A Machine That Would Go of Itself: The Constitution in American Culture (New York: Vintage Books, 1986), 73–74.

30. Peter Applebome, "David Duke Battling in Dark as Spotlight Trails Buchanan," *New York Times,* 6 March 1992, pp. A1, A12, at A1.

31. Elizabeth Kolbert, "Abortion, Dole's Sword in '74, Returns to Confront Him in '96," *New York Times,* 8 July 1996, pp. A1, A8, at A8.

32. Ibid.

33. Richard Rovere, *Senator Joe McCarthy* (New York: Harper and Row, 1959), 122–27.

34. Lukas, *Common Ground,* 129.

35. Marshall Frady, *Wallace* (New York: Meridian, 1968), 125. See also Dan T. Carter, *The Politics of Rage* (New York: Simon and Schuster, 1995).

36. Frady, *Wallace,* 133.

37. Ibid., 133–34.

38. See Robert Harmel and Kenneth Janda, "An Integrated Theory of Party Goals and Party Change," *Journal of Theoretical Politics* 6 (1994): 259–87; Kenneth Janda, Robert Harmel, Christine Edens, and Patricia Goff, "Changes in Party Identity: Evidence from Party Manifestos," *Party Politics* 1 (1995): 171–96.

39. James L. Sundquist, *Dynamics of the Party System* (Washington, DC: Brookings Institution Press, 1983), 195–96.

40. Ibid., 185.

41. Ibid., 184.

42. Schattschneider, *Semisovereign People,* 74–75.

43. Lukas, *Common Ground,* 137–38.

44. Williamson, *Rage for Order,* 78.

45. C. Vann Woodward, *The Strange Career of Jim Crow,* 3d rev. ed. (New York: Oxford University Press, 1974), 48.

46. Ibid., 56–57.

47. C. Vann Woodward, *Origins of the New South* (Baton Rouge: Louisiana State University Press, 1971), 257.

48. Ibid., 259.

49. Williamson, *Rage for Order,* 118.

50. Ibid., 119.

51. See Anthony Downs, *An Economic Theory of Democracy* (New York: Harper and Row, 1957), 100: "Three factors in our model explain how wide ideological variance can develop out of our vote-maximizing hypothesis. They are heterogeneity of society, the inevitability of social conflict, and uncertainty."

52. Williamson, *Rage for Order,* 119.

53. Woodward, *Strange Career,* 88–89.

54. Williamson, *Rage for Order,* 131.

55. Ibid., 178–81.

56. Ibid., 186.

57. Ibid., 193.

58. Schattschneider, *Semisovereign People,* 67.

59. Woodward, *Strange Career,* 83.

60. Michael Rogin, *The Intellectuals and McCarthy* (Cambridge: MIT Press), 216. See also Edwin R. Bayley, *Joe McCarthy and the Press* (Madison: University of

Wisconsin Press, 1981); Thomas C. Reeves, *The Life and Times of Joe McCarthy* (New York: Stein and Day, 1982); Nelson W. Polsby, "Towards an Explanation of McCarthyism," *Political Studies* 8 (1960): 250–71.

61. Rogin (ibid., 256) also suggests that there was unspoken Democratic guilt over hints of truth in McCarthy's charges about subversives and sympathizers in the national government.

62. See James L. Gibson, "Political Intolerance and Political Repression during the McCarthy Red Scare," *American Political Science Review* 82 (1988): 511–29.

63. See Jon Elster, "Arguing and Bargaining in Two Constituent Assemblies," The Storrs Lectures, Yale Law School (1991), manuscript; and "Transmutation and Misrepresentation," *Nordic Journal of Political Economy* 23 (1996): 3–23.

64. See Elaine Walster, Elliot Aronson, and Darcy Abrahams, "On Increasing the Persuasiveness of a Low Prestige Communicator," *Journal of Experimental Social Psychology* 2 (1966): 325–42; Alice Eagly, Wendy Wood, and Shelly Chaiken, "Causal Inferences about Communicators and Their Effect on Opinion Change," *Journal of Personality and Social Psychology* 36 (1978): 424–35. On persuasion, see Anthony Pratkanis and Elliot Aronson, *Age of Propaganda* (New York: W. H. Freeman, 1991); Elliot Aronson, *The Social Animal* (New York: W. H. Freeman, 1984); Richard E. Petty and John T. Cacioppo, *Attitudes and Persuasion* (Dubuque, IA: Brown, 1981) and *Communication and Persuasion* (New York: Springer-Verlag, 1986).

65. Sundquist, *Dynamics,* 44.

66. John Higham, *Strangers in the Land* (New Brunswick, NJ: Rutgers University Press, 1992), 101.

67. Nina Bernstein, "Battles over Lawyer Advertising Divide the Bar," *New York Times,* 19 July 1997, pp. A1, A9.

68. Pam Belluck, "Landmark End to Hispanic Bias in Housing," *New York Times,* 8 August 1997, p. A14.

69. One principle may also be used to cover for another principle. Following the passage in California of Proposition 209, a 1996 legislative initiative eliminating affirmative action policies in state programs and institutions of higher learning, the University of California at Berkeley has tried to devise new admissions criteria that are correlated with, but not based explicitly on, race and ethnicity. By giving greater weight in the admissions process to students who have had to overcome economic disadvantages, substandard schools, or other hardships, the university has managed to increase the proportion of minority students in its entering classes by a modest amount.

70. Friedman, *History of American Law,* 506.

71. George M. Fredrickson, *The Black Image in the White Mind* (New York: Harper and Row, 1971), 46–47.

72. Ibid., 48.

73. Ibid., 61.

74. Williamson, *Rage for Order,* 170.

75. Iver Peterson, "In Its Reward in Cosby Case, Tabloid Tapped a Tradition," *New York Times,* 16 March 1997, p. A12.

76. Lukas, *Common Ground,* 27.

77. Woodward, *Strange Career,* 75.

78. Dennis Chong, "All-or-Nothing Games in the Civil Rights Movement," *Social Science Information* 30 (1991): 677–97.

79. Woodward, *Strange Career,* 216–17. See also Gary Orfield, "Race and the Lib-

eral Agenda: The Loss of the Integrationist Dream, 1965–74," in Margaret Weir, Ann Shola Orloff, and Theda Skocpol, *The Politics of Social Policy in the United States* (Princeton: Princeton University Press, 1988).

80. Schattschneider, *Semisovereign People,* 13.

81. Boulding, *Conflict and Defense,* 281–82.

82. See, e.g., Lukas, *Common Ground;* Rieder, *Canarsie.*

83. Schattschneider, *Semisovereign People,* 72–73.

Chapter Five

1. Sam Howe Verhovek, "County in Texas Snubs Apple over Unwed Partner Policies," *New York Times,* 2 December 1993, p. A1.

2. In June 1995, with the assistance of Anna-Maria Marshall, a doctoral student in political science at Northwestern University, I interviewed sixteen people in Williamson County, including all five of the county commissioners and several community leaders who took an active interest in the decision. During the interviews, each of which lasted about two hours, we asked a variety of questions about (among other things) their views on the Apple vote, their perception of the costs and benefits of the Apple plan, their social and political ties, and their feelings about maintaining social and moral values in the community. In addition, we interviewed, by telephone, seven residents who had written letters to David Hays, one of the county commissioners. Four supported Hays's initial vote against the abatements, while three were opposed to it. We also reviewed all of David Hays's correspondence, which included 195 letters opposing the abatements and 77 letters in favor. The public opinion data reported in the chapter were collected by Opinion Analysts for the *Austin American-Statesman* shortly after the first commissioners' vote. A random sample of 401 respondents participated in the telephone survey.

3. David Scott and Beth Snyder, "Location, Location, Location," *Texas Business* (June 1995): 74–82, 98–100, at 74.

4. Verhovek, "County in Texas Snubs Apple."

5. Ibid.

6. Carol Ness, "Apple Firm on Texas Plans," *San Francisco Examiner,* 4 November 1993, p. B1.

7. Charlotte-Anne Lucas, "Two Officials Cite Gay Policy, Oppose Apple Tax Breaks," *Dallas Morning News,* 5 November 1993, p. 1A.

8. Ness, "Apple Firm."

9. Laura Evenson, "Apple Draws Fire over Gay Benefits," *San Francisco Chronicle,* 4 November 1993, p. B1.

10. Lucas, "Two Officials."

11. Diana Kunde, "Job Benefits for Gay Pairs on Increase," *Dallas Morning News,* 2 December 1993, p. 1D.

12. Charlotte-Anne Lucas, "County Near Austin Kills Apple Tax Break," *Dallas Morning News,* 1 December 1993, p. 1A.

13. Verhovek, "County in Texas Snubs Apple." Hays told me that he was misrepresented. He recalled that, following the initial vote, an *Austin American-Statesman* reporter asked him why he changed his mind. He explained that he got a lot of calls pressuring him to vote against the abatement. One caller asked, "How are you going to walk into your church knowing that you let this thing happen to all of our children

and knowing that you brought homosexuality into Williamson County?" Hays claimed that he recounted this call to the reporter, but that she reported it as his own remark.

14. Lucas, "County Near Austin Kills Apple Tax Break."

15. Charlotte-Anne Lucas, "Officials Feel Heat to Reverse Apple Vote," *Dallas Morning News,* 6 December 1993, p. 1D.

16. Charlotte-Anne Lucas, "Williamson County Panel OKs Incentive for Apple," *Dallas Morning News,* 8 December 1993, p. 1A.

17. Apple never built its facility in Williamson County. In February 1995 the company shelved its plan, citing a need to expand production capacity at computer plants in other cities. In July 1997 Apple put its 129-acre Williamson County site up for sale.

18. Riker, *Liberalism against Populism* and *The Art of Political Manipulation.*

19. See the references above in chap. 4, n. 10.

20. A general discussion of rationalization can be found in Leon Festinger, *A Theory of Cognitive Dissonance* (Evanston, IL: Row, Peterson, 1957).

21. While this is the stock interpretation of morality as a visceral issue, we will see later that there is a more cognitive rationale not far beneath the surface.

22. See Glenn, "Values, Attitudes and Beliefs"; Jennings and Niemi, *Generations and Politics;* Sears, "Persistence of Early Political Predispositions"; Alwin, Cohen, and Newcomb, *Political Attitudes.*

23. In a prescient note, dated November 2, 1993, to the Round Rock Economic Development Committee, Heiligenstein urges members to "please call Judge John Doerfler and emphasize that good paying jobs are the best insurance against family disintegration. A reinforcement call to David Hays wouldn't hurt." The same theme is reiterated in Heiligenstein's press release following the second vote: "Nothing in the world promotes a strong family better than a vibrant economy and a well paying job."

24. See, e.g., Lipset and Raab, *Politics of Unreason.*

25. The literature on social capital also features interpersonal trust as an important element in fostering cooperation and political participation. See Robert D. Putnam et al., *Making Democracy Work* (Princeton: Princeton University Press, 1993) and "Bowling Alone: America's Declining Social Capital," *Journal of Democracy* 6 (1995): 67–78; Coleman, *Foundations of Social Theory,* 300–321.

26. In several of these interviews, the subjects insisted on a view of community that included psychological features in addition to a territorial dimension. A community not only is geographically bounded, but its members share common tastes and outlooks and a commonality of interests.

27. Lianne Hart, "Texas County Draws Static for Apple Tax Vote," *Los Angeles Times,* 2 December 1993, p. A35.

28. Chong, "How People Think."

29. See, e.g., the introduction to Elster, *Rational Choice;* Simon, "Human Nature in Politics."

30. See the references above in the introduction, n. 11.

31. See the references above in chap. 1, n. 31.

32. Rodney Stark and William Sims Bainbridge, *The Future of Religion: Secularization, Revival and Cult Formation* (Berkeley: University of California Press, 1985).

33. See Levine and Campbell, *Ethnocentrism,* 29–42.

34. See, e.g., Martin Fishbein and Icek Ajzen, *Belief, Attitude, Intention, and Behavior* (New York: Wiley, 1975); Martin Fishbein, ed., *Readings in Attitude Theory and*

Measurement (Reading, MA: Addison-Wesley, 1976); Anthony R. Pratkanis and Anthony G. Greenwald, "A Sociocognitive Model of Attitude Structure and Function," *Advances in Experimental Social Psychology* 22 (1989): 245–85.

35. Nisbett and Ross, *Human Inference;* Schneider, "Social Cognition"; Kahneman, Slovic, and Tversky, *Judgment under Uncertainty;* Markus and Zajonc, "Cognitive Perspective"; Lee, Ross, and Lepper, "Biased Assimilation and Attitude Polarization."

36. Albert O. Hirschman, in *The Rhetoric of Reaction* (Cambridge: Harvard University Press, 1991), suggests that the objective uncertainties of a situation will not necessarily produce a corresponding subjective uncertainty: "This argument, which might be called the imminent-danger thesis, has two essential characteristics in common with its opposite, the jeopardy thesis. First of all, both look at only one category of dangers or risks when a new program is discussed: the jeopardy camp will conjure up exclusively the dangers of action, whereas the imminent-danger partisans will wholly concentrate on the risks of inaction. Second, both camps present their respective scenarios—the harm that will come from either action or inaction—as though they were entirely certain and inescapable" (153). In the Texas study, people were confident about the scenarios that they presented to support their position on the Apple issue. The difficulty of adducing evidence to evaluate arguments may increase the role that ideology plays in people's thinking. Because it is difficult if not impossible to evaluate competing claims, the claims are presented dogmatically.

37. Barry, *Sociologists, Economists, and Democracy;* Hardin, *One for All;* Dennis Chong, "Values versus Interests in the Explanation of Social Conflict," *University of Pennsylvania Law Review* 144 (1996): 2079–2134.

38. Jonathan Baron, *Thinking and Deciding* (Cambridge: Cambridge University Press, 1994). See also Nozick, *Nature of Rationality,* 74–75.

CHAPTER SIX

1. Hadley Cantril, *Public Opinion, 1935–1946* (Princeton: Princeton University Press, 1951).

2. Herbert H. Hyman and Paul B. Sheatsley, "Attitudes toward Desegregation" *Scientific American* 211 (1964): 16–23, at 17.

3. Herbert H. Hyman and Paul B. Sheatsley, "Attitudes toward Desegregation," *Scientific American* 195 (1956): 35–39, "Attitudes toward Desegregation" (1964); Andrew M. Greeley and Paul B. Sheatsley, "Attitudes toward Racial Integration," *Scientific American* 225 (1971): 13–19; D. Garth Taylor, Paul B. Sheatsley, and Andrew M. Greeley, "Attitudes toward Racial Integration," *Scientific American* 238 (1978): 42–51; Tom W. Smith and Paul B. Sheatsley, "American Attitudes toward Race Relations," *Public Opinion,* 7 (Oct.–Nov. 1984): 14–15, 51–53; Howard Schuman, Charlotte Steeh, and Lawrence Bobo, *Racial Attitudes in America* (Cambridge, MA: Harvard University Press, 1985).

4. However, a puzzling finding in the study by Schuman and his colleagues is that ratings of blacks by white respondents on a "thermometer" scale ranging from 0 (cold) to 100 degrees (warm) have remained virtually unchanged at around 60 degrees since the mid-1960s (Schuman, Steeh, and Bobo, *Racial Attitudes in America*). Schuman, Steeh, and Bobo admit that "it is not entirely clear what a question like this measures, since it does not deal with any issue and does not seem to vary with external events or show a secular trend" (120). Nevertheless, they venture that "the lack of temporal

change despite the relation of the question to other volatile issues suggests that people respond to these issues over time in terms of their policy content, but do not generalize them to influence overall feelings toward blacks" (121–22). Still, this does not account for the increased tolerance that whites display on social distance indicators. These indicators, it would seem, reflect how whites "feel" about blacks.

5. Paul B. Sheatsley, "White Attitudes toward the Negro," *Daedalus* 95 (1966): 217–38, at 223.

6. Taylor, Sheatsley, and Greeley, "Attitudes toward Racial Integration" (1978), 43.

7. Donald R. Kinder and David O. Sears, "Prejudice and Politics: Symbolic Racism versus Racial Threats to the Good Life," *Journal of Personality and Social Psychology* 40 (1981): 414–31; Paul M. Sniderman and Philip E. Tetlock, "Reflections on American Racism," *Journal of Social Issues* 42 (1986): 173–88; James H. Kuklinski, Michael D. Cobb, and Martin Gilens, "Racial Attitudes and the New South," *Journal of Politics* 50 (1997): 323–49. See also *Public Opinion Quarterly,* Special Issue on Race (Spring 1997).

8. Patricia G. Devine, Margo J. Monteith, Julia R. Zuwerink, and Andrew J. Elliot, "Prejudice with and without Compunction," *Journal of Personality and Social Psychology* 60 (1991): 817–30, at 829.

9. Nicholas Lemann, *The Promised Land* (New York: Vintage, 1991), 343.

10. Black and Black, *Politics and Society,* 197: "Because most white adults were thoroughly socialized to white supremacist beliefs, embracing integration would appear to be too radical a shift for most white southerners to accept."

11. Dennis Chong, "Tolerance and Social Adjustment to New Norms and Practices," *Political Behavior* 16 (1994): 21–53.

12. All quotations in this and the previous paragraph are from "Gloucester Is Calmer on Moon's Followers," *New York Times,* 9 January 1984, p. A11.

13. See Festinger, *Cognitive Dissonance;* Aronson. *The Social Animal;* Jon Elster, *Sour Grapes* (Cambridge: Cambridge University Press, 1983).

14. To give another example of this "in between" feeling, an article by Jane Gross in the *New York Times* carried the headline "Homosexuals Finding New Empathy" (4 February 1988, p. A13). The gist of the story was that homosexuals, at least in New York and San Francisco, were being treated with greater sympathy and understanding by heterosexuals in spite of, or maybe because of, publicity about AIDS (acquired immune deficiency syndrome). The author of the story was quick to point out that the changes were subtle: "The [new] attitude is hard to define. . . . It is not a matter of total acceptance—many heterosexuals are far from treating homosexuals as social equals. Instead, it seems to amount to a new sensitivity and attempts to be less discriminatory in behavior, if not always in attitude." Anecdotes were offered as evidence of this change in attitude. For example, a gay man observed that a male friend of his was no longer nervous that, as a result of their association, others might think that he too was a homosexual. Another gay man had been recently assured by a heterosexual friend that his homosexuality was no bar to their friendship.

15. Hazel Erskine and Richard L. Siegel, "Civil Liberties and the American Public," *Journal of Social Issues* 31 (1975):13–29, at 17. A similar process took place in the former Soviet Union. In the midst of glasnost, the Soviet people began to express views in public criticizing conditions in their country, questioning state policy, demanding greater individual rights, and challenging the state's distortions of history—all of which would have been taboo previously. The public expression of these sentiments was sur-

prising initially (and, undoubtedly, disturbing to many) but became less so as it grew more widespread. The editor of *Ogonyok,* a small weekly magazine, noted that the volume of reader mail climbed dramatically after 1986 following a relaxation of censorship. Moreover, most letters, in addition to expressing bolder views, arrived complete with the authors' names and addresses. The magazine's editor cautioned at the time, however, that not everything was permissible; some things remained out of bounds: "Letters proposing a multiparty political system I am not prepared to publish. As a small boss, I understand what the situation is around me, and I'll probably wait until *Pravda* publishes it first" (David K. Shipler, "Soviet Letters Editor Tests Limits," *New York Times,* 24 April 1988, p. A6).

16. Anthony Lewis, "You Can't Go Home Again," *New York Review of Books,* 29 September 1983, pp. 16–17, at 16.

17. The writer Margo Kaufman observed that almost nothing is confidential or private any more. "What used to be airing dirty linen is now small talk," she lamented, as her friends and casual acquaintances speak indiscreetly about their affairs, sexual preferences, bulimia, drug dependency, abortions, therapy, cosmetic surgery, and other formerly sensitive subjects. "Nothing . . . is shameful anymore. This is the golden age of full disclosure" ("Hers," *New York Times,* 4 February 1988, p. A18).

18. Felice Flanery Lewis, *Literature, Obscenity, and Law* (Carbondale: Southern Illinois University Press, 1976).

19. Lawrence Tribe, *American Constitutional Law* (Mineola, NY: Foundation Press, 1978), 668.

20. For instance, as Edward de Grazia and Roger Newman explain, the inability of a Houston district attorney to prevent the showing of *Deep Throat* prompted him to declare that future obscenity prosecutions would be limited to films portraying "bestiality, excretory functions, or sex acts involving minors" (*Banned Films* [New York: R. R. Bowker, 1982], 144). For a general historical analysis of changes in sexual attitudes and relations, see John D'Emilio and Estelle B. Freedman, *Intimate Matters* (New York: Harper and Row, 1988).

21. In his splendid social history of the United States, William Manchester frequently tries to recapture how popular sensibilities have changed. For example, he recounts how moviegoers in the Depression era, watching a Mae West film, *Night after Night,* "gasped" when "in reply to a friend's remark, 'Goodness, what beautiful diamonds,' Mae replied, 'Goodness had nothing to do with it, dearie.'" Also, he describes how people reacted in 1935 when Dennis King sang "to *Hell* with Burgundy": "A thrill ran through the audiences, as though a naked woman had run among them." *The Glory and the Dream: A Narrative History of America* (Boston: Little, Brown, 1974), 66, 120.

22. The process by which people adjust to change plays a critical role in the development and expansion of tolerance. Tolerance involves, in this view, not only the ability to withstand or put up with those groups, ideas, and activities that one disagrees with or fears, but also the capacity to reduce one's apprehensions about things that are unconventional in response to changes in norms and practices. This stands in contrast to the more conventional view of tolerance, which (1) holds that something cannot be tolerated unless it is disliked, and (2) implies that increases in tolerance are synonymous with increases in self-restraint. Comparing the tolerance of different generations, in this view, involves comparing the reactions of each generation to the most unpopular groups and ideas in its day. The justification for this approach is that it ensures that

people will be responding to things that are salient to them, and guards against expressions of tolerance that merely reflect indifference.

The conventional view, however, does not take into account that Americans—for reasons quite apart from changes in salience—no longer disapprove of various groups, ideas, and activities with the same vigor as they once did. Focusing only on the reactions of society to the things that cause great consternation therefore overlooks the process by which people become acclimated or inured to things that once bothered them. As society has become more heterogeneous, with the emergence of new groups, ideas, lifestyles, habits and customs, standards of morality, and norms of individual rights and freedoms, people have on the whole adapted to many of the changes that have occurred despite having initially resisted them. Americans in particular have become more tolerant on matters of politics, race, and morality insofar as they now countenance a much greater degree of individual freedom within these realms than they did in the past. Many of the dramatic developments in these areas cannot be understood without recognizing that changes in popular feelings and sentiments have paved the way to increases in tolerance.

For background on the conceptualization and measurement of tolerance, see Bernard Crick, "Toleration and Tolerance in Theory and Practice," *Government and Opposition* 6 (1971): 144–71; Preston King, "The Problem of Tolerance," *Government and Opposition* 6 (1971): 172–207; John L. Sullivan, James E. Piereson, and George E. Marcus, "An Alternative Conceptualization of Political Tolerance: Illusory Increases, 1950's–1970's," *American Political Science Review* 73 (1979): 781–94; John L. Sullivan, James E. Piereson, and George E. Marcus, *Political Tolerance and American Democracy* (Chicago: University of Chicago Press, 1982). For an early alternative view of tolerance that is consistent with my own, see Gordon Allport, *The Nature of Prejudice* (Garden City: Anchor Books, 1958).

23. The innovators in the "coolhunt," for example. See Gladwell, "The Coolhunt"; Furchgott, "For Coolhunters."

24. Stability conditions: In addition to exploring the components of the equilibrium values of the system, we also want to know under what conditions these values will actually be reached. Intuitively, we might expect that, if the system is to stabilize in the long run, there will have to be some balance between the forces promoting change, the forces of resistance, and the rate of adjustment. Plainly, if the influence of the entrepreneurs of change is not constrained by a "sufficient" countervailing influence stemming from public pressure, mass resistance, and limited adjustment, the system will be unstable and unbounded in the long run, as the opinion leaders change the norms in each succeeding time period and drag the mass public along for the ride.

To ascertain the precise conditions for stability, we examine the auxilliary or characteristic equation associated with the system:

$$\begin{vmatrix} 1 - m - \rho & m \\ e & 1 - e - r + rd - \rho \end{vmatrix} = 0 \qquad (1)$$

After multiplying out this equation, we are left with the following quadratic characteristic equation:

$$\rho^2 + [(m + e) + r(1 - d) - 2]\rho + \{(1 - m)[1 + r(d - 1)] - e\} = 0 \quad (2)$$

The behavior of the system will be determined by the roots, ρ_1 and ρ_2 of this quadratic equation; it is a well-known result in the analysis of dynamic systems that if the absolute value of both roots is less than 1, the system will be stable (i.e., it will reach equilibrium in the limit).

An important theorem in this regard stipulates that the roots of the characteristic equation will be less than 1 in absolute value if the coefficients of the equation satisfy three necessary and sufficient conditions:

$$\text{(a) } 1 + a_1 + a_2 > 0$$
$$\text{(b) } 1 - a_1 + a_2 > 0$$
$$\text{(c) } 1 - a_2 > 0$$

where a_1 and a_2 are the coefficients of the characteristic equation (for the theorem, see Goldberg, *Introduction to Difference Equations,* 172).

Substituting the coefficients of equation (2) into the first inequality gives us:

$$1 + [(m + e) + r(1 - d) - 2] + \{(1 - m) [1 + r(d - 1)] - e\} > 0. \quad (3)$$

Fortunately, most of the terms in this unwieldy expression cancel each other and it reduces simply to:

$$d < 1. \quad (4)$$

Consequently, if the system is to be stable, attitude adjustment to changes in compliance cannot be perfect, nor can there be an overcompensatory effect whereby attitude change continually races ahead of changes in compliance. Notice that when d equals 1, the denominators in the equilibrium become 0.

Both restrictions appear reasonable. While popular attitudes adjust in concert with mass compliance to changing social and political norms, the adjustment is not so complete that compliance is given without reservation. In other words, people will tolerate social conditions that are not entirely to their liking $(C > A)$. On the other hand, "overcompensation" is counterintuitive, since this would mean that people will not comply with norms that are agreeable to them.

The remaining two conditions for stability are best treated together:

$$1 - [(m + e) + r(1 - d) - 2] + \{(1 - m) [1 + r(d - 1)] - e\} > 0. \quad (5)$$

$$1 - \{(1 - m) [1 + r(d - 1)] - e\} > 0. \quad (6)$$

These inequalities reduce to:

$$\{[r(1 - d) - 2] (m - 2)\}/2 > e > m[r(1 - d) - 1] - r(1 - d). \quad (7)$$

I do not have an easy intuitive interpretation of these inequalities except to say that they identify the balance that needs to be maintained between the relative influences of opinion leaders and the mass public if the system is to reach a stable equilibrium. System stability can be achieved whether the coefficients are very large or very small so long as the relative sizes of m, d, r, and e continue to satisfy the inequalities in equation (7).

25. Richard Kluger, *Simple Justice* (New York: Vintage Books, 1975), 722–46.

26. Frederick M. Wirt, *Politics of Southern Equality* (Chicago: Aldine, 1970), 301.

27. Numan V. Bartley, *The Rise of Massive Resistance* (Baton Rouge: Louisiana State University Press, 1969), 191.

28. Ibid., 192, 193, 195–96.

29. See Wirt, *Politics of Southern Equality;* William K. Muir, *Law and Attitude Change* (Chicago: University of Chicago Press, 1973); Stuart A. Scheingold, *The Politics of Rights* (New Haven: Yale University Press, 1974); Harrell R. Rodgers Jr. and Charles S. Bullock III, *Law and Social Change* (New York: McGraw-Hill, 1972).

30. Wirt, *Politics of Southern Equality,* 195–214; see also his follow-up study almost thirty years later, Frederick M. Wirt, *We Ain't What We Was* (Durham, NC: Duke University Press, 1997).

31. In reply to critics of Christian Science who contend that medical treatment should not be withheld from infants even if the parents' religious beliefs prohibit scientific medicine, defenders of Christian Science argue that they are entitled to religious freedom under the First Amendment. The availability of a defensible principle fortifies their opposition to change. It is instructive that Canadian and British Christian Scientists nevertheless have been able to adapt to laws requiring them to seek medical treatment for their children, whereas in the United States, where the rights of children and religious freedom have not been resolved, Christian Scientists continue to resist such a law. See Fraser, "Suffering Children," 118, 120.

32. Wirt, *Politics,* 286.

33. Wirt, *Politics,* 299–305.

34. Black and Black, *Politics and Society,* 199.

35. Lawrence M. Friedman, *American Law* (New York: W. W. Norton, 1984), 220. When Frederick Wirt returned in the 1990s to the Mississippi county that he studied in the late 1960s, he found that black registration and voting were now taken for granted and that controversies that once divided communities no longer merited coverage in local newspapers because they have been resolved (Wirt, *We Ain't What We Was*).

36. Black and Black, *Politics and Society,* 209.

37. For an early study of the effects of racial integration, see Morton Deutsch and Mary Ellen Collins, *Interracial Housing: A Psychological Evaluation of a Social Experiment* (Minneapolis: University of Minnesota Press, 1951). See, more recently, Howard Schuman and Shirley Hatchett, *Trends in Racial Attitudes* (Ann Arbor: University of Michigan, Institute for Social Research, 1974); David L. Hamilton and George D. Bishop, "Attitudinal and Behavioral Effects of Initial Integration of White Suburban Neighborhoods," *Journal of Social Issues* 32 (1976): 47–67; Lee Sigelman and Susan Welch, "The Contact Hypothesis Revisited: Interracial Contact and Positive Racial Attitudes," *Social Forces* 71 (1993): 781–95.

38. For data on generational differences in racial attitudes, see Schuman, Steeh, and Bobo, *Racial Attitudes,* 127–35.

39. Dirk Johnson, "Old List of Klan Members Revives Racist Past in Indiana City," *New York Times,* 2 August 1995, p. A7.

40. For this reason, it is arguably difficult to assign blame in retrospect to those who abided by the social conventions of their day. In Indiana, some of the local Klan members joined because they were pressured by others or because the Klan organization provided companionship and social contacts (ibid.). However, because we are prone to assign blame for past conformity, so that people are not forgiven for complying with beliefs that are no longer socially acceptable, we unintentionally reduce the incentives for these individuals to change their values.

41. Allegations of racism in the treatment of Denny's restaurant customers resulted in a multimillion dollar legal settlement and comparable losses in sales (Floyd Norris, "Buyout Kings Flee Disaster at Denny's," *New York Times,* 23 March 1997, sect. 3,

p. 1.) Texaco recently paid out $140 million to settle a lawsuit accusing the corporation of discriminating against minorities in its hiring and promotion practices after secretly taped conversations between Texaco executives disparaging black employees became public (Kurt Eichenwald, "Blowing the Whistle, and Now Facing the Music," *New York Times,* 16 March 1997, sect. 3, pp. 1, 12, 13).

42. Woodward, *Strange Career,* 7.

43. Ibid., 105–6.

44. Ibid., 106.

45. For an analysis of the arguments commonly marshaled against social change, see Hirschman, *Rhetoric of Reaction.*

CHAPTER SEVEN

1. See, e.g., the array of criticisms of rational choice theory, and responses to them by defenders of the theory, in *Critical Review* 9, nos. 1–2 (1995), Special Issue on Rational Choice Theory and Politics.

2. Will Kymlicka, *Multicultural Citizenship* (Oxford: Oxford University Press, 1995), 76.

3. Jere Longman, "Slow Down, Speed Up," *New York Times,* 1 May 1996, p. B11.

4. Dennis Chong, "Reputation and Cooperative Behavior," *Social Science Information* 31 (1992): 683–709. On the rules and regulations of personal presentation, see the collection of classic and contemporary essays in Dennis Brissett and Charles Edgley, *Life as Theater,* 2d ed. (New York: Aldine de Gruyter, 1990).

5. Kenneth Clark, *Prejudice and Your Child,* 2d ed. (Boston: Beacon Press, 1963).

6. Hardin, *One for All,* 108.

7. Ibid., 110.

8. Howard Zinn, *The Southern Mystique* (New York: Knopf, 1964), 9.

9. Ibid., 22–23.

10. Hardin, *One for All,* 90.

11. Anthony Downs, *An Economic Theory of Democracy* (New York: Harper and Row, 1957), 270.

12. Donald P. Green and Ian Shapiro, *Pathologies of Rational Choice Theory* (New Haven: Yale University Press, 1995), 34–38.

13. Laudan, *Progress,* 115–17.

14. Thomas L. Friedman, "Envoy to Iraq, Faulted in Crisis, Says She Warned Hussein Sternly," *New York Times,* 21 March 1991, p. A1.

15. Ibid., p. A7.

16. Abelson, "Secret Existence," 27.

17. See, e.g., Mark R. Lepper, D. Greene, and Richard E. Nesbitt, "Undermining Children's Intrinsic Interest with Extrinsic Reward: A Test of the 'Overjustification' Hypothesis," *Journal of Personality and Social Psychology* 28 (1973): 129–37.

18. Boyle, *The Desegregated Heart,* 75.

19. See Abby Goodnough, "Volunteering Helps Volunteers, Too," *New York Times,* 26 December 1994, p. A10.

20. Kristen Renwick Monroe, *The Heart of Altruism* (Princeton: Princeton University Press, 1996); Phil Gailey, "Four Rescuers Praised; Courage of the Fourth is Known, But Not the Name," *New York Times,* 15 January 1982, p. D15.

21. Rick Bragg, "She Opened World to Others; Her World Has Opened, Too," *New York Times,* 12 November 1996, pp. A1, A10.

22. Abelson, "Secret Existence," 27–28.

23. Kevin Sack, "The Final Refrains of 'Dixie,'" *New York Times,* 1 November 1998, Education Life Section, pp. ED 20–21, 32–33, 35.

24. David Garrow, "All Over but the Legislating," *New York Times Book Review,* 25 January 1998, pp. 14, 16.

25. Nozick, *Nature of Rationality,* 26–27.

26. Kathlyn Taylor Gaubatz, *Crime in the Public Mind* (Ann Arbor: University of Michigan Press, 1995), 158.

27. Nozick, *Nature of Rationality,* 29.

28. Bernard Weinraub, "Hoffman: A Fresh Face Even as Age Catches Up," *New York Times,* 17 February 1998, pp. B1, B5, at B5.

29. Barry, *Sociologists, Economists, and Democracy,* 32.

30. For a discussion of the prisoner's dilemma and assurance game, and their relation to collective action problems, see Chong, *Collective Action;* Hardin, *Collective Action;* Michael Taylor, *The Possibility of Cooperation* (Cambridge: Cambridge University Press, 1987).

31. Taylor, "Structure, Culture and Action."

32. Barrington Moore, *Social Origins of Dictatorship and Democracy* (Boston: Beacon Press, 1966), 486.

33. Charles Lave and James March, *An Introduction to Models in the Social Sciences* (New York: Harper and Row, 1975), 73.

34. See Donald Davidson, *Inquiries into Truth and Interpretation* (Oxford: Oxford University Press, 1986); Fay, *Contemporary Philosophy of Science.*

BIBLIOGRAPHY

Abelson, Robert P. "The Secret Existence of Expressive Behavior." *Critical Review* 9 (1995): 25–36.

Achen, Christopher H. "Social Psychology, Demographic Variables, and Linear Regression: Breaking the Iron Triangle in Voting Research." *Political Behavior* 14 (1992): 195–211.

Adorno, Theodor, et al. *The Authoritarian Personality.* New York: Norton, 1950.

Akerlof, George. *An Economic Theorist's Book of Tales.* Cambridge: Cambridge University Press, 1984.

Alba, Richard D. *Ethnic Identity.* New Haven: Yale University Press, 1990.

Aldrich, John. "Rational Choice and Turnout." *American Journal of Political Science* 37 (1993): 246–78.

Aldrich, Nelson W. *Old Money.* New York: Vintage Books, 1988.

Allport, Gordon W. *The Nature of Prejudice.* Garden City: Anchor Books, 1958.

Almond, Gabriel, and Sidney Verba. *The Civic Culture.* Princeton: Princeton University Press, 1963.

Alwin, Duane F. Ronald L. Cohen, and Theodore M. Newcomb. *Political Attitudes over the Life Span.* Madison: University of Wisconsin Press, 1991.

Anderson, Elijah. *Streetwise.* Chicago: University of Chicago Press, 1990.

————. "The Code of the Streets." *Atlantic Monthly,* May 1994, pp. 81–83, 86–89, 92–94.

Applebome, Peter. "David Duke Battling in Dark as Spotlight Trails Buchanan." *New York Times,* 6 March 1992, pp. A1, A12.

————. "Orval Faubus, Segregation's Champion, Dies at 84." *New York Times,* 15 December 1994, pp. A1, C19.

Aronson, Elliot. *The Social Animal.* New York: W. H. Freeman, 1984.

Asch, Solomon E. "Forming Impressions of Personality." *Journal of Abnormal and Social Psychology* 41 (1946): 258–90.

————. "Effects of Group Pressure upon the Modification and Distortion of Judgment." In Harold Guetzkow, ed., *Groups, Leadership, and Men.* Pittsburgh: Carnegie, 1951.

————. "Opinions and Social Pressure." *Scientific American* 193 (1955): 31–35.

————. "Studies of Independence and Conformity: A Minority of One against a Unanimous Majority." *Psychological Monographs* 70 (1956): no. 9, whole no. 416.

Asch, Solomon E., and Hans Zukier. "Thinking About Persons." *Journal of Personality and Social Psychology* 46 (1984): 1230–40.

Aumann, Robert J. "Agreeing to Disagree." *Annals of Statistics* 4 (1976): 1236–39.

Axelrod, Robert. *The Evolution of Cooperation.* New York: Basic Books, 1984.

Ayers, Edward L. *The Promise of the New South.* New York: Oxford University Press, 1992.

Baron, Jonathan. *Thinking and Deciding.* Cambridge: Cambridge University Press, 1994.

Barry, Brian. *Sociologists, Economists, and Democracy.* Chicago: University of Chicago Press, 1978.

Bartley, Numan V. *The Rise of Massive Resistance.* Baton Rouge: Louisiana State University Press, 1969.

Bayley, Edwin R. *Joe McCarthy and the Press.* Madison: University of Wisconsin Press, 1981.

Beck, Roy. "The Ordeal of Immigration in Wasau." *Atlantic Monthly,* April 1994, pp. 84–86.

Becker, Gary. *Accounting for Tastes.* Cambridge, MA: Harvard University Press, 1996.

Bell, Daniel, ed. *The Radical Right.* New York: Anchor Books, 1964.

Belluck, Pam. "Landmark End to Hispanic Bias in Housing." *New York Times,* 8 August 1997, pp. A1, A14.

Bem, Daryl J. "Toward A Response Style Theory of Persons in Situations." In Monte M. Page, ed., *Personality: Current Theory and Research.* Lincoln: University of Nebraska Press, 1983.

Bem, Daryl J., and A. Allen. "On Predicting Some of the People Some of the Time: The Search for Cross-Situational Consistencies in Behavior." *Psychological Review* 81 (1974): 505–520.

Bem, Daryl J., and D. C. Funder. "Predicting More of the People More of the Time: Assessing the Personality of Situations." *Psychological Review* 85 (1978): 485–501.

Benn, Stanley I. "The Problematic Rationality of Political Participation." In Peter Laslett and James Fishkin, eds., *Philosophy, Politics and Society,* 5th series. Oxford: Blackwell, 1979.

Berelson, Bernard R., Paul F. Lazarsfeld, and William N. McPhee, *Voting.* Chicago: University of Chicago Press, 1954.

Berkeley, Bill. "The Warlords of Natal." *Atlantic Monthly,* March 1994, pp. 85–100.

Bernstein, Nina. "Battles over Lawyer Advertising Divide the Bar." *New York Times,* 19 July 1997, pp. A1, A9.

Bicchieri, Cristina. "Methodological Rules as Conventions." *Philosophy of Social Science* 18 (1988): 477–95.

Bicchieri, Cristina, Richard Jeffrey, and Brian Skyrms, eds. *The Dynamics of Norms.* Cambridge: Cambridge University Press, 1997.

Birmingham, Stephen. *America's Secret Aristocracy.* Boston: Little, Brown and Co., 1987.

Black, Donald. *The Behavior of Law.* New York: Academic Press, 1976.

Black, Earl, and Merle Black. *Politics and Society in the South.* Cambridge, MA: Harvard University Press, 1987.

―――. *The Vital South.* Cambridge, MA: Harvard University Press, 1992.

Bobo, Lawrence. "Whites' Opposition to Busing: Symbolic Racism or Realistic Group Conflict." *Journal of Personality and Social Psychology* 45 (1983): 1196–1210.

Bodnar, John. *Steelton.* Pittsburgh: University of Pittsburgh Press, 1977.

Bollinger, Lee. *The Tolerant Society.* New York: Oxford University Press, 1986.

Boulding, Kenneth. *Conflict and Defense.* New York: Harper, 1962.

Bourdieu, Pierre. *Distinction*. Translated by Richard Nice. Cambridge, MA: Harvard University Press, 1984.

Boyd, Robert, and Peter J. Richerson. *Culture and the Evolutionary Process*. Chicago: University of Chicago Press, 1985.

Boyer, Paul, and Stephen Nissenbaum. *Salem Possessed*. Cambridge, MA: Harvard University Press, 1974.

Boyer, Peter J. "The Ogre's Tale." *New Yorker,* 4 April 1994, pp. 36–48.

Boyle, Sarah Patton. *The Desegregated Heart*. New York: William Morrow, 1962.

Bragg, Rick. "She Opened World to Others; Her World Has Opened, Too." *New York Times,* 12 November 1996, pp. A1, A10.

Brissett, Dennis, and Charles Edgley. *Life as Theater*. 2d ed. New York: Aldine de Gruyter, 1990.

Brody, Richard A., and Paul M. Sniderman. "From Life Space to Polling Place: The Relevance of Personal Concerns for Voting Behavior." *British Journal of Political Science* 7 (1977): 337–60.

Brown, Roger. *Social Psychology*. 2d ed. New York: Free Press, 1986.

Bruce, Steve. *The Rise and Fall of the New Christian Right*. Oxford: Clarendon Press, 1990.

Calvert, Randall. "The Rational Choice Theory of Social Institutions: Cooperation, Coordination, and Communication," In Jeffrey S. Banks and Eric A. Hanushek, eds., *Modern Political Economy*. Cambridge: Cambridge University Press, 1995.

Campbell, Angus, Philip E. Converse, Warren E. Miller, and Donald E. Stokes, *The American Voter*. New York: John Wiley and Sons, 1960.

Campbell, Donald T. "On the Conflicts between Biological and Social Evolution and between Psychology and Moral Tradition." *American Psychologist* 30 (1975): 1103–26.

Cantril, Hadley. *Public Opinion, 1935–1946*. Princeton: Princeton University Press, 1951.

Carter, Dan T. *The Politics of Rage*. New York: Simon and Schuster, 1995.

Cash, W. J. *The Mind of the South*. New York: Vintage, 1941.

Casson, John. *Rudeness and Civility*. New York: Hill and Wang, 1990.

Chartier, Roger. *A History of Private Life*. Vol. 3: *Passions of the Renaissance*. Cambridge, MA: Harvard University Press, 1989.

Chong, Dennis. *Collective Action and the Civil Rights Movement*. Chicago: University of Chicago Press, 1991.

———. "All-or-Nothing Games in the Civil Rights Movement." *Social Science Information* 30 (1991): 677–97.

———. "Creating Common Frames of Reference on Political Issues." In Diana Mutz, Richard A. Brody, and Paul M. Sniderman, eds., *Political Persuasion and Attitude Change*. Ann Arbor: University of Michigan Press, 1996.

———. "How People Think, Reason, and Feel about Rights and Liberties." *American Journal of Political Science* 37 (1993): 867–99.

———. "Rational Choice Theory's Mysterious Rivals." *Critical Review* 9 (1995): 37–58.

———. "Reputation and Cooperative Behavior." *Social Science Information* 31 (1992): 683–709.

———. "Social Incentives and the Preservation of Reputation in Public-Spirited Collective Action." *International Political Science Review* 13 (1992): 171–198.

———. "Tolerance and Social Adjustment to New Norms and Practices." *Political Behavior* 16 (1994): 21–53.

———. "Values versus Interests in the Explanation of Social Conflict." *University of Pennsylvania Law Review* 144 (1996): 2079–2134.

Chong, Dennis, Herbert McClosky, and John Zaller. "Patterns of Support for Democratic and Capitalist Values in the United States." *British Journal of Political Science* 13 (1983): 401–40.

———. "Social Learning and the Acquisition of Political Norms." Chapter 8 in Herbert McClosky and John Zaller, *The American Ethos*. Cambridge: Harvard University Press, 1984.

Chong, Dennis, and Melissa Miller. "Racial Attitudes and Identifications over the Life Span." Paper presented to the Annual Meeting of the American Political Science Association, Washington, DC, 1997.

Christie, Richard. *Studies in Machiavellianism*. New York: Academic Press, 1970.

Citrin, Jack, and Donald Philip Green. "The Self-Interest Motive in American Public Opinion." *Research in Micropolitics* 3 (1990): 1–28.

Clark, Kenneth. *Prejudice and Your Child*. 2d ed. Boston: Beacon Press, 1963.

Clausen, John. "The Life Course of Individuals." In Matilda W. Riley and Anne Foner, eds., *Aging and Society*. New York: Russell Sage Foundation, 1972.

Coben, Stanley. *Rebellion against Victorianism*. New York: Oxford University Press, 1991.

Coleman, James S. *Foundations of Social Theory*. Cambridge, MA: Harvard University Press, 1990.

Connor, Walker. *Ethnonationalism*. Princeton: Princeton University Press, 1994.

Converse, Philip E. "Information Flow and the Stability of Partisan Attitudes." *Public Opinion Quarterly* 26 (1962): 578–99.

Cook, Karen Schweers, and Margaret Levi, eds. *The Limits of Rationality*. Chicago: University of Chicago Press, 1990.

Cooley, Charles H. *Social Organization*. New York: Charles Scribner's Sons, 1909.

Crawford, Alan. *Thunder on the Right*. New York: Pantheon, 1980.

Crawford, Vincent P., and Hans Haller. "Learning How to Cooperate: Optimal Play in Repeated Coordination Games." *Econometrica* 58 (1990): 571–95.

Crews, Harry. *A Childhood: The Biography of a Place*. New York: Harper and Row, 1978.

Crick, Bernard. "Toleration and Tolerance in Theory and Practice." *Government and Opposition* 6 (1971): 144–71.

Critical Review 9, nos. 1–2 (1995), Special Issue on Rational Choice Theory and Politics.

D'Emilio, John, and Estelle B. Freedman. *Intimate Matters*. New York: Harper and Row, 1988.

Davidson, Donald. *Actions and Events*. Oxford: Oxford University Press, 1986.

———. *Inquiries into Truth and Interpretation*. Oxford: Oxford University Press, 1986.

Davis, Kingsley, and Wilbert E. Moore. "Some Principles of Stratification" *American Sociological Review* 10 (1945): 242–49.

De Graaf, Nan Dirk, Paul Nieuwbeerta, and Anthony Heath. "Class Mobility and Political Preferences: Individual and Contextual Effects." *American Journal of Sociology* 100 (1995): 997–1027.

de Grazia, Edward, and Roger Newman. *Banned Films.* New York: R. R. Bowker, 1982.

de Tocqueville, Alexis. *Democracy in America* [1840]. Edited by Phillip Bradley. New York: Vintage, 1945. [The Henry Reeve text as revised by Francis Bowen, now further corrected and edited with introduction, editorial notes, and bibliographies by Phillip Bradley]

Deutsch, Morton, and Mary Ellen Collins. *Interracial Housing: A Psychological Evaluation of a Social Experiment.* Minneapolis: University of Minnesota Press, 1951.

Devine, Patricia G., Margo J. Monteith, Julia R. Zuwerink, and Andrew J. Elliot. "Prejudice with and without Compunction." *Journal of Personality and Social Psychology* 60 (1991): 817–30.

Diamond, Sara. *Roads to Dominion.* New York: The Guilford Press, 1995.

Dimaggio, Paul. "Cultural Entrepreneurship in Nineteenth-Century Boston: The Creation of an Organizational Base for High Culture in America." *Media, Culture, and Society* 4 (1982): 33–50.

Dittes, James, and Harold Kelley. "Effects of Different Conditions of Acceptance upon Conformity to Group Norms." *Journal of Abnormal and Social Psychology* 53 (1956): 100–107.

Dobrzynski, Judith H. "Glory Days for the Art Museum." *New York Times,* 5 October 1997, sect. 2, pp. 1, 44.

Dollard, John. *Caste and Class in a Southern Town.* New York: Harper, 1937.

Dolnick, Edward. "Deafness as Culture." *Atlantic Monthly,* September 1993, pp. 37–40, 46–48, 50–53.

Downs, Anthony. *An Economic Theory of Democracy.* New York: Harper and Row, 1957.

Eagly, Alice, Wendy Wood, and Shelly Chaiken. "Causal Inferences about Communicators and Their Effect on Opinion Change." *Journal of Personality and Social Psychology* 36 (1978): 424–35.

Easton, David, and Jack Dennis. *Children in the Political System.* New York: McGraw-Hill, 1969.

Eddy, Mary Baker. *Science and Health.* Boston: Published by the Trustees under the will of Mary Baker G. Eddy, 1906.

Edelman, Murray. *Politics as Symbolic Action.* Chicago: Markham, 1971.

———. *The Symbolic Uses of Politics.* Urbana: University of Illinois Press, 1964.

Edgerton, Robert B. *Rules, Exceptions, and Social Order.* Berkeley: University of California Press, 1985.

Edsall, Thomas Byrne, with Mary D. Edsall. *Chain Reaction.* New York: Norton, 1991.

Eichenwald, Kurt. "Blowing the Whistle, and Now Facing the Music." *New York Times,* 16 March 1997, sect. 3, pp. 1, 12, 13.

Elias, Norbert. *The History of Manners,* trans. Edmund Jephcott. New York: Pantheon, 1978.

Ellickson, Robert. *Order without Law.* Cambridge, MA: Harvard University Press, 1991.

Elster, Jon. *The Cement of Society.* Cambridge: Cambridge University Press, 1989.

———. *Sour Grapes.* Cambridge: Cambridge University Press, 1983.

———. *Ulysses and the Sirens.* Cambridge: Cambridge University Press, 1984.

———. "Arguing and Bargaining in Two Constituent Assemblies." The Storrs Lectures, Yale Law School (1991), manuscript.

————. "Rationality, Emotions, and Social Norms." *Synthese* 98 (1994): 21–49.

————. "Transmutation and Misrepresentation." *Nordic Journal of Political Economy* 23 (1996): 3–23.

Elster, Jon, ed. *Rational Choice.* New York: New York University Press, 1986.

Erskine, Hazel, and Richard L. Siegel. "Civil Liberties and the American Public." *Journal of Social Issues* 31 (1975):13–29.

Etzioni, Amitai. *The Moral Dimension.* New York: Free Press, 1988.

Evenson, Laura. "Apple Draws Fire over Gay Benefits." *San Francisco Chronicle,* 4 November 1993, p. B1.

Fay, Brian. *Contemporary Philosophy of Social Science.* Oxford: Blackwell, 1996.

Feldman, Stanley. "Economic Self-Interest and Political Behavior." *American Journal of Political Science* 26 (1982): 446–66.

Feldman, Stanley, and John R. Zaller. "The Political Culture of Ambivalence: Ideological Responses to the Welfare State." *American Journal of Political Science* 36 (1992): 268–307.

Festinger, Leon. *A Theory of Cognitive Dissonance.* Evanston, IL: Row, Peterson, 1957.

Festinger, Leon, Stanley Schachter, and Kurt Back. *Social Pressure in Informal Groups.* New York: Harper & Brothers, 1950.

Fiorina, Morris P. *Retrospective Voting.* New Haven: Yale University Press, 1981.

Fishbein, Martin, ed. *Readings in Attitude Theory and Measurement.* Reading, MA: Addison-Wesley, 1976.

Fishbein, Martin, and Icek Ajzen. *Belief, Attitude, Intention, and Behavior.* New York: Wiley, 1975.

Forbes, H. D. *Ethnic Conflict.* New Haven: Yale University Press, 1997.

Formisano, Ronald P. *Boston against Busing.* Chapel Hill: University of North Carolina Press, 1991.

Frady, Marshall. *Wallace.* New York: Meridian, 1968.

Frank, Robert H. *Choosing the Right Pond.* New York: Oxford University Press, 1985.

Frankfurt, Harry G. "Freedom of the Will and the Concept of a Person." *Journal of Philosophy* 68 (1971): 5–20.

Fraser, Caroline. "Suffering Children and the Christian Science Church." *Atlantic Monthly,* April 1995, pp. 105–8, 110–20.

Fredrickson, George M. *The Black Image in the White Mind.* New York: Harper and Row, 1971.

Friedman, Lawrence M. *American Law.* New York: W. W. Norton, 1984.

————. *History of American Law.* New York: Touchstone, 1973.

Friedman, Robert I. "An Unholy Rage." *New Yorker,* 7 March 1994, pp. 54–56.

Friedman, Thomas L. "Envoy to Iraq, Faulted in Crisis, Says She Warned Hussein Sternly." *New York Times,* 21 March 1991, pp. A1, A7.

Furchgott, Roy. "For Coolhunters, Tomorrow's Trend is the Trophy." *New York Times,* 28 June 1998, Business Section, p. 10.

Gailey, Phil. "Four Rescuers Praised; Courage of the Fourth is Known, But Not the Name." *New York Times,* 15 January 1982, p. D15.

Gamson, William A., and Kathryn E. Lasch. "The Political Culture of Social Welfare Policy." In Shimon E. Spiro and Ephraim Yuchtman-Yaar, eds., *Evaluating the Welfare State: Social and Political Perspectives.* New York: Academic Press, 1983.

Gans, Herbert J. *Popular Culture and High Culture.* New York: Basic Books, 1974.

Garrow, David. "All Over but the Legislating." *New York Times Book Review,* 25 January 1998, pp. 14, 16.

Gaubatz, Kathlyn Taylor. *Crime in the Public Mind.* Ann Arbor: University of Michigan Press, 1995.

Geertz, Clifford. *The Interpretation of Culture.* New York: Basic Books, 1973.

Gibbard, Allan. *Wise Choices, Apt Feelings: A Theory of Normative Judgment.* Cambridge, MA: Harvard University Press, 1990.

Gibson, James L. "Political Intolerance and Political Repression during the McCarthy Red Scare." *American Political Science Review* 82 (1988): 511–29.

Gilens, Martin, and James Glaser. "Interregional Migration and Political Resocialization." *Public Opinion Quarterly* 61 (1997): 72–86.

Gladwell, Malcolm. "Black Like Them." *New Yorker,* 29 April and 6 May 1996, pp. 74–81.

———. "The Coolhunt." *New Yorker,* 17 March 1997, pp. 78–88.

Glenn, Norval D. "Values, Attitudes and Beliefs." In Orville G. Brim Jr. and Jerome Kagan, eds. *Constancy and Change in Human Development.* Cambridge, MA, Harvard University Press, 1980.

"Gloucester Is Calmer on Moon's Followers." *New York Times,* 9 January 1984, p. A11.

Goffman, Erving. *Relations in Public.* New York: Basic Books, 1971.

———. *Stigma.* Englewood Cliffs, NJ: Prentice-Hall, 1963.

Goldberg, Samuel. *Introduction to Difference Equations.* New York: John Wiley and Sons, 1958.

Goode, Erich, and Nachman Ben-Yehuda. *Moral Panics.* Oxford: Blackwell, 1994.

Goode, William J. *The Celebration of Heroes.* Berkeley: University of California Press, 1978.

Goodnough, Abby. "Volunteering Helps Volunteers, Too." *New York Times,* 26 December 1994, p. A10.

Goodstein, Laurie. "Women in Islamic Headdress Find Faith and Prejudice, Too." *New York Times,* 3 November 1997, pp. A1, A14.

Gose, Ben. "Cornell President Seeks Racial Integration in Campus Housing Areas." *Chronicle of Higher Education,* 17 October 1997, p. A52.

———. "Gay Students Have Their Own Floor in a U. of Massachusetts Dormitory." *Chronicle of Higher Education,* 21 February 1997, pp. A37, A38.

Greeley, Andrew M., and Paul B. Sheatsley. "Attitudes toward Racial Integration." *Scientific American* 225 (1971): 13–19.

Green, Donald Philip, and Jonathan A. Cowden. "Who Protests: Self-Interest and White Opposition to Busing." *Journal of Politics* 54 (1992): 471–96.

Green, Donald P., and Ian Shapiro. *Pathologies of Rational Choice Theory.* New Haven: Yale University Press, 1995.

Greenstein, Fred I., and Michael Lerner, eds. *A Sourcebook for the Study of Personality and Politics.* Chicago: Markham, 1971.

Grimes, William. "Should Only Blacks Make Movies about Blacks?" *New York Times,* 28 March 1994, pp. B1, B2.

Gross, Jane. "Homosexuals Finding New Empathy." *New York Times,* 4 February 1988, p. A13.

Gurr, Ted Robert. *Why Men Rebel.* Princeton: Princeton University Press, 1970.

Gurr, Ted Robert, and Barbara Harff. *Ethnic Conflict in World Politics.* Boulder, CO: Westview Press, 1994.

Gusfield, Joseph R. *The Culture of Public Problems*. Chicago: University of Chicago Press, 1981.

———. *Symbolic Crusade*. 2d ed. Urbana: University of Illinois Press, 1986.

Hall, Kermit. *The Magic Mirror*. New York: Oxford University Press, 1989.

Hamilton, David L., and George D. Bishop. "Attitudinal and Behavioral Effects of Initial Integration of White Suburban Neighborhoods." *Journal of Social Issues* 32 (1976): 47–67.

Hardin, Garrett. *The Limits of Altruism*. Bloomington: Indiana University Press, 1977.

Hardin, Russell. *Collective Action*. Baltimore: Johns Hopkins University Press, 1982.

———. *One for All*. Princeton: Princeton University Press, 1995.

———. "The Emergence of Norms." *Ethics* 90 (1980): 575–87.

Hare, A. Paul, Edgar F. Borgatta, and Robert F. Bales, eds. *Small Groups*. New York: Alfred A. Knopf, 1955.

Harmel, Robert, and Kenneth Janda. "An Integrated Theory of Party Goals and Party Change." *Journal of Theoretical Politics* 6 (1994): 259–87.

Harris, Neil. "American Manners." In Luther S. Luedtke, ed., *Making America*. Chapel Hill: University of North Carolina Press, 1992.

Harsanyi, John C. "A Bargaining Model for Social Status in Informal Groups and Formal Organizations." *Behavioral Science* 11 (1966): 357–69.

———. "Rational Choice Theories of Politics vs. Functionalist and Conformist Theories." *World Politics* 21 (1969): 513–28.

Hart, Lianne. "Texas County Draws Static for Apple Tax Vote." *Los Angeles Times,* 2 December 1993, p. A35.

Hechter, Michael. *Principles of Group Solidarity*. Berkeley: University of California Press, 1987.

Heider, Fritz. *The Psychology of Interpersonal Relations*. New York: Wiley, 1958.

Heng, Liang, and Judith Shapiro. *Son of the Revolution*. New York: Vintage, 1983.

Higham, John. *Strangers in the Land*. New Brunswick, NJ: Rutgers University Press, 1992.

Hirschman, Albert O. *The Rhetoric of Reaction*. Cambridge: Harvard University Press, 1991.

———. *Shifting Involvements*. Princeton: Princeton University Press, 1982.

———. "Against Parsimony: Three Easy Ways of Complicating Some Categories of Economic Discourse." In *Rival Views of Market Society, and Other Recent Essays*. New York: Viking, 1986.

Hirshleifer, David, and Eric Rasmusen. "Cooperation in a Repeated Prisoners' Dilemma with Ostracism." *Journal of Economic Behavior and Organization* 12 (1989): 87–106.

Hodge, Robert W., and Donald J. Treiman. "Occupational Mobility and Attitudes toward Negroes." *American Sociological Review* 31 (1966): 93–102.

Hofstadter, Richard. *The Paranoid Style in American Politics*. Chicago: University of Chicago Press, 1955.

Hogg, Michael A., and Dominic Abrams. *Social Identifications*. London: Routledge, 1988.

Holmes, Steven A. "Wilder Seeks to Mix Black Support with Middle-Class Votes." *New York Times,* 30 December 1991, p. A10.

Homans, George C. *The Human Group*. New York: Harcourt, Brace, 1950.

Huckfeldt, Robert, and John Sprague. *Citizens, Politics, and Social Communication: Information and Influence in an Election Campaign.* Cambridge: Cambridge University Press, 1995.

Hunter, James Davison. *Culture Wars.* New York: Basic Books, 1991.

Huntington, Samuel P. *American Politics: The Promise of Disharmony.* Cambridge, MA: Harvard University Press, 1981.

Hyman, Herbert H., and Paul B. Sheatsley. "Attitudes toward Desegregation." *Scientific American* 195 (1956): 35–39.

———. Attitudes toward Desegregation." *Scientific American* 211 (1964): 16–23.

Inkeles, Alex. *Becoming Modern.* Cambridge, MA: Harvard University Press, 1974.

Iyengar, Shanto, and Donald R. Kinder. *News That Matters.* Chicago: University of Chicago Press, 1987.

Jacobs, Lawrence R., and Robert Y. Shapiro. "Issues, Candidate Image, and Priming: The Use of Private Polls in Kennedy's 1960 Presidential Campaign." *American Political Science Review* 88 (1994): 527–40.

James, Henry. *The American Scene* [1907]. New York: Horizon Press, 1967.

Janda, Kenneth, Robert Harmel, Christine Edens, and Patricia Goff. "Changes in Party Identity: Evidence from Party Manifestos." *Party Politics* 1 (1995): 171–96.

Jennings, M. Kent, and Richard G. Niemi. *Generations and Politics.* Princeton: Princeton University Press, 1981.

———. *The Political Character of Adolescence.* Princeton: Princeton University Press, 1974.

Johnsen, Thomas. "Healing and Conscience in Christian Science." *The Christian Century,* 29 June 1994, pp. 640–41.

Johnson, Dirk. "Old List of Klan Members Revives Racist Past in Indiana City." *New York Times,* 2 August 1995, p. A7.

Jones, Edward E. "The Rocky Road from Acts to Dispositions." *American Psychologist* 34 (1979): 107–17.

Jones, Edward E., and Richard E. Nisbett. "The Actor and the Observer: Divergent Perceptions of the Causes of Behavior." In Edward. E. Jones et al., eds., *Attribution: Perceiving the Causes of Behavior.* Morristown, NJ: General Learning Press, 1971.

Kahneman, Daniel, Paul Slovic, and Amos Tversky, eds. *Judgment under Uncertainty: Heuristics and Biases.* Cambridge: Cambridge University Press, 1982.

Kammen, Michael. *A Machine That Would Go of Itself: The Constitution in American Culture.* New York: Vintage Books, 1986.

Katz, Daniel. "The Functions of Attitudes." In Fred I. Greenstein and Michael Lerner, eds. *A Sourcebook for the Study of Personality and Politics.* Chicago: Markham, 1971.

Katz, Elihu, and Paul F. Lazarsfeld. *Personal Influence.* New York: Free Press, 1954.

Kaufman, Margo. "Hers." *New York Times,* 4 February 1988, p. A18.

Kazin, Michael. *The Populist Persuasion.* New York: Basic Books, 1995.

Kennedy, Duncan. "Legal Education as Training for Hierarchy." In David Kairys, ed. *The Politics of Law.* New York: Pantheon, 1982.

Kinder, Donald R. "Opinion and Action in the Realm of Politics." In Daniel T. Gilbert, Susan T. Fiske, and Gardner Lindzey, eds., *The Handbook of Social Psychology,* 4th edition. Boston: McGraw-Hill, 1998.

Kinder, Donald R., and Lynn M. Sanders. *Divided by Color.* Chicago: University of Chicago Press, 1996.

———. "Mimicking Political Debate with Survey Questions: The Case of White Opinion on Affirmative Action for Blacks." *Social Cognition* 8 (1990): 73–103.

Kinder, Donald R., and David O. Sears. "Prejudice and Politics: Symbolic Racism versus Racial Threats to the Good Life." *Journal of Personality and Social Psychology* 40 (1981): 414–31.

———. "Public Opinion and Political Action." In volume 2 of Gardner Lindzey and Elliot Aronson, eds., *The Handbook of Social Psychology*. 3d ed. New York: Random House, 1985.

King, Preston. "The Problem of Tolerance." *Government and Opposition* 6 (1971): 172–207.

Kluger, Richard. *Simple Justice*. New York: Vintage Books, 1975.

Knight, Jack. *Institutions and Social Conflict*. Cambridge: Cambridge University Press, 1992.

Knutson, Jeanne, ed. *Handbook of Political Psychology*. San Francisco: Jossey-Bass, 1973.

Kolbert, Elizabeth. "Abortion, Dole's Sword in '74, Returns to Confront Him in '96." *New York Times*, 8 July 1996, pp. A1, A8.

Kornhauser, William. *The Politics of Mass Society*. Glencoe: Free Press, 1959.

Kristof, Nicholas D. "Chic Japan is Dyeing (Natural It Is Not)." *New York Times*, 29 April 1996, p. A4.

———. "Lamas Seek the Holy Child, but Politics Intrude." *New York Times*, 1 October 1990, p. A4.

Krosnick, Jon A. "The Stability of Political Preferences: Comparisons of Symbolic and Nonsymbolic Attitudes." *American Journal of Political Science* 35 (1991): 547–76.

Krosnick, Jon A., and Donald R. Kinder. "Altering the Foundations of Support for the President through Priming." *American Political Science Review* 84 (1990): 497–512.

Kuklinski, James H., ed. *Thinking about Political Psychology*. Cambridge: Cambridge University Press, forthcoming.

Kuklinski, James H., Michael D. Cobb, and Martin Gilens. "Racial Attitudes and the New South." *Journal of Politics* 50 (1997): 323–49.

Kunde, Diana. "Job Benefits for Gay Pairs on Increase." *Dallas Morning News*, 2 December 1993, p. 1D.

Kymlicka, Will. *Multicultural Citizenship*. Oxford: Oxford University Press, 1995.

Laitin, David D. "The Tower of Babel as a Coordination Game." *American Political Science Review* 88 (1994): 622–34.

Latané, Bibb, and John M. Darley. *The Unresponsive Bystander*. New York: Appleton-Century-Crofts, 1970.

Laudan, Larry. *Progress and Its Problems*. Berkeley: University of California Press, 1977.

Lave, Charles A., and James G. March. *An Introduction to Models in the Social Sciences*. New York: Harper and Row, 1975.

Lemann, Nicholas. *The Promised Land*. New York: Vintage, 1991.

Lepper, Mark R., D. Greene, and Richard E. Nesbitt. "Undermining Children's Intrinsic Interest with Extrinsic Reward: A Test of the 'Overjustification' Hypothesis." *Journal of Personality and Social Psychology* 28 (1973): 129–37.

Levine, Lawrence W. *Highbrow, Lowbrow.* Cambridge, MA: Harvard University Press, 1988.

LeVine, Robert A., and Donald T. Campbell. *Ethnocentrism.* New York: John Wiley, 1972.

Lewin, Leif. *Self-Interest and Public Interest in Western Politics.* Oxford: Oxford University Press, 1991.

Lewis, Anthony. "You Can't Go Home Again." *New York Review of Books,* 29 September 1983, pp. 16–17.

Lewis, David K. *Convention.* Cambridge, MA: Harvard University Press, 1969.

Lewis, Felice Flanery. *Literature, Obscenity, and Law.* Carbondale: Southern Illinois University Press, 1976.

Lewis, Oscar. *Five Families.* New York: Basic Books, 1959.

———. *La Vida.* New York: Random House, 1966.

Liebenstein, Harvey. *Beyond Economic Man.* Cambridge, MA: Harvard University Press, 1980.

Lippmann, Walter. *Public Opinion.* New York: Free Press, 1922.

Lipset, Seymour Martin. *Political Man.* Garden City, NY: Doubleday, 1960.

Lipset, Seymour Martin, and Reinhard Bendix. *Social Mobility in Industrial Society.* Berkeley: University of California Press, 1959.

Lipset, Seymour M., Paul F. Lazarsfeld, Allen H. Barton, and Juan Linz. "The Psychology of Voting: An Analysis of Political Behavior." In Gardner Lindzey, ed., *The Handbook of Social Psychology,* vol. 2. Reading, MA: Addison-Wesley, 1954.

Lipset, Seymour Martin, and Earl Raab. *The Politics of Unreason.* New York: Harper, 1970.

Lipset, Seymour Martin, and Hans Zetterberg. "A Theory of Social Mobility." *Transactions of the Third World Congress of Sociology* 3 (1956): 155–77.

Litsky, Frank. "Gerrit Jan van Ingen Schenau, Clap Skate Creator, Dies at 53." *New York Times,* 7 April 1998, p. C28.

Little, Daniel. *Varieties of Social Explanation.* Boulder, CO: Westview Press, 1991.

Longman, Jere. "Slow Down, Speed Up." *New York Times,* 1 May 1996, p. B11.

Lord, Charles, Lee Ross, and Mark Lepper. "Biased Assimilation and Attitude Polarization: The Effects of Prior Theories on Subsequently Considered Evidence." *Journal of Personality and Social Psychology* 37 (1979): 2098–2109.

Lotwis, M. A. "The Gun Toter and the Gun Controller: Self Interest and Ideology in Political Attitudes about Gun Control." Paper presented at the Annual Meeting of the Midwest Political Science Association, Chicago, IL, 1989.

Lucas, Charlotte-Anne. "County Near Austin Kills Apple Tax Break." *Dallas Morning News,* 1 December 1993, p. 1A.

———. "Officials Feel Heat to Reverse Apple Vote." *Dallas Morning News,* 6 December 1993, p. 1D.

———. "Two Officials Cite Gay Policy, Oppose Apple Tax Breaks." *Dallas Morning News,* 5 November 1993, p. 1A.

———. "Williamson County Panel OKs Incentive for Apple." *Dallas Morning News,* 8 December 1993, p. 1A.

Luce, R. Duncan. "Analyzing the Social Process Underlying Group Voting Patterns." In Eugene Burdick and Arthur J. Brodbeck, eds., *American Voting Behavior.* New York: Free Press, 1959.

Luenberger, David. *Introduction to Dynamic Systems.* New York: Wiley, 1979.

Lukas, J. Anthony. *Common Ground.* New York: Vintage, 1985.

Luker, Kristin. *Abortion and the Politics of Motherhood.* Berkeley: University of California Press, 1982.

Manchester, William. *The Glory and the Dream: A Narrative History of America.* Boston: Little, Brown, 1974.

Mansbridge, Jane J., ed. *Beyond Self-Interest.* Chicago: University of Chicago Press, 1990.

Margolis, Howard. *Selfishness, Altruism, and Rationality.* Chicago: University of Chicago Press, 1982.

Markus, Hazel, and R. B. Zajonc. "The Cognitive Perspective in Social Psychology." In volume 2 of Gardner Lindzey and Elliot Aronson, eds., *The Handbook of Social Psychology.* 3d rev. ed. New York: Random House, 1985.

Martin, William. *With God on Our Side.* New York: Broadway Books, 1996.

McAdam, Doug. *Political Process and the Development of Black Insurgency, 1930–1970.* Chicago: University of Chicago Press, 1982.

———. "Social Movements." In Neil J. Smelser, ed., *Handbook of Sociology.* Beverly Hills, CA: Sage, 1988.

McAdams, Richard H. "The Origin, Development, and Regulation of Norms." *Michigan Law Review* 96 (1997): 338–433.

McClelland, David C. *The Achieving Society.* New York: Free Press, 1961.

McClosky, Herbert. "Conservatism and Personality." *American Political Science Review* 52 (1958): 27–45.

McClosky, Herbert, and Alida Brill. *Dimensions of Tolerance.* New York: Russell Sage Foundation, 1983.

McClosky, Herbert, and Dennis Chong. "Similarities and Differences between Left-Wing and Right-Wing Radicals." *British Journal of Political Science* 15 (1985): 329–63.

McClosky, Herbert, and Harold E. Dahlgren. "Primary Group Influence on Party Loyalty." *American Political Science Review* 53 (1959): 757–76.

McClosky, Herbert, and John Zaller. *The American Ethos: Public Attitudes toward Capitalism and Democracy.* Cambridge, MA: Harvard University Press, 1984.

McGuire, William J. "The Poly-Psy Relationship: Three Phases of a Long Affair." In Shanto Iyengar and William J. McGuire, eds., *Explorations in Political Psychology.* Durham: Duke University Press, 1993.

McGuire, William J. "Personality and Susceptibility to Social Influence." In E. E. Borgatta and W. W. Lambert, eds., *Handbook of Personality Theory and Research.* New York: Rand-McNally, 1968.

McWhiney, Grady. *Cracker Culture.* Tuscaloosa: University of Alabama Press, 1988.

Mead, George Herbert. *Mind, Self, and Society.* Chicago: University of Chicago Press, 1934.

Merton, Robert K. *Social Theory and Social Structure.* Enl. ed. New York: Free Press, 1968.

Miles, Jack. "Blacks vs. Browns." *Atlantic Monthly,* October 1992, p. 55.

Miller, Dale T., and Rebecca K. Ratner. "The Power of the Myth of Self-Interest." In Leo Montada and Melvin J. Lerner, eds., *Current Societal Concerns about Justice.* New York: Plenum Press, 1996.

Miller, Neil, and John Dollard. *Social Learning and Imitation.* New Haven: Yale University Press, 1941.

Miller, Warren E., and J. Merrill Shanks. *The New American Voter.* Cambridge: Harvard University Press, 1996.

Mischel, Walter. *Personality and Assessment.* New York: Wiley, 1968.

———. "The Interaction of Person and Situation." In D. Magnusson and N. S. Endler, eds., *Personality at the Crossroads.* Hillsdale, NJ: Erlbaum, 1977.

Mischel, Walter, and Philip K. Peake. "Analyzing the Construction of Consistency in Personality." In Monte M. Page, ed., *Personality: Current Theory and Research.* Lincoln: University of Nebraska Press, 1983.

Mohr, James C. *Abortion in America.* Oxford: Oxford University Press, 1978.

Monroe, Kristen Renwick. *The Heart of Altruism.* Princeton: Princeton University Press, 1996.

Monroe, Kristin Renwick, ed. *The Economic Approach to Politics.* New York: Harper/Collins, 1991.

Moore, Barrington. *Social Origins of Dictatorship and Democracy.* Boston: Beacon Press, 1966.

Morris, Aldon. *The Origin of the Civil Rights Movement.* New York: Free Press, 1984.

Muir, William K. *Law and Attitude Change.* Chicago: University of Chicago Press, 1973.

Mussen, Paul H., and Norma Haan. "A Longitudinal Study of Patterns of Personality and Political Ideologies." In Dorothy H. Eichorn, John A. Clausen, Norma Haan, Marjorie P. Honzik, and Paul H. Mussen, eds., *Present and Past in Middle Life.* New York: Academic Press, 1981.

Naipaul, V. S. *A Turn in the South.* New York: Vintage Books, 1990.

Ness, Carol. "Apple Firm on Texas Plans." *San Francisco Examiner,* 4 November 1993, p. B1.

Neugarten, Bernice L. "Age Groups in American Society and the Rise of the Young-Old." *Annals of the American Academy of Political and Social Sciences* 415 (1974): 187–98.

Newcomb, Theodore M. "Some Patterned Consequences of Membership in a College Community." In Theodore M. Newcomb et al., eds., *Readings in Social Psychology.* New York: Henry Holt, 1947.

Newcomb, Theodore M., Kathryn E. Koenig, Richard Flacks, and Donald P. Warwick. *Persistence and Change.* New York: Wiley, 1967.

Nisbett, Richard E. "The Trait Construct in Lay and Professional Psychology." In Leon Festinger, ed., *Retrospections on Social Psychology.* New York: Oxford University Press, 1980.

Nisbett, Richard E., and Lee Ross. *Human Inference.* Englewood Cliffs, NJ: Prentice-Hall, 1980.

Nisbett, Richard E. and Timothy DeCamp Wilson. "Telling More than We Know: Verbal Reports on Mental Processes." *Psychological Review* 84 (1977): 231–59.

Norris, Floyd. "Buyout Kings Flee Disaster at Denny's." *New York Times,* 23 March 1997, sect. 3, p. 1.

Nozick, Robert. *The Nature of Rationality.* Princeton: Princeton University Press, 1993.

Olson, Mancur. *The Logic of Collective Action.* Cambridge, MA: Harvard University Press, 1971.

Omi, Michael. "Racial Identity and the State: Dilemmas of Classification." *Law and Inequality* 15 (1997): 7–23.

Orfield, Gary. "Race and the Liberal Agenda: The Loss of the Integrationist Dream, 1965–74." In Margaret Weir, Ann Shola Orloff, and Theda Skocpol, *The Politics of Social Policy in the United States*. Princeton: Princeton University Press, 1988.

Parsons, Talcott. *The Social System*. Glencoe, IL: Free Press, 1951.

Peterson, Iver. "In Its Reward in Cosby Case, Tabloid Tapped a Tradition." *New York Times,* 16 March 1997, p. A12.

Petty, Richard E., and John T. Cacioppo. *Attitudes and Persuasion*. Dubuque, IA: Brown, 1981.

———. *Communication and Persuasion*. New York: Springer-Verlag, 1986.

Polsby, Nelson W. "Towards an Explanation of McCarthyism." *Political Studies* 8 (1960): 250–71.

Pomper, Gerald. *The Election of 1996*. Chatham, NJ: Chatham Press, 1996.

Popkin, Samuel L. *The Reasoning Voter*. Chicago: University of Chicago Press, 1991.

Popkin, Samuel L., John Gorman, Jeffrey Smith, and Charles Phillips. "What Have You Done for Me Lately? Toward an Investment Theory of Voting Behavior." *American Political Science Review* 70 (1976): 779–805.

Popper, Karl. *The Poverty of Historicism*. New York: Harper and Row, 1961.

Powdermaker, Hortense. *After Freedom: A Cultural Study in the Deep South*. New York: Russell and Russell, 1939.

Pratkanis, Anthony, and Elliot Aronson. *Age of Propaganda*. New York: W. H. Freeman, 1991.

Pratkanis, Anthony R., and Anthony G. Greenwald. "A Sociocognitive Model of Attitude Structure and Function." *Advances in Experimental Social Psychology* 22 (1989): 245–85.

Public Opinion Quarterly 61 (Spring 1997), Special Issue on Race.

Putnam, Robert D. "Bowling Alone: America's Declining Social Capital." *Journal of Democracy* 6 (1995): 67–78.

Putnam, Robert D., with Robert Leonardi and Raffaella Y. Nanetti. *Making Democracy Work*. Princeton: Princeton University Press, 1993.

Rabinowitz, Howard N. *Race Relations in the Urban South, 1865–1890*. Urbana: University of Illinois Press, 1980.

Raines, Howell. *My Soul Is Rested*. New York: Penguin, 1977.

Reeves, Thomas C. *The Life and Times of Joe McCarthy*. New York: Stein and Day, 1982.

Restle, Frank. "A Theory of Discrimination Learning." *Psychological Review* 62 (1955): 11–19.

Rieder, Jonathan. *Canarsie*. Cambridge, MA: Harvard University Press, 1985.

Riker, William H. *The Art of Political Manipulation*. New Haven: Yale University Press, 1986.

———. *Liberalism against Populism*. San Francisco: Freeman, 1982.

Rodgers, Harrell R., Jr., and Charles S. Bullock III. *Law and Social Change*. New York: McGraw-Hill, 1972.

Rogin, Michael. *The Intellectuals and McCarthy*. Cambridge: MIT Press.

Rosenbaum, David E. "90-Cent Dose of Bluster." *New York Times,* 30 April 1996, pp. A1, A12.

Ross, Lee. "The Intuitive Psychologist and His Shortcomings: Distortions in the Attribution Process." In Leonard Berkowitz, ed., *Advances in Experimental Social Psychology,* vol. 10. New York: Academic Press, 1977.

Ross, Lee, and Craig A. Anderson. "Shortcomings in the Attribution Process." In Daniel Kahneman, Paul Slovic, and Amos Tversky, eds., *Judgment under Uncertainty: Heuristics and Biases.* Cambridge: Cambridge University Press, 1982.

Rovere, Richard. *Senator Joe McCarthy.* New York: Harper and Row, 1959.

Rubinstein, Ariel. "The Electronic Mail Game: Strategic Behavior Under 'Almost Common Knowledge.'" *American Economic Review* 79 (1989): 385–91.

Sabini, John, and Maury Silver. *Moralities of Everyday Life.* New York: Oxford University Press, 1982.

Sack, Kevin. "The Final Refrains of 'Dixie.'" *New York Times,* 1 November 1998, Education Life Section, pp. ED 20–21, 32–33, 35.

Schattschneider, E. E. *The Semisovereign People.* New York: Holt, Rinehart and Winston, 1960.

Scheingold, Stuart A. *The Politics of Rights.* New Haven: Yale University Press, 1974.

Schelling, Thomas C. *Micromotives and Macrobehavior.* New York: Norton, 1978.

———. *The Strategy of Conflict.* Cambridge, MA: Harvard University Press, 1960.

Schemo, Diana Jean. "'Victim' Tokens Illuminate a Suspect." *New York Times,* 1 July 1993, p. A9.

Schneider, David J. "Social Cognition." In Mark R. Rosenzweig and Lyman N. Porter, eds., *Annual Review of Psychology.* Palo Alto, CA: Annual Reviews, 1991.

Schuman, Howard, and Shirley Hatchett. *Trends in Racial Attitudes.* Ann Arbor: University of Michigan, Institute for Social Research, 1974.

Schuman, Howard, Charlotte Steeh, and Lawrence Bobo. *Racial Attitudes in America.* Cambridge, MA: Harvard University Press, 1985.

Scitovsky, Tibor. *The Joyless Economy.* New York: Oxford University Press, 1976.

Scott, David, and Beth Snyder. "Location, Location, Location." *Texas Business,* June 1995, 74–82, 98–100.

Scott, John Finley. *Internalization of Norms.* Englewood Cliffs, NJ: Prentice-Hall, 1971.

Searing, Donald D., Joel J. Schwartz, and Alden E. Lind. "The Structuring Principle: Political Socialization and Belief Systems." *American Political Science Review* 67 (1973): 415–32.

Searing, Donald D., Gerald Wright, and George Rabinowitz. "The Primary Principle: Attitude Change and Political Socialization." *British Journal of Political Science* 6 (1976): 83–113.

Sears, David. O. "On the Persistence of Early Political Predispositions: The Roles of Attitude Object and Life Stage." In Ladd Wheeler, ed., *Review of Personality and Social Psychology.* Beverly Hills, CA: Sage, 1983.

———. "Political Behavior." In volume 5 of Gardner Lindzey and Elliot Aronson, eds., *The Handbook of Social Psychology.* 2d ed. Reading, MA: Addison-Wesley, 1969.

———. "Symbolic Politics: A Socio-Psychological Theory." In Shanto Iyengar and William J. McGuire, eds., *Explorations in Political Psychology.* Durham: Duke University Press, 1993.

Sears, David O., and Jack Citrin. *Tax Revolt.* Cambridge, MA: Harvard University Press, 1982.

Sears, David O, and Carolyn Funk. "Self-Interest in Americans' Political Opinions."
    In Jane J. Mansbridge, ed., *Beyond Self-Interest.* Chicago: University of Chicago
    Press, 1990.

————. "The Role of Self-Interest in Social and Political Attitudes." *Advances in Ex-
    perimental Social Psychology* 24 (1991): 1–91

Sears, David O., Carl P. Hensler, and Leslie K. Speer. "Whites' Opposition to 'Busing':
    Self-Interest or Symbolic Politics?" *American Political Science Review* 73 (1979):
    369–84.

Sears, David O., Richard R. Lau, Tom R. Tyler, and H. M. Allen Jr. "Self-Interest vs.
    Symbolic Politics in Policy Attitudes and Presidential Voting." *American Political
    Science Review* 74 (1980): 670–84.

Sen, Amartya K. "Rational Fools: A Critique of the Behavioral Foundations of Eco-
    nomic Theory" *Philosophy and Public Affairs* 6 (1977): 317–44.

Sheatsley, Paul B. "White Attitudes toward the Negro." *Daedalus* 95 (1966): 217–38.

Shenon, Philip. "Admiral, in Suicide Note, Apologized to 'My Sailors,'" *New York
    Times,* 18 May 1996, pp. A1, A9.

Sherif, Muzafer. *The Psychology of Social Norms.* New York: Harper, 1936.

————. "Group Influences upon the Formation of Norms and Attitudes." In Guy E.
    Swanson, Theodore M. Newcomb, and Eleanor L. Hartley, eds., *Readings in Social
    Psychology.* Rev. ed. New York: Henry Holt, 1952.

Sherif, Muzafer, and Carolyn W. Sherif. *Reference Groups.* Chicago: Henry Regnery,
    1964.

Shipler, David K. "Soviet Letters Editor Tests Limits." *New York Times,* 24 April 1988,
    p. A6.

Sidanius, James. "The Psychology of Group Conflict and the Dynamics of Oppression."
    In Shanto Iyengar and William J. McGuire, eds., *Explorations in Political Psychol-
    ogy.* Durham: Duke University Press, 1993.

Sigelman, Lee, and Susan Welch. "The Contact Hypothesis Revisited: Interracial Con-
    tact and Positive Racial Attitudes." *Social Forces* 71 (1993): 781–95.

Simmel, Georg. *The Sociology of Georg Simmel.* Translated by Kurt H. Wolff. Glen-
    coe: Free Press, 1950.

Simon, Herbert. "Human Nature in Politics: The Dialogue of Psychology with Political
    Science." *American Political Science Review* 79 (1985): 293–304.

Sims, Verner M., and James R. Patrick. "Attitude toward the Negro of Northern and
    Southern College Students." *Journal of Social Psychology* 7 (1936): 192–204.

Skocpol, Theda. *States and Social Revolutions.* Cambridge: Cambridge University
    Press, 1979.

Smelser, Neil J. *Theory of Collective Behavior.* New York: Free Press, 1962.

Smith, Tom W., and Paul B. Sheatsley. "American Attitudes toward Race Relations."
    Public Opinion 7 (Oct.–Nov. 1984): 14–15, 51–53.

Sniderman, Paul M., and Philip E. Tetlock. "Reflections on American Racism." *Journal
    of Social Issues* 42 (1986): 173–88.

Snow, David, and Robert D. Benford. "Ideology, Frame Resonance, and Participant
    Mobilization." *International Social Movement Research* 1 (1988): 197–217.

Snow, David, E. Burke Rochford Jr., Steven K. Worden, and Robert D. Benford.
    "Frame Alignment Processes, Micro-Mobilization, and Movement Participation."
    American Sociological Review, 51 (1986): 464–81.

Snyder, Mark, and Edward E. Jones. "Attitude Attribution When Behavior is Con-
    strained." *Journal of Experimental Social Psychology* 10 (1974): 585–600.

Sowell, Thomas. *The Economics of Politics and Race.* New York: William Morrow and Co., 1983.

Sperber, Dan. *Rethinking Symbolism.* Translated by Alice L. Morton. Cambridge: Cambridge University Press, 1975.

Stark, Rodney, and William Sims Bainbridge. *The Future of Religion: Secularization, Revival and Cult Formation.* Berkeley: University of California Press, 1985.

Steckenrider, Janie S., and Neal E. Cutler. "Aging and Adult Political Socialization: The Importance of Roles and Transitions." In Roberta S. Sigel, ed., *Political Learning in Adulthood.* Chicago: University of Chicago Press, 1989.

Steinberg, Stephen. *The Ethnic Myth.* Boston: Beacon Press, 1989.

Stewart, James B. "Moby Dick in Manhattan." *New Yorker,* 27 June and 4 July 1994, pp. 46–66.

Stinchcombe, Arthur. "The Conditions of Fruitfulness of Theorizing about Mechanisms in Social Science." *Philosophy of the Social Sciences* 21 (1991): 367–88.

Stokes, Donald E. "Spatial Models of Party Competition." In Angus Campbell, Philip E. Converse, Warren E. Miller, and Donald E. Stokes, eds., *Elections and the Political Order.* New York: John Wiley and Sons, 1966.

Sudit, M. "Ideology or Self-Interest? Medical Students' Attitudes toward National Health Insurance." *Journal of Health and Social Behavior* 20 (1988): 376–84.

Sugden, Robert. *The Economics of Rights, Co-operation and Welfare.* Oxford: Basil Blackwell, 1986.

Sullivan, John L., James E. Piereson, and George E. Marcus. *Political Tolerance and American Democracy.* Chicago: University of Chicago Press, 1982.

————. "An Alternative Conceptualization of Political Tolerance: Illusory Increases, 1950's–1970's." *American Political Science Review* 73 (1979): 781–94.

Sundquist, James L. *Dynamics of the Party System.* Washington, DC: Brookings Institution Press, 1983.

Tajfel, Henri. *Human Groups and Social Categories.* Cambridge: Cambridge University Press, 1981.

Tajfel, Henri, ed. *Social Identity and Intergroup Relations.* Cambridge: Cambridge University Press, 1982.

Tarrow, Sidney. *Power in Movement.* Cambridge: Cambridge University Press, 1994.

Taylor, Charles. "The Politics of Recognition." In Amy Gutmann, ed., *Multiculturalism and "The Politics of Recognition."* Princeton: Princeton University Press, 1992.

Taylor, D. Garth, Paul B. Sheatsley, and Andrew M. Greeley. "Attitudes toward Racial Integration." *Scientific American* 238 (1978): 42–51.

Taylor, Michael. *The Possibility of Cooperation.* Cambridge: Cambridge University Press, 1987.

————. "Battering RAMS." *Critical Review* 9 (1995): 223–34.

————. "Structure, Culture and Action in the Explanation of Social Change." *Politics and Society* 17 (1989): 115–62.

Tribe, Lawrence. *American Constitutional Law.* Mineola, NY: Foundation Press, 1978.

Turner, John C. *Rediscovering the Social Group.* Oxford: Basil Blackwell, 1987.

Tyler, Tom R., and Renee Weber. "Support for the Death Penalty: Instrumental Response to Crime, or Symbolic Attitude?" *Law and Society Review* 17 (1982): 21–45.

Ullmann-Margalit, Edna. *The Emergence of Norms.* Oxford: Clarendon Press, 1977.

Valentine, Charles A. *Culture and Poverty.* Chicago: University of Chicago Press, 1968.

Verba, Sidney. *Small Groups and Political Behavior.* Princeton: Princeton University Press, 1961.

Verhovek, Sam Howe. "County in Texas Snubs Apple over Unwed Partner Policies." *New York Times,* 2 December 1993, p. A1.

Walster, Elaine, Elliot Aronson, and Darcy Abrahams. "On Increasing the Persuasiveness of a Low Prestige Communicator." *Journal of Experimental Social Psychology* 2 (1966): 325–42.

Walzer, Michael, Edward T. Kantowicz, John Higham, and Mona Harrington. *The Politics of Ethnicity.* Cambridge, MA: Harvard University Press, 1980.

Wattenberg, Ben. *Values Matter Most.* New York: Free Press, 1995.

Weddle, David L. "The Christian Science Textbook: An Analysis of the Religious Authority of *Science and Health,* by Mary Baker Eddy." *Harvard Theological Review* 84 (1991): 273–97.

Weinraub, Bernard. "Hoffman: A Fresh Face Even as Age Catches Up." *New York Times,* 17 February 1998, pp. B1, B5.

Williamson, Joel. *A Rage for Order.* New York: Oxford University Press, 1986.

Wilson, Glenn D. *The Psychology of Conservatism.* New York: Academic Press, 1973.

Winerip, Michael. "In School." *New York Times,* 20 April 1994, p. B13.

Wirt, Frederick M. *Politics of Southern Equality.* Chicago: Aldine, 1970.

———. *We Ain't What We Was.* Durham, NC: Duke University Press, 1997.

Wood, Michael, and Michael Hughes. "The Moral Basis of Moral Reform." *American Sociological Review* 49 (1984): 86–99.

Woodward, C. Vann. *Origins of the New South.* Baton Rouge: Louisiana State University Press, 1971.

———. *The Strange Career of Jim Crow.* 3d rev. ed. New York: Oxford University Press, 1974.

Young, H. Peyton. *Individual Strategy and Social Structure.* Princeton: Princeton University Press, 1998.

Zald, Mayer N. "Culture, Ideology, and Strategic Framing." In Doug McAdam, John D. McCarthy, and Mayer N. Zald, eds., *Comparative Perspectives on Social Movements.* Cambridge: Cambridge University Press, 1996.

Zaller, John R. *The Nature and Origins of Mass Opinion.* Cambridge: Cambridge University Press, 1992.

Zaller, John R., and Stanley Feldman. "A Simple Theory of the Survey Response: Answering Questions Means Revealing Preferences." *American Journal of Political Science* 36 (1992): 579–618.

Zinn, Howard. *The Southern Mystique.* New York: Knopf, 1964.

Zurcher, Louis A., and R. George Kirkpatrick. *Citizens for Decency.* Austin: University of Texas Press, 1976.

INDEX

Abelson, Robert P., 24, 223, 224, 226
abolitionism: principled debate over, 143; southern opposition to, 53–54
abortion rights: attitudes toward, as guided by past decisions, 103–4; motives of opponents to, 224–25; opposed by Bob Dole in 1974 campaign, 131; opposition to among scientifically trained physicians, 99–100; principled debate over, 120
ad hoc modifications to a theory, 221
Adams, John, 252n.29
addictions, as impediments to rationality, 4
African National Congress, 50
agenda-setting, 131
aging, and conservatism, 101
alcohol, as a symbolic issue, 23
Alpert, Leo, 190
altruism, admiration for, 142, 223–24
Anderson, Craig, 91
Anderson, Elijah, 19
anomalies, compared to unsolved problems, 16
anticommunism, 131–32. *See also* McCarthy, Joseph; McCarthyism
Apple Computer controversy: Apple's development plans in Williamson County, 155–56, 256n.17; described, 9, 153–54; economic interests at stake, 180; moral arguments of Apple's opponents, 169–70; motivations of participants, 180–84; national media coverage, 157; origins, 130, 131, 159–60; Perryman Report, 179, 180, 181; role of political entrepreneurs, 158, 185. *See also* Williamson County, Texas
assurance game, 228
attitude change: accomplished by changing frames of reference, 118, 150–51, 251n.9; in response to behavioral change, 9–10, 90, 193, 196, 198, 220. *See also* individual choice, model of; social adjustment; social adjustment model

attitude structure, 118
a-type: characteristics, 100; environment, 78; group, 67; individual, 78, 79, 90, 109
autokinetic effect, 67–68

Barry, Brian, 37
Becker, Gary, 101
Bennington College study, 39–40
Berelson, Bernard R., 65
Black, Donald, 108
Black Power salute, 224–25
Boatright, Greg: on the centrality of morality in politics and economics, 164–65, 166–67, 174, 176; perception of public opinion, 161; position on second vote, 158; on shared values and trust, 171–72; surprised by outcome of first vote, 158; troubled by Apple's domestic partners benefits policy, 156; view of commissioners' attitudes toward homosexuality, 163
Bodnar, John, 111
Bollinger, Lee, 119
Boorda, Jeremy, 47
Boulding, Kenneth, 124
Boyd, Robert, 69
Boyle, Sarah: attributional errors committed by, 93; ethnocentric beliefs of, 87–88; motives behind moral actions of, 223; socialization of, 2, 233n.5
Brewer, Phil: on the appropriate decision rule for development issues, 162; on the attractions of Williamson County, 158; on the business community's support for Apple, 180–81; characterization of Apple's opponents, 168; confidence prior to first vote, 160; on costs and benefits of Apple's development plan, 177; criticism of media coverage, 168; on the relationship between economics and morality, 166–68
Brown, Roger, 92, 248n.53